THE BEST OF CHIEF EXECUTIVE

Edited by
J. P. Donlon

BUSINESS ONE IRWIN
Homewood, Illinois 60430

Sponsoring editor: Jeffrey A. Krames
Project editor: Jane Lightell
Production manager: Mary Jo Parke
Compositor: The Wheetley Co.
Typeface: 11/13 Palatino
Printer: Book Press

Library of Congress Cataloging-in-Publication Data

The Best of Chief executive / edited by J.P. Donlon.
　　p.　　cm.
　　ISBN 1-55623-781-2
　　1. Chief executive officers.　2. Industrial management.
　I. Donlon, J. P.　II. Chief executive (New York, N.Y. : 1977)
HD38.2.B483 1993
658.4—dc20　　　　　　　　　　　　　　　　92-11983

Printed in the United States of America

1 2 3 4 5 6 7 8 9 0 BP 9 8 7 6 5 4 3 2

To my wife Jean, and to my sons Ian and Keith

Foreword

Anthony J.F. O'Reilly
Chairman, President and Chief Executive Officer
H.J. Heinz Company

The following volume of Chief Executive Magazine is a highly readable and very useful compendium of articles. Seldom is leading corporate opinion assembled with such insightful effect. Nor has the theme of global competition been more timely. The breathtaking changes in Central and Eastern Europe have accelerated greatly the evolution of a global economy. The conclusion of the Cold War puts squarely on the shoulders of both the business and political sector the responsibility for recasting a world order shaped by commerce rather than conflict.

One notion I would carry through from my interview published here is that "the globalization of markets is not a future dream; it's a daily reality." That certainly has been our experience at Heinz. As a basket of companies, currencies, and brands, we must continually transform ourselves to fit the evolving shape of the global economy.

Out of globalization has arisen the truly multinational, multicultural corporation. The old colonial model—an American business with overseas outposts—has given way to the paradigm of a global corporation with decentralized, cosmopolitan management.

This in turn has enriched the world's consumers and enlarged their expectations. The desire for global brands is extending ever outward as more people are becoming participants in the worldwide consumer economy.

This is the environment for global competition in the 1990s and beyond. The companies most likely to prevail will be those with powerful global brands, nimble marketing strategies, regionally integrated supply, alert financial planning, state-of-the-art production, and management sensitive to both local preferences and universal consumer desires.

The essays in this volume touch on these and other elements in the global equation. They afford the astute reader a unique opportunity to share the counsel, instruction and example of some of the world's most successful global competitors.

Acknowledgments

Napoleon once said that victory has many fathers, but defeat is an orphan. So, too, the credit of putting a volume like this together is owed to many people, not the least of whom are the chief executives and other contributors whose essays are featured here. My former assistant, Susan Moore Hanchett, deserves unreserved appreciation for her administrative help and preparation, without which I would not be able to have completed the manuscripts. Special thanks are due to the many capable people who have made the magazine and its roundtables possible: Elizabeth Bayles, Jeanine Garaban, and Betsy Hughes. I thank Laurie Grube for her help in copyediting and above all Alma Phipps for the creativity in design that has become a *Chief Executive* hallmark. I am grateful for Peter Callahan's encouragement to me in completing this effort and to Manny Rabinowitz for his professional help in removing obstacles in our path.

These are two figures, grey eminences of *Chief Executive*, who merit my deepest appreciation. Robert Lear, formerly of F&M Schaefer, and Jock Ritchie, formerly of Royal Dutch/Shell, have been generous with their time and wise counsel in helping *Chief Executive* and myself in ways too numerous to mention. Their insight and advice have proved invaluable.

Contents

Chapter Two
WORLD-CLASS MARKETING   91

Chapter Three
WORLD-CLASS MANUFACTURING   183

Introduction to
"The Best of Chief Executive"

There are few classes of people about whom much is written but less is understood than the chief executive of a major enterprise. In the popular imagination there are numerous stereotypes. There is the imperious autocrat such as Armand Hammer, who when he was alive had a gift for having himself photographed with as many heads of state (Soviet dictators and Middle East potentates were a specialty) as there were members of the U.N. Hammer was rarely seen in the company of the average Occidental employee. There is the tabloid CEO such as Lee Iacocca or Donald Trump, who is forever dispensing advice on subjects somewhat removed from his competence in front of TV cameras. Then there's the made-for-TV-villain CEO such as Charles Keating, he of the 19-count conviction for defrauding depositors and investors of Lincoln Savings.

Such knaves do exist, of course, but in the 14 years of editing Chief Executive magazine, I have found that most CEOs—and I meet about four score a year—are boringly unsordid. More typical of the contemporary chief executive are such people as John Hall of Ashland Oil, David Beatty of Weston Foods, and Charlie Sanford of Bankers Trust. Hall runs a $9 billion refiner and marketer of petroleum, and worries enough about declining education levels that he has Ashland pay cash "bonuses" to teachers in his home state of Kentucky who excel in raising those levels for their students. Beatty operates the $1.5 billion Toronto-based unit of George Weston Holdings, a multinational food company. He grapples with the competitive implications of the North American Free Trade Agreement not only as it relates to Weston's operations in Ontario, Buffalo, and New York City, but in remaining competitive in an industry where governments of every persuasion feel it's their birthright to rig agricultural prices. Sanford, a soft-spoken but tough-minded Georgian, spent the first three years of his chairmanship getting Bankers Trust out of commercial banking and into the resolute merchant bank it had to become if it was to survive. Although the restructuring succeeded, Sanford must still deal with the increasing marginalization of U.S. banking as a source of capital for transnational companies that issue their own commercial paper.

Hall, Beatty, and Sanford will most likely never be featured in *Vanity Fair*, are not intimates of Warren Beatty, don't hang out with Frank Sinatra, and have never been interviewed by Diane Sawyer. (Since each is still wed to his original spouse, I think we can forget about a photo spread in *People*, too.) Yet the decisions of these and other CEOs who run today's wealth-producing engines of civilization, in fact, affect our society if not our daily lives, in a fundamental way. Most are highly talented. Some are lucky. A few are gifted. All are fallible and subject to self-doubt (despite healthy egos). Each asks himself, "How best can our company add value to our products and services? Do we have the right people for the challenges we face? How do our costs and prices compare with our competitors'? Do we have the right technology and are we using it effectively? Does our strategy make sense in these tumultuous times, and if so, does our organization carry it out clearly and coherently?" (Do our people, in fact, understand what our mission really is?) Finally, the sensible CEO asks himself, "How do we know what we think we know about all this?" Or, as Peter Drucker once advised the management of Philips, the Dutch electronics multinational, "What are the new things you will do for your customers; what are the old things you need to abandon?"

Enter *Chief Executive* magazine. It is said that the essence of a top executive's job is making decisions. Not true. It is more a matter of making choices (or creating choices if none seem to be available) within a scheme of goals and objectives. Management must be based on judgment, knowledge, and technique. The last of these receives the most attention in the news media and the business schools, but it is the first two that are most important. Very often the best advice a CEO can use comes not from his board or executive reports, but from another CEO who has experienced a similar tough choice. Since its inception in 1977, *Chief Executive* has been a journal of opinion and analysis where CEOs have shared ideas, concerns, and judgments through its pages. Sometimes the best counsel is a fellow CEO who "has been there." This is why most of the articles are authored by CEOs and presidents both at the corporate and divisional level. This anthology of recent essays reflects diverse "over the horizon" thinking among top executives on the principal issues chief executives tell us they face today, namely:

- Global Competitiveness
- Total Quality
- Revitalizing Growth
- Total Customer Orientation
- Productivity (particularly in services)
- Strategic Use of Information Technology
- "Teaming" the Organization
- Reducing Time-to-Market
- Strategy Implementation
- Alliance Building

I deliberately list those over which the CEO has direct influence at the managerial level. Executives are nearly unanimous in worrying about deteriorating national educational standards, and their impact upon the work force. They gripe that the tax system punishes capital and investment relative to the U.S.' principal trading partners. And apart from the consultants and service providers, CEOs are not amused by the rise in health care costs and environmental liabilities. These are regarded as the twin scud missiles aimed at U.S. competitiveness. Everyone recognizes the menace, but no one is able to find the source and destroy the threat.

Through surveys and direct contact, *Chief Executive* encourages its 35,000 readers to participate in an exchange of views and is guided in its editorial selection by the issues and concerns CEOs themselves say are important to them. Some of the CEO authors here may be well-known to the casual business reader, but many may not. Advanced practices and thinking are not the monopoly of the biggest or best-known companies. Many household names live off past glory. In all cases, the material in this volume was selected for its continuing usefulness for those who seek to know what today's chief executive regards as "best practices."

What are the challenges CEOs confront today?

Thinking globally, but acting locally is now a cliche of business. But consider that approximately half of all imports and exports are transacted between companies and their foreign affiliates or parent organizations around the world. One-half of all products made in the U.S. have one or more foreign-made components. What makes the international economy so fascinating, according to Murray Weidenbaum, director of the Center for the Study of American Business at Washington University in St. Louis, is that "the forces of technology and economics are outpacing current management thinking and traditional politics." The demise of the Soviet threat to Western security serves curiously to highlight Western economic insecurity. Trade rivalry is not new, but in the past 46 years it had been subordinated to the deadlier superpower rivalry.

A majority of chief executives are convinced globalization is critical to winning in the 1990s. In a 1991 survey of 500 CE readers, CEOs predicted their foreign operations will represent a greater share of total corporate profits during the following four years. In fact, they projected that by 1995 overseas profits will increase to 50 percent of the total. Currently it ranges from 21 to 34 percent of profits for companies with annual turnover over $500 million. To take advantage of the worldwide opportunities, three-fourths of the CEOs have put in place aggressive strategies for international expansion. The trouble is only 10 percent reckon their implementation was on target. Why? The obstacles are overwhelmingly cultural. The two biggest barriers to success in international markets are a lack of globally minded executives and a short-term profit focus. Even McDonalds, that ubiquitous symbol of transnationalism learned the hard way. When it first entered foreign markets 20 years ago it attempted to transplant its decidedly American philosophy and experience to the Netherlands by opening several units in suburban Amsterdam. Each of the Dutch outlets was closed in short order. Today McDonalds seeks predominantly urban locations with high visibility, and favors linking up with dedicated national entrepreneurs over partnerships with foreign companies.

One of the more internationally oriented CEOs, H. J. Heinz's Tony O'Reilly, calls Europe "the new frontier," a place where "global branding" can be implemented in strength, because in its sophisticated markets Europeans have only half the line items available to the consumer than are available to American consumers. For the first time since the mid-1980s, cross-border investments in Europe exceeded that of North America. In 1991, EC investments reached $23.3 billion, North America had $20.3 billion, according to KPMG Peat Marwick. Although the EC is generating greater investment activity, the trade wall around the community shows no sign of coming down. If anything, a more inward-looking EC, to some degree, is strengthening barriers to external competition. Hence the importance of operating within the Community as a Europe-based enterprise becomes more vital. For example, the U.S. biotech leader Genentech, which is 60 percent owned by Roche Holding, the parent of Swiss pharmaceutical giant Hoffmann La Roche, recently formed a European marketing and development subsidiary to ensure having its own presence and distribution for its products independent of La Roche. IBM Europe, long an advocate of open trade, recently joined the crypto-protectionist chorus of France's Bull, Italy's Olivetti, and Germany's Siemens in slowing the advance of Hitachi and NEC within the EC. Coupled with the growing economic tension between Japan and the U.S.—this despite a 120 percent increase in American manufactured exports to Japan since 1985—changes in international trade dynamics will force CEOs to rethink their long-term growth strategies. As some companies have learned to their cost there are very few unchanged world-products (Coca-Cola, Sony Walkman, and Perrier are exceptions) but there are numerous world-class companies. The reason is capabilities (manufacturing, operations, technology, finance) have become internationalized, but markets themselves have become more and more segmented. Even Heinz's ubiquitous worldwide staple, tomato ketchup, is reformulated for local tastes.

Just as CEOs will have to adjust their strategies for growth and development to adjust to what McKinsey's Kenichi Ohmae calls the interlinked economy, their marketing and manufacturing methods will be judged by world-class standards. Nowhere is this more evident than in the power of international brands. Pepsico CEO Wayne Calloway discourses on how having eight brands each generating $1 billion at retail can only work when basic operating skills are honed every day. David Kearns, former CEO of Xerox and current Undersecretary for Education under Lamar

Alexander, reveals his personal odyssey in turning Xerox back into a world-class manufacturer.

The corollary of this trend is that competitors aspiring to global status must be world class in all operations. This means first-class products and service, quality and cost, fast cycle times in both operations (from order to delivery) and innovation (from idea to market). This will prove to be a double-edged sword. Consider the example of the world automotive industry—the first to internationalize in this century, but the most rapidly consolidating sector of the world economy today. Only a fraction of the number of car makers that existed 50 years ago are still in business today. But the range of car choices among autos available to consumers has grown exponentially. Product quality and value have also increased. Soon cars essentially will be made to order with hundreds of specifications becoming available through computer terminal. Yet quality—the rallying cry of the 1980s—is not sufficient in itself to ensure competitive advantage anymore. After all, the customer has paid for quality; he expects to be satisfied. The world-class marketer or manufacturer in the 1990s will need to distinguish itself by transforming satisfaction into delight.

One of the more enduring notions about international business is that the rapid deployment of technology either in product commercialization or in information systems is the key to competitiveness. The truth is that technology alone is not enough. Annual U.S. expenditure on information technology is about $20 billion. But as Apple CEO John Sculley notes in this volume, this activity has had almost no discernible impact on office productivity. The dilemma faced by CEOs is that few have the technical background sufficient to give them an intuitive feel for their company's enormous investment in information technology. Executives who can spot a flaw in a marketing plan or acquisition proposal in a nanosecond become nervous about IT. For a decade or more they have been at the mercy of the IT mandarins, the systems professionals and CIO wannabes. And the computer industry itself has not helped matters by trying to lock customers into proprietary systems for so many years.

The issue is not one to be solved by interconnectivity and "open architecture." CEOs must face up to their responsibility in overcoming the cultural problem of how to use IT strategically—not just tactically as most use it today. There are perhaps three CEOs in the U.S. today who grasp intuitively the importance of, say, expert systems as a strategic tool, that is when IT is completely integrated to the enterprise in all of its operations to advance the business as a whole, not just automate back office parts of it: American Airlines' Bob Crandall, American President Companies' Bruce Seaton, and Mrs. Field's Cookies' Randy Fields. Inference Corp. Founder and Chairman Alex Jacobson maintains "that the abdication of authority by U.S. CEOs with regard to IT initiatives, poses a serious threat to U.S. companies' long-term viability in global markets. Playing not-to-lose rather than to win, exacerbates the challenge."

This volume closes with a discussion of two vexing challenges chief executives must overcome in the remaining years of this decade. What is the relationship of the employee to the corporation and the organization's responsibility to the employee? What ought to be the role of the chief executive in relation to employees, shareholders, and directors? In other words, what is the CEO being paid for and how much should he be paid to get that result? The decade of the 1980s, demonized by the popular press as the decade of greed, was for business a desperate search for renewal and redefinition. During the first half, the threat from vigorous competitors from Japan and to a lesser degree, Europe, precipitated alarm followed by reappraisal. The reappraisal took two principal forms: Let's adopt what the Japanese keiretsu do but do it better; or let's return to what the U.S. once did so well, i.e. become entrepreneurial. The financial maneuvering and restructuring of the latter half of the period was an attempt to do one or the other in searching for a sustainable competitive advantage. U.S. business never quite had to do this because before World War II American market dominance across the board didn't exist and wasn't on anyone's national agenda.

When John D. Rockefeller ran Standard Oil or Alfred Sloan led General Motors, capital and economies of scale were clear advantages. Today, information technology allows economy of scope to obviate economy of scale (and the heavy capital requirement to sustain it). Also, the integration of world financial markets means money flows instantaneously to where it gets the best return anywhere in the world. No monopoly is possible. When Reginald

Jones ran General Electric and John Opel ran IBM controlling proprietary technology was a sure way to win. But technology became almost as fungible as money. Rivals can get access to competitive technology far easier. And carefully controlling the introduction of next-generation technology (without losing the last drop of remaining sales from the obsolete product), which was IBM's gift, cannot be done now. (Does anyone remember the U.S. government's 20-year antitrust case against IBM because of its presumed lock on the market?)

In the end there is only one source of sustainable advantage: people. This is why one reads so much today about "empowerment," "decentralization," "flattening the [organizational] pyramid." "Most competitive improvements can't be bought," writes labor economist Anthony Patrick Carnevale in his book, *America and the New Economy.* "Sixty percent of competitive improvements come from learning to make better use of the resources we buy." The trouble is, that in turning companies upside down and inside out in attempting to restructure, management destroyed the social compact—the bond—that kept people's loyalty, and more importantly, their faith with the organization. One recalls the sign posted in front of a U.S. Steel plant earlier in the century: "Firings will continue until morale improves." It has belatedly dawned on many CEOs that they had better fix this "soft" issue before they go on to do anything else. Look closely at management strategy today. Getting the work force to share the vision of the business and allowing people a say in how they can contribute is close to the top of the CEO's agenda. If it isn't; short the stock. Rivals that are able to "get to team" will eat their competitor's lunch.

In future, directors ought to judge the worth of a CEO by his organization's return of human capital, as well as by the return on financial resources employed. They are already being pushed to examine the return on the company's most visible human resource, the CEO himself. PCA's David Meredith argues convincingly that it's spurious to say that CEO pay is too high on an absolute basis. What matters is setting pay in relation to the performance rendered. Part of the confusion on this subject centers on the widely different compensation numbers that are commonly attributed to an executive. Given that proxy statements and annual reports serve as the common database for everyone's research, how can the conclusions be so different? The answer lies in the methodology used to calculate total compensation. The PCA/*Chief Executive* analysis includes long-term incentive grants such as stock options rather than the gain on long-term incentives that may have been granted two, five, or even ten years ago but are only now being exercised. This approach ensures that we calculate current compensation rather than the value of pay packages in previous years. When measuring company performance, we take the shareholder's view. How much gain in stock price and dividends has the company delivered in comparison with its competitors? By plotting the pay versus performance on an axis, one can readily see which CEO's pay packet exceeds his grasp, but also which CEOs are, relative to their performance, bargains for the shareholders even if the absolute pay seems high.

Top executive pay is, however, not a narrow, technical issue. It goes directly to the fundamental notion of accountability and control. It is also a "team" issue in that pay that is perceived to have no link with performance or accountability becomes a barrier to teamwork in the organization, causing productivity to suffer. Executive pay also concerns leadership. During the Italian campaign against Austria's numerically superior and better-trained armies, Napoleon insisted on eating the same rations as those of his troops because he needed "to know how far they can go." According to Richard E. Dauch, former executive vice president of worldwide manufacturing for Chrysler, "When provided the right leadership, the average worker is full of resolve to compete globally and accepts the realities of world competitiveness." There is an old expression in the British army, "There is no such thing as poor soldiers; only poor officers."

—**J.P. Donlon**

1

STRATEGY FOR GROWTH AND DEVELOPMENT

Heinz Meanz Branz

The worldly Tony O'Reilly argues that brands are transcending their national origins and are becoming "citizens of the world." If this sounds like Irish levity (or Ted Levitt-y), consider two truths: It helps to be the low-cost producer with widening operating margins and, more tellingly, O'Reilly meanz persistenz.

I n anointing Anthony J.F. O'Reilly of H.J. Heinz, the $6 billion Pittsburgh-based food processor, 1990 Chief Executive of the Year, the committee of his peers were mindful of a number of accomplishments. There was no doubt about consistent financial performance. Since he became CEO 10 years ago the average annual return for shareholders who have reinvested dividends was 31 percent, which compares with an annual average of 17.5 percent for the S&P 500 and 21.4 percent for the S&P food index. Over the same period market capitalization went from $908 million to $9 billion with the same number of shares outstanding. Financial performance is also matched by internal performance. During the 1980s Heinz led the charge in corporate America as a cost cutter. Its gross operating margins grew from 33.4 percent in 1980 to 38.8 percent in 1989—this in a tight "nickel and dime" business.

Developing and extending such powerful names as Heinz, Weight Watchers, StarKist, Ore-Ida, and 9-Lives to the point where 55 percent of sales derive from number one brands marketed in over 200 countries is nice work if you can get it. But what drove the panel of judges to their selection was the sensibility behind these accomplishments. Using global strategies while satisfying local markets is not unique. Nor is employing a decentralized management structure to respond to local tastes. What set O'Reilly apart in their minds is the degree to which vision, leadership, skillful marketing, and an empowered employee base can execute the strategy on a consistent basis.

Much ink is spilt describing the company's low-cost operator techniques and its Phil Crosby-inspired Total Quality Management discipline. Both are important. But what funnels the vital oxygen driving the organization—Heinz's core competency if you like—is a collegiality and consistency that permits execution. Much of what is represented as America's competitiveness problem stems from organizational rigidity. O'Reilly's gift, other than his Jamesian urbanity (how many CEOs quote T.S. Eliot, the Duke of Wellington, and Will Rogers in one conversation?) lies in striking the right balance between control and anarchy. "He's bright, witty, intelligent and also highly intimidating, highly demanding," reflects Heinz Pet Products CEO Bill Johnson. "If somebody has a problem typically other managing directors are willing to pitch in to compensate for the financial shortfall or resource allocation. It makes this a demanding place because you have to satisfy your peers." Other senior managers and Heinz customers suggest that O'Reilly leads not as a general marching at the head of troops, but more like a physicist leading a team of biologists, geologists, and astronomers planning a space mission. The team is assembled periodically and the team leader probes via question. The Socratic method comes naturally to a Jesuit-trained mind. Says Weight Watchers International president Chuck Berger, "We tend to tell him everything because you don't wish to displease him. He has that effect on people. Besides he never erupts. You know you've disappointed him if he responds with silence. And if you get white-lipped silence, it's uh-oh."

Even customers succumb to the charm. "He's my hero," says IGA CEO Tom Haggai. "Heinz couldn't go up against Campbell in launching a line of soups or maybe it didn't work as anticipated. So he developed a store branded line with IGA. He can be ruthless. Peck's Bad Boy. He enjoys being different, as if to say, 'I know we're going to succeed no matter what you think of me.' He's taken a stuffy company and internationalized it." Safeway CEO Peter Magowan says, "Tony has done an outstanding job with Heinz. All Heinz operating companies are focused businesses, responsive to industry and consumer needs. Heinz is one of our very best suppliers."

There is one anomaly. At a time when CEO pay is subject to increasing scrutiny, the judges have selected a man who is generously compensated, even allowing for the company's strong performance. His 1989 total cash equivalent pay (salary and incentives, the proxy lumps the two) consisted of $2,756,545, which is a tad under the $3.2 million competitive total pay offered in the food industry. (CE's annual pay for performance analysis appears in the next issue.) But Heinz also gave him 1,269,160 options, exercisable with restrictions in a ten-year period, that grant the right to purchase shares at an approximate average price of $22.50 each. With Heinz common trading at $32.50, those options if used would provide a net gain exceeding $12 million. At this rate O'Reilly will barely see Ross Johnson's taillights (the RJR chief walked away with $53 million), but it will be interesting to see if future performance justifies the long-term gain.

At 56, life is not all ketchup and baked beans for the Dublin-born former rugby star, ex time and motion consultant, and youngest CEO of an Irish state-owned enterprise. Former Mobil vice chairman and now Bekaert CEO James Riordan remembers him (O'Reilly had served on Mobil's board) as intelligent and quick with the charming epigram. ("What is the Irish definition of a queer? Someone who prefers women to whisky.") In Kilcullen, Ireland, he is master of a 500-acre estate, Castlemartin, with an 18th-century Georgian manor house. His entrepreneurial interests include stud farms for race horses, cattle breeding, oil and gas exploration, and hotels, and he is Ireland's leading press baron. Total investments exceed $100 million.

A reflective man, Heinz's chief identifies most with Winston Churchill, "because he was absolutely dauntless and had the courage to learn. We are sometimes slow to make up our minds to do a lot of things, but once we decide to do something we stick with it. We stuck with Weight Watchers. In the first four years it was not a great success. We couldn't find a formula to unlock what we knew to be something quite important. But we eventually put it together by sticking to it."

What is the core competency of Heinz?
Professional collegiality is something we prize greatly. By that I mean a form of community within the organization that promotes support, openness, and candor and is underwritten by our structure of goal setting, compensation, and the sense of ownership that all the senior executives have.

We are probably unique in the United States in percentage of ownership by way of option that is controlled by management and the employees. In an era of LBOs, we're probably the only management and work team to have in a sense created an LBI, a leveraged buy-in, in that we probably have about 17 percent of the company, which is worth $9 billion, owned by management and the work force. That's very unusual.

This has been created over a long period of time. My predecessor, Burt Gookin, made a major contribution to our system by structuring an incentive program that had been very short-term goal oriented, until he brought in a long-term incentive program. When I took over in 1979 as chief executive—I'd been president since 1973—I emphasized the notion of the symmetry between shareholder and executive by introducing a vigorous stock option program.

Base salaries at Heinz are way below industry norms. The incentive programs are based on the year's results and certain subgoals. The long-term incentive program is based on three-year aggregate earnings per share calculations that give an intermediate-term focus to the way you manage your business.

If you miss any of the targets, 75 percent of your total compensation is at risk. And in many cases, people just have failed to get any compensation bonus in a particular year.

What did you bring to this culture?
A sharply redefined marketing focus. This has basically transformed the company. Our marketing expenditure went from about 2.5 percent of sales to 9 percent, which is really very big spending, even by Procter & Gamble's standards.

One of the reasons why I am often identified with marketing is that I am very responsive to demographic changes and I am fascinated by media changes in the world. I'm going to read a paper in Berlin entitled, "The Brand: Citizen of the World." Until mass marketing techniques were facilitated by television, the brand was citizen of a nation.

The advent of television in America heralded the great era of brand expansion in this country. It's my thesis that the advent of satellite television will transform the marketing map of Europe. Instead of having numerous brands that are being marketed in different ways in Portugal, Spain, France, and so on, manufacturers will embrace the notion of international brands which they mass market simultaneously through satellite television to 12 countries in 12 different languages.

Manufacturers will ask themselves, what inherently are the great brands that Heinz has, or General Mills has, or Procter & Gamble has? In our case we probably have over 700 brands of which interestingly enough, only 35 percent of our total sales are under the Heinz name. Sixty-five percent are our other brands: StarKist, 9-Lives, Ore-Ida, Weight Watchers, Near East, and so on.

We are considering the notion of extracting the major international brands that we think stand for the universal potential of the corporation, like Heinz ketchup, like Weight Watchers, like Heinz baby food. And we're thinking in global terms now, whereas prior to that, we never did. The "Dallasization" of the world, the "McDonaldization" of the world will be the most startling facet of the next decade.

"Dallasization" and "McDonaldization" imply that American tastes are being absorbed or grafted onto other societies? Don't French tastes remain French, even after 1992?

No. Don't you like Perrier?

But is that really "French"?

It's French. It's imported. It's from the Perrier springs. I think that that's a classic example of the way things are coming this way. Maxwell House is Swiss. But we are going to absorb an awful lot of European tastes, Ramen noodles from Japan, Mexican dishes (if there is a great Mexican food manufacturer), Benetton clothing, Gucci watches and shoes. The world is moving toward global brands.

I used to be a skeptic about that. But it is this powerful new agent, the magic of this eye in the sky that has so changed the marketing potential of the great brands. The Europeans are ahead of us on this. The most admired company in France with the largest capitalization on the Paris bourse, is LVMH, the company that has Dior. [CEO] Bernard Arnault may not be overwhelmed with the burden of his own humility, but he's done a good job. They are basically capitalizing on the social insecurity of the newly rich. It's a fascinating world that's opened up before us.

**How will Heinz ketchup or Weight Watchers be
marketed differently as a result?**

We have a recipe in Holland that wins hands down against our
British product in Holland and Belgium and Germany. We tested
the Dutch recipe in Britain and it loses hands down. So there is a
standard thing called Heinz ketchup, but it's quite different in the
two markets. It's the same product, but it just has a slightly different texture to it. The palate of the Brit requires a sweeter-tasting
product, and the palate of the German and the Dutch requires a
slightly spicier, sour taste. But the actual marketing message for all
of them is roughly the same.

The prospect of 1992 has changed our view of our British company. We're now thinking of factories that happen to be located in
Britain as "Eurofactories." We have built in Kitt Green, U.K., the
world's most modern food factory. With the Channel tunnel opening up soon, we will be able to deliver truckloads of our products.
We've moved into Spain and Portugal and Greece. They're countries that excite us very strongly. So we are very European and
non-nationalistic. We harbor great ambitions to globalize our
brands, particularly ketchup, baby food, and Weight Watchers.

**Observers assert that Nestlé and Unilever are mopping
the floor with American food companies in Europe.**

That's completely untrue. The fact of the matter is that, this year,
we have probably got the two most profitable food companies in
Europe—a lot more profitable than Nestlé or Unilever. I don't
know how you rank success, but my method includes margin on
sales, sales growth, profit growth, return on equity, return on
invested capital. By any of these criteria, we're better than Nestlé,
better than Unilever. You can buy Unilever stock for 11 times
earnings. One pays 17 times earnings for ours. And obviously, 40
percent of our business is outside the United States.

**Will international competition become cutthroat,
thereby putting pressure on your gross margins?**

We don't see any intensification of international competition
because of 1992. More damaging, particularly in Europe, is the
growth of the power of the retailers. The retailers in Europe are
extremely powerful and given very substantial latitude under the

antitrust laws by their individual governments. We have situations of almost oligopolistic strength in Great Britain, France, and Germany, where the three or four dominant retailers control 85 percent of all the buying decisions in each market.

That's very daunting, but if you have a great brand like Weight Watchers, they have to stock your product. Because you create the consumer demand by going directly to the consumer saying, buy our product, because it promises longevity, and a smoother figure, and a more elegant step in your stride, and the prettiest girl in the room. That's what Weight Watchers is all about. It promises control over your life, control over your calorie count and nutrition.

So that's the way you do it there, and you do it by inventive copy and you do it by strong marketing. This is an unrelenting nickel and dime business.

Will the "green marketing" phenomenon endure?
People now realize that there are real hazards, paradoxically, in fresh foods, which don't really get processed. After Chernobyl, in our Italian business, people ceased to eat fresh produce that they thought had been affected by the radium fallout. They used up virtually all our pre-Chernobyl stocks of processed products. We assumed after three or four months of stock that they would revert back to a mixture of fresh and processed foods. They didn't—they stayed with our products.

One of the reasons was that our Italian company was able to say, look, we conduct checks that no fresh produce manufacturer conducts. We actually start at the farm level. We in effect put up an "environmental oasis" around our products, and we guarantee that the manufacturer polices and controls procedures that ensure that the minimum amount of pesticide, of fungicide, of insecticide, of fertilizer, is ingested by anyone who eats their food. This has had an enormous appeal.

Five years before Alar was rejected by the Food and Drug Administration, we had ceased to use it. We believe that the purity of our brands is extremely vulnerable to this sort of criticism, unless we're extremely careful and extremely innovative about the future.

I don't think we'll get to organic farming, but one of the biggest opportunities opening up for food manufacturers in the next decade will be the public's concern about their own health and the ingestion of all sorts of toxic substances that hitherto they have assumed were not present in their food.

Proposition 65 in California, on the other hand, is a classic example of overkill. California has seceded from the rulings of the FDA. Soon we'll see an FDA for Californians that will dictate the tolerance level of carcinogens in each product. Then we'll have a label for California, a label for Idaho, a label for Iowa, and a label for Mississippi. It reflects an enormous upsurge in people's awareness that we are slowly poisoning the universe.

Won't it be easy for protectionists to hide behind the label of food purity?

This is what they call—the Japanese are masters of it—nontariff protection. I didn't think that the fidelity of the Japanese monetary or import system was threatened by our ketchup, and yet they managed to exclude our ketchup by the subtle business of abandoning all quotas but almost trebling the tariff.

The Europeans are no slouches at it.

Oh, absolutely perfect at it. The Americans have picked up on it, too. You won't see too many New Zealand dairy products around here in the United States, despite the fact that New Zealand can produce at half the price of an American farm. So, they shelter behind veterinary regulations, and so on. But I was in the milk industry in the early 1960s and you had no chance of getting around any of these barriers. At least now, you have a chance. Irish farmers will be supplying milk into Great Britain in the not too distant future. Dublin could easily supply it at a very much lower cost. Hitherto, there were all sorts of regulations. But they're going to go.

How much further can you reduce operating costs? One recalls the anecdote about your eliminating the back label from the ketchup bottle to save $1.5 million. What do you do for an encore? Eliminate the front label?

You would be absolutely amazed at what cost savings can be accomplished. Our North American task force now looks on North America as an entity. It's rather like the unification of

Germany in commercial terms. We just see the 20 million Canadians as an extension of the U.S. market, and we've found, to our surprise, that many things are substantially cheaper in Canada than they are in the United States. So we are supplying quite a lot of our packaging now from Canada to the United States.

Their costs are lower, which surprised the hell out of us. It may be that their suppliers were prepared to accept a lower profit margin. It may be that they are actually more efficient. Canadians are supplying our U.S. factories now. That may change. So we are very much now globalized by the power of satellite television and by the political and cultural integration of Europe and North America.

If you ask, where do we get growth from? We get growth from our power brands like Weight Watchers. We assiduously try to expand our share of ketchup and sauces and Ore-Ida brand potatoes. We took an initiative on dolphin-free tuna, which has a great deal of approval by the public. And while it may cost us a little more in sourcing, I think it will expand the market for tuna.

What does it cost to be seen as an environmental good guy?
The costs are quite significant, or could be quite significant because we walked away from one ocean, we walked away from a source—the eastern tropical Pacific, which contributes 20 percent of our total catch and is adjacent to our largest plant, our cannery in Puerto Rico. So we know there are going to be some cost increases for the raw material.

Fundamentally, the environmentalists won the battle. And they won the battle particularly with the young consumer, the kids. This particular cause is unique in that Flipper was part of American folklore.

It may seem clever to ride the green marketing wave, but what will you do when animal rights activists declaim against hamburger consumption and put your ketchup business at risk?
Well, at the end of the day, you have to decide. Society has its own particular agenda, and there are many agendas that can rally a cause. But I can't imagine that will ever be a universal cause in this beef-loving land.

**You've got task forces looking into Eastern Europe—
Poland and the U.S.S.R. What might we expect to see
there?**

My response would be all or nothing. I mean, you could see us in
the U.S.S.R. making a range of our products. You can see us in
Poland, which is the largest apple producer in Europe and the
largest potato producer. You can see us in both areas that we are
very big in. We're very big in juices for children and we're very big
in frozen french fries.

So obviously, we have the capacity to go into both countries to
satisfy what we've identified to be consumer needs. We think we
can help improve the diet in both Poland and Russia. The problem
is that there is no convertibility with their currency. And unless
we can get convertibility, we will not go in. I don't want rusty razor
blades, and I'm not sure I want to be the world's largest battle-
ship vendor.

**Having been selected by your peers as chief executive
of the year confers a kind of most valuable player
status. What advice would you give other CEOs who
compete internationally? What do they most have to get
right to face the challenges of the 1990s?**

The globalization of markets is not a future dream; it's a daily
reality. So the first thing they've got to do is to realize that they
have enjoyed the security and prosperity afforded them by the
first great experiment in common marketing, which is the United
States of America, and that now the world is a much more
ubiquitous thing than it was 10, 15, 20 years ago.

Don Petersen touched upon it in *Chief Executive's* interview with
him last year, which I found most interesting. We're not going to
engineer a car for Europe and a different car for America. The ex-
ternals may look different, but underneath it has the same basic
engineering.

We are all—all manufacturers of the world—going to have to
think that way. We're going to have to engineer global products. To
do that, you have to develop a global attitude. We cannot assume
that the way to do it in Tokyo is the way we do it in Wichita or
Pittsburgh. We have to go there and try to understand the market.

One of the things that Heinz enjoys to an enviable degree is cultural flexibility and enormous pluralism within its work force. Just listening to our managers is absolutely fascinating. The Chinese talking about their own market, the Japanese talking about theirs. The accents alone indicate the diversity of the company and the universality of it at the same time. We're a very attentive company.

The Interlinked Economy

Kenichi Ohmae
Director
McKinsey & Co., Japan

Forget us versus them. The world is becoming increasingly interconnected and we will eventually be part of one large, global community.

T he United States takes great pride in the Declaration of Independence, but now it is time for the United States to join the interdependent and borderless interlinked economy (ILE) forming around the world. We have to recognize that in today's world, the notion of national boundaries is not clear anymore. To which country does Honda-USA belong? To whom does IBM-Japan belong? IBM-Japan is a $10 billion company with 20,000 employees and last year reported a $2 billion profit, which corresponds to almost one-third of IBM's global profits. So does IBM-Japan belong to the Americans or to the Japanese?

The truth is, it belongs to neither. IBM-Japan is IBM and Honda-USA is Honda. They exist because they have the support of their customers and appreciation for their employees. They have connections with vendors and dealers, not with governments. Corporations survive as long as they serve their purpose and act as "social entities." Therefore, the concept of national borders—treating American-born companies as carrying the stars and stripes and Japanese-born companies as belonging to Japan—will soon become obsolete or irrelevant.

The fundamental reason for the obliteration of national borders is the power of information. Consumers today can tell which personal computer or laptop is best for them, whether made by Toshiba or Compaq. In the old days, international enterprise followed an exploitative system; in the case of Japan, once a foreign manufacturer received a production license from the government, he could exploit the consumer because he knew there would be no competitors. This kind of system still exists in developing countries, unfortunately, but in most developed countries, access to information is giving people the ability to choose the best quality for the best value. Therefore, the role of the government is no longer as integral or as powerful, nor should it be.

UPDATING JAPAN

In this context, the Japanese government is one of the most backward. The government has brought up the Japanese per capita GNP from $500 after the war to the current $26,000, but it still wants to sit in the driver's seat. The government should now let the people be in charge. In my book, *Zero Based Organization*, I analyze each of the Japanese ministries and propose a new constitution.

I discovered, for example, that the reason why Japan cannot communicate with the rest of the world lies with the Ministry of Education. In Japan, English classes teach literature, composition, and grammatical rules, instead of how to speak English. After six years of English education, students are still afraid to speak up and cannot even introduce themselves properly. American or British teachers could come to Japan and teach proper English, but they usually cannot speak Japanese, which is required for obtaining the Ministry of Education's license for teaching English. As long as the ministry maintains this bureaucratic attitude, the Japanese will not be able to communicate with the rest of the world.

I also looked at the Japanese Ministry of Health and Welfare, which oversees the pharmaceutical and medical electronics industries and certifies drugs. Should patients have adverse reactions to a drug, however, the government denies any responsibility. There are many lawsuits against the ministry protesting the approval of problem drugs. My recommendation is that if the ministry does not want the responsibility, it should not interfere but simply approve any drug certified by American or European authorities.

Also, if a medical doctor is certified by an accredited institution of a developed nation, he or she should be allowed to practice in Japan based on those credentials.

In order to fulfill the notion of a borderless economy, we have to change regulations and systems that are remnants of the 19th century nationalistic, mercantilist world.

WHAT IS AN IMPORT TODAY?

There are 2,000 U.S. companies operating successfully in Japan. Texas Instruments (TI) is the largest memory chip producer in Japan. TI once closed its Texas plant for memories (now reopened) and moved its memory chip production as well as its headquarters to Japan. Hewlett-Packard and AMR also make large profits from their Japanese operations. Coca-Cola comprises 70 percent of Japanese soft drink sales, is Japan's largest producer of canned coffee, and has many other successful product lines. The collective production and sales of the U.S. companies in Japan amount to $50 billion annually. But none of this is reflected in trade figures because these products are not imported into Japan. IBM-Japan's $10 billion output is produced in Japan. Texas Instruments is Japan's largest exporter of memory chips. Still, the U.S. government looks at memory chip imports from Japan and complains. Another aspect that is ignored: A large slice of Japan's exports to the United States these days is comprised of American companies' shipments to their parent companies and Japanese auto components for Detroit's Big Three.

The Japanese, like people elsewhere, buy products based on their comparative value and not their nationality. Per capita spending of the Japanese on U.S. goods is twice the U.S. per capita spending on Japanese products. Why do people not know this? The Japanese bureaucrats believe that silence is golden and have decided that when Americans are so upset, it is best to just listen to them; instead of solving a problem, they prefer to swallow it.

Many U.S. companies have expanded into Mexico also, and when their goods come back into the United States, they are registered as imports from Mexico. Again, Congress worries about lost competitiveness. A trade deficit is not the result of loss of competitiveness; it is the corporate decision to produce or procure elsewhere.

Corporations can migrate between countries because customers look for the best and cheapest products as long as supply is stable. And supply is stabilized when goods are produced within the market. That is why U.S. corporations represent one-fifth of European corporate activities. But the U.S. government, at least that part of it which publishes statistics, chooses to ignore this fact. The government does not track down U.S. corporations worldwide; instead, it remains within the borders and only measures the ins and outs of the measurable transfer of goods. In effect, it remains in the last century.

NEED FOR STABLE CURRENCY

The 19th-century trade model looked at export and import in terms of how many tons of goods crossed national borders. Nowadays, not just goods but money is transported across borders as a result of corporate activities. IBM's return on equity out of Japan was 120 percent last year; in other words, in a single year they recovered 100 percent of the equity they invested. No merchandise traveled across national borders, but statistics suggest there is a trade imbalance. By the old macroeconomic model, a trade imbalance drains the country's wealth. But this is also incorrect, because America does not use foreign currency for payments. In this sense, the United States has no foreign trade per se, only domestic purchases. When buying goods from Taiwan, Japan, Korea, or Mexico, the United States pays in dollars, which means that these commercial activities are identical to buying California oranges or Louisiana tea. America does not have "foreign" trade and foreign currency reserves, but statistically it is supposed to be involved in foreign trade, making government officials worry about the "trade deficit."

The United States is probably the only country that does not have to worry about foreign currency reserves because the government can simply use its high-speed printing presses to finance the purchase of foreign goods and services. America can buy easily from abroad because the dollar is and will be nearly universally accepted, as long as its value does not decline significantly.

During the Plaza meeting, Secretary of State James Baker and his advisers suggested that the dollar be weakened to gain competitiveness and correct the trade deficit. This kind of thinking is based on the antiquated models of David Ricardo and Adam Smith, which worked in the days when commodities were traded and price was elastic. Today, however, price elasticity is low. More fundamentally, to increase international competitiveness, we need to improve productivity and quality, not adjust currency. The manipulation of currency acts as a handicap, which lowers motivation. The U.S. government gives corporations a 20 percent handicap overnight in the form of a currency adjustment. So neither productivity nor competitiveness is improved.

Furthermore, the devaluation of the dollar has made America itself the most competitively sought-after product: the buildings, the corporations, the real estate. When Baker made his proposal, the exchange rate was 240 yen to the dollar; within several months the dollar dropped to 120 yen. This has not changed the trade balance, but it has made America a bargain because assets—both tangible and intangible—are also tradable. At 120 yen to a dollar, if you could collateralize the city of Tokyo, you could buy the entire United States and all its corporations. If you could collateralize the Japanese Imperial Palace, you could buy the whole state of California. The trade deficit amounts to only 0.4 percent of U.S. GNP, but when you change the currency exchange rate, you make a fundamental aspect of a country (i.e., the assets) cheap. In the borderless world, Rockefeller Center does not have to be transported to Tokyo to be owned by the Japanese.

The economies in Japan and the United States have been steadily growing 2 to 4 percent per year for the past eight years. Inflation has been unchanged at 2 to 3 percent, which means that the currency exchange rate between the two countries should also have been rather stable. Each time the exchange rate changes, this means something went wrong, and economists erroneously attribute this to factors such as the trade imbalance, which is minuscule compared with the size of our economies.

ECONOMICS UNBOUND

With the disappearance of national borders, everyone can participate in everyone else's real estate market as well as stock market. Therefore, currency exchange rates should be set to equalize purchasing power of goods, assets, and financial fundamentals (the expectation of return on certain investments), reflecting the differences in inflation rate and interest rate. This also requires political providence, because politicians can have a tremendous influence on the foreign exchange rate. Some $600 billion changes hands every day over the markets of Tokyo, New York, and London, compared with $20 million of goods traded among Japan, the United States, and Europe. Hence, the impact of these currency exchange rates is enormous, especially because currency traders do not really understand the workings of the economy. The markets, however, have not properly reflected the tradability of assets.

Today, we can literally see the forming of an ILE; people and corporations routinely crisscross between national borders. The emergence of a gigantic ILE, which behaves in a totally new and complex way, renders existing macroeconomic theories obsolete and requires our rethinking and reshaping of models and standards. Lower interest rates traditionally stimulate the economy, but in the borderless world, if the U.S. economy increases, jobs are created in Korea, for example.

In Keynes's day, there were national economies modified only by export/import. Hence, if his theories do not accurately describe current economic conditions, it is the fault of contemporary scholars who are still applying the nation-state model to changed circumstances. Instead of realizing that a new and more global model is required, they simply try to adjust the Keynesian model by adding modifications and writing academic papers about them. What happens if money supply gets tight in a country in today's world? It comes in from abroad in the form of, say, impact loans. In 1988, 90 percent of the new bonds of Japanese corporations were issued in Europe. If the government raises the interest rate, cheaper capital comes in from abroad.

SPECULATIVE MARKETS

Interest-bearing instruments have lost much of their allure these days; speculative ones such as real estate and stocks, which do not bear interest, have become more compelling. The largest of these financial instruments is the foreign exchange market itself, which, as mentioned before, moves $600 billion daily. Without this kind of "pocket" in the form of the speculative market, the money created by the governments' sloppy money supply policies, known as superliquidity, would flow into the real market, causing tremendous inflation. Politicians and bureaucrats say we have learned how to curb inflation, but this is not true. The money is simply routed into a much more speculative and risky market instead of the inventories in the real marketplace. Inflation is measured by misleading indicators, the Consumer Price Index and the Wholesale Price Index, neither of which is based on prices of speculative items.

In the old days, when speculative instruments were not available, the excess money bought up goods for the future. Excess liquidity created inflation. Now we have speculative instruments that absorb the excess money and prevent the symptoms of inflation, though we actually live in an enormously inflationary world (50 percent per annum in some speculative markets). Tokyo's real estate market has gone up five times in five years. Now Osaka real estate is going up. Toronto's market is going up because Hong Kong is moving in. The speculative market knows where the activities are, and currently, they are burgeoning on a global basis. This is another characteristic of the ILE: Even inflation is restrained by being contained within these speculative market "pockets." After the crash of the Tokyo Stock Exchange in early 1990, the money migrated to New York and Frankfurt. Eventually, it will go to France and Italy.

JUST SAY PARTNER

In a recent book, *The Japan That Can Say No*, by Sony Chairman Akio Morita and politician Shintaro Ishihara, the authors are mistaken. The book is based on the old mentality that it is America versus Japan and Japan can't say no in this relationship. America, however, is an abstract noun. Does Morita mean to say no to Rep. Richard Gephardt (D-Mo.)? Probably not. There is no such thing as America saying yes, Japan saying no. A country is an abstract entity. One must distinguish between various parts of a country—Osaka and Tokyo are both in Japan but are quite different from each other.

Americans think that all Japanese are out to punish America. But in Japan, as in the United States, there are vast differences of opinion among residents. In the same way, when Rep. Helen Delich Bentley (R-Md.) smashes a Toshiba radio, the Japanese think all Americans want to smash Toshiba radios. Our two countries have lived together for over a century now and yet, when it comes to Japan-U.S. issues, we do not have the prudence to examine the fine structures of this relationship. But more and more leaders realize that we have to start doing so, and we will come to see that most Japanese attitudes are not very different from many American attitudes; the Japanese are also beginning to enjoy the benefits of the ILE.

We have to establish that the real economy is the entire world and devise new guiding principles accordingly. Some parts of the economy are completely international, whereas others are very provincial, so not everything crosses national borders and the borders are not perfectly permeable. Yet money moves easily across borders. We have to figure out appropriate theories and frameworks to deal with this complex ILE. We also have to work out a "Declaration of Interdependence" and devise a super-governmental structure to regulate this new economic environment, geared toward the year 2005, around which time we can expect the ILE to take full shape. Under the new structure, even the tax I pay in Japan will not end up 100 percent with the national government: one-third may go outside of Japan, one-third to Japan, and one-third to my local community. We are all global citizens. We should be citizens of the interlinked world first, before we are citizens of a specific country.

Kenichi Ohmae, Ph.D., is the director in charge of McKinsey & Company's offices in Japan, the author of *The Borderless World*.

The Uses of Failure

Dr. Kent G. Stephens
Chairman and Chief Executive
Sage Analytics International, Inc.

If at first you don't succeed, fail, fail again!

P aradoxes abound in the 20th century, and I would like to suggest another one: the best way to achieve success is to determine—as carefully as you can—how you are apt to fail.

When a company or organization engages in long-range planning or sets the time frame for a particular project, the assumption is that careful strategic thinking will lead to success. After all, managers are supposed to be success-oriented. To consider the possibility of failure is negative thinking.

As a consequence of this predisposition, however, often these goal-oriented strategies go wrong unexpectedly. The reason is that success was factored in from the beginning as the inevitable end result, excluding any possibility of failure. Whatever the plan or project may be, the motivations and decisions of those who want the plan to work—and therefore are designing it for success—create inevitable biases.

This holds true no matter what the topic may be for structured planning: plans for a new product introduction, setting goals for next year, establishing a means to evaluate continuing performance, and seeking means to make operations more efficient.

The failure-avoidance technology I've been advocating to management is essentially an outgrowth of the old "fault-tree" analysis pioneered by Bell Laboratories 30 years ago, and further refined at Boeing Aerospace by a team of mathematicians, including myself. For obvious reasons, the nuclear and aerospace industries were in the forefront of serious efforts to develop a fail-safe system. During the course of this research, it soon became apparent that failure could be defined, measured, and analyzed much more easily and accurately than success. In those days the focus of the research was on the development of computer hardware and software to model scenarios and process data quantitatively. Again, to an extent, what went into the computer reflected the predispositions and assumptions of management.

Today, we are getting a more accurate end result due to technological enhancements and breakthroughs. Failure-avoidance technology—to be truly effective—must consider the opinions and observations of management and employees. This subjective information—in addition to hard data about the plan or project under study—is part of a detailed information-gathering process preferably carried out by impartial investigators or analysts.

Truly effective failure analysis involves three kinds of interaction: component to component, person to component, and person to person. With this input, it is possible to get a comprehensive portrait that helps to separate the critical problems from the insignificant, and to rank each potential problem area in terms of importance. Organizations, from the U.S. Army to the California public school system—along with a wide range of manufacturers—have been successful using this method of failure analysis.

Component to Component

A case in point is Syncrude Canada Ltd., a company that separates tar sands into crude oil and sand. Refining crude oil requires the use of massive machines called fluid cokers. Syncrude wanted to find out why recently installed cokers were plugging up so rapidly, causing frequent shutdowns. In the first 18 months of use, the cokers were operating at only 53 percent of capacity.

Failure analysis studies were carried out in two waves: The first wave identified what areas in the production setup seemed most likely to blame. The second study took those areas apart and dug deep down to root causes. The first big discovery: the study spotted 250 engineering deficiencies in the design of the coker installation. The second big finding: these deficiencies could be eliminated by making changes in operational procedures, which Syncrude began to implement. Within two weeks, the cokers were running with an efficiency rate of 85 percent of capacity; the company reported that the operations transformation was adding $2 million a day in increased revenues.

Person to Person

Scientific application of failure-avoidance technology also works well when the subject under the microscope is strictly personnel. One example is Vaughn Manufacturing Corporation—a family-owned business in Salisbury, Massachusetts, manufacturing a high-grade water heater—which was trying to cut costs and increase productivity in a shifting marketplace. However, the recently unionized, small workforce didn't seem to be cooperating. There was friction with management, and a general perception that morale was down.

What could be done to get everybody up to speed again? The underlying objectives were to inspire workers to cooperate in an overall effort to increase productivity by cutting down on rework, slashing overhead, and reducing the costs of manufacturing. Management realized these goals would be hard to accomplish with disgruntled workers.

The failure analysis study at Vaughn included in-depth confidential interviews with employees on the subjects of employee job satisfaction and on improving lines of communication with supervisors. Research identified 26 root-cause problems that would have to be addressed; study results were presented to management and supervisors, which provoked a great deal of discussion.

Person to Component

One foreman, a veteran at Vaughn, said 90 percent of the critical deficiencies identified could be immediately corrected without spending any of the company's money—if modifications in the way management and workers related to one another were made.

Vaughn took the foreman's advice and changes were made. There was an immediate improvement in morale, which translated into greater productivity. The company became more competitive and is in a strong position today. Workers at Vaughn recently voted out their union, a sure sign of worker contentment.

Failure analysis has proved that motivation is all-important. Even seemingly innocuous changes in management style can result in incredible improvements. The challenge is to identify problem areas that may have been institutionalized years ago.

FAILURE ANALYSIS OUTSIDE OF INDUSTRY

Outside of industry, failure analysis has also proved extremely effective among schoolchildren and the military. The California State Department of Education decided to try failure-analysis technology in a pilot project. This involved seven schools in the Sacramento area where some 40 percent of the students were at high risk for failure or dropout because of such indicators as poor test scores, frequent absences, and disruptive behavior.

Research was conducted that probed the many ways in which students and teachers interrelate during a typical school day. The study identified several critical areas where failure seemed to be built into the system. Recommendations went into effect. A turnaround took place and all indicators rose: test scores went up, absentee rates dropped, and behavior problems diminished.

Scientific failure analysis technology has benefited the U.S. Army as well. It helped to improve its M1 battle tank, to field the improved tank on schedule, and it provided valuable information to the army that went into a new battlefield doctrine—the Airland Battle. Other recent military applications of failure analysis technology range from the highly technical Airborne Optical Adjunct to the Strategic Defense Initiative (Star Wars) to the development of a new "total army personnel model," a study of the personnel system.

I've been involved with hundreds of major applications of advanced failure analysis technology studies. These almost always have a common theme: failure is usually a result of people's perceptions of how they are being treated.

FAULT ZONES

I've identified what I call three categories of failure or "fault zones" that characterize all the critical paths to failure that have harmed a project or blunted an organization's objectives.

Fault Zone One

Fault zone one is defined by how people in an organization perceive they are being treated and has nothing to do with competence. No matter how efficient an engineer may be, for example, he will not make the contribution he is capable of if he feels he is being mistreated.

Fault Zone Two

Fault zone two includes the inadequacies inherent in what kinds of jobs people do—the technical aspects and competency requirements of the job. These problems may or may not be remedied by providing additional training to individuals in their specialized fields.

Fault Zone Three

Fault zone three—which is inextricably bound to the other two fault zones—is made up of inadequacies that are inherent in an organization's vision of itself: what it could become and the direction it believes it is taking.

Based on an analysis of several hundred failure-avoidance studies, most of the weaknesses we've identified lie in fault zone one—people performing inadequately because they perceive they are being mistreated—whereas the majority of efforts to improve motivations and job performance of these alienated people are misguided attempts within fault zone two. In other words, if you're having a problem with your personnel department, you don't solve it by sending personnel to advanced equal-opportunity training. Most often, inadequacies have nothing to do with the credentials of the person doing the job; it's how he or she is being treated within the system that's causing the trouble.

Failure analysis illustrates over and over again the many pitfalls involved in strategic planning and in the organization—and reorganization—of people who want to do a good job, if they're comfortable with their environment and secure about their share of the responsibility for the company's success.

Dr. Kent G. Stephens is chairman and chief executive of Sage Analytics International, Inc., the Provo, Utah-based firm that provides Sage Analysis™ to firms both in the United States and abroad. Dr. Stephens is the world's foremost authority on theory of failure avoidance and its companion stewardship management; he is the creator of the internationally acclaimed Sage Analysis™; he has consulted and advised in the management principles and decision-process design for industry and government.

Does U.S. Industry Lack the Standard Advantage?

Jawed Wahid
President
Recognition Technology

Standardized development of high-tech industries can make the difference between having an edge in the market and being an also-ran.

I n an increasingly competitive world, it is not enough to have access to, or to make use of, high technology. The advanced technologies that can give American—or German or Japanese—industries a considerable competitive edge do exist, but it is the environment in which it is used that spells the difference between effectiveness and waste, or between having an edge and being an also-ran.

As has been proven in the field of personal computers, companies employing high technology will each go their own way unless a set of standards is in place. Before IBM's disk operating system (PC-DOS) became the industry standard, each manufacturer of personal computers had its own operating system, and each was incompatible with all the others. The emergence of IBM's PC-DOS (also sold under the name MS-DOS), more than anything else, has put a personal computer on every desk.

The personal computer is reflective of much of what is high-tech. It has many uses in any industry, but it does nothing in and of itself: It must have specific applications programs for it to work. The adoption of PC-DOS and MS-DOS as industry standards made the computer revolution possible. Software packages that would run on a broad range of machines could now be mass produced at affordable prices.

Another field that could have the same revolutionary impact is image processing, the uses of which range from adjusting the contrast on a TV screen to discovering stress patterns in jet engine parts. Image processing systems can duplicate tasks of interpretation and recognition performed by humans, but without their fallibility.

We started our company knowing that the medical industry had a dire need for visual image processing. Our aim was to sell the image processing hardware, the basic technology, to OEMs (original equipment manufacturers) in the belief that industries servicing the medical field would find solutions to their specific problems. Unfortunately, we found that none knew enough to harness the new technique.

PROHIBITIVELY UNIQUE SOLUTIONS

The dilemma is evident in the failure of MVI (Machine Vision Incorporated), a high-tech company in our industry that had the technology, the people, and the money. It found solutions to many industrial problems, but all were unique solutions to problems in single installations. MVI produced everything from pharmaceutical to fruit inspection packages. They harnessed machine vision for equipment to preset analog watches that could do nothing beyond that one function. That was fine for a while, but then they found out that they could not grow that way. The manpower requirements would be immense. They needed experts for almost every industry. Now MVI is virtually out of business.

The problem in image processing right now is that every application is unique. Imagine if only one user wanted a spreadsheet and asked IBM to write this one program. The cost would be prohibitive, and that is the problem shared by much of the high-tech world. There are no standard packages for any one industry. The hardware exists, but the software is missing.

Almost every industry could benefit from image processing, but only a few know of it, and much of the technology remains on the shelf. The techniques will spread only after our universities and technical schools turn out more electrical engineers with degrees in image processing. This is beginning to happen as some colleges and universities now offer courses in image processing, but obviously, more is needed. Those entering traditional industries must be educated to the possibilities of high-tech, and the older engineers should also be taught by cycling them through seminars and symposia.

The bind comes when high-tech companies such as ours are too small and cannot afford to run such programs. Some of the larger high-tech companies do offer training, but much of this is product-specific for they, of course, are interested in teaching only about their own product. Larger traditional companies who could afford programs to disseminate such information mostly lack the knowledge to do so.

The aim should be to standardize applications industry-wide so it pays to produce software that can be broadly applied throughout an industry. Without standards, that software is simply too expensive. If U.S. industry could get together, as I believe Japanese industry has done, and set industry-wide standards, then such software could be developed.

If industries set standards they all could buy the same software package and benefit from it. The industry could better meet domestic and foreign competition. Instead, manufacturers choose not to use new technology because of the cost of custom-designed software.

Standardization could take many directions. The pharmaceutical industry might, for instance, settle on an optical inspection standard for pill sizes. If most manufacturers agreed to inspect their pills by the same criteria, the development of software to perform that task would be economically feasible. Some customizing might be needed at low levels, but that could simply be a matter of choosing an item from the program's menu.

Although existing hardware platforms allow certain levels of applications, they, too, could be greatly improved were industry-wide standards set. Speed of working is an example. Much development work today is directed toward making hardware work faster. In many cases, problems can be solved but the hardware is too slow for the solution to be practical. Returning to the pharmaceutical example, existing methods may allow the inspection of five pills a second, when the industry calls for a minimum inspection rate of 50 pills a second. A tenfold improvement in speed might cost 100 times more. Were a firm willing to spend $500,000 to solve a problem it would be solved. However, as this is not cost-effective, the project dies. Yet, it would be feasible were the industry to set standards and apportion costs. The dilemma, in the absence of such standards, is that machines that can do the work are not cost-effective, and cost-effective machines cannot do the job.

Another example is the automobile industry, which has great need for machine vision for various aspects of inspection and design. Each manufacturer develops some technology in-house and then funds a number of outside companies to develop this technology and feed it back to them. Each of these companies works unto itself, on whatever it believes is the best technology. This approach has not been overly fruitful: The offshoot company gets money coming from the parent company but not the overall guidance, cooperation, and information that would flow to it in a joint effort with other companies. Consequently, the solutions that such firms come up with too often disappoint their sponsors. Each manufacturer cuts the cord once it realizes that it is getting an inadequate return on its investment.

STANDARDIZATION: AN OPPORTUNITY?

A whole industry might do better by establishing a consortium, or "think-tank," with the resources to develop both algorithms and technologies. Many problems can be reduced to common factors that, once solved, can be applied to different fields. Automobile manufacturers and other traditional industries could jointly develop techniques to solve classes of machine vision problems to benefit all involved.

One of the first tasks of such a research center would be to define what could be standardized, and to decide on the problems that might be solved by higher technologies. The consortium would set priorities on what could reasonably be done immediately, in the long term, and in the very longest term. In this way, standards and dominant technologies could evolve together.

Although a consortium of this kind could successfully be based on one industry, it would work best were it to embrace a broader spectrum. Instead of working on narrow solutions or applications, it should aim to encompass the variants of different classes of problems. It would involve basic technological developments applicable to problems across industry lines. Automobile and aircraft manufacturers could join together with industries from what has come to be known as the "rust belt" to, say, solve many machine vision problems.

A central clearinghouse for the initial investigation of new technologies and the circulation of its findings among its members could be established. Members would be informed that technology "X" exists, with various future uses and applications. They would then be invited to join in its development. Companies would explain their problems, as well as the technological barriers to their resolution. The central clearinghouse could then combine the information from all sources, and determine which problems share some common ground and organize the research to solve them drawing on those with the ability and the inclination to participate.

High-technology firms could provide the basic knowledge and experience. They are expert in many fields, each able to do some things very well. These companies, funded by the consortium, could guide the group research. It would prevent duplication of effort. If, for example, smaller companies inform a central clearinghouse of which directions they are taking, the clearinghouse could approach the larger industries to assess the potential uses of this technology. The users would define what this technology could do for them.

MEETING THE JAPANESE CHALLENGE

Under the scheme I suggest, the central body would set standards once needs are defined. At the very least, one of its functions would be to drive the research to make it happen. The consortium or foundation could also specify standards for providers of an application so that companies wishing to use it know exactly what it does and how it will do it. No longer would there be 10 different solutions to the same problem.

One of the tragedies of our present chaotic situation is that the high-tech industry seems to be moving away from, rather than toward, standards. In machine vision, for instance, slow scans, line scans, variable scans, and direct digital outputs are among a number of different scanning techniques now available. These may improve machine vision, but in the absence of a central standard-setting committee, they encourage everyone to do their own thing.

Gaining acceptance of standards, much as they are needed, will not be easy. People will still refuse to take part, believing that they are giving up their own secrets, losing their creativity, or surrendering their competitive edge. Whenever companies in an industry wish to get together and work for the common good, there will be those that feel it will infringe on their intellectual freedom or personal gain.

Although there is no foolproof way of overcoming these natural reservations, it may be possible to make sure that no one picks up the ideas of others, develops them, and then runs off with them. The consortium would also have to act as a policing agency, making sure that the firms contributing to development of a "star" technology are properly rewarded. Obviously, if one company got burned, the word would soon spread and everyone would back out. Ground rules must be established to ensure that those who discover and develop a technology will benefit from their labors.

The Japanese channel funds in directions that they consider to be desirable. A smaller company developing a technology that is seen as beneficial to the growth of the country and the industry is sure of getting funding. Once the technology is developed, that company sells the product or supplies it down line to larger corporations.

If we see standardization as an opportunity and not as an obstacle, and if we cooperate to achieve it, we can go a long way toward regaining our industrial preeminence. Americans could then, conceivably, put the fruits of our industrial inventiveness to better use, and meet the German and Japanese challenges head on well into the 21st century.

Jawed Wahid is president of Recognition Technology, Inc., the Westborough, Massachusetts-based company specializing in the design and manufacture of image processing and machine vision software and hardware for science and industry. Prior to founding Recognition Technology in June 1983, Wahid served as director of hardware engineering for Data Translation, Inc., where he was responsible for all board-level hardware design.

Getting Everyone to Think Strategically

Benjamin B. Tregoe
Chairman

Peter M. Tobia
Vice President
Kepner-Tregoe

More and more top executives seek strategic input from the lower rungs of the corporate ladder, and find that broader participation helps translate vision into reality.

O nce upon a time and not too long ago, there was a widely held perception that strategy was the exclusive preserve of the CEO and a few of his trusted subordinates. The annual retreat became a metaphor for top management's sovereignty over strategy, with key executives meeting away from the hubbub and *hoi polloi* to toil through pressing directional issues. Few managers down the line knew what transpired up on Mount Olympus. Often, they were left to divine the latest strategy from whatever moves top management began to make.

In many organizations, however, top management's monopoly on strategy is giving way. Strategy or vision is no longer hidden in the vest pockets of a few executives. It is being brought into the open and becoming everyone's property. Participation, for years the mantra of gurus promoting operational excellence, has now become the imperative for strategic success. And with good reason. A mid-level manager of a New Jersey utility summed up the need for involvement this way: "Don't ask me to kill for somebody else's vision."

Rambo rhetoric aside, there is great need to make top management's vision "ours." Otherwise, vision will not become action. Commitment requires broad and deep participation in further refining and executing the organization's strategy.

In addition, the day of the CEO as superman is over. Economic, sociopolitical, and technological change puts all the old axioms up for grabs, and well beyond the reach of one person to understand, interpret, and act upon. Today's CEO needs to tap an array of resources, especially when the future of his organization is on the line.

Zuheir Sofia, president of the Columbus, Ohio-based Huntington Bancshares, faces change and stiff competition in the markets his bank serves. According to Sofia, "Banking today is sailing in uncharted waters. Competition is different. Traditional answers no longer hold. This means we need as many people as possible thinking creatively. This can be done only by being free to participate—and the place to start is with the organization's strategy."

GUIDELINES FOR STRATEGIC PARTICIPATION

Granted, broader participation is essential for implementing strategy, but how should the CEO proceed to encourage participation without inducing chaos? There are three key ways.

First, recognize that the future direction of the organization remains the unique responsibility of the CEO. Participation should not dilute that responsibility. Arguably, the CEO wields more power over the organization's future than over its current operations. As Bob Morrison, the recently retired CEO of Consumers Packaging in Canada, observes:

"A key to my role is concerning myself with the future health and prosperity of the operation. This means I must take a longer-term view than the people who are charged with day-to-day responsibilities. I must look further out, set a direction, and meet whatever challenges come along to the future of this business."

Second, the key to strategic success is to gain broad commitment through participation rather than striving for consensus. Participation in the strategic process does not mean that strategy should become an exercise in Athenian democracy. Not only is the CEO ultimately responsible for an organization's vision, but his is always the deciding vote.

Victor Rice, CEO of Varity Corporation (formerly Massey-Ferguson) is shifting his company's strategic direction away from a concentration on agricultural equipment to a broader, more diversified enterprise. Concerning his company's new direction and the issue of participation, Rice remarks:

"Yes, there are different management styles, but they only represent different ways for getting the organization to follow the CEO's vision. In the final analysis, the CEO establishes the vision and constantly pushes it. He may, in the process, gather the judgments of those around him. But ultimately, he is the one responsible for saying, 'This is the way we're going!'"

Third, have a clear idea of the various roles people should play in the strategic process, from the CEO right on down. In a study of 19 organizations we conducted, CEOs felt they were responsible for articulating the vision, ensuring strategic consistency throughout the organization, establishing strategic reward mechanisms, involving the board of directors, communicating the vision, and keeping the strategy updated and relevant.

On the other hand, senior management viewed itself as a kind of alter ego of the CEO. Its responsibilities are summed up by Ned Richardson of the Federal Reserve Bank of Cleveland when he says, "My responsibilities as vice president of service management include helping to formulate the strategy and then motivating, pushing, shoving, coaxing, and cajoling so the strategy gets implemented."

But participation should not stop with the top team. In most organizations, the great black hole of strategic involvement is the middle-management tier that includes business unit managers, functional managers, managers of geographical areas, staff department heads, and key individual contributors. This black hole need not exist.

Organizations that are successfully implementing strategy have redefined the role of middle managers to include significant strategic responsibility. Such firms expect the middle managers to understand the organization's vision and all the nuances that apply to their function.

In many instances, middle managers (1) clarify top management's initial thinking about the kinds of products it wants to offer and the markets it plans to serve and then (2) develop specific action plans. Some managers are also responsible for seeing that systems are in place to support and monitor the strategic direction. Although middle managers have different roles in implementing strategy, one connecting thread is the shared responsibility for effectively communicating strategy to subordinates.

Malcolm Vinnicombe, a divisional chief executive of Courtaulds Furnishing and Textile Furnishing Group in the United Kingdom, spoke about detailing corporate strategy at the middle-management level. Vinnicombe explains, "Understanding the relative emphasis of different products or markets as defined by our corporate strategy was immensely useful at unit level. At this level, we had all the facts and could refine top management's product and market thinking as it applied to our area of the business."

Information is the raw stuff of strategic thinking and the middle managers can help the top team answer the crucial question: "How viable is the vision when looked at through the narrower prism of a middle manager's job?" Middle managers and key contributors are closest to the action and are top management's best sources of information, whether that information tests assumptions that underlie the strategy or indicates how well strategy implementation efforts are proceeding. Providing this information may involve the marketing and sales functions in testing customer intentions and reactions. It may involve research, product designing, and engineering in verifying product requirements. Finance, management information systems, and accounting may be required to provide the appropriate performance measures. Personnel, training, and human resource groups may provide information on levels of commitment and strategic understanding.

One other important strategic role of middle management involves them in setting the vision for their own units. Ideally, strategy should cascade down through the organizational hierarchy. Strategy should proceed from corporate, to global and area business groups, to business units, with progressively more detail and refinement added to corporate's thinking about products, markets, and capabilities at each step. Much of this refining can be done by middle managers, with approval from the next level up. But what about those less-than-ideal situations where there is a strategic vacuum in an organization? Here, middle managers can seize the initiative. Chet Marks, director of planning for Dow Chemical's U.S. Plastics businesses, says:

"People who manage small businesses, or functions, or small geographical regions don't have the same size job as people who manage big businesses or large geographical areas. But they have similar strategic responsibilities.

"They have a responsibility for setting a strategic direction. But if nobody tells them what to do strategically, they should decide what they will do and communicate it up to their superiors and down to their subordinates. If your superiors don't like what you're doing, they'll tell you not to do it. If they do, maybe you'll be promoted."

Middle managers should be proactive in fulfilling their strategic responsibility. If the vision is unclear, or the information needed to implement it is inadequate, these managers must take the initiative and probe for answers at the next level up.

In organizations that effectively manage strategic participation—"strategically excellent" companies—even employees at first levels can and should participate in the organization's vision. Ed Lowell manages an electronics plant for the Minnesota-based OTC Group. Ordinarily, someone with his operational responsibility doesn't pay much attention to strategic vision. But Lowell sees communicating the vision to his work force as critical:

"It is essential that people feel they are contributing to the vision. We take pains to ensure that our people, from the shop floor right on up, understand where they fit into the whole process and that their role is important. If they understand the vision, the end products they are working on, and the importance of their contribution, they will be responsive, work toward higher quality, and reduce costs."

Although first-level employees do not require the same depth of understanding as higher-level managers, they should realize the benefits of working in an organization that integrates day-to-day operational activities with the longer-term success promised by the vision. Tim Smucker, CEO of The J.M. Smucker Company, cites an example that demonstrates the payoff from that understanding:

"Typically, I arrive at a plant a little early, before the formal strategy/operations review. I try to meet informally with as many plant people as I can.

"Once I sat beside a woman and asked her how long she had been with us and what shift she worked on. It turned out she had been with us for seven years and worked on the night shift. Noting that it was only 2:30 in the afternoon, I asked her why she came in for this meeting. She said she wanted to know what the company was doing and that she appreciated being included."

Employees at grass-roots levels should be able to relate their jobs and priorities to the company's overall strategy. Achieving quality standards on the assembly line may be the critical factor in product differentiation that makes a strategy succeed. At the sales level, taking time with the customer to probe for new needs can be critical. At the technical level, in the research function, staying on top of the relevant literature might just unlock the door to keeping the strategy on the leading edge.

OPPORTUNITIES FOR STRATEGIC PARTICIPATION

Whatever model for setting and implementing strategy your organization employs, the strategic process offers great opportunities for participation. For example, in our consulting work, we ask the top team first to consider the organization's basic beliefs. These "self-evident truths" can exercise a gravitational pull on the strategy. They must be made explicit so they can be revised or reaffirmed to square with the strategic direction. Once there is agreement on the basic beliefs or values of the organization, the next question becomes, "Are we living up to these beliefs?"

At the Washington Mutual Financial Group in Seattle, chairman Lou Pepper formed a committee on values and staffed it with middle managers. The committee's charge is to take a good, tough look at the organization to uncover any gaps between rhetoric and reality. When the two diverge, the committee then reports back directly to Pepper and changes are made swiftly.

One crucial challenge in setting strategy is achieving a tight definition of the future scope, emphasis, and mix of products and markets. Top management at Washington Mutual met to set strategy and did some initial product and market thinking for the future. But that thinking had to be refined. As Kerry Killinger, the Group's senior executive vice president explains:

"When the top team set strategy, we agreed on the broad range of financial services we would offer now, and on those we might consider offering in the future."

"We let this settle in for a while, then reconvened the original small group of executives, as well as a much broader group of middle managers. We wanted them to work through the issues involved in developing future opportunities."

Strategic thinking requires careful testing against the hard facts of reality. The initial judgments that top management makes about the future nature and direction of the business must be confirmed, modified, or discarded. The reality-testing process opens up yet another opportunity for broad participation in the organization's vision.

At Consumers Packaging in Canada, a significant strategic shift led the company away from dependency on glass packaging to other forms of packaging, especially plastics. This required considerable investment in new plant equipment and acquiring new technology.

CEO Bob Morrison raised the key question about the new strategy when he said to his top team, "That's what we think. Now, what do our customers think we should be?" Morrison's question led to considerable involvement of his people, right down to the individual salespeople.

Reality testing was done initially at the corporate level by executives talking with their counterparts from customer organizations, and then by personnel down the line who talked with respective customer contacts in marketing, sales, product development, and service and support.

Organizations are vast storehouses of information waiting to be tapped. Much of this information is operational in nature. This is as it should be. But hidden in most organizations is information about environmental trends, customer needs, competitive moves, technological change and the like, all of which is vital for setting and testing strategy. Yet for many organizations, that rich storehouse remains an unused asset and a missed opportunity for broadening participation in the organization's vision.

STRATEGIC PARTICIPATION: ELEMENTS FOR SUCCESS

Broadening involvement adds complexity to the strategic process. It would be far simpler to go it alone. But setting and living by a vision of the future is a social act. A vision that does not touch every employee's head, heart, and hands remains an idea in waiting. For vision to come alive, participation is needed. This requires careful management.

Strategically excellent companies possess five common elements that mark them for success: a common strategic language, a simple and specific strategy, managed participation, a motivated work force, and CEO involvement.

By "strategic language," we mean a common vocabulary of expression that everyone in the organization understands. One way to attain the common language is to have an agreed-upon strategic process. By "process" we mean a necessary sequence of logical steps for collecting and analyzing information and then drawing inferences.

A strategic process provides a common road map for participation, which is especially important when an organization has a great number of disparate businesses or operates in a multinational environment. Explains Peter Barton, Varity's vice president of business development, "We had a common strategic process and language at the corporate level and rolled it into each business. Our divisional vice presidents understand what we're talking about when we use strategic concepts, and we at the corporate level can understand the businesses when they talk about their strategic objectives and action plans."

Second, strategically excellent companies keep strategy simple and specific so mere mortals can understand and contribute to it. A strategy entombed in a thick three-ring binder will never rise from the dead. Tim Smucker observes that his organization's strategy is "simple and specific enough to be carried around in everyone's head." Not surprisingly, just about everyone at Smucker's participates in implementing the vision and uses the company's vision to make day-to-day decisions, from personnel selection to inventory control.

Third, strategically excellent companies carefully manage participation. The last thing any CEO needs is a strategic free-for-all.

Managing participation down through the organization entails clearly defining roles along the lines already discussed and carefully creating opportunities for managers and key contributors to become involved. A growing number of companies employ cross-functional task forces to stimulate creativity and commitment and to resolve key strategic concerns.

The fourth element making for strategic success, a motivated work force, keeps vision an ongoing, vital influence. Top management has to provide the enthusiasm so that managers down through the organization *want* to get involved; participation should not come off as a command performance.

Middle managers and other key contributors should participate in the strategic effort because they see an opportunity to provide input into the organization's future, to gain valuable experience in developing their strategic capability, and to gain exposure to the next level up.

Ben Goodman, a mid-level manager at Consumers Packaging, reflects on his experience as a member of a strategic task force:

"The results we produced were much more than the recommendations made. We learned from one another about what type of questions to ask our customers and how to probe for need. The updates we provided gave us a unique opportunity to exchange ideas with senior management and to further shape our perspective."

There are many other ways CEOs are keeping vision vibrant, from rewarding strategic initiative and not just operational accomplishment, to building discussions about strategy into the management routine of meetings and planning cycles. Larry Reed, president of Dow Corning, keeps enthusiasm high the old-fashioned way. It is important, he maintains, to "repeat, repeat, repeat the specifics of the strategic message." When enthusiasm is in the air, everyone wants to be involved.

The fifth element for strategic success, CEO involvement, is the most crucial. Without the personal involvement and encouragement of the CEO in every step along the strategy continuum, from initially formulating strategy to action planning, vision will not come to fruition.

CEOs who have labored mightily to broaden participation in the strategic process have rarely been disappointed with the results. They found that when the key elements for success are present, participation energizes vision. It tests and refines strategic conclusions and is essential for translating management's vision into action.

Benjamin B. Tregoe, Ph.D., is chairman of Kepner-Tregoe, Inc., a Princeton, New Jersey-based organization specializing in strategic and operational decision making. He is the author of several books on top management strategy, including the recently published *Vision in Action*. Peter M. Tobia, Ph.D., is vice president of Kepner-Tregoe, Inc. Tobia is coauthor of *Vision in Action*, along with John W. Zimmerman and Ronald A. Smith.

Speed Kills the Competition

Richard D. Stewart
President and Chief Executive
Computer Corporation of America

Quality is not enough; you have to be quick.

As a competitive advantage, the use of time is shaping up as critical in today's fluid and highly charged business frontiers. The drive to deliver new products or services, and to respond to a changing marketplace in the least time possible, has become the growing obsession of industries all over the world, with astonishing and powerful results. The agile injection of speed into development, manufacturing, distribution, and most recently into sales and marketing, constitutes the ultimate competitive weapon. Doing it fast defines a winner; not keeping pace identifies certain losers. Even the previously "safe" businesses, such as the old, regulated airline, trucking, telecommunications, and often, insurance industries, are realizing the compelling need to do it fast and right the first time.

In the insurance industry, one not historically known for flexible operations, there is innovation brewing to decrease the time involved in purchasing a health insurance policy. Soon, companies and individuals will also be able to tailor health insurance plans to suit their unique requirements, and input that plan directly to the provider. In addition, the information gathered from all sectors of the health care field will enable health care consumers to make more cost-effective use of health care services.

A graphic illustration is an oft-told story about the nature and consequences of business competition in today's markets. It's about the Honda-Yamaha war that exploded in 1981. Yamaha tried to unseat Honda as the world's largest motorcycle producer. To the battle cry of "Yamaha wo tsubusu," translated into a chilling, "We will crush, squash, slaughter Yamaha," Honda vigorously, even mercilessly, defended its title and market presence.

Using the products of effective time-based management—speed and flexibility—as its major weapons, Honda brilliantly introduced or replaced 113 new product models in one-and-a-half years, though it had entered the war with 60 models. Honda also raised the sophistication of its product lines through the addition of such features as four-valve engines, and beat Yamaha into the market at every turn. Yamaha publicly conceded defeat and pledged respect for its competitor, while Honda returned its attention to breaking into the automobile market.

WINNING THE FIGHT

Not all competitive situations have the legendary quality of the Honda-Yamaha war, but most competitive crises offer three choices to management: fight, join the competition, or concede and walk away. Those companies that understand the competitive value of time and have the organizational flexibility to use time to their advantage have the best chance of winning the fight. In fact, companies who use speed as a tactic to "kill the competition" generally stay ahead of the pack and avoid these costly battles altogether.

George Stalk, Jr., a senior partner at Boston Consulting Group, eloquently describes the advantage speed brings to companies. "As a strategic weapon," Mr. Stalk writes, "time is the equivalent of money, productivity, quality, even innovation. . . . The ways leading companies manage time—in production, new product development and introduction, sales and distribution—represent the most powerful new sources of competitive advantage."

Companies that have recognized the competitive value of time and its products, speed and flexibility, are known now by various labels, including "time-based competitors," "fast-cycle companies," and "third-wave companies," to name just a few. These keep moving; they anticipate change. They've collapsed their decision cycles and use technology, information, and organizational flexibility as a foundation for product and market decisions.

SPEED IN MANUFACTURING

In the 1970s the introduction of new technologies to automate various product processes suggested a revolution in the way products could be brought to market. At that time, though, these new technologies, such as CAD/CAM (computer-aided design, computer-aided manufacturing) and robotics, were typically adopted to automate familiar product development or manufacturing tasks. One of CAD/CAM's pioneers, Computervision founder Martin Allen, began his role in the industry when he realized that the drafting tools of the 1960s were almost identical to those of the 1760s. His goal was to automate the drafting process. He used the same basic approach, but with quicker execution. This was the beginning of a technology revolution.

The early corporate appetite for automation technologies, which ranged somewhere in the hundreds of millions of dollars, bordered on gluttony. Purchase decisions focused on machine-versus-man, or rather machine-mimic-man cost analysis, particularly in the adoption of robotics.

But with the on-site presence of these technologies soon came the realization that the traditional foundations of product design, high-volume manufacturing, and market distribution—though automated—were grossly underutilizing the potential of these new productivity tools. Technology enabled business to cut costs, but corporate structures and systems and the way business competed for market share anchored it securely to the past. Business paused and considered.

INDUSTRY'S PRODUCTIVITY TOOLS

The revelation came with the recognition that the same tools that automated the labor efforts of the engineer or production worker could also be used to add flexibility to a company's product offerings; to respond rapidly to change; or even better, to create change by rapidly introducing new products and services in time periods not previously thought possible.

The use of productivity tools such as just-in-time (JIT) manufacturing processes made dramatic inroads toward changing business methodology and philosophy, changes that were key to both speeding up processes and reducing costs. Traditional thinking emphasized economy and efficiency in manufacturing achieved as a result of quantity. New thinking created processes that ensured the manufacture of a million widgets. But the ultimate benefit of the automation process, the CAD/CAM and JIT methodologies, came from the ability of the company to respond faster to customer demands, to offer new features and services that met a changing environment before the competition could react.

AT&T's Shreveport Works plant, designed for manufacturing business and consumer phone and phone systems, adopted JIT processes and the concept of the focused factory as one important response to deregulation, and a new competitive environment. The Shreveport program improved its manufacturing processes by designing materials flow based on the pull of materials from customer to vendor, reducing waste and eliminating non-value-adding steps, and installing a continuous flow assembly scheme. The program has produced inventory reductions, substantial cuts in materials handling costs, and decreases in required testing. The ultimate paybacks are faster time to market, reduced waste, and increased customer satisfaction—all decided competitive advantages.

But what about marketing, sales, and product distribution? If companies can't reduce time in the marketing, sales, and distribution cycles, gains in production time may disappear from the total picture.

INFORMATION TECHNOLOGY

Information technology (IT), the productivity tool of marketing, sales, and distribution, has been advancing just as meteorically as other technologies. And the appetite for IT is just as robust. In 1950 much less than 10 percent of corporate investment occurred in the area of IT, and even in 1978, investment in IT only reached about 20 percent of all new investment in plants and equipment. However, in the 1980s the IT explosion began. By 1984 more than 40 percent of all new investments in plants and equipment were for IT.

Just as was the case with initial CAD/CAM and other automation technology investments, business may now be in danger of choking on its huge investment in information tools, technology, and capability, without an efficient way of accessing information the way managers want it, when they want it. The IT investment of the 1980s allowed companies to change from being product-oriented to being market-oriented. But being market-oriented has its own pitfalls, which might be compared to the problems associated with a large, inflexible manufacturing plant—it is too big a unit to use as a competitive tool. Rather, the companies must be customer-oriented to be able to identify and market to smaller, targeted sets of customer requirements.

FLEXIBILITY

The creative and effective use of IT can achieve this second most desired product of time: flexibility. To restate a blunt truth, in rapidly changing economies and markets, companies that exhibit flexibility to anticipate change and respond quickly will survive and prosper. The others won't.

One constant in business today is change. The key to success is the ability to use information as a value-added entity to enable quick response where and when change is taking place. For example, European countries are gearing up for 1992. According to John F. Magee, chairman of Arthur D. Little, "A renewed European economy is a real threat to those American and other non-European businesses that fail to react quickly and flexibly to a change as potentially profound—economically—as any in European history. . . . The forces driving change in Europe are specific to each industry, and effective responses need to be specific to each company."

If a company is not positioned to "play," and no one knows for certain now what the competitive environment will be like, that company will not be among the competition.

"Playing" in the world economy today means anticipating change and responding quickly. For example, a midsize company today in a European country with a customer base of 15 million may find itself in 1992 with a potential customer base of 100 million. To react intelligently and maximize opportunity, company management must be able to gather the right information, use it to analyze the impact of the situation at hand, and design possible actions or orchestrate changes to the situation. In competitive battles, company management must use information to make decisions on fighting, joining the competition, or walking away from opportunity. Unfortunately, in most companies, the kind of information required to make strategic decisions isn't always readily available.

Roadway Express, a leader in the "less than truckload" (LTL) trucking industry, broke forth from deregulation with an idea about information. Roadway believed that to be a leader it had to treat information as a product or service to its customers. In the LTL industry, shipments often make their way via a number of trucks. Tracking a particular shipment is a complex process that required extensive handling of information, but tracking individual shipments and providing quick and accurate information about shipment progress was just what Roadway's customers wanted.

Roadway adopted advanced information technology in the form of a networked computer system with distributed computing capability and intelligent workstations at each trucking terminal, connected by a data management product designed for rapid response and large capacity. This system allows Roadway to instantly track the location and arrival time of every shipment.

Further, Roadway has proved to be a leader in implementing voice response system technology, a method of allowing instant on-line access to shipment status information. A Roadway customer simply calls a phone number, keys in the specific freight number, and receives a voice-simulated update on exactly where the shipment is and when it is expected to arrive. The database is updated continuously from each workstation on the network. Once again, the use of information to strip time from the cycle provides the competitive advantage.

MARKETING AND SALES

Although tools and technology that increase productivity in product development and manufacturing have captured the attention of business management, little technology and few tools have been successfully applied to actually increasing productivity in marketing and sales.

One only has to look to the sky to see other good examples of companies using IT to gain a competitive advantage. Most U.S. airlines offer a frequent flyer program. These programs have used information-based marketing to inject brand loyalty into an industry where convenience of flight time had previously dictated purchase patterns. Information about customers gathered instantly from frequent flyer programs is then available to analyze route offerings, flight schedules, fares, customer preferences, and other factors. Quick reaction to customers' needs is possible through the availability of the right data.

An exceptionally clever use of IT to achieve competitive advantage occurs within Gelman Sciences, a manufacturer of scientific filters. In the past, Gelman sold exclusively through its dealer network, which blocked its view of specific customers and users and hampered its ability to respond as quickly and effectively as it wanted to market changes and user preferences. This really affected its reputation.

To get to know their customers and reward customer loyalty, Gelman launched its "frequent flyer program." As part of this program, coupons are included inside product packaging for return to Gelman, which tallies individual accounts for each responding customer.

Gelman expected that the program would encourage customer loyalty and heighten name recognition of its filters. What came as a pleasant by-product was its ability to use this new database to gain a competitive advantage. When a distributor chose to carry a competitor's product, Gelman used the muscle of its identifiable loyal customers to maintain its clout. It also uses the frequent flyer group to test-market new products or new directions, achieving significant marketing productivity. In Gelman's case, the speed inherent in its ability to implement IT to achieve its goals provided the edge.

Marketing is, of course, an area rich in opportunity for productivity gains. For example, Information Resources Incorporated (IRI), a leading and innovative market research firm, has pioneered the marriage between scanning technology and market testing in a product it calls Behavior Scan, to provide its clients with timely data on consumer buying patterns as a result of exposure to the client's advertising campaigns.

The sample consumer (IRI uses a test market of 3,500 households) is selectively shown specific television advertisements from an IRI client. That same consumer brings a coded identification card to the supermarket, which is scanned before purchases are scanned and recorded. Combined with data gathered from the specially directed cable television showings of the client's ad, the data collected from scanning systems identify clear preferences and buying patterns.

Using leading-edge information systems with enormous capacity, flexibility, and rapid response time, IRI in turn provides proprietary information to its clients. This measurement leads to concrete decisions on advertising investments and airtime purchases for specific markets.

NOW AND TOMORROW

One can easily imagine the day when all individuals will carry coded cards that capture all the data a retailer needs to know as soon as a customer walks through the door. Or better yet, store personnel would anticipate customer requirements by using specific past buying patterns stored in databases. By quickly accessing this information, they would then send the merchandise directly to the home. The dramatic rise in the number of narrow niche catalogs is surely a precursor to this scenario.

Collapsing the selling cycle by using specific information of target markets is the goal of most of today's consumer product companies. In the last two to three years, one of the nation's leading food and consumer products conglomerates has developed and used an enormous marketing database—built by customer response to offers or surveys—to execute more and more precisely targeted marketing programs. Because their database software provides extremely large capacity, exceptional response time, and flexibility of query, the marketing group can now see buying patterns more clearly and more quickly and can convert these data into meaningful findings and recommendations. As one company manager explains, "The technology is here. The real challenge is rapidly developing the application to take advantage of the opportunity."

Companies that have recognized and met the challenge of increasing sales and marketing productivity early on are already way ahead of the competition and have made it difficult to be overtaken. These companies have been the "firsts"—the first to recognize opportunity, the first to introduce the right product, the first to gather market share, and the first to use information access and manipulation as the cornerstone of time-based marketing.

These companies tend to put information into the hands of those who can use it to make quick and effective decisions, whether those people are on the factory floor or the executive floor. These companies have recognized that new business frontiers, in fact, require new ways of doing business, new thinking on organization structures and processes. They have, in effect, begun to restructure and flatten out the organization, and have found that giving people an opportunity to use more and better information actually fosters ideas and creativity.

Competition now or tomorrow is certainly not for the fainthearted. There will be the well-rewarded winners and some losers, and the rest will be "survivors." The calculated injection of speed and flexibility into the decision-making process will be the edge needed to "kill the competition."

Richard D. Stewart heads the Cambridge, Massachusetts-based Praxis International Inc. Established in 1992, Praxis International Inc. evolved from Computer Corporation of America, a software and applications company founded in 1965. Previously, Stewart was president and chief operating officer of GCA Corp., a manufacturer of equipment for integrated circuit production and factory automation. Prior to joining GCA, Stewart spent 20 years at GE in a broad range of operations, from applied research and development to product planning and marketing to general management.

The New Calculus of Growth

Michael Allen
President
The Michael Allen Company

In the 1990s companies will have to grow more from within.

T he era of restructuring and LBOs has been a sobering re- minder of corporate management's responsibility to provide attractive returns to shareowners. An extraordinary shakeout and buyout of underperforming corporations has occurred. Over 30 percent of the *Fortune* 500 list of 1979 (162 corporations) have been acquired or taken private in the decade. These companies failed to shape and execute an appropriate strategy for profitability and growth. To survive in the 1990s, CEOs will need to maintain required levels of profitability, but they will also need to sustain wealth creation by real growth. Internal growth, as opposed to acquired growth, should return to favor as the acquisition market becomes more efficient and bargains become scarce. Growth will not be limited by lack of market potential. Global opportunities abound, fueled by the changing needs of consumers, the chang- ing structure of business customers, the productivity power of expanding technology, and the desire of companies and countries to participate in global economic expansion. Nor will growth be limited by management's inability to identify market growth segments and develop new product or service ideas; these skills can be found in plenty. Rather, the limits to growth will be found in organization behavior, risk aversion, and protection of the status quo. A recent Reebok management meeting epitomizes the degree of change that inevitably accompanies rapid growth: Only one of the 200 attendees had been with the company for four years. We believe that the direction of cause and effect is that change in behavior leads to growth. Therefore, real growth can be thought of as the rate at which a business can change. In that sense, there are real barriers and limits to growth in many enterprises. They are unwilling to seek out opportunities that derive from change and cannot provide an enabling culture for growth. The subject of this article and the challenge to CEOs will be their ability to accelerate the pace of change in their increasingly far-flung and potentially cumbersome enterprises. The new calculus of growth identifies six axes along which CEOs can prompt their organizations to change and grow. Each needed behavioral shift is relevant to the 1990s, but represents a change from the popular management prescriptions of the 1980s.

FROM MARKET DRIVEN TO MARKET ANTICIPATION

We have seen a renaissance of market and customer sensitivity in the 1980s, which has brought with it remarkable structural change in many industries: Retailers have shifted from multipurpose, standard formats to specialized formats for different customer segments; lodging providers have introduced new property types, price points, and service levels to meet specialized and shifting travel behavior; packaged goods companies have proliferated stock keeping units (SKUs) to meet increasingly sophisticated consumers' needs for variety, nutritional, and quality products; and advertising industries have reflected shifts in media use to magazines, cable, and radio.

In short, business planners and marketers are tracking customer behavior and responding to changes with new products, services, channels, packaging, and so on. We've heard of companies becoming "obsessed" with customers and being market driven. As a result, market information providers have experienced spectacular growth.

While this renaissance is an advance, the market driven philosophy as practiced in many companies is still limiting. It relies much too heavily on researching present and past customer behavior. It often gives late warning of market shifts. By the time a new buying pattern is observed, someone else is already supplying it. Consequently, we continue to find former market leaders with lots of market data preempted in new market segments by newcomers who did a better job of anticipating customers' unmet needs. For instance, the growth of delivered pizza, ready-to-assemble (RTA) furniture, eye care chains, and bottled water all exemplify market myopia by former category leaders. Table 1-1 shows that the growth leaders typically have not been the size leaders and have generated stockholder value at a higher rate.

The techniques and methods that prove useful in anticipating new market needs are different from data-based, analytic, market research. They aim to identify small, fast-growing, emerging needs—not large, established needs. They focus on customer problems—not established preferences and loyalties. They identify new, small competitors rather than analyze large, established competitors. They use unstructured, nonevaluative thinking sessions—not rigorous, analytic, data validation. In sum, the market-oriented company of the 1990s will turn its efforts to anticipating and testing market needs—much more than monitoring, measuring, and analyzing past market behavior.

The CEO who wants his organization to lead market change will look beyond the market driven paradigm and test carefully his company's style of market evaluation. The CEO will accept that new market opportunities cannot be documented and analyzed as well as might be desired. Successful marketers will not be able to prove their ideas. The CEO will reward and encourage those willing to risk their credibility in anticipating change—and penalize those who are surprised by it.

FROM BUSINESS ANALYSIS TO BUSINESS UNDERSTANDING

Business analysis, like traditional market research, also suffers from a tendency to develop static, historical perspectives. A preoccupation with the question of how the business is performing is also limiting. Management's attention is focused on performance comparison with history, with goals, or with peer groups.

TABLE 1-1
Growth Leaders Build Shareowner Value More Rapidly

Business Category	Size Leader				Growth Leader				$ Mkt Value Per $ Sales	
	$ Billion	78	88	Δ	$ Billion	78	88	Δ	Size Leader	Growth Leader
Discount Retailing	Sears	17.5	50.3	32.8	Wal-Mart	1.2	16.0	14.8	0.30	1.06
Specialty Retailing	Woolworth	4.8	7.1	2.3	Melville	2.0	6.8	4.8	0.46	0.56
Autos*	GM	63.2	121	57.8	Toyota	9.8	29.1	19.3	0.29	0.48
Apparel	Nike	0.2	1.7	1.5	Reebok	0	1.8	1.8	0.67	0.71
Components	Texas Inst.	2.5	6.3	3.8	Intel	0.4	2.8	2.4	0.50	1.55
Food Processing	Sara Lee	3.5	10.4	6.9	Borden	3.8	7.2	3.4	0.47	0.57
Pharmaceutical Medical	Johnson & Johnson	3.5	9	5.5	Merck	2.0	5.9	3.9	1.57	4.30
Entertainment	Warner	1.3	4.2	2.9	Disney	0.8	3.4	2.5	1.69	2.46
Financial Services**	Citicorp	87.2	207.7	120.5	Amex	17.1	142.7	125.6	0.05	0.10
Computers	IBM	21.1	59.7	38.6	DEC	1.4	11.5	10.1	1.17	1.03
Insurance	Aetna	9.5	24.3	14.8	AIG	2.0	13.6	11.6	0.25	1.00
Office Equipment**	Xerox	5.9	16.4	10.5	Canon	1.4	8.6	7.2	0.34	0.39
									7.76	14.31

*Stockholders equity used in place of market value

**Assets used in place of sales

If the CEO wants his team alert to change, he will insist not on more analysis, but on "understanding" how business performance changes as the environment changes. He'll require more understanding and action to deal with the impact of product and market complexity, shorter technology cycles, new channel economics, functional competitors, increased quality and service levels, and the impact of transnational supply and demand.

Although these prevalent, environmental forces are often raised as issues, they are not converted to growth opportunities. Traditional financial analysis and functional performance evaluations often fail to show how a business's economics are impacted. Worse still, poor analysis may suggest that these market changes merely increase costs and erode margins. Therefore, it may be inferred, a slowdown is called for in product, market, channel, technology, service, or international investment and development—at just the time when they represent new value-added opportunities. Business analysis shows change to be a cost; business understanding can show which changes are, in fact, a profit opportunity.

FROM STRATEGIC THINKING TO CREATIVE THINKING

There has been wide growth in the application of strategic management principles during the last 15 years. Recently, the strategic thinking of CEOs, their teams, and advisors appears to have been heavily oriented toward the concepts of developing and sustaining competitive advantage. In the process the strategic vision of many businesses may have been limited.

The focus on competitive advantage, augmented by intensive competitive analysis, has had persuasive supporters. They argue that in maturing, consolidating, and increasingly globally competitive markets, growth and profitability depend on market share wins to achieve segment scale, leadership, and barriers to displacement. The work of The Strategic Planning Institute on the profit impact of market strategy (PIMS) theory and the writings of Michael Porter have documented this reasoning.

However, this pattern of strategic thinking is based heavily on the premise of zero-sum or limited-sum markets. It leads to heavy attention to supply-side competitiveness (low-cost leadership, productivity, global sourcing, etc.). It has been a major contributing factor in the numerous acquisitions, restructurings, and consolidations of the last decade. Companies have made a virtue of refocusing on competitive leadership in their core businesses. However, preoccupation with the competitor has also detracted from attention to the market and to opportunities for value-added growth. Markets remain hugely elastic to effective innovation of good-quality products ("lite" foods and beverages), good service (Club Med), useful technology (fax machines and car telephones), and new information or entertainment (the VCR boom). Unfortunately, these illustrations are the exception, not the rule. Preoccupation with competitiveness seems to squeeze out innovativeness. Strategic thinking and its analytic support disciplines have been the forte of a breed of executives less adept at creative thinking. Techniques of portfolio analysis, business segmentation, and value analysis have thrived—and may have optimized results—but they are not powerful techniques for generating real growth, creating market demand and innovating products or services with higher value added.

Therefore, we believe the CEO who is dedicated to growth will rejuvenate his enterprise's commitment to supporting the innovator and the creative thinker. Just as the bureaucracy of staffs has come under attack in the 1980s, so the CEO might strip away the negativism and risk aversion that stifles creative thinking. CEOs who insist on "thinking outside the box" will be rewarded by a stream of ideas and the growth they produce.

FROM ORGANIZATION STRUCTURE TO ORGANIZATION CAPACITY

The organization approach of a company should be strongly influenced by the degree of change that is called for in its plan. The pressures for profitability in the 1980s have driven organizations to eliminate all but lean, functional staffs and to manage around decentralized units. Improved planning, budgeting, and information systems have put stronger performance controls in place. However, these flatter, leaner, more tightly managed organization structures have, as frequent side effects, limited capacity to adapt to and reinvest in change.

To be more dynamic requires discarding organization structure as an end. There is no final or end point structure, only the capacity to recognize and adapt to a continuum of change. This capacity includes increasing the mental ability of the enterprise, developing the aptitude to lead and coach new behavior, supplementing the existing business resource with new expertise, and expanding the utility of the business resource to play multiple roles.

A crucial attribute of the change-responsive organization is strong horizontal linkages. These may take the form of market managers, business unit general managers, regional general managers (but not committees, councils, or internal boards). In a dynamic environment strong multifunctional or multiproduct team leadership is required to recognize and adjust to new market opportunities. For example, in the last two years, Procter & Gamble shifted from brand management to category management, and Pepsi-Cola from a functional structure to an integrated, regional business structure.

Whereas functional excellence was important to each of these great marketers in the 1980s, it is now clear that their organizations need greater capacity or "band width" to handle the complexity, variety, and pace of change required of leaders in the 1990s.

FROM MANAGEMENT DEPTH TO MANAGEMENT STRUCTURE

The 1980s have seen profound shifts in the basic contract between manager and corporation. In many cases of corporate ownership change, wholesale management cuts have taken place, ending or revising careers. Even in surviving enterprises, the loyalty of a company to its employees—particularly middle and upper management—has given way to a harsher, performance-based contract. Massive early retirement programs have taken place at such great "management development" companies as IBM and GE, and the pressure for star performers has increased outside managerial hiring over internal training and development. For many, this is a disturbing set of changes, but they appear to be in tune with the times.

Major public enterprises have their survival on the line and are frequently examined and ranked according to shareowner value creation. In this spotlight they want top managerial talent now. Increasingly, corporate management teams are like professional sports teams, with high pay for heavy hitters and quick relegation for the scoreless. These teams are becoming smaller in number but more elite, with managers of greater stature taking on bigger responsibilities. To grow, businesses require talent and energy of a high order, which is scarce. Therefore, it's better to have one manager with a big job paying $200,000 than four with more limited responsibilities earning $50,000 each. This trend is leading to a rethinking of traditional job evaluation systems that define pay levels by points that reflect the size of the management task. The system of paying market rates is also being questioned as yielding "me, too" managers, not distinctive talent. Levels need to be reset and reevaluated to allow a corporation to pay for the people who can exploit a business's real growth potential.

Management depth and training may have been key when controlling organization size was the primary corporate mission. In the 1990s, in contrast, management stature is needed to lead the growth of complex enterprises.

MANAGING THE CHANGE AGENDA

A centerpiece of leadership style in the 1980s was to manage around issues. The identification, analysis, definition, and discussion of critical issues led to ongoing changes in the agenda of management meetings. Management consultants adore issues because they require study, analysis, and objective resolution. But what has all this issue paralysis to do with change? If anything, it deferred the need for action and limited execution of growth ideas.

The change-driven CEO worries less about the issue management agenda and more about managing the change agenda. He draws a map of the basic changes required in how the organization must behave to execute growth strategies in a new environment (Table 1–2). These changes in style start with the leader

TABLE 1-2
An Extensive Change Management Agenda

From	To
Leadership, Shared Vision	
Clear, in charge of agenda	Less clear, agenda changing
Independent unit plans	Integrated, single business strategy
Strong centralized direction, narrow band width	Decentralized management, greater variety
Management Effectiveness	
Do it all, run faster	Selective, do it smarter
Marketing by brand, channel	Marketing integration by segment
National sales, distribution programs	Localized planning, funding, and tailoring
Human System Productivity	
Functional duplication	Functional integration
Output at all cost; spend budget	Output at economic cost; beat plan
System Leverage	
Distributor as executional partner based on support level, constraints	Distributor as strategic business partner based on commitment, ownership
Initiative at the top	Initiative at all levels
Culture and Attitudes	
Individual performance and career advancement	Team performance and business growth
Upward performing; high turnover	Downward developing; growth in job

himself. He articulates a different vision of the enterprise and must win his team's commitment and support. His management team will probably have to change radically to deal effectively with a major shift in business strategy. The dynamic growth leaders have been characterized by substantial turnover and upgrading of top management—witness Apple, Reebok, Wal-Mart, AIG, and others. The degree of top management change has been much smaller at the size leaders. Changing the productivity of the human system remains a difficult and unresolved challenge for many companies. Crude approaches like overhead value analysis lose more, long run, in employee alienation than they gain, near term, in headcount reduction. Continuous improvement philosophies and "work out" programs are being rediscovered by U.S. corporations after a 25-year hiatus. They require sustained leadership and commitment, which is sometimes difficult in today's corporate environment of changing ownership and mobile management. A crucial improvement need in productivity management is to separate the costs of operating the business today from the expenses of reinvesting in programs for tomorrow's growth. CEOs should change their vision from low-cost producer to lowest-cost operator and most aggressive reinvestor. The days of cutting "futures" expenditures to make today's numbers have to be banished.

Culture and attitude shifts have been heavily worked in the management literature of the 1980s, but the pace of change in some corporate behavior would still make snails seem like sprinters. The leaders appear to be talking less about empowerment and more about real ownership interest in the enterprise's growth. One clarion signal of the 1980s restructuring trend is that ownership provides far stronger management motivation than even the most sophisticated compensation schemes.

A second powerful tool in changing organization attitudes is effective, simple, inspiring communication to the troops of what their jobs and lives are all about. Ford's "Quality Is Job One" stands out as a unifier of employee and customer. CEOs would do well to discard the tired and sometimes fake exaltation of employee commitment, pride, and teamwork. Better than bragging about something that is in doubt, the CEO should daily explain and promote the win-win game between employee and customer.

Michael Allen is president of The Michael Allen Company, consultants specializing in strategic management. He was formerly vice president of corporate strategy at General Electric and created the Nine Block concept for GE.

The Strategic Choice of Markets

Harry F. Bunn
President and Chief Executive
Ronin Development

Guided by a rigorous framework for assessing current and future markets in a uniform and unemotional manner, the CEO can make better and more balanced decisions.

C onsider the following scenario: It was XYZ Corporation's annual strategic planning session. Managers from each of the firm's operations presented their business plans for the next four years to the chairman. Most had done their homework; each had lobbied the members of the executive committee for support of his plan; some had used emotional arguments stressing the link of their line of business (LOB) to corporate roots. Everyone wanted corporate resources.

The CEO and his executive committee, on the other hand, were facing the realities of the overall financial condition of the corporation. They needed to decide how to allocate scarce resources. Courage meant closing down certain LOBs and channelling the resources into more attractive businesses. Their argument was that the corporation should be marketplace-driven, but could the CEO choose between funding $50 million for development of a cross-LOB market in the health care field and $50 million for development of a new component for a major product line? The CEO was fed up with wrangling, lobbying, and emotional plays.

In the past the outcome of the planning session had been a compromise. The corporation kept the status quo, which upset the fewest people, but resulted in a bland continuation of traditional approaches. None of the poorly performing businesses were shut down and too little investment had been made in new and emerging units. A fellow CEO had used a much more authoritarian approach and had made radical changes. Unfortunately, many of his decisions had been wrong.

Clearly the time had come for a rigorous framework; one that would provide a uniform way to compare one business/market with another and determine the "bang for the buck" of investing in each. The framework had to be developed, proven to be "fair," and then implemented.

The aforementioned scenario illustrates the importance of establishing a framework for decision making. Using an eight-point approach, the following questions should be answered: (1) Which markets will you assess? (2) Which parameters should you use? (3) How important are these parameters? (4) How attractive is each market? (5) What does it take to succeed? (6) How do you match attractive markets to success rate? (7) What should your strategic investment portfolio contain? And (8) How can you improve your position?

NARROWING IN ON THE PLAN

Corporations often begin market analysis by asking the question, "What business are we in?" This is a useful exercise depicted in Peter Drucker's classic example of railroad management's breakthrough when they realized that the business they were in was not railroads, but transportation. Their real competitors were the airlines, and their marketing strategies had to relate to that environment. Instead, the railroads could have decided that they were in the real estate business. They could have built office complexes at prime sites around their stations or invested in residential real estate in remote locations and then provided high-speed links for commuters.

If management assesses the current environment correctly, it must look beyond the present and decide what businesses fit in with the future. A more useful approach, however, is to dismiss businesses the corporation will not operate in by a process of elimination. After that, all remaining markets or businesses offering some hope of success become the overall "arena of interest." Within the arena of interest you need to take each business/market and determine how attractive it is compared with others.

What are the businesses whose attractiveness you want to define? They are not necessarily the established SBUs (strategic business units) currently in the corporation. Most companies set up their business units based on product and/or geography. Neither of these is appropriate. Instead, we should allow the market to define our segments.

THE TARGET IS SMALL

The concept of the corporation as a "diverse portfolio" of businesses is outdated. Increasing competition will be the byword of business in the next decade. The smallest corporations will globalize and use the increasing speed of communications and information processing systems to challenge subsidiaries of even the largest corporations.

The generalized resources and broad market participation viewed as strengths in the 1980s will be inappropriate in the 1990s. Competitive fronts will be in narrower and narrower niches, where both large and small corporations will contend on a relatively level battlefield. Market selection will be the key issue facing the CEO.

We must allow the market to define our segments. Who are the customers and what do they want to buy? These market segments may include product, but must start first with a market definition. Valid segmentation implies a commonality of customer needs and wants, so that only a single strategy is applicable to all customers in the segment. The segment can be broad (e.g., households in the United States) or narrow (e.g., mid-price, one-family homes with fireplaces in the Northeast).

MARKET FOCUS

Markets can be identified by the CEO, or a planning team, or they can be based on market research using cluster analysis, regression techniques, or expert systems—including such algorithms as

ID3. By grouping similarities of customer needs and forming segments, these statistical approaches allow the market to define itself.

In the final stages, assessment helps you decide how to allocate resources between competing markets. This can result in exiting some markets altogether, and entering some new ones. But the first step is to go back to the success factors that were developed in each market and think about improving them. You should also determine an estimate of the cost relating to each level of improvement.

Establish a base case scenario of the business the corporation is in today. The base case sets out current levels of revenue, profitability, and market share relative to the market leader. Next, check on the cost of implementing the incremental steps required for improvement. Databases like PIMS will help you estimate the effect on profitability. Then the market attractiveness approach can be applied.

WHICH PARAMETERS?

Decisions about market attractiveness typically focus on two traditional parameters: the size and the growth rate of the market. There are a wide range of other parameters, however, that also must be considered.

In judging market attractiveness, CEOs should take into account the competitive environment, the power of suppliers and customers, the potential for new market entrants or substitute products, the susceptibility to various environmental factors, and the current levels of profitability of a "typically successful" player.

In comparing the PC market versus the typewriter market, for instance, the size and growth rate would greatly favor PCs. This conclusion would be dramatically modified, however, when other competitive aspects are analyzed.

There are seven major factors that affect the parameters for rigorous market assessment: (1) size and growth rate; (2) competitive environment; (3) supplier power; (4) customer power; (5) new entrants/substitutes; (6) environmental factors; and (7) profitability. These seven subdivide into 32 parameters that are loosely based on Michael Porter's approach to describing industries.

TABLE 1–3

Assessment of the U.S. Consumer Electronics Market
(Factor: Customer Power)

	Weight	Rate	Score
Concentration	.75	7	5.25
Switching Costs	1.00	3	3.00
Importance of Purchase	.50	5	2.50
Attitude to Price	1.00	2	2.00
Differentiation	1.50	1	1.50
Totals	4.75		14.25

Let's break out the individual cell that focuses on customer power. Analyzing the customer power cell means asking the following questions: How concentrated are the customers? What level of switching costs are involved? How important is purchasing this product to the customer? How price-conscious are the customers? How differentiated are the customer's available products?

The answers to these individual parameter questions are translated into a rating score on a 10-point scale. A low concentration of customers (e.g., thousands of customers for luxury automobiles) translates to a high attractiveness rating, seven out of a possible ten.

Each parameter should be weighted to determine its relative importance. Using its weighting in combination with the rates, one arrives at an overall score. Table 1–3 shows an assessment of the U.S. consumer electronics market.

The weight assigned to each parameter also reflects the overall objectives of the assessment. How will profitability be measured? By ROS, ROE, or ROA? When will profitability be optimized, in five years or more?

In most cases the answer is strategic, where the emphasis is optimized profitability over the planning period. In capital intensive businesses, ROE or ROA are the usual measures, whereas in a service business, ROS is the best gauge. When a corporation is evaluating both manufacturing and service businesses, it is important to use both indicators. Otherwise, comparison will be impossible.

TABLE 1–4
Market Attractiveness Scores*

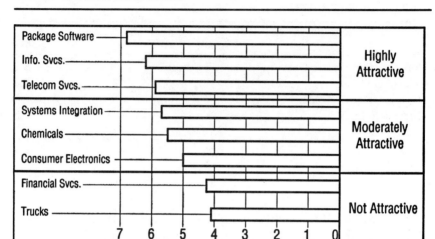

In one case a manufacturing company with heavy capital investment—necessary for its traditional businesses—was lured by the magic of noncapital intensive service businesses, where the return on net assets was significantly higher. What seemed attractive on that single, traditional measure was shown to be much less attractive when viewed more comprehensively.

ATTRACTIVENESS QUOTIENT

Each potential market segment is analyzed and its attractiveness calibrated by considering each of the 32 parameters (see Table 1–4). An overall score can be calculated for each of the segments.

The methodology allows analysis of widely divergent segments in a way that is both uniform and demonstrably fair, since each is being assessed using the same parameters and weights.

For example, we can compare the attractiveness of mid-sized trucks sold on lease in Canada with four-wheel-drive trucks sold in Thailand, or even personal computer software sold through dealers to the financial services industry. This analysis also gives an indication of the level of profitability that might be expected from a typically successful player in each market, regardless of how diversified.

FIGURE 1–1
Hierarchy of Success Factors for Packaged Software

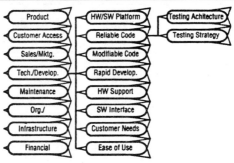

REQUIREMENTS FOR SUCCESS

The preceding analysis may identify several attractive market segments. The next step specifies those in which the corporation can be successful. What does it take to succeed and does the corporation have what it takes? If the answer is no, can improvements be made or an outside unit be acquired?

To determine a corporation's success rate, a generic set of success factors can be used, each of which can be expanded into a more detailed set of required capabilities. An example for the success factors required in the packaged software market is illustrated in Figure 1–1.

Employees, consultants, and industry gurus are all good sources for identifying the right set of success factors. Another method, and perhaps the best, is to list the factors considered responsible for the success of each of the three to four top competitors in the market. For each of the factors, a judgment must be made of how well the corporation matches up. This is often done by an independent group using market research, soliciting the views of consultants and industry leaders, or talking to competitors.

MATCHING ATTRACTIVENESS TO SUCCESS

Consider a corporation that is currently in a variety of businesses—consumer electronics, financial services, trucks, chemicals, and packaged software. It is actively considering entering the systems integration, information services, and telecommunications services

TABLE 1-5
Attractiveness Matched to Success Scores

	Highly Attractive	Moderately Attractive	Not Attractive
Packaged Software	+0.5*		
Info. Services	−4.5**		
Telecom Services	−6.0**		
Systems Integration		−9.5**	
Chemicals		+2.0**	
Consumer Electronics		−2.0**	
Financial Services			+7.5*
Trucks			+7.8*

*Strong position.
**Weak position.

markets. What should it leave? What should it enter? And how should its investment dollars be divided?

As shown in Table 1-5, the illustrative corporation is not well positioned for the most attractive markets. Management must weigh carefully the risk of staying with relatively unattractive markets where it is well positioned, against pursuing attractive markets where it is not.

This analytical approach can assist greatly in making the first level of assessments. If you have a strong position in the most attractive markets, it is good news. More often, however, some of the best matches are with those markets that are least attractive and vice versa. The CEO should explore the cost of investment to improve the match.

A simple resource allocation model can be used to determine what combination of businesses and investments will give the best payback. For example, the corporation we described in our opening scenario may see a range of ways to improve its performance in its consumer electronics division. These include increasing its sales force, improving sales force productivity, manufacturing a less expensive line of products, and changing the advertising program. We costed out each of these improvements and estimated its effect on profitability. The resource allocation model determined the percentage of increased profitability that will be derived from a wide range of alternative actions, netting it down to the optimal profit relative to levels of investment.

The method we have just described for assessing market attractiveness is a powerful tool for executive decision making. Although a significant amount of the data used in the analysis is, by definition, judgmental, the goal is not pinpoint accuracy. Rather, the aim is to provide a formalized framework for what executives are expected to do—establish corporate priorities.

Harry F. Bunn is president and CEO of RONIN, a Princeton, New Jersey-based strategy consulting firm. RONIN's practice is based on strategy development and planning with the use of expert systems and a technology enhanced "war room."

50/50 or Nothing

Gordon Lankton
President
Nypro

The 51/49 business partnership doesn't work. Actually, 50/50 joint ventures encourage the partners to do more than their share.

M arriage is the oldest type of partnership in the world. Every good marriage has evolved into a real 50/50 partnership. Likewise with business partnerships, a decade or two ago we often heard of 60/40 partnerships or more commonly 51/49 partnerships. From Nypro's perspective, these partnerships are meaningless. It's not so much a matter of the one percent. This is not significant at the bottom line.

The critical element is the basic mentality from which the two partners operate. I never want to be a 49 percent partner. Likewise, I never want to be a 51 percent partner. Every 49 percent partner goes to the table as a second-class citizen. It's a mentality that can't be avoided. Who wants to sit at a table concentrating on issues and developing strategic plans, all the while knowing that he or she really doesn't count as much as the other person? No one wants to be in that position. In this day and age, it spells doom for the partnership from day one. By the same token, it is not comfortable to be the dominant partner. Who wants to go to a board meeting that will clearly not be a free and open relationship between equals? Not me. I want everyone present to have the same voice.

A DIFFICULT FRENCH LESSON

We learned this lesson the hard way. We went into France in 1975 with a 100 percent owned acquisition. It wasn't long before all our French customers were letting us know by subtle means that they weren't about to do business with an American subcontractor. Furthermore, the French labor bureau began informing us (not so subtly) that the rules were different in France. If a business downturn occurs, the French labor bureau calls the shots.

The unemployment compensation system familiar to us in the United States does not exist in France. So you don't lay people off easily in France (or in other European countries). You must first submit your plan to the Labor Board. They deliberate for a few weeks or months, demand to scrutinize your financial statements for another month or so, then ask for the names of those who are to be laid off. Some six months after the initiation of the process, they let you lay off maybe five of the 15 you wanted to lay off and they tell you the names of the five that they have chosen for layoff after having studied their individual political preferences.

The lesson Nypro learned in this process, most importantly, was the necessity of local partners. If we had had a local 50/50 French partner, there would have been an understanding of the idiosyncrasies of French customers and government red tape.

THE LUCK OF THE IRISH

Ultimately, we moved our operations out of France and into Ireland, where we have a local 50/50 partner. The relationship has been extremely successful. We would never go back to France without a 50/50 French partner.

Global strategic alliances develop out of 50/50 partnerships. As in marriage, the contributions of the partners will not be identical, but they should be equal in importance. One may provide the potential for opening new markets, whereas the other may provide technology. The secret to success is that both partners recognize their need to contribute equally. Both will strive to do more and to carry more than their 50 percent of the load. This is what pushes the partnership forward.

During the 1980s Nypro developed three significant strategic alliances. The first was with Netstal Machinery of Switzerland. Netstal wanted to introduce its closed-loop process control injection molding machines into the U.S. market. Nypro, at the same time, wanted access to European injection molding machine technology, which was considerably ahead of the American technology.

A 50/50 partnership was formed. Netstal established a strong position in the U.S. market (where other European machinery manufacturers had often stumbled) and Nypro gained intimate access to the latest and best world-class technology. A single partnership in Clinton, Massachusetts, brought about additional partnerships in Singapore and Burlington, North Carolina. The Nypro-Netstal strategic alliance has developed and strengthened over a 10-year period.

JAPANESE EFFICIENCY

In Japan, Nypro has developed a strategic alliance with Sailor Pen Co., Ltd. In the late 1970s we learned that 70 percent of the injection molding machines in Japan used robots. In the United States, that figure was less than 5 percent. Nypro seized upon this as a double opportunity. First, we could form a partnership to be the exclusive distributor of Sailor robots in the United States through our automation affiliate, Automated Assemblies Corp. Second, through development of end-of-arm tooling technology and downstream automation, Nypro could be the first plastics custom injection molder in the United States to robotize all operations.

Now, 10 years later, Nypro has robots at every molding machine. Our competition is still only 15–20 percent robotized. And Automated Assemblies has established a very profitable $10 million robotics business in the United States.

The Sailor strategic alliance has also moved forward in an oblique manner. Sailor is a major producer of pens and pencils in Japan. Through our association with them, we have established a molding plant for pen components in Mt. Pleasant, Iowa—a truly international joint venture among Nypro, Sailor, and Sheaffer Pen.

Nypro's third strategic alliance is with Mitsui & Co., the largest company (in terms of revenues) in the world. While it is humbling to find ourselves 50/50 partners with a company of over $100 billion in sales (over 1,000 times our size), Mitsui considers Amitech Inc., our joint venture in Atlanta, one of their most successful operations. Mitsui brings relationships with Japanese manufacturers that are establishing plants in the United States (the fastest-growing segment of U.S. manufacturing) and Nypro brings Mitsui insight on how to sell their plastic materials to the U.S. plastics processing industry. The Amitech partnership was followed by a new 50/50 joint venture recently started in San Diego, California.

DON'T GO IT ALONE

Nypro has learned that there's a big world out there. It's a world we need to be a part of, but we can't do it alone.

We only have $100 million in sales. If we could afford a staff of experienced international lawyers, financial analysts, and multilingual business executives, we might be able to do it alone. But I doubt we would want to do it alone.

Fifty/fifty joint venture partnerships are the way to grow and develop world-class businesses. Marriages based on 51/49 relationships used to be acceptable, but are no longer. Likewise, 51/49 business partnerships are obsolete. Fifty/fifty partnerships prosper and as they do, they develop into global strategic alliances.

Gordon Lankton is president of Nypro, a $100 million plastics components manufacturer based in Clinton, Massachusetts.

Transfer Pricing

Peter R. Scanlon
Former Chairman and Chief Executive
Coopers & Lybrand

Going global is no longer the way to escape to a low-tax frontier. The IRS is targeting pricing between multinational corporate subsidiaries and developing complex regulations in the transfer pricing area. CEOs need a price review now.

T ransfer pricing is a tax concept that has existed for many years. But it was generally only of academic interest to U.S. corporations—unless they had manufacturing operations in Puerto Rico, where transfer pricing has helped firms enjoy significant tax benefits. Because of this relative inattention, and the fact that in the past many companies with related party transactions were subject to only a perfunctory IRS review, some firms may have developed a false sense of security about their transfer pricing policies. This is changing quickly. Senior management may soon find itself having to become very "expert" about transfer pricing, as U.S. corporations significantly expand their international operations.

U.S. tax law, as is the case in most other industrialized countries, requires that the pricing for transactions between related parties be at "arm's length." The price between related parties should be the same as it is between one member of a group and a company unrelated to that group. This arm's length standard applies to most related party transactions, including loans, rentals, services, inventory, and the use of know-how, trademarks, patents, and other intangibles. The purpose of the arm's length standard is to ensure an appropriate measure of taxable income between tax jurisdictions, internationally and even among states.

But some companies going global may find that they have non-arm's length pricing arrangements because they have not fully considered tax implications when creating or changing their operational structures. Frequently, non-tax professionals determine, monitor, and change transfer prices without consulting the tax department or their tax advisers. As a result these companies' transfer prices may lose their arm's length status, and, more importantly, the companies lack the documentation needed to justify and support their transfer prices at the time of audit by tax authorities.

GLOBAL TAX TARGETS

The IRS is under pressure from Congress to generate additional revenue. The tax bill passed in 1990 contains a revenue projection of $9.4 billion. This is to be raised by the IRS over five years from more vigorous audit and enforcement actions. The IRS has reorganized its examination process for large companies, in part to ensure that key issues such as transfer pricing are carefully and fully developed. Clearly, the IRS has made transfer pricing audits an important element in meeting its revenue goals. Spurred on by reports that foreign-owned U.S. companies were paying less U.S. income tax than their U.S. counterparts, Congress in 1989 and 1990 granted an IRS request to strengthen enforcement provisions for multinationals. The IRS already has employed and trained many more agents who will work in the transfer pricing area. And companies that have not been audited on this issue before are now being challenged by teams of IRS international examiners.

The United States, of all developed countries, has the most highly evolved set of transfer pricing rules, and the most experience in determining transfer prices. It also has the most tax controversy in this area, having been the leader in challenging intercompany pricing arrangements, and the most active in auditing such arrangements. Now this audit activity is about to be increased dramatically. In the past the IRS heavily focused its audit resources on tax shelter cases. As this issue dwindles in importance, and related audits wind down, largely as a result of the new "at risk" rules introduced in the Tax Reform Act of 1986, the IRS is redirecting its energies and resources to what it perceives to be more promising revenue sources. Transfer pricing audits will certainly be high on the source list.

While some provisions of the new tax legislation, such as those regarding record keeping, apply only to foreign-owned companies, the 1990 tax act also included enforcement regulations intended for application in the auditing of U.S. companies with overseas subsidiaries, as well as foreign-owned U.S. companies.

The law added a new 20 percent penalty if transfer pricing adjustments exceed $10 million of taxable income unless a company can show reasonable cause for its existing pricing arrangement. This nondeductible penalty increases to 40 percent if the IRS makes an adjustment of more than $20 million and reasonable cause cannot be shown.

These penalty provisions are complex and obviously are intended to root out perceived abuses. The provisions will apply to taxable years ending after November 5, 1990; therefore the penalties will apply to companies filing calendar-year returns beginning in 1990. Because of the far-reaching consequences of transfer pricing adjustments, it is likely that for many companies the total proposed adjustments in this area would exceed $10 million, leaving corporations open to a penalty assessment by the IRS. Moreover, the penalty provisions put a powerful lever in the hands of the IRS in negotiating any resolution of a substantial transfer pricing dispute.

Transfer pricing is not solely a U.S. tax issue. Foreign tax authorities, for example, in Germany, Japan, Canada, and the United Kingdom, partly in response to the IRS emphasis on this issue, have increased their audits in the case of transfer pricing issues. In addition, many countries such as Sweden, Finland, South Korea, and Taiwan that were not especially interested in transfer pricing are now instituting transfer pricing laws and having their audit staff undertake IRS training on transfer prices.

PRICE REVIEW IS NEEDED

The combination of new penalties, increased IRS staff, Congressional pressure for increased revenues, and new awareness by foreign tax authorities means that multinational corporations can expect more substantive challenges to their transfer prices. In keeping with the principle that the best defense is a good offense, a company should take steps now to review its transfer pricing arrangements and related documentation to prepare for likely tax audits.

Additional reasons now compel companies to review and document their transfer pricing arrangements with foreign-related parties now. Doing so serves three important purposes:

• Transfer pricing review will minimize tax controversy in the United States and overseas by establishing a reasonable basis for transfer pricing arrangements.

• Review provides protection against the U.S. tax penalties arising out of substantial tax adjustments.

• Review can help avoid the possibility of two countries taxing the same income. Generally, tax treaties provide relief from this risk, however, the procedures are complex and slow. Further, the United States does not have tax treaties with some of its major trading partners (e.g., Mexico), and this relief may not be available.

From the IRS perspective, it's not enough for a company to have reasonable transfer prices; those prices must be supported by appropriate documentation. Although there is little formal guidance in this area (regulations are expected later in 1991), a "white paper" from the Treasury Department asserted that such records should be contemporaneous. Congress appears to have embraced this standard by adding the penalties previously described. Many tax accountants believe that a review and analysis of transfer pricing, performed internally or by third parties, will be sufficient to avoid an IRS penalty assessment because it will demonstrate good faith. This assumes, of course, that the positions taken have merit. But resolution will remain unclear until the IRS issues its formal rules.

Although documentation supporting a transfer pricing policy may not cause a tax examiner to drop his or her investigation, the scope of that inquiry—and its associated costs—probably will be more limited. Ideally, a company's transfer pricing documentation will mirror the information the IRS traditionally seeks when conducting an audit in this area. For this reason it is useful to understand the IRS approach to a transfer price audit. The tax laws of the United States and most other developed countries require that pricing for each of these types of transactions be at "arm's length," or "market" prices. As mentioned earlier, the price charged between related parties must reflect the price that would have been charged had the parties been unrelated. Obviously, this requirement does not lend itself to a neat formula. For this reason, the IRS uses a group of specialists on the transfer price audit team.

First the IRS (and to a more limited extent, tax authorities in other countries) examines each company's operation relevant to the transactions at issue. In the case of manufacturing and distribution, the IRS determines the functions performed by each legal entity involved in the transaction, for example, the unit that develops marketing strategy, the unit responsible for manufacturing activity, the unit that provides customer service, and so on. In addition, it determines the business risks (credit risk, foreign exchange risk, inventory risk, etc.) borne by each legal entity, and the intangibles (patents, trademarks, customer list, etc.) developed or used by each. This process can be lengthy and involves interviews with key operating personnel of the U.S. company and the relevant foreign affiliates. Since this is one of more complicated procedures administered by the IRS, companies must use extra diligence in complying.

The purpose of the functional analysis is to understand each legal entity's contribution to overall profits. After its completion, the IRS conducts an industry analysis. This is done to understand the economics of the industry in which the company competes. The best evidence of "arm's length" transfer prices is found in comparable transactions between unrelated companies. In many cases, such comparables can be found—although they frequently must be adjusted to account for differences between the comparable and the related-party transaction. For example, adjustments are made by economists to account for differences in the amount of marketing done by a comparable distributor and the selling affiliate of the company under audit.

Other exceptions to the strict use of comparables include the price effects of market penetration and market maintenance situations. When a company is trying to establish itself in a new market, it may discount prices to win new customers. Market maintenance price effects come about when a product is threatened by competition, and the manufacturer discounts prices in order to maintain market share. In the absence of comparables, economic modeling is sometimes used to determine true "arm's length" prices. Several companies have asked us for assistance in determining royalty rates for transfers of intangibles where, because of the unique products involved, no comparable prices were available. We developed an economic model to explain the profitability in each of those companies to determine the income attributable to the intangible in question. Having done so, we were able to determine an "arm's length" royalty rate. This work constitutes the mandated effort needed to keep transactions at a distance.

EXPANDING THE CONTEXT

A transfer pricing review also offers a company the opportunity to conduct a strategic review of all its international operations because it involves many areas of focus, for example, review of the use of intangibles, manufacturing costs, distribution centers, sales activities, and research and development activities. These reviews can be the catalyst for a challenge to traditional or long-standing arrangements, and help determine whether or not they still meet the needs of the marketplace. Transfer pricing reviews that indicate a need to modify intercompany prices or charges frequently identify other related problem issues. For example, a modification to a royalty rate may require a correlative major change in a unit's operating budget. Performance-driven compensation plans may have to be adjusted, or currency hedging plans may have to change. It obviously is more efficient and easier if these changes can be implemented in the context of an overall strategic business plan.

A transfer pricing review also can serve as an overall aid to effective multinational corporate tax planning. While evaluating the potential for transfer pricing tax exposure, companies should consider whether or not they would like to maximize income in a foreign country where liabilities of this nature exist. They may also wish to pursue opportunities to minimize their worldwide tax rate. Questions involving these issues are frequently put to us—and we have found that we can almost always help a company achieve its broad goals while putting a defensible transfer pricing policy in place. For example, assume a U.S. corporation has an arrangement with its German subsidiary for the distribution of U.S.-manufactured consumer goods. If the corporation assumes responsibility for advertising, credit risk, and product warranty costs formerly borne by the German subsidiary, it can justify a higher transfer price and shift income from the higher tax system in Germany to a system with a lower tax rate. If the German subsidiary's profit was 10 percent of sales, it could be reduced to 5 percent or less under this new arrangement.

Although customs duty specifications differ from transfer pricing rules, it is important to consider the customs duty implications of transfer pricing policy. Many of our clients have found that an evaluation of the method they use for pricing goods for entry into the European Economic Community (EEC) can save a large amount of duty dollars. U.S. law requires that the price declared for duty purposes (for imports into the United States) must not be lower than the transfer price used for income tax purposes. In the EEC, no such requirement currently exists. This means that for exports to the EEC, it may be possible, following existing rules, to declare a price for customs purposes that is lower than the transfer price. Obviously, many other tax and business issues must be considered in making such a pricing decision. But the potential savings can be significant enough to warrant further exploration.

Transfer pricing seems an esoteric issue for many non–tax-oriented executives. But senior management must become more knowledgeable about transfer pricing to encourage a broad effort in this area. Such an effort is necessary if multinational companies are to avoid costly and time-consuming tax audits. An IRS with finite resources is likely to focus its energies on audits where the financial opportunities are greatest. A transfer price audit can be very intensive and can consume significant amounts of senior management time. But making the effort to determine appropriate transfer prices now has the added advantage of assisting evaluations of global operating performance and future planning. Doing so will also minimize costly and time-consuming audits.

From 1982–1991 Peter R. Scanlon was chairman and CEO of Coopers & Lybrand, a professional services firm with 65,000 employees worldwide, and revenues exceeding $4 billion.

Six Early Warnings of Business Failure

Ian Sharlit
President and Chief Executive
Durkee, Sharlit

Paul Tobias

Don't expect to find clues to early corporate deterioration in financial ratios. The "numbers" are, if anything, a lagging indicator. Watch instead the behavior of key executives.

B usiness failures are often preceded by personality dysfunctions on the part of the executives involved. More often than we think, the root causes of many business problems and failures lie in the executives' own personality traits, which are (or become) mismatched with the requirements of the business challenges that confront them, and the perceptions or remedial actions required.

Some instances amount to no more than the wrong person being in the wrong position at the wrong time. This happens when a performer in one setting goes astray when the environment abruptly changes to one they have difficulty acknowledging, still less accommodating.

We see this "square peg in the round hole" situation often in entrepreneurial companies where the second generation tries to live up to the (usually heroic) performance of the parent-founder. The progeny usually have various admirable qualities, but rarely would they be selected for the position they hold on an objective basis. Their most important qualifications are frequently genetic, which is one principal reason that family-controlled companies so rarely survive, and even more rarely prosper, from one generation to the next.

More often, however, we see a situation where executives whose traits and qualities fit the time and place well, begin to change their behavior in a destructive way. For instance, they become addicted to self-serving rationalizations and illusions, "blind" to certain types of input, paralyzed from a decision-making point of view because of their own uncertainties and fears. They begin reacting to their colleagues and subordinates in a prejudicial and perverse way because of their own difficulty in coping with challenges that they are unsure how to resolve.

Consider, for instance, the recent case of Q.T. Wiles, a legendary business consultant who, in his late 60s, took over as chairman and CEO of MiniScribe, then a major computer disk-drive manufacturer that had fallen on hard times.

The Wall Street Journal relates that, at a meeting, Wiles asked two controllers to stand and then fired them on the spot, saying, "That's just to show everyone I'm in control of the company." Wiles is described as throwing, kicking, and ripping briefing books, and showering his audience with paper while yelling, "Why don't you understand this?"

A year later, Wiles is reported to have said, "I no longer want to be remembered as a turnaround artist. I want to be remembered as the man who made MiniScribe a billion dollar company," even though he had previously been reported as saying that the faster he could sell MiniScribe, the better. According to a former MiniScribe accountant, Wiles would specify the objectives for each quarter, and the results were amazingly close. The apparent reason for the forecasting accuracy, as the *Journal* article notes, was falsification on a massive scale.

When he resigned in 1988, Wiles was devastated by what his re-examination of the company revealed and acted as though he'd been blindsided. After investigators showed him several memos that had been distributed at a meeting he had attended, Wiles denied having seen them. At last report, Wiles has resigned from all the positions he held in various companies, and lives in virtual seclusion.

In our opinion, the tragic story of Wiles's downfall does not reflect his lack of executive experience or stamina. After all, he had been hugely successful in similar situations for decades. Neither does it simply reflect poor judgment. At the risk of reaching conclusions based on the media, we see Wiles's poor judgment as a direct result of the personality dysfunction we have been describing. The consequences for MiniScribe have been nothing short of catastrophic.

RED FLAGS

Every experienced and alert executive we know tries to anticipate crises and manage around or through them, looking for signs that events are getting out of control. So-called red flags have been developed over the years, and the literature is full of them. However, most are tied to financial statements and are numerically oriented. They seek to reflect objective measures of changes in performance (e.g., sales, profit and loss, margins, liquidity, and leverage), either in an absolute sense or relative to prior years or comparable companies in an industry.

Our consulting experience suggests that executives' personality dysfunctions underlie many business crises and failures, that traditional financially oriented relationships are often "lagging indicators," and that comparable red flags are needed to detect danger early enough to take effective remedial action.

As with financially oriented red flags, the key is to look for significant changes, which in this context translate into behavioral changes. Individuals become successful executives by using their strongest personality traits. However, each of these strengths has a darker aspect. When executives begin to dysfunction, their internal balance of forces becomes distorted and the destructive personality traits begin to dominate. This compelling pattern of behavior, which destroys the very thing they are trying to achieve, is what we call executive failure syndrome (EFS).

In what follows, we will describe several—but by no means all—of the most prominent early warning signs of executives who are "at risk," drawing from our experience.

Isolated

An executive becomes increasingly isolated and uncommunicative over a period of time, canceling meetings, refusing to return phone calls, and not reacting to reasonable needs of colleagues and customers. This sort of individual is often seen as a master strategist who focuses all available energies on a problem and eliminates all distractions; but actually is a fearful and depressed person who is hiding because reality has become too demanding and frightening.

Obsessed

An executive becomes increasingly "locked in" with a single objective, seemingly irrespective of evidence to the contrary and, in effect, marches to the beat of a different drummer. This individual is sometimes thought of as a true leader but is actually a rigid person with only one "note" or "gear" to offer. He does not know how to accommodate change constructively.

Angry

An executive becomes increasingly angry, abusive, and even violent to colleagues and outsiders, often without any apparent provocation. This individual is often seen as someone who sets such high performance standards that abuse is rationalized as a small price to pay for the results achieved; but in reality has low self-esteem, if not an actual self-hatred, which is inflicted on those who are nearby and usually subordinate.

Indecisive

An executive increasingly finds ways to delay taking any meaningful action, no matter how urgent the situation. This person is often thought of as careful to assess and intellectualize every possible alternative and protect against every conceivable contingency; but really is a perfectionist terrified at the possibility of being seen as losing control or making a mistake, and will often go to irrational lengths to avoid such an outcome.

Capricious

An executive increasingly seems to respond to circumstances in an arbitrary manner. This individual is often thought of as an action-oriented and decisive leader; but really has difficulty living with uncertainty for a prolonged period of time, has a self-concept that borders on the heroic, needs a crisis to demonstrate worth, and lacking one, will often create one to alleviate internal stress.

"Workaholic"

An executive increasingly spends endless hours, and even days, visibly "on duty." This individual is often idealized as the epitome of self-denying dedication; but in fact finds no fulfillment or satisfaction in anything but work, and has an internal meter ticking away toward emotional (if not mental and physical) burnout or collapse.

CAUSES OF EXECUTIVE DYSFUNCTION

Successful, hard-driving executives usually engage in an intense search for "specialness," which often involves a denial of their own mortality and, in the recesses of their subconscious, a belief that there is an ultimate "rescuer" inside themselves.

In these terms, the executive may believe that the laws of nature "don't apply to me." Death (or its organizational equivalent, retirement) is not acceptable because there is too much yet to be done that "only I can do."

An example of how these elements come together to cause dysfunction is the middle-aged executive who in his search for meaningfulness has difficulty coping with a mid-life crisis and (like John DeLorean) affects the image of a much more youthful person, becomes distrustful of everyone around him, and believes that his "specialness" puts him above the rules by which others operate a business.

A variation is the self-defeating syndrome, where a high achiever begins a repetitive pattern of "explained" failures that result from an internal conviction that success is not deserved. This has been speculated for Bill Lear, the inventor and entrepreneur.

Sometimes personality dysfunction may be triggered by changes in relationships brought about by the death of a parent, mate, or mentor, or the breakup of a family. Outward evidence may include changes of habits such as drinking, gambling, or smoking. Sometimes there are behavioral changes that are perceived by others as withdrawing or attacking.

However, the causes of executives' personality dysfunctions do not lie mainly outside the workplace. In particular, the concept of business competition as a kind of combat has invaded the popular culture. For instance, such titles as *The Art of War* and *Winning Through Intimidation* have become best-sellers; and slogans such as "Winning is the only thing," "Giving 110 percent," "When the going gets tough, the tough get going," and "No guts, no glory" are heard everywhere.

When executives operate under this sort of unremitting pressure, aided and abetted by incentive compensation and management-by-objectives, there are going to be casualties—and they will not be limited to opposing organizations. Some executives, who to all superficial evidence are still functioning, will, in reality, have caught a psychological bullet.

Regardless of the specific cause, EFS occurs when elements of a person's positive personality traits are distorted under stress and lead to such maladaptive behavior that a "blind spot" is created, which turns success into failure.

A practical difficulty in recognizing, not to speak of remedying, such dysfunctions is that an excess of personal "denial" is built into most ambitious executives. It is a primary defense to their anxieties. Driven executives often have little conscious insight concerning adverse changes in their own behavior patterns. This implies that executives are, in general, poorly equipped to spot their own transitional steps toward self-defeating behavior.

There are, however, four groups of people who often perceive these personality changes. Unfortunately, each group has built-in motivations to keep their insight from the dysfunctioning executive.

The first, of course, are the executive's peers, subordinates, and other colleagues. However, even if these staff people or executives see harmful changes in an executive's behavior, many times it is too threatening, or even prejudicial to their position, to admit to these perceptions or actually confront the executive.

The second group are the lenders and suppliers to the business. They are often aware that a person who was reasonable is now rigid and irascible. However, lenders and suppliers deal with this person at a distance, and have a vested interest in keeping the relationship harmonious. They tend to do this by performing their own assessment of how the executive has changed, but usually avoid the risk of losing the relationship unless pressed by credit problems, impending bankruptcy, default, or other crises.

Third are the attorneys, CPAs, physicians, and other professionals who serve the company and the individual. These people, particularly the physicians, may have the training to assess dysfunctional behavior, but often have built a personal relationship that effectively puts them in collusion with the destructive changes that are occurring.

The executive's own family is the fourth group capable of seeing changing patterns such as increased drinking, isolation, sleeplessness, and conflict. Until the problem becomes a crisis, however, they seldom ask for help or are able to confront the changes that vitally affect their own lives. Yet, it is most often a spouse or adult offspring who first calls a professional and says, "We need to do something."

CORRECTIVE MEASURES

Fortunately, a few companies are beginning to employ various programs to highlight, and often heal, what can be potentially destructive behavioral changes among their executives.

First, there is a periodic upward evaluation or appraisal. Many well-managed companies have institutionalized the idea of executive appraisal-feedback that is confidential, and handled in such a way that it effectively minimizes intimidation to both executives and their assessors. As a result, senior executives or owners are provided with observations about their own behavior from subordinates. The difficulty here is that many executives reject the idea that anyone who works for them could objectively evaluate them. They feel that their concept of and drive for "specialness" puts them outside the realm where ordinary people could observe their behavior and make sense of it.

Second, some companies have their own or the individual's physician review the behavior of executives annually. This mental fitness evaluation can be built into an executive health program to coincide with the annual physical. The physician or psychologist performing the mental fitness evaluation should have access to information regarding past years for perspective. Among the behavioral changes the physician looks for are mood swings that can be detected with brief psychological tests; use of medications, alcohol, and other chemicals; changing patterns of sleep and sexual activity; increased numbers of conflicts and fights; evidence of "the blues" or feeling "down"; and breakup of the home due to separation or divorce. Changes in these behavior patterns will be weighed against major business stresses or reverses in an effort to estimate the likelihood of impending personality dysfunction. Such behavioral patterns not only reflect increased inner stress, they also aggravate existing stress.

Third, some companies rely on excellent mental health programs where executives can recharge along with peers under the supervision of qualified professionals. A major function of these programs is to administer a thorough personality assessment with feedback to the participant. Programs like the one at the Menninger Foundation, for instance, give this kind of assistance.

When the aforementioned remedial programs are not available or effective, calling in a qualified outside professional often represents the only practical way to help a dysfunctional executive, and frequently his company as well.

Ian Sharlit is president and CEO of Durkee, Sharlit, a Los Angeles-based planning firm specializing in profit improvement, growth management, and financial turnaround services.

Paul Tobias is an independent clinical and industrial psychologist, who assists Durkee, Sharlit clients. For many years, he was associated with IBM.

CHAPTER

2

WORLD-CLASS
MARKETING

A Different Brand
Of Leader

PepsiCo's Wayne Calloway inherited a strong, well-run global marketer of powerful brands. That was luck. He gave it sharper focus, greater attention to cost control, and most importantly, pushed people forward with the power of ownership. That was ability. Beyond the placid country-boy manner lies a shrewd judge of character who leads by indirection.

F rito-Lay CEO Roger Enrico, formerly the Norman Schwarzkopf of the cola wars of the 1980s when he ran Pepsi-Cola, remembers the nervousness he felt when he sat down to tell his boss that Michael Jackson wanted $10 million instead of $5 million to re-enlist as a Pepsi promoter. "I told him it was an outrageous amount of money, but that it looked to me like a good idea and we ought to do it," recalls Enrico. "Wayne just looked at me and said, 'well, it sounds like a big idea to me,' and that was the end of that. Wayne works through decisions by dealing with his people."

Pizza Hut marketing director John Lauck got stuck with $5 million in sunglasses when a sales promotion tied to the launch of *Back to the Future, Part 2* misfired badly. The result? Lauck was later promoted. Pizza Hut CEO Steve Reinemund told Tom Peters in *On Achieving Excellence,* "People here don't get shot for taking risks."

People make the difference. Politicians say it. Military officers (when they are not stumbling over compound acronyms) say it. And CEOs, nodding like so many backseat auto kewpie dolls, say it. With massive downsizing (oops, "rightsizing") of U.S. corporations because of restructurings and a recession, why believe PepsiCo's chief executive anymore than the others? "His example gets us to act on it, not just talk about it," Enrico shoots back. The notion of employee empowerment, ever the buzzword of today's management high priests, is difficult to dismiss lightly even at this $18-billion soft drink, snack food, and restaurant company with 308,174 employees—not when a Florida employee in personnel on her own initiative convinces her local school board to consider a Pizza Hut concession in the school's lunch program, or when a Mississippi Pepsi truck driver comes up with a money-saving scheme by using back roads to shave 100 miles off his delivery route. Then there's the Texaco executive, who in going out to dinner one evening, met a PepsiCo accountant, with no sales responsibilities, who talked the oilman into selling pizzas in Texaco's new European convenience stations.

Isolated anecdotes? Maybe. Yet in 1989 the Purchase, New York-based company offered to *all* eligible employees something that is normally reserved for the corner office types with blue suits and snappy red ties: stock options. Sharepower is a Calloway brainchild that almost didn't happen. "The lawyers and many at corporate headquarters were dubious because no one had ever done anything like this before," says PepsiCo vice president, compensation and benefits, Charles W. Rogers. (The number of options is based on employee's earnings; 83,175 employees participate today with 19.5 million options granted, of which only 0.2 percent have been exercised. Dilution is not significant.) Sharepower is being closely watched by other companies. "The plan is the best expression of fairness and internal consistency in employee incentives today," says Douglas Reid, senior vice president, human resources, Colgate-Palmolive.

The effects are often spontaneous: Oklahoma City KFC restaurant manager Ken Hardin scours local manufacturers for a more durable hot water hose that annually saves his store, and ultimately 12 others to whom he's passed the idea on, $600 per restaurant. Frito-Lay employees in Plano, Texas, start the work day checking PepsiCo's stock price in the financial pages. A senior corporate vice president is taken aback when a secretary filling out his expenses asks, "Couldn't you have stayed at a less expensive hotel?"

"We want to change the way this company is managed," says the 55-year-old Elkin, North Carolina-born CEO with a soft Blue Ridge accent. How does one do this in a company already enjoying 15 percent annual growth? Michael Jordan, CEO of Pepsico Foods International who has worked in the company for 17 years says, "It's much calmer today compared to the days of Don

Kendall. Don was dynamic, always pulsating. Since 1986 (when Calloway became CEO), we focus on consistency—margin improvement as well as growth. Cost reduction was always important, but we're more consistent at it."

PepsiCo more than anything is a global marketing engine with eight turbo brands, each generating more than $1 billion yearly at retail. (Brand Pepsi exceeded $14 billion worldwide retail in 1990. Coke still dominates with 40.9 percent of the overall market versus Pepsi's 33.2 percent, nearly a two-point gain since 1985, according to *Beverage Digest*. Each of its three business lines—soft drinks (37 percent), snack foods (28 percent), and restaurants (35 percent)—have managed double-digit sales growth and record operating profits. Frito-Lay, with which Pepsi-Cola merged in 1965 and which Calloway ran from 1976 to 1983, commands almost half the $12 billion salty snack market in the United States. Use of hand-held computers by Frito-Lay's representatives allows increased distribution control and quicker line extension introductions.

Although the U.S. market will continue to dominate, the future lies beyond. International operating profits were 7.6 of the total in 1987, but will be 20 percent by 1992. Coke has a 2.5-to-1 lead over Pepsi due mostly to its being in Europe directly after the war. Pepsi plans to grow by building the category and taking share from lesser players. Coke's formidable distribution system in Europe, now extended throughout Germany, will assure its supremacy there unless Coke does something really stupid. Yet Pepsi's early lead in the Soviet Union, pioneered by predecessor Don Kendall, and its presence in India, as well as recent acquisitions in Mexico, should keep the folks in Atlanta from being too smug.

Although he came up through finance (as he did earlier with ITT under Harold Geneen), Calloway sees PepsiCo's challenge in choosing "the right people." "He's a mentor and cheerleader to these guys," says John Nelson, analyst with Brown Brothers Harriman, "and generous enough to pass along plenty of the credit." Nelson sees the stock growing 16 percent versus the S&P 500's 7 to 8 percent over the next three to five years. However relentlessly upbeat, the company faces acute challenges in such areas as its fountain wars with Coca-Cola, where Coke argues to restaurant customers that buying Pepsi's syrup funds competing PepsiCo restaurants. Burger King's switch to Coke represented a loss of Pepsi's biggest fountain customer. Snack profit declined 4 percent overall and 12 percent internationally in the first quarter of 1991 due to price cutting, a troubling sign since snack food profit hasn't seen a decline since 1986.

Since PepsiCo doesn't participate in rapid growth industries with favorable demographic trends in its favor, how long do you think PepsiCo can continue to be such a terrific cash machine?
First of all, I have to disagree somewhat with the premise that we aren't in a growth industry. Last year, people said that restaurants had a bad year. Actually, the restaurant industry in the United States grew about six percent. Packaged goods companies, at least, would think that is terrific.

And if you look back at the history of the soft drink business and the snack food business, they've both averaged four or five percent growth as well. So, compared to most packaged goods businesses, we're in a very good business for growth. We've doubled our business every five years for 25 years since PepsiCo was formed in 1965. So we expect to continue that for at least another 25 years. We don't see any reason we couldn't. The market will grow. Since we are market leaders in our business, we expect to get more of our share of that growth.

We also have to look at the international marketplace. Much of the world, as you know, is underdeveloped. The United States still represents the bulk of our business. Even in a developed country such as Canada, the consumption of soft drinks is considerably less than in the United States. And the United Kingdom would be half the United States. In India, someone will drink in a year what an American would drink in soft drinks on a weekend. So, we have an enormous growth potential all around the world, and that's true now with soft drinks as well as with pizza or chicken or snacks.

BUILDING A BETTER BRAND

There are a lot of firms that are very good at marketing consumer products. What do you have that sets you apart from what other people do?
One is that we have outstanding people. I'm sure you hear that from a lot of CEOs, but I think it's clearly true in our case. We

work hard at that. So we have an outstanding group of associates at PepsiCo around the world, and a culture that says, take this, be bold.

Our second strength, which is evident, is our strong brands. We have 25 brands that have sales over $100 million. We have enormous strength in that.

The third—and probably the most overlooked for PepsiCo's growth—is the fact that we are quite good at operating things. Generally, people think of us in terms of being a good marketing company. We do pretty well at that, but in addition, we know how to operate lots of businesses in a detailed manner.

For example, Pepsi-Cola has 10,000 sources. A normal packaged goods company—maybe a Kellogg or a General Mills—might have five or six hundred sources; we have 10,000. When you're operating 6,000 Pizza Hut restaurants in the United States, a lot of little transactions add up to big numbers. That is a real strength that we have that most people don't realize.

That is a very sustainable competitive advantage, if you think, for instance, about McDonald's. They're not the largest hamburger chain in the world because they're the world's greatest hamburger. But they have very wide distribution, a large number of restaurants, they operate them very well, and they're clean. That is a strength that competitors have not been able to overcome.

Those operating skills are really critical for us, because we don't sell boxcars of anything—we don't sell million dollar orders or billion dollar orders. We sell one pizza at a time, one pack of potato chips at a time.

> **You continually emphasize the "power of big brands," brand building, and brand equity. But surely your chief soft drink rival has a brand that is every bit as formidable, and some would argue is even more formidable, than any product made anywhere in the world. If your emphasis is becoming a brand company and you're up against the world's biggest, most powerful brand, is this going to be enough to win at the end of the game?**

Coke clearly does have the world's strongest brand, and that's recognized by everybody. That's why they have a great company. So, in our case, that shows we have a great brand—among the top four or five in the world—because that gives us the strength to play against a brand as strong as Coke.

The good news for all of us is that the soft drink business is so huge, and it's growing around the world at tremendous rates. There's plenty of room for both of us. The beverage business is not a zero sum game.

In fact, one of the reasons we've done very well is that there really is a cola war, so we both keep each other on our toes. Nobody's going to sleep in the beverage business because it's so competitive. And so as a result of that, you're constantly seeing innovations and improvements in the business.

> **Speaking of the cola war, PepsiCo lost Burger King and Wendy's to Coke last year, but it won from Coke Marriott and Howard Johnson. Will we continue to see a titanic struggle for distribution control where points of sale are lost back and forth like so many pawns and knights?**

Oh, certainly. As I said, the cola war is real. Every time we get one of their customers they're going to try to get back, and every time they get one of ours, we're going to try to get back. So, that will continue. It keeps everybody sharp.

> **Considering that Pepsi has 15 percent of the share of the international market versus Coke's 46 percent, how is Pepsi going to narrow that market-share gap?**

The international market is so huge and it's growing so fast that it is not a zero sum game. There's plenty of room for Coke to grow very well and for Pepsi to grow quite rapidly as well. It's not a question of, do we have to take share from them or they have to take share from us?

The underdevelopment in all of those markets is so astounding that as they are rapidly developing, they are rapidly picking up the habits of soft drink consumption that we have in the United States. So we can certainly grow our business at an accelerated rate, and certainly, Coke will as well. I don't think that either one of us is going to worry much about market share. But Coke has said on many occasions that the name of the game is growing the market, really raising our market share, and that's exactly what we're both going to do.

DISTRIBUTION HITS THE SPOT

**What sort of things do you pay special attention to in
the international marketplace that might not receive the
same consideration in the domestic operation?**
In many of the international markets, the real issue is distribution
and having the product available. One of the great things about
this country is that almost anywhere you go, a Pepsi is available
through a vending machine or fountain. That's the real drive in
international marketing.

**How will the role of snack foods and restaurants be
advanced in the international market?**
We have enormous opportunity in the restaurant side of this
business. We're in about 60 countries now with Pizza Hut and we
have almost the same number of Kentucky Fried Chicken. That
relates to 150 countries we're in with Pepsi. So we have a lot of
opportunity with geographic distribution. And again, the development is far behind the United States. We have 6,000 Pizza Huts
in the United States, and we have two in Brazil. That's quite a big
spread here that we can develop. The same is true in the snack
business. Frito-Lay is in about 27 countries now, and we'll be in
three or four times that number before it's all over.

We've more than quadrupled our investment in the international markets outside the United States over the last four years.
We'll do that again, I suspect, in the next four or five years as well.
We have enormous potential in restaurants and snack foods as
well as beverages in the international scene. That's why we're very
comfortable about continuing to grow.

**In each of your three principal businesses, it appears
that PepsiCo is modifying or reorganizing the
distribution system. Are we approaching the day of
perhaps even eliminating the middle man?**
If you look at our business over the years, like everything else, it
changes. If you went back 20 years ago, Coke and Pepsi would
have had maybe 500 bottlers apiece in the United States, built on
a franchise system. As the world changed, as the supermarkets
got more regional, as the cost pressures began to get much

tougher over the years, that began to force a restructuring of the business. So certainly, PepsiCo had to participate in the restructuring. The net result of that today is that Pepsi-Cola owns and operates about half of all the bottling themselves. It's likely to continue consolidating, but at a slower pace than it has been happening.

We won't live to see the day that we're going to control all of that distribution. We're going to always have partners ultimately getting to the consumer. Now, that doesn't mean that we don't have our eyes on the consumer. But we also better have in our mind that getting from the manufacturer to the consumer, there is a partnership in there in many of those cases that will be a retailer or wholesaler, restaurant operator or bowling alley operator, or whatever the case may be. Ultimately, the consumer is the customer. That's why brands are so important, because the ultimate customer is the one that consumes the product. If they have in their mind that this brand is better than that brand or no brand, then that is where you begin to have a viable business transaction. That will help you get through the distribution system in a partnership.

> **In the age of micromarketing, allowing ever-greater customization of products, do you anticipate making soft drinks or potato chips or foods that are so customized that you can almost customize it to one brand per family?**

That would be difficult. On the other hand, if that's ultimately what the customer wants, you can bet your boots that's what we'll be doing, because whether we like it or not, the customer is king. We aren't down yet exactly to the household, but if you pick any supermarket in the country, we have an idea of the demographics around that one supermarket, what the income is, whether there are 30,000 people or 40,000 people within three miles, what ethnic background that might be, and whether they would like a hot flavor or not so hot flavor or whatever their preferences might be. How far that kind of micromarketing is going, we don't know, but we want to be out in front of it, not behind it.

You have extended a lot of your brands—made variations of them—as have other companies. Just how long can you keep extending a brand?

The elasticity of the brand is a subject that is very important, and it is something for which your information system has to be very well developed. You have to listen again to the consumer. When you see that you're not getting the incremental sales, that one extension is pulling from one extension, then you have to be sensitive enough to say, maybe it's time to pull back.

On the other hand, the drive to get to every individual consumer is still there. One consumer wants sour cream and onion, and somebody else wants barbeque, and somebody else wants banana, and somebody else wants whatever. You constantly have to keep testing that limit. But you'd better do it very carefully, because there will come some point where you can dilute the brand strength until there's nothing left to sell.

INTEGRITY AND RESULTS

One of the reasons that your peers nominated you—and ultimately selected you—is that they regarded your efforts at encouraging executive talent as being exemplary. How tolerant are you of failure when you push people to change?

Our business is built on two foundations: one is integrity, and the other is, get results. If you do those two things around here, you are very successful. We don't care how old you are, how young you are, what race you are, what sex you are, what school you went to, whether you even went to school or not. What's important is integrity and results. And everybody would agree on results. But the integrity part is that, in order to get people to take risks, in order to get people to change, you have to have a nurturing and a trusting environment.

That's why when you talk to people at PepsiCo, you're talking about integrity. We're constantly expanding on what that means and dealing with people in an open and above-board manner. We do encourage risks, and if you blow it, you blow it. We don't fire

you, and we don't shoot the wounded. We don't even put you in
the penalty box.

On the other hand, if you keep making a lot of dumb mistakes,
we would probably suggest that maybe there's a better place for
you to work. But if you're going to get results in the long term,
you've got to have integrity—openness, honesty with your customers, suppliers, and associates, and even with your competitors. All of that has to be part of it.

> **Some of the people who work for you describe you as
> being almost Japanese-like in your management style in
> that you're not prone to giving direct orders by fiat, but
> you tend to urge by indirection or inference or
> persuasion. Is that accurate?**

I never thought about being Japanese in style. But my style is
clearly to delegate. Our businesses are all different, they're all
decentralized, and we've always run them that way. It's my job to
make it a collaborative effort between the CEOs of the different
businesses and myself about whatever areas we're going to pursue. We have an agreement about where we want to be three years
from now or five years from now. Within the integrity framework
that we all understand around here, we're pretty much open to
however they want to make it happen, as long as they get results.

> **How has sharepower changed the way PepsiCo
> operates? Can you quantify the difference that
> it's made?**

The entire reason that we're successful around here is hustle at
everyday business. We haven't sold a single pizza tomorrow, we
haven't sold a single Pepsi tomorrow. It's that kind of business. So
all of our associates have to feel that this is their business, that
they are the steward of these assets, wherever they might be, in
Des Moines or in Thailand or wherever. We have always said that,
we want you to take responsibility, we want you to be your own
CEO. We have seen enormous instances of people responding to
that. People who have never thought of themselves as salespeople
are now out going in the supermarket and checking the shelves to
see if it's okay. And they work in the accounting department, but
now they feel, hey, this is my company.

What would you tell another chief executive that he most has to get right if he's to adopt some form of sharepower for his company?

Communication is really important. We had people who understood stock options right to the fourth decimal place, and we had people out in some parts of the businesses who never heard of a stock option. And we had everybody in between who'd heard about it but didn't know exactly what it was. What we have found is that it is a continuous process.

A lot of your peers are using the buzzword "empowerment," and they're looking for a silver bullet. Is that what it is?

There are no silver bullets. But empowerment is important. You need that to feel, "This is my business and my company, and I'm the steward of these assets." It's really important to us.

What advice would you give other CEOs who want to compete on your level internationally.

The key for us has been to think about the world in the global sense, and we've been trying to do that by our focus on the customer. When you think about that customer, it becomes clear in your mind that the customer in Thailand is different from the customer in Des Moines, who's different from the customer in Rio, who's different from the customer in London. The buzzwords that are being used for that are think globally and act globally. One of the reasons that you keep hearing that cliche is it's true. But in order to do that, you have to have a diversity about your way of doing business and be willing to change and to take risks. Part of it is really being willing to fix it even if it's not broken, and keep evolving.

When Global Markets Get Tough

James Espey
President and Chief Executive
United Distillers, North America

*International competitors are scrambling for share in a product
category facing marginal sales declines in leading national markets.
Of the 200 brands you offer, arguably two are truly global. What to
do when there's no place to hide?*

T he Red Queen said, "Now here, it takes all the running you
can do to keep in the same place. If you want to get somewhere else, you must run at least twice as fast as that!"

Were she reigning in today's global-market world, in which
twice as fast might seem a snail's pace, the Red Queen doubtless
would need to recommend a speed of far greater order of mag-
nitude. Clearly it is a global economy in which one no longer can
take refuge in merely being successful in one's own protected
backyard. There simply is no place to hide.

As barriers to entry tumble, and as international marketing
courses proliferate amoeba-like in graduate school of business catalogs, global competition from anywhere and everywhere becomes increasingly intense. Thus, on those too rare occasions
when I can find the time to teach a marketing class, I enjoy having
students contribute to a "Who would have guessed . . ." scenario.
For example: "Thirty years ago, who would have guessed that the
Japanese auto industry would so dramatically dominate the U.S.

auto market?" Or, "Five years ago, who would have guessed that U.S. bourbon whiskey would find its primary growth market in Japan? Yes, Japan!"

While there is no doubt that the world has moved into a new dimension of global competitiveness, there is some doubt about management's ability to know what in the world to do about it.

BIG FOUR THEORY

Some companies do, of course, know quite a bit about facing up to global marketing challenges. For the most part these are probably the giant players, and would certainly include companies that come under the umbrella of my "Big Four Theory." This theory, which I postulated some years back, suggests that by the year 2000 most major sectors of economic activity will be dominated by four large entities.

This certainly has come to pass in the beverage alcohol industry, with its reigning foursome of Guinness Plc and United Distillers spirits arm; Seagram; Allied-Hiram Walker; and Grand Metropolitan with its spirits arm International Distillers and Vintners.

What the Big Four paradigm really says is that, broadly speaking, only a limited number of large organizations will come to dominate most spheres of business worldwide. The actual number may be three, perhaps as many as five. But the inevitable result is for a small number of major firms to become truly dominant global forces via their internal growth as well as their increasing propensity for acquisitions and joint-venture alliances. Noteworthy, too, is that the Big Four paradigm applies both to the retailing and the manufacturing sectors of the world economy.

All of which suggests, in turn, some quite severe competitive hurdles for lesser-sized companies that may lack the financial resources to support infrastructures and overheads attendant to attaining Big Four status. What the writing on the wall clearly spells out is the essentiality of mastering marketing strategies and techniques that will enable them to survive, and quite nicely so, as niche players adept at walking among the giants.

US VERSUS THEM

One of the world's truly great global companies, Nestlé, does only two percent of its business in Switzerland, and the remaining 98 percent abroad. They are, however, most unusual. By contrast, most global companies have sizable operations in their home country, and often view themselves as domestic rather than international entities.

No matter how firms perceive themselves, global success, which is, after all, the aggregate of success and failure in individual markets, is traceable to attitudes and actions from the interplay between home/office management and management at the country level. Sometimes the home/office view myopically says there is only one way to operate and that is our way. Conversely, at the local level, one often faces the "not invented here" syndrome, and thus ideas from abroad are firmly unwelcome. Clearly, neither approach is right.

By remaining vigilant to the dangers of the "us versus them" mentality, and by literally outlawing it from the marketing equation, broad-vision managements are, in fact, thinking globally but acting locally. In their lexicon, the term "international" communicates an implicit sense of national and regional diversities within an overall global unity. Twenty years ago, who would have guessed that local, country, and regional variations would so greatly impact upon international marketing decisions?

Fundamental research can help generate awareness and understanding of values, perceptions, and attitudes in varying parts of planet Earth. World-vision executives contribute to the process by providing intuitive and intellectual interfaces with the nuances of differing countries and cultures. Sadly, there still are far too few executives able to shift readily from a domestic mode that innately gives greater credence and priority to us than to them. Perhaps we need to be looking to the world-class schools of cultural anthropology as well as to the preeminent graduate schools of business in our quest for tomorrow's world class global executives.

A WORKING PLATFORM

United Distillers (UD), the spirits arm of Guinness Plc, is a world leader in the international marketing of prestigious branded spirits. UD only came into being in 1986 when Guinness, in what was then the largest takeover in Britain's history, acquired Distillers Company Limited. In terms of respective size, it was an instance of the fish swallowing the whale. The acquired whale was composed of 20 virtually independent spirits companies respectively marketing their brands worldwide and frequently in competition with one another. With over 200 separate brands in the pipeline, it was evident that the acquired giant had to be drastically slimmed down and energized if it were ever to realize its equally giant promise.

An initial step was to determine which brands offered the greatest national, regional, and international potentials. Once that was accomplished, we could allocate the resources required to fully support and grow the targeted brands. Two overriding principles governed. Firstly, in order to practice the directed-marketing philosophy that we preached, we had to simultaneously think globally and act locally. Secondly, we had to design an organizational structure that would better enable us to get and remain close to the ultimate consumer.

A REGIONAL STRUCTURE

That structure was to encompass the five separate regions: the United Kingdom, continental Europe, North America, Asia Pacific, and international (Africa and South America). The five have since become four, with the United Kingdom being placed within the continental Europe region. Under the direction of its own regional managing director, each region has full profit responsibility for the company's brand portfolio in its part of the world.

One of the inevitable outcomes of such regionalization is that it ensures more logical management of the brand portfolio. Under the old preaquisition system, the chief executive of each of the 20 companies endeavored to maximize performance by literally selling his brands whenever and wherever possible; this strategy often involved a whatever price. By contrast, the postacquisition system has each of the four regions focusing upon a balanced brand portfolio that will maximize long-term potentials and profitabilities.

The old system led to a degree of internecine warfare, with Johnnie Walker, for example, competing head-on with Bell's, Dewar's, or our other scotch whiskies. In all too many cases this competition went beyond fighting for consumer hearts and minds, and to the point of extreme pricing that all but eliminated profits. Portfolio management, to its lasting credit and reward, conversely allows one to select which brands should be marketed in which parts of the world, as well as to determine how these brands can best be positioned, distributed, and priced to the consumer in each of these markets.

One of our early conclusions was that among a portfolio of over 200 brands, only two could arguably qualify as global brands—Johnnie Walker Red and Johnnie Walker Black, and Gordon's Gin. Accordingly, one of our first key decisions was to arrive at a balanced menu of brands for each region and for each country within that region. In the process, we culled those brands that seemed to offer little or no marketplace promise. The dollars thus saved were then allocated to brands that would likely profit from the added support.

From a portfolio perspective, it is interesting to note that the brand leader in premium scotch whiskey in the United States is Dewar's, which in the United Kingdom proves to be a modest seller. Bell's, which leads the category in the United Kingdom, happens to be a brand that we no longer sell in the United States. What's the most popular premium imported gin in the United States? Tanqueray, an outstanding member of our brand portfolio, albeit one that remains relatively unknown in most other countries.

Put another way, one does not find our marketers naively sitting in London and conceptualizing what products are best for Australia, Japan, or the United States. These subjective calls are being made at regional levels by mortals who function close to the consumer and are thus best positioned to interact with the overviews of headquarters. In essence, world statements are dangerous, regional statements are better, and country statements are best of all.

While there appears to be a few truly global brands, these also tend to exist in varying stages of development in different markets. Here again, country and regional orientations are essential to the formulation of a correct global strategy. Even though Johnnie Walker ranks as the leading scotch brand worldwide, we continue to research, rethink, and revitalize. This has resulted in redesign of the label and packaging for both Johnnie Walker Black and Red. To further enhance the world image of both brands, we have created new but differing advertising campaigns for Asia Pacific, Europe, North America, and South America. Historically, for example, Japanese advertisements have not shown men and women together. Yet our new Johnnie Walker ads are showing happy couples, and the consumer response is very positive. In the United States, we have moved away from the traditionally dull product-with-glass ad theme, and have brought a new dimension of excitement to scotch whiskey advertising.

At all times, however, the different interpretations of Johnnie Walker advertising in individual markets is compatible with the strategic direction provided by London, and indeed it is important to know that London also has a right of veto in terms of proposed strategic changes for our major brands in individual markets. At the end of the day, it boils down to "intelligent balance."

GEOCENTRISM

How we perceive others and the correct way of doing business with such others is very much influenced by our own cultural orientation. This is the root cause of ethnocentrism, which sees the ways of the home country as best and, as such, fully meriting adoption by other cultures with whom we interact. Equally debilitating in terms of international marketing is polycentrism, a state of acceptance that views the ways of doing business in the host country as being automatically right and correct.

This brings us to geocentrism, connoting a worldwide orientation that embraces a positive attitude of inquiry and analysis toward all people and cultures. It favors neither the home nor the host country, but tries to understand and borrow what is best from all.

When an executive being considered for international assignment displays this geocentric orientation, and the multicultural adaptability that flows from it, one need not be concerned as to whether he/she is French, American, British, or other. In essence, it is the state of mind rather than the state or country of birth that truly counts.

James Espey, former president and CEO of United Distillers, North America, a unit of Guinness Plc., is now President and CEO of the Chivas and Glenlivet Division of The Seagram Company.

Turn Up Your Marketing Candlepower

Michael Allen
President
The Michael Allen Company

To be a leader, learn how to change your business faster than its markets are changing.

I f a CEO wants to stay in the running, he can follow several standard prescriptions. He can cut corporate staff, reject strategic planning and become a low-cost (but quality) producer. He can manage by flying around, and build company culture with two-week executive outward-bound courses. He can hope that growth will emerge from some varied inventors in hidden skunkworks. However, these actions will make him indistinguishable from other "supply-side executives," for whom market change represents a threat.

Should a CEO want to become a leader, however, he will have to accept that his business must change faster than its environment. He will have to reshape its basics to deal with markets that are experiencing earthquakes and face the hard fact that many lieutenants are "marketing in the dark." He will be forced to give them fresh vision, illuminated with more strategic marketing candlepower. He will have to build a team of "market smart executives," for whom market change spells opportunity.

MARKETING IN THE DARK

Can a CEO run a business without knowing and understanding his customers? You may not think so; however, it's happening in many prestigious corporations. The signs and the reasons are not difficult to discern: marketing blindness, cheap introspection, and denial that change is taking place.

Marketing blindness

This occurs when companies are preoccupied with their technology, their channel intermediaries (distributors/agents/retailers), their plant automation, or brand awareness. When these drivers dominate, volume and scale preoccupy management. They lose sight of special end-user needs, service requirements, loyalty, and profit potential. Years ago, Ted Levitt diagnosed "Marketing Myopia" as a prevalent disease; regrettably, it has brought many corporate patients close to blindness. Why?

Cheap introspection

A generation of managers skilled only in overhead value analysis (perhaps McKinsey's worst contribution to the art of management), asset-stripping, leveraged financing, and portfolio restructuring have squeezed out the most important investments a business can make—those needed to understand its customers. Even big spenders of market research services spend more to protect their ideas than to change them, tracking their past instead of planning their future. The widespread use of third-party information services is evidence of how little value is placed on proprietary market insight.

Change denial

The consumer marketing equation continues to change in profound and irreversible ways—eventually impacting all businesses. So a basic change in attitude is needed—from managing businesses to managing change. Whereas managing a business requires regular data on operating performance, managing change requires more frequent information on business structure. As GE's vice chairman, Larry Bossidy, noted, "Don't fix it if it ain't broke is a dangerous and silly adage." When you sum it all up, supply-side introspection has supplanted demand-side vision and this trend could not be happening at a worse time.

STRATEGIC MARKETING CANDLEPOWER

Few CEOs will doubt that in a world of market structure change, there is a premium on competitive advantage—and innovation must spark share shift in market-driven organizations.

In this world, each marketing activity must concentrate on strategic positioning and competitive advantage. Yet very few companies can be most innovative in all segments of a market while still maintaining dominance in times of market change. Not IBM in business machines, nor Xerox in document processing, nor Kodak in photography, nor Citicorp in money center banking.

Here's what we see as the genesis of strategic marketing: the need to select that market opportunity and segment where unassailable competitive position can be developed and sustained and where the business can be a competitive killer.

Thus strategic marketing has been shaped by the pressures for companies to manage strategically and to become more sensitive to market change. It is a pivotal phase in a company's strategic evolution—taking planning from macro to micro; from static annual treatment to dynamic development; from an emphasis on evaluation to an emphasis on innovation; from operating data to strategic intelligence; from thinking to action. In this phase the CEO should change his leadership message and rewrite the management agenda.

FROM SUPPLY-SIDE THINKING

In this mode, management sees its mission as efficiently serving customer needs; its profit philosophy is to invest for growth and scale. Its priorities are to get more customers, build unit market share, achieve higher sales per customer, and increase customer benefits while being a low-cost producer. In addition, its goals are to increase distribution coverage, extend advertising reach through power advertising, and conduct market research into the market potential for leveraging existing brand imagery, products, or sales channels; management's style is to make company rules and manage them.

TO DEMAND-SIDE INSIGHT

Management, with this different mindset, defines its mission as creating a competitively unassailable customer franchise. The profit philosophy is to invest for market leadership. The priorities are to build share of profitable customers, achieve higher loyalty per customer, and increase service valued-added by solving customer problems. Additional priorities are to build relevant channels, focus media usage with finesse advertising, and to use strategic intelligence about the reasons for market change to innovate, to create a relevant image, to change product preferences, and to shift purchase behavior. Management's objective is to change the rules and exploit them competitively.

WINNING PRACTICES IN SERVICES

Nowhere does this thinking apply more than in the world of consumer services. I have observed eight strategic marketing practices that appear to be critically important to winning in the fields of consumer service: define the business in terms of service, not product; understand service values; focus and concentrate on segment or niche; shape a strategy of sustained service enhancement; develop a localized delivery system; create and leverage the service contract; and use information power strategically.

Winners define themselves by service

They know that all businesses have service opportunities; that service is not a cost to be eliminated but a source of revenue and profit. They therefore define themselves, not by product, feature, or price, but in terms of customer need and satisfaction. A classic winner is Club Med's "The Antidote for Civilization"; it has double-digit sales and earnings growth and the highest unsolicited brand inquiry of any resort group. *The Wall Street Journal* is "The daily diary of the American Dream." McDonald's says "You deserve a break today," but Burger King is "The Home of the Whopper"—perhaps explaining its recent rethinking in its advertising strategy.

Understand service values

There are six dimensions of service value: utility, reliability, advisory, personal treatment, convenience, and enjoyment. Utility value increases as "reach" increases (e.g., ATM networks, phone service, charge cards, or FTD flower delivery). Reliability value comes into play when consumers want help with uncertain quality of services and want to avoid having to try different providers (e.g., reliability in car warranties or HMOs).

Advisory value is important to consumers facing big (but infrequent) decisions, but who cannot learn for themselves or from enough experience, so they value advice in home buying, legal, medical, financial planning, and even undertaking.

Everyone wants to fight back the alienation and impersonality of our complicated world. With the personal treatment value, a person prefers to be referred to as an honored guest or as a private or preferred client, not just a 14-digit computer number.

The convenience value is especially important. Busy people want 24-hour service availability, speedy response and problem-solving on such things as insurance claims or reservations. Consumers, most importantly, want the most out of their shrinking leisure time and want fun when shopping, exercising, or catching up on the news—and not just in conventional entertainment.

Winners in consumer services build as many of these values into their offering as possible. The stunning success of the American Express platinum card and premier service are great examples.

Focus and concentrate on segment or niche

It's critical to segment consumer needs to pinpoint where potential service value is greatest and to decide how to tailor the service offering. Mediocre service for everyone loses to specialists.

The segmentation importance of affluence in services is clear: Affluent consumers have higher relative usage of services like accountants, private schools, and travel agencies, while the less affluent spend more on basics like medical insurance. A service company needs a strong consumer franchise with the emerging affluents and the delivery capability to get to them.

Shape a strategy of sustained service enhancement

The winning concept here is that service enhancement requires the recognition and solution of customer problems. Consumers are better at articulating problems they have with a service than expressing the benefits they want. For example, local newspapers can be improved by responding to readers' concerns about a lack of local news or complaints of smudging newsprint.

Deer Valley has quickly earned a reputation as the hot ski area in the West by solving skiers' top problems: the time needed to get there, long lift lines, poor food, and unfriendly service. Deer Valley has concentrated on providing superlative service in each of these areas.

To identify service enhancements, the service company is constantly getting feedback on customer problems (Domino's pizza arrives with a questionnaire that asks "Satisfied?" on the very top, with nine requests for comment—from temperature to toppings. Domino's has grown from sales of $626 million in 1984 to $1.5 billion in 1986).

Swiss Air—one of the superb on-time airlines in terms of flight precision—still searches for additional service excellence: babies that won't cry through the night of a transatlantic flight. How do they do this? The baby hammock. They are able to enhance their service by receiving constant customer feedback through surveys. Great service commands loyalty.

Develop a localized delivery system

An interesting example, applicable in several service industries, is that of newspaper or magazine distribution. Rack or news agent outlets must intercept the target reader traffic pattern.

One newspaper increased rack sales 70 percent in three months applying this principle. For example, concentrating racks at a "Yuppie" commuter railroad station caused sales to increase five-fold. This principle applies to home delivery service, specialty retailing, restaurants, and other household services whose usage varies with affluence.

Create and leverage the service contract

Many examples exist—from credit card contracts to a hotel-honored guest program. These programs, if done well, reinforce a consumer's need for reliable, personalized treatment. The supplier also gains several strategic advantages: service expectations are set, service can be differentiated, and loyalty can be rewarded. There are also marketing and operating benefits.

One major hotel chain examined its productivity in converting members of its preferred guest program to loyal users of their hotels. There were a substantial number of frequent travelers who were "rejectors." Now the preferred guest program has a range of features tailored for each type of guest.

Maintain a service culture with the personal touch

Leading service companies know that service quality is strongly influenced by human interaction. Service companies like Marriott, Federal Express, and Sears, with millions of customer interactions per day, spend millions of dollars in training to make them successful. They establish service standards and operating procedures that provide quality assurance before delivery. They train personnel, measure customer satisfaction, and provide feedback and rewards to employees.

Training schools for service personnel who deliver the service to the customer have several objectives beyond procedures and technical knowledge. They also stress courtesy, friendliness, and problem management.

I experienced good selling skills from the "Oliver Twist" chimney service. At night, by phone, they sold me a contract to clean two chimneys at $45 each. The chimney sweep arrived three days later and coaxed my wife into allowing him to clean four flues, remove a squirrel's nest, and replace some dangerously absent fire bricks, which came to a total of $420! The company called back that evening to see if we were satisfied.

Use information power strategically

As the Michelin guide for the restaurants of France demonstrates, customer information is a great tool to manage service quality. Information power can also personalize service (e.g., the receptionist at the Ritz pulls out your card and says, "Welcome back, Mr. Allen").

Information power can also extend the service offering. American Express has made a service extension with its gold card year-end summary of charges. We are beginning to see data base information power generate new service industries. "Infomediaries" are emerging (i.e., Council Travel, Shelternet, Job Net, Compu Card, Yellow Voices, Telerate) that enhance, or displace the information functions in travel planning, home buying, job hunting, investing, and so on. We are on the verge of fundamental changes and huge growth in information-intensive service businesses.

SELF-EVALUATION

Table 2–1 summarizes the eight strategic marketing practices that contribute to success in consumer service businesses. The differences between the winning company and the loser can be observed; you can use these calibration points to rate your own service behavior against the best practices of the winners, as illustrated in the table.

It is my observation that companies using these practices achieve superior growth compared to those who do not (see Table 2–2). They are escaping from the marketing dark ages into a more enlightened era. They are using higher strategic marketing candlepower; the American consumer continues to voice consider-

TABLE 2–1
Your Service Rating?

Practice	Calibration Standards		Illustrative Scores (Relative to Industry)				
	Strong (5)	Weak (1)	Wall Street Journal	American Airlines	Merrill Lynch	Wool- worth	Howard Johnsons
1. Define in Terms of Service	Defines business in terms of customer need and satisfaction.	Defines business in terms of product, activity, or price.	5	4	3	2	1
2. Understand Service "Value Added"	Combines utility, reliability, advisory, personal treatment, convenience, and enjoyment.	Provides only some, if any. Regards them as a "cost."	4	5	3	2	2
3. Focus on Segment or Niche	Focuses attention on important service segment defined by: affluence, household type, geography, and activity.	Lack of focus. Service target too broad, quality too low. Specialists more successful.	5	4	2	2	2
4. Sustain Service Enhancement	—Searches for problems —Helps customers —Responsive	—Ignores problems —Blames customers —Defensive	4	4	3	2	1
5. Develop "Localized" Delivery	—Dispersed —Maximizes customer access —Fulfills service guarantee	—Centralized —Minimizes delivery cost —No commitment	5	5	4	2	3
6. Leverage "Service Contract"	—Bills against "contract" —Provides membership —Differentiates service	—Sells transaction —No —No	5	5	5	1	1

	Positive indicators	Negative indicators					
7. Maintain "The Personal Touch"	—Builds loyalty —Cross-markets —High employee quality —Professional training in activity and total business —Delivery person has soft sales skills —Surveys of customer satisfaction —Service person reward tied to service level	—Low repeat —No —High turnover —Amateur on-the-job training —Delivery person doesn't sell —Surveys of customers —No connection	3	4	2	1	1
8. Use Information Power	—Major investment —Interaction points used for proprietary data collection —Client records built —Answer services provided	—Major cost —Not used —Client records discarded —Can't get answers	5	5	3	2	1
Position			4.5	4.5	3.1	1.7	1.5
Assessment			4.0–5 Winner		3.0–3.9 Vulnerable	2.0–2.9 Unprofitable	1.0–1.9 Won't Last

TABLE 2–2
Service Company Growth (Revenues, 1981–1986, Percent Per Year)

	Strong Strategic Marketing		Weak Strategic Marketing	
Retailing:	The Limited	+58.0%	Woolworth	−2.1%
Lodging:	Marriott	+21.0%	Hilton	3.1%
Health Care:	Hospital Corp. of America	+19.0%	Omnicare	−4.2%
Insurance:	Executive Life	+16.9%	Aetna	6.7%
Financial Advice:	H&R Block	+16.1%	E.F. Hutton	13.8%
Financial Services:	American Express	+15.2%	Bank America	6.4%
Publishing:	Gannett	+15.4%	Grolier	0.3%
Information:	Dow-Jones	+12.1%	CBS	3.4%
Airlines:	American	+7.9%	Pan Am	−4.3%

able dissatisfaction about the quality of services he or she receives. The field is ripe with opportunity and the rewards are great for those who are prepared to become "market smart."

Michael Allen is president of the Michael Allen Company of Rowayton, Connecticut.He was formerly vice president of corporate strategy at General Electric and created the Nine Block concept for GE.

What to Do When You're Not No. 1 or No. 2

Robert M. Donnelly
President and Chief Executive
RAC America

Though GE wrote it in stone, you can still succeed by breaking the commandment.

A common characteristic of being either the leader or number two in any market is the ability to supply a wide range of products to a diverse group of customers. Typically, this requires a lot of overhead since the majority of the firm's efforts are directed at providing more, not less, and it also limits responsiveness to change. These characteristics create an opportunity for any smaller and more focused competitor who identifies some unsatisfied customer requirement and then works diligently to satisfy it, initially within a narrow product or service niche.

Smaller, more focused competitors slip unnoticed by the big guys long enough to establish a dominant position with key customers in their niche. By the time market leaders respond, it is often with too little, and frequently whatever they do is too late to change the minds of the customers they have already lost. Market leaders create these windows of opportunity by becoming victims of their past success.

This is especially true when they feel that they own a comfortable share of the market. Once that happens they start to make assumptions about what the customer wants, rather than asking them about current needs. Once you start to market by assumption and define quality internally from your product's own marketing design, you are creating an opportunity for a more focused competitor. This was the window GM left open, which Honda among others brilliantly exploited.

AUTO INDUSTRY MONOLITHS

From 1980 to 1989 GM's share of the U.S. auto market went from 59 percent all the way down to 33 percent. GM sells one-third fewer cars now than it did in 1979. In 1989 GM lost close to $1 billion in North America and entered 1990 with $1 billion worth of unused factory capacity. The auto-making monolith is turning to stone. This is a very expensive price to pay for not paying attention to customers and marketing only by assumptions about customer desires. Honda on the other hand has experienced unprecedented success during the same period.

Americans are buying more foreign cars, and especially Hondas, not because they are foreign, but because they have been more intelligently designed, more carefully put together, and are more economical to operate than American-made cars. These reasons stand out when we compare the GM Chevette and the Honda Civic. What's the basic difference between these cars? They both have about the same amount of plastic, rubber, chrome, and steel, but one is superior in design, craftsmanship, and peformance—the key criteria customers use to evaluate a car.

The fundamental assumption has to be that quality is whatever the customer says it is. It naturally follows that companies must talk directly to customers to find out what they value. Those that best adapt their products to meet customer requirements, over time, will naturally displace their competitors no matter how big they are. Basic marketing strategy advocates a deliberate search for unsatisfied consumer requirements because few competitive advantages last forever. In reality, the best way to beat your bigger competitors is probably staring you right in the face. GM has been an obvious target for Honda and others for the last 10 years.

Let's look at another example of how important it is to understand what customers value. In the 1970s Hanes, a manufacturer of women's stockings and panty hose, asked women what they wanted and couldn't find in these products. The answers, as always, were simple: a heavier denier or sheerness, which makes stockings less likely to develop a run; a good fit; and a convenient source of supply. Obviously, improved quality of material, better fit, and more convenient availability at the local supermarket was the solution. "L'eggs" was born. Creative packaging in colorful plastic eggs and the masterful play on words contributed to one of the most successful consumer products of the 1970s. It was clearly a case of those that adapt best, by targeting consumer needs, displacing the rest. The more highly focused competitors changed the competitive equilibrium because they realized that playing by the leader's rules is competitive suicide. Each delivered a new value to customers and changed the nature of the existing competition for market share by waging the war on newly defined grounds.

NICHE-CONSCIOUS MARKETERS

The niche marketer must become totally customer conscious. Successful niche marketers recognize that innovation is really as much about customers as it is about products. The key to beating number one and number two is finding out how customers behave, what motivates them, and what they really need and value. Customer requirements are becoming ever more sophisticated and thus more easily segmented. Niche marketers create value by changing the perceptions specific sets of customers have about existing products or services, making those products more closely fit current requirements.

Customer profiling identifies groups of similar customers who have sets of unsatisfied requirements. These customer groups are usually subsets of existing market segments and can be sizable and uniquely profitable unto themselves. By determining the special requirements of these subset segments and creating or modifying a product or unique service approach to satisfy their special needs, a viable and very profitable niche can be developed. Notice what Volvo has done to appeal to the safety-conscious driver. Volvo's overall emphasis in the last 10 years has been on the safety and durability of its cars. Repetitive promotions that illustrate life-saving crash results and cars stacked on top of cars to demonstrate strength of construction have allowed Volvo to carve a profitable niche out of the highly competitive luxury car segment of the auto market. The unsatisfied customer requirement prior to a Volvo was as basic as the fear of dying or becoming seriously injured in an automobile accident because of weak vehicle construction. In this case the value feature staring all the auto manufacturers in the face was safety. Volvo was neither one nor two in terms of overall market share, but today safety is synonymous with Volvo.

The best way to determine what you need to do to become more customer conscious is to go through your own consumer decision-making process and apply the same logic to your customers. You know there are some products you care about and others you don't care about. Your value thresholds have been established in your mind and the minds of your customers since childhood. They've been embellished over the years by input from parents, peers, and virtually thousands of advertising messages.

But many CEOs never go to the supermarket anymore. A business philosopher said a long time ago, "A desk is a dangerous place from which to view the world." My advice to every CEO is to get out to see your customers as frequently as possible. Apparently, Roger Smith never got out, not even to see a GM dealer. Designing cars by committee obviously produced cars only a committee can love.

SEGMENTING CONSUMERS

Most consumers have a mental product grid. We separate the products we care about and those we don't care about. Those we do not value highly we buy as cheaply as possible. When it comes to products we do care about, we look for the best quality product or a set of attributes whose appeal is unique to us. In the quality category a single cell in our mental product grid usually has room in it for about three brand alternatives in descending order of grade. Whatever gets into your mental product grid displaces something that was already there. Apparently, European, Japanese, and Korean cars have recently been displacing American cars in many consumers' minds.

FIGURE 2–1
Customer Segmentation Flow Chart

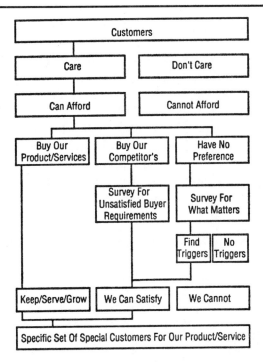

Your goal as a niche marketer is to segment customers in order to target unmet needs (see Figure 2–1). First, you must identify customers that care and those that don't care about the kinds of products or services you offer. For example, if you're selling something new and innovative certain customers won't care about it because they're not interested in new things, and consequently you'll never sell anything new or innovative to this group.

Next, separate existing and potential customers into those that can afford your product and those that cannot. You're not going to sell too many Rolls Royces in Appalachia. Then segment customers into those that buy your products or services now. Why? So you can keep them and treat them as an appreciating asset, by serving them well and by finding out what else you can do or get for them in the way of additional, new, or modified products.

Don't forget—stay close to the customers. Ask them if they're happy. Ask them what else you can do to keep them happy and shopping at your particular supermarket. Then look to your competitors' customers and find out if there is anything they are unhappy about. Survey them for unsatisfied buyer requirements. Why? To determine if there is something missing that you can provide.

Marketing is really a battle for the customer's mind. The more customers you can attract the bigger and more profitable you will become. The forces of social change have created micromarkets made up of clusters of many different kinds of customers with very different backgrounds, desires, and requirements. If you are totally customer-focused and you deliver the services your customers want, everything else will follow. But be careful, if you ever get to be number one or two in terms of market share, not to become a victim of your own marketing strategy.

Robert M. Donnelly, is president and chief executive of RAC America and the Honorary Chairman and Managing Partner of Alpha International Management Group Ltd.

International Marketing Myopia

Philip Voss, Jr.
President and Chief Executive
Zotos International

"When in Rome" is still true when it comes to global marketing, but "going local" has its surprises, too.

S uccessful consumer product companies share a particular approach to international marketing. Each has a structure that allows it to treat every region differently. For every cultural and linguistic nuance, a successful multinational always has a carefully researched and targeted marketing response. But far too many executives suffer from "global myopia." If they have any awareness at all of markets away from home, they expect overseas consumers to accept new products "as is."

Mars, Inc., for example, finally decided the United Kingdom was ready to accept a candy bar called "Snickers." For years the company had been convinced that the similarity of its most popular candy's name and the British slang for women's underwear would lead to problems. Similarly, when Exxon was considering a name change from Esso/Humble, it searched long and hard for a one-word corporate moniker that had no negative meaning anywhere.

The designers behind Chevrolet's Nova should have been as thorough. When that car was first shipped outside the United States no one could understand why sales were so slow overseas until someone realized that "No va" means "It doesn't go" in some Romance languages. The translation hardly bred optimism in the minds of consumers. Such examples pointedly illustrate the need for careful research and targeting (and what may befall a marketer when they are neglected).

DISSOLVING OLD BORDERS

Large, successful international marketers are positioning themselves to meet the opportunity presented by a unified European Community in 1992 (and by the increasingly market-driven economies of the Soviet Union, Eastern Europe, the Pacific Rim, and Latin America). Some have grown both through strategic acquisitions and the creation of their own manufacturing, distribution, and sales operations within targeted countries. Others have taken less straightforward routes.

But while Europe may be without frontiers after 1992, there will continue to be myriad cultural differences—which can affect a product's appeal—waiting to trip up unsuspecting or unprepared consumer marketers. And although Eastern Europe and much of Asia have opened themselves to freemarket principles and beckon companies of all sizes, nationalism will remain a powerful force, making it even more necessary for companies to market country by country.

Exceptions are few; there are only a handful of truly global products. Coca-Cola has succeeded among different consumer populations in dissimilar markets by following the same formula for success that has gained it a dominant market position in the United States—a uniform product and message. It must be doing something right. In the last three years Coke has made more money in the Pacific Rim and Western Europe than in the United States.

But few products have the potential to be so universally accepted and consumed—most successful introductions into new markets are consumer, rather than product, driven. More companies will have to learn to appeal to consumers by thinking and marketing globally. For the vast majority of marketers that will require different formulas for success in different parts of the world, whether the revisions consist of new advertising, new packaging, or changes in the products themselves.

Product revisions, and the difficulties in discovering what exactly must be changed, are pertinent to CEOs of multinational companies, especially those in the United States. As our domestic markets mature and our populations age and decline, growth and the possibilities of untapped markets continue to shrink. It behooves all U.S. and European companies to look beyond their traditional borders for opportunities.

LOCAL EMPLOYEES FOR LOCAL MARKETS

Many of the most successful multinationals have developed a cadre of bosses of different nationalities who have all had several international postings. After attempting to run its overseas operations from Cincinnati, Procter & Gamble eventually found success when it decided to staff much of its overseas organization with local people—from top management on down. At the same time, P&G learned that once you know the consumer in Japan, Germany, or Australia, it's only logical that you revise your products' marketing strategies. Several large U.S. companies— such as Colgate-Palmolive, Bristol-Myers, and Warner-Lambert— have become successful multinationals in the same way.

Today, many of P&G's top managers have come up from the international side, bringing a distinctly global outlook to one of the world's top marketers. Colgate CEO Reuben Mark and several of his top executives have had a number of foreign posts and many are multilingual. Increasingly, in fact, experience abroad is a prerequisite for a shot at the top echelon management jobs in the *Fortune* 500.

Executives of mid-sized concerns need to trust and apply local talent to their overseas marketing effort as well; their reluctance to do so too often renders them oblivious to local consumers' wants and needs. Nevertheless, they just don't have the resources to engage in trial and error abroad. They must learn from the experiences of their larger predecessors and apply the lessons on a smaller scale.

Rather than attempt to run an overseas effort from an offshore headquarters, which is the current practice of many mid-sized concerns, a company should make every attempt to run overseas operations locally. Regional managers who know their markets and are supported by their international employer vastly improve a company's chances for success. Local managers bring with them a firsthand knowledge and understanding of the company's potential customers and the marketing techniques needed to reach them. Coca-Cola, for example, has a multinational management group that is making a big international push. IBM relies heavily on locals to manage non-U.S. operations, while it continually increases the number of international executives in top corporate positions.

There are, of course, difficulties in staffing an overseas unit entirely with local employees. Sometimes, the driving force behind a company's success—its culture—can be diluted or lost entirely when marketing efforts are expanded far afield. In response to this risk, many large corporations go out of their way to provide home office training in the company's values and business practices to their international management. This ensures that a shared value system becomes integral to each branch, no matter what its location. For example, Colgate works hard to ensure that it is a local company in every country it enters. But at the same time, local executives have responsibilities to New York-based product managers and the company as a whole.

For the smaller company, the advantages to using local employees far outweigh the risks. By "going local," a business finds it easier to win acceptance and avoid political hassles. Often, units perceived to be "local" can sidestep bureaucratic obstacles and red tape that confront offshore companies. Other benefits include lower labor costs and new products, often created to take advantage of particular consumer needs or to meet competitive pressures in overseas markets, that can be successfully marketed elsewhere.

Reliance on local managers should not be confined to single-country marketing efforts. As mid-sized companies grow, they will find that their global product managers will require fluency in a variety of languages and cultural mores as they assert more power over country and regional managers. This means opening top ranks as well as command of offshore operations to managers from every foreign market. The number of companies that have gone that far are few, but a look at their ranks, which include

Unilever PLC, Sony, Gillette, Hewlett-Packard, and Heinz, should give others the incentive to try.

For the most part, Shiseido, the Japanese company that acquired Zotos in 1988, chose to have its U.S. subsidiary managed by Americans. In my case, this means that I've embarked on a regimen of Japanese lessons that give me the necessary feel for Japanese culture and implicitly say to Shiseido executives that I respect them.

ENTERING THE MARKET

Unlike their smaller brethren, successful multinationals often have the funds to enter a new market directly, either through the development of proprietary manufacturing, distribution, and sales channels, or through the acquisition of a complementary local business. These two strategies help ensure central control even in the face of rapid expansion into new markets.

But for the CEO of a mid-sized company looking to enter a new country, the thought of creating an overseas twin to his or her domestic manufacturing, sales, and distribution system or acquiring an overseas company can be daunting. The costs alone of such a strategy place global expansion out of the reach of all but the most prosperous mid-sized companies.

However, market development through joint ventures or limited partnerships with other mid-sized firms can be a viable substitute for direct acquisitions. Such inter-firm business arrangements can give any size company a foothold within a marketplace that otherwise might have taken years to develop.

Even large companies recognize the benefits. Compaq, the second-largest PC company in Europe, works with thousands of dealers rather than selling direct. According to Eckhard Pfeiffer, president of Compaq's Munich-based international operations, working with dealers who also carry other brands is an advantage because end users need a range of supplies that no single manufacturer can provide.

Indeed, joint ventures and partnerships effectively address a danger zone that has tripped up many large multinationals. Let's call this risky area the "indigenous component." Friendly joint ventures, partnerships, and mergers are vital in many countries if relations with the local community or government are to be good. Without an indigenous connection to meet local content regulations, for example, market entry can be impossible in some countries.

But advantages beyond dodging local trade barriers also exist for multinationals working with local units. Our acquisition is a good example. We offered a safer and less capital-intensive route into the professional beauty business in the United States. In addition, since we emphasize R&D, a number of other product breakthroughs are available to be re-marketed globally. And the backing of a financially secure corporate parent has allowed us to upgrade domestic marketing and sales operations, while at the same time investing in new production and R&D facilities.

THE LICENSING ALTERNATIVE

For those companies that can't yet swing an outright acquisition or find a suitable joint venture partner, the most feasible technique may be the development of a licensing agreement with a local company.

Licensing offers a mid-sized company the opportunity to contract out manufacturing, distribution, and sales to a locally established firm. Given that the cost of entry is so high in the international arena, many mid-sized companies are unable to cover all markets within a specified area in the manner necessary for success. The return on investment just isn't big or fast enough. By turning over selected operations to an overseas licensee, a company can build its business to a pre-determined threshold level that will later support company-owned manufacturing, distribution, and sales efforts or the creation of the critical mass necessary to attract a partnership with a strong local entity.

The threshold level for determining complete commitment to a market should be based on market share, after ascertaining that the market is large enough to sustain a major capital investment in local facilities.

For example, an outside hair care company would be foolish to challenge L'Oreal directly for its market share in France. A more feasible route into that highly competitive market would be to ship from an outside manufacturing facility through locally based distribution channels and work from there to gain a respectable market share.

Obviously, determining such a competitive situation beforehand is essential—an incoming mid-sized company must commit to the same high degree of research as larger companies if it is to determine accurately what sort of strategy is appropriate given the competition within a particular market.

There are, of course, difficulties in taking the licensing route to penetrate new markets. Chief among them is that a licenser gives up the ability to be the master of its fate—it largely relinquishes control of its product's presentation to consumers. A licensee is primarily a local entrepreneur and, as such, fairly autonomous. The difficulty lies in making use of that entrepreneurial spirit while maintaining a minimum of central control.

Companies need a global communications network. Following the lead of other international marketers, Zotos recently initiated European Council meetings to maintain contact and to simulate a corporate culture among our diverse European licensees. Gathering everyone together at least twice a year instigates a valuable cross-fertilization of ideas on subjects from product formulations to advertising. Discussions range from our plans for the future to workshops on how to improve relationships with local retailers.

SUCCESS IN THE GLOBAL MARKET

Achieving a successful global product requires more than just a good marketing team. It requires in-depth market research, a solid understanding of the consumer habits in the chosen market, and a good negotiation team to hammer out a successful partnership or licensing agreement with local players.

Failure to recognize that marketing efforts need to change market to market will, in the long run, hurt a company's global competitiveness. Nations and industries prosper as they increase their productivity, which in turn results from continuous improvements in quality, market penetration, and technology.

Global competition and its rigors cannot help but make companies stronger and more adaptable. The road to success, although fraught with hazards, inevitably leads to leaner, more effective companies that are at much lower risk of succumbing to market vagaries.

Philip Voss, Jr. is president and chief executive of Zotos International, a Darien, Connecticut-based manufacturer and distributor of hair care products.

Green Marketing

James R. McManus
Chairman and CEO

James H. Carter
Partner
Marketing Corporation of America

Are the new "green" marketers only after the "green" in customer pockets? Or is the proliferation of environmentally safe, biodegradable products more than a go-for-it marketing gimmick?

M ore than 90 percent of U.S. consumers claim to be concerned about the quality of the environment. Retailers and manufacturers, particularly those in the grocery and packaging industries, are now attempting to come to grips with the new consumer awareness by enhancing the environmental safety of their wares.

There's no question that environmental concerns are real, and they should be a major agenda item for every CEO. Any company not addressing the critical dimensions of this issue is not serving its customers, employees, and stockholders. It's a strategic offensive and defensive imperative that companies develop and execute a "green" plan. But despite the flurry of green marketing activity and the barrage of media coverage in recent months, almost nothing substantial has resulted. Yet the green movement will continue to gain unprecedented attention as the issues (solid waste, pollution, safety, natural resources, etc.) become better understood and involvement broadens.

But green won't become a reality to most Americans until it has an impact at home, until it noticeably changes our lives. Helping to change attitudes is the recent barrage of environmental information in the popular media, particularly surrounding last spring's catalyst, the Earth Day celebrations. By the end of last year, network news coverage of environmental issues had increased from an average of one story every second night in 1988, to two stories per night. Popular magazines such as *House Beautiful*, as well as trade publications such as *Advertising Age*, now have designated environmental sections.

TRASH CONSCIOUSNESS

Until now, convenience issues have largely overridden consumer environmental concerns. Demand for easy-to-use, time-saving products, which require more packaging, ballooned in the last decade. Nevertheless, when trash sorting becomes mandatory for millions of households, Americans will truly change their behavior, and green will become a way of life. That change is rapidly headed our way in the form of a dramatic reduction in this country's landfill capacity. Current sites simply can't hold America's throwaways. That message was brought home clearly by New York's infamous wandering garbage barge, as it was turned away from port after port, unable to dump its pungent cargo. By 1995, half of our current 6,000 landfills will be closed (there were 16,000 sites in 1970), forcing large-scale recycling of our solid waste. Meanwhile, dumping fees at most municipal landfill sites are skyrocketing. And the Environmental Protection Agency (EPA) is calling for 25 percent recycling by 1992, up from last year's 11 percent recycling rate.

Meanwhile, the public has already been exposed to an alarming rate of environmental statistics on the waste problem:

• Discarded plastic litters the earth for centuries, discarded glass for up to 1,000 years, and aluminum cans for 500 years.

• It takes more than 500,000 trees to supply Americans with their Sunday newspapers every week.

• The amount of garbage produced by Americans has doubled since 1960.

• Recycling one aluminum can saves enough energy to operate a TV set for three hours.

All of these memorable statistics notwithstanding, the solid waste crisis has also resulted in many public misconceptions. For example, it's generally perceived that packaging is the principal component of solid waste. In reality, only 30 percent is from packaging. Many people point the finger at plastic as the major source of packaging waste, when plastic represents only some 7 percent by weight—far less than paper and paperboard or glass, the real culprits. And there is growing evidence of less disparity between paper and plastic in terms of their rate of degradability in modern landfills. Yet packaging, and plastics in particular, have become the "bad guys" of the solid waste problem. On the government front, more than 800 pieces of environmental legislation were introduced in 1989 alone, and more than 130 laws were enacted in 38 states. This year, state legislatures will consider more than 1,000 solid waste bills. Several proposals—some extreme—are being considered as potential solutions:

• A one cent tax on each component of a package has been proposed.

• Disposal fees may be charged on containers not being recycled in high enough specific quantities.

• Bans and surcharges on non-degradable containers will become law.

• There are plans to ban retail sale of foods or beverages in non-recyclable containers.

• Prohibition of retail sale of products packaged in multi-material containers may be instituted.

• Mandatory national container-deposit fees have been proposed.

ALL CLAIMS ARE SUSPECT

Concurrently, the media, environmental groups, and government agencies are moving to expose companies for making misleading or irrelevant packaging claims. *The New York Times* recently reported that McDonald's will test new container materials following charges that some of its current packaging is not as recyclable as it claims. Under pressure from environmental watchdogs and a task force of state attorneys general, Mobil dropped the word "degradable" from its plastic bags. It's been pointed out that products may be designed to degrade, but that process is inhibited through lack of water and sun exposure when waste is buried in most landfill sites. Mobil dropped the claim quickly, thereby getting itself off the environmental hit list and gaining credit for trying to do the right thing.

So-called degradable diapers have been widely castigated as failures. Yet many public institutions that promote hygiene, such as hospitals and day care centers, continue to mandate their use. White Rain Styling Mousse was attacked for its "Ozone Friendly" labeling based on the omission of chlorofluorocarbons (CFCs). The claim was true enough; however, the Food and Drug Administration banned CFCs in all such products back in the 1970s, so it wasn't exactly unique. Furthermore, the product was criticized on the ground that its substitute propellant contributed to smog. Even Heinz's recent announcement on new recyclable plastic packaging for ketchup has drawn criticism. The reason has nothing to do with the change—but environmentalists claim that it addresses only half the problem because no established recycling programs currently exist in much of its marketplace.

RETAILERS CHANGE COLORS

Despite these problems, many retailers and manufacturers are taking steps to assume leadership and provide consumer education. Some attempts are working, some aren't. But most companies win points for trying. Wal-Mart, one of the first U.S. retailers to launch a major green offensive, ran full-page ads in major media urging consumers to choose environment-friendly products and calling on manufacturers to produce them. Focusing on recycled and recyclable products, the advertising's message was, "We're looking for quality products that are guaranteed not to last." Wal-Mart also introduced in-store signing to flag "greener" products.

Big Bear Markets, a San Diego-based retail chain, is taking the offensive with a fully integrated green marketing program. Its consumer efforts focus on changing purchasing and personal habits—more careful product selection, for example, and recycling are both emphasized. Initiatives to improve or eliminate a number of its in-store products, such as foam deli trays, are in progress. And the chain switched back to paper bags at checkout on the grounds that paper is preferable in coastal areas because plastic bags can entangle and trap marine life. Company research indicated that a switch to bags made from recycled paper was a sound business decision. The San Diego City Council applauded the chain's efforts, declaring last October "Big Bear Markets Appreciation Month."

Loblaw's, a major Canadian retail chain, used its size and innovative marketing skills for a preemptive green line launch throughout Canada in 1989. It included healthy, or "body friendly," products to fill out the line. The company won product endorsements from environmental groups, but at least one product was withdrawn, when the question of biodegradable diapers become an issue. The initiative was criticized as "just another marketing ploy," but controversy surrounding the green line introduction actually helped spur initial sales. The jury is still out on its long-term success.

Meanwhile, the Grocery Manufacturers Association is becoming proactive in solving waste problems, while protecting the business rights of its membership. A number of other trade associations— such as the Food Marketing Institute, the National Grocers Association, and the Council on Plastics and Packaging in the Environment—promote educational materials that help answer packaging complaints, report major retailer programs, and assist in writing consumer education brochures. And the National Food Processors Association published its own policy on solid waste, asking for firm commitment from and participation by members.

THE PRODUCT SIDE

With an eye on events in Canada and Europe, where environmentalists have also attacked green marketing campaigns for unsubstantiated claims, a number of major U.S. manufacturers are nevertheless adopting a green position. In all likelihood, however, most of green products will be slow to reach the market. When it comes to implementation, Procter & Gamble is perceived as the real leader. The company is testing diaper recycling in Seattle and diaper composting in Minnesota. It has also announced tests on recycled plastics for use in soap and cleaning product packaging. P&G is also introducing a concentrate refill package for Downy, a laundry product, which it says uses 75 percent less packaging material. The refill is a crushable, paper-based package with a spout to pour into a larger, plastic container. It contains concentrate, which, when mixed with warm water, makes the equivalent of 64 ounces of fabric softener.

Heinz has made a major commitment to gaining a green leadership position and has even established a green public relations program. It was also the first tuna processor to announce a ban on using tuna caught by nets that also kill dolphins. Another food industry giant, Campbell Soup Co., has established a task force to keep abreast of environmental issues. Its Pepperidge Farm subsidiary is testing recycled packaging and package size reductions.

While there are no clear product successes from a green point of view as yet, there are some promising product categories with lots of activity—paper goods, plastic bags, unbleached coffee filters, cereal packaging using recycled paperboard, to name a few. For the most part, the real changes are in packaging reduction and recycled or recyclable products. The green movement promises to produce sizable business opportunities throughout the 1990s. But CEOs should also recognize the pitfalls. The stakes are high. And corporate reputations are in play through high visibility and close scrutiny.

HOW TO MARKET GREEN

Green will be a constantly moving target. What is apparent today will change tomorrow. Knowledge is evolving and so are solutions, as well as expectations. Indeed, increased expectations mean the playing field will never be completely level. To prepare themselves, retailers and packagers need to get serious about going green or be prepared for negative publicity about their companies and products. Companies must address the issue of environmental marketing in a comprehensive manner, putting together a master plan with a sense of urgency that prioritizes internal and external areas of concern. Anything short of a comprehensive action plan will be viewed as ad hoc and opportunistic. It will place your company in the position of operating under crisis management, instead of in a proactive manner. Avoid a defensive posture.

The plan should be manageable, traceable, and have the required resources to back it up. Develop a green philosophy at corporate and department levels. An internal plan should include active employee information sharing in the form of workshops, newsletters, and feedback opportunities. The troops have to develop a commitment; corner office commitment alone won't work. We strongly recommend that CEOs follow the recent example set by Disney, General Electric, and Unilever by appointing an individual with clout to be totally responsible for environmental policy. That executive should oversee policy implementation and help manage its consistency, both internally and externally. Keep your eyes open for opportunities to take the initiative, while at the same time calculating the business risks of turning green too quickly.

Defining green too narrowly (e.g., plastic, by definition, justified or not, may never be green enough) or too broadly (body friendly) will defeat your purpose. While right choices may be unclear, it is clear that there are wrong choices. Look out for the bad guys of environmentalism. And don't expect a total win. Regardless of your actions, some consumers won't be happy; some environmentalists and regulators won't be satisfied. There will always be those who argue the benefits of certain products, while others believe them to be an unnecessary evil.

In summary, there are two key points for CEOs to keep in mind. One is that green must be a comprehensive program in the form of a corporate strategy, not merely a promotion. Moreover, we suggest that you instill green as a way of life in your company. It's sure to strike a responsive chord with your customers, employees, and others who are experiencing recycling and other environmental legislation that affects their everyday lives.

James R. McManus is the chairman, CEO, and founder of the Marketing Corporation of America, a full-service consulting and venture development firm based in Connecticut.

James H. Carter is a partner and director of the Marketing Corporation of America's environmental and customer marketing practices.

When Niche Marketing Confuses Consumers

Wilder Baker
President and Chief Executive

Robert Fiore
Vice Chairman and Chief Operating Officer
Warwick Baker & Fiore Advertising

Niche marketing has overshot its target. Now, only consumer-friendly niches will succeed in attracting shoppers confused by massive product welter.

Everywhere, American shoppers find themselves with less time to do the things they used to do. And it seems that there really is much more to do, in terms of today's economic needs. One would think that CEOs would seize the opportunity to make life simpler for consumers. And they've tried. Niche marketing became all the rage in the 1980s. Consumers could have exactly what they wanted, custom-tailored for their physiological and psychological needs. What could be simpler?

From the marketer's standpoint, niche marketing has been the only way to enter crowded product categories where huge marketing budgets reign. Identify an untapped market, uncover an unmet consumer need, reveal an emerging trend, seek out an ignored demographic group—and watch those dollars rush in.

The marketers could also reach their niche target through segmented media. TV sets with 100 channels, over 1,500 targeted magazines, doctor's office or classroom advertising. Now you can select your audience and talk directly to them—no mass media vehicles like the *Cosby* show or *People* magazine for you. A marketer's dream had come true—or did it? Along the way, did something go wrong with niche marketing?

PRODUCT NICHES: THE ROOT OF CONSUMER CONFUSION?

The latest research indicates a very different result of niche marketing—a result that could turn a marketer's dream into a nightmare overnight. Instead of simplifying consumers' lives, marketers have created consumer confusion, dissatisfaction, and frustration. In an attempt to make product selection easier for the consumer, marketers have made it harder, if not impossible, for consumers to shop. Overall, this is because manufacturers have defined product niches based on product attributes, rather than creating consumer niches driven by consumer need and communicated in consumer language. The difference between product niches and consumer needs, and the impact of this difference on the consumer and business success, is the focus of this article.

There are three clear reasons for the confusion that has resulted from the niche marketing of the past.

1. By not totally committing to their niche, even niche marketers who appear to be successful have confused their consumers:

By definition, niche marketing requires a finite marketing focus in order to better meet the needs of a specific consumer group. In other words, marketers decide to focus 100 percent of their marketing effort on somewhere between 5 percent and 25 percent of the population that is perfectly suited to their product. Unfortunately, many marketers are unwilling to truly commit to a limited consumer group. One of our favorite stories is of the manufacturer who developed a product for women. In test marketing, the product did so well among women that the manufacturer suggested it be expanded to men.

Selecting a niche requires the courage to walk away from a living, breathing percentage of the population. If your commitment to your niche wavers, you will end up with a fuzzy or confused brand image—and perhaps a decline in sales. To your consumers, you are no longer made for them. This discovery is

confusing and alienating to your loyal customers, and may damage your relationship with them.

For example, Tiffany had always been the high-end name in
jewelry. Tiffany became a metaphor for the best: People spoke of
the Tiffany of carpets, the Tiffany of cosmetics, even the Tiffany
of dishwashing liquids. But after its acquisition by Avon in 1979,
Tiffany began to expand outside of its upscale niche. "Why restrict
the appeal only to a select few?" became the cry from corporate
headquarters. Quickly, we began to see a new focus on $15 stem-
ware rather than $2 million diamond pendants. By the mid-1980s,
Tiffany had lost its prestige to Cartier. Tiffany is now feverishly
trying to recapture its former niche, with new print ads focusing
on $100,000 necklace and earring sets.

The message: Don't succumb to the temptation to expand
beyond your niche unless you've carefully assessed the benefits,
recognized the risks, and are convinced that expansion will work.

*2. Products are too often marketed from the manufacturer's perspec-
tive, not the consumer's perspective. When a niche is identified and a
product is marketed, the manufacturer, the advertiser, and perhaps the
retailer know exactly who it is meant for:*

Unfortunately, the consumer doesn't. In many cases, the consumer has not been clearly told which product in the wide array
of options is for her.

Take the cold remedy category, for example. Manufacturers
have a full range of products, ostensibly to meet any consumer
need. There are prescription and nonprescription products lasting
4, 8, or 12 hours. Medications are available in liquid or tablet, for
multiple or single symptoms, with or without analgesic. And if
you are lucky enough to know the cause of your problem in
addition to the symptom, you can also choose between cough,
cold, sinus, or allergy products. With this many products, there
must be something for everyone, right?

Wrong. In one study on consumer confusion, the cold category
was ranked by consumers as one of the most confusing regularly
purchased product categories. In fact, it ranked right after insurance. Obviously, the segmentation created by manufacturers does
not necessarily match the consumer's approach to buying in a
given category.

The drug category is not the only one that confuses consumers,
however. In a separate consumer study, consumers said that 80

percent of all products available have no point of difference at all. What's more, 64 percent said that products did not deliver on their promises. Claims like "new and improved" have worn out their welcome (not considered important by 86 percent), and contemporary promises such as "light," "low fat," and "cholesterol free" are important, but not widely believed or understood. In the end, consumers' skepticism and confusion may be the basis for a return to the safety of familiar brands from yesteryear. Not a result most manufacturers would be thrilled with, except possibly Procter & Gamble.

The message: Listen to what consumers tell you about how they perceive segments in the category and what factors and attributes motivate their purchase—in their language, not in manufacturers' production line terms.

3. Successful product niches are inevitably exploited by leading brands:

It's an old story—an innovative, entrepreneurial product marketer identifies an opportunity, spends lots of time, money, and effort to develop and qualify a product for brand introduction. The product is a smashing success—until the market leaders realize the potential, duplicate the technology or formulation, and introduce it as a line extension of their top-selling brand name.

Even patented innovations are subject to duplication. In all likelihood, the innovation will be copied, with a minor alteration, for immediate introduction. If it is not, a manufacturer must capitalize on his seven-year "window of opportunity" to survive the competition when his patent runs out.

The examples are endless. Check-up toothpaste pioneers the pump and tartar control formulations, only to be superseded by line extensions of Crest, Colgate, and every other major brand. Pritikin's diet salad dressing competes with Kraft Free. Almay Sensitive Skin lotion now sits next to Oil of Olay's Sensitive Skin line. Caffeine-free soda is now an option in Coke and Pepsi. Nondrowsy formulations are alternatives for the major cold remedies. High-protection sunscreens compete with Bain de Soleil's SPF 30. And Cheerios, the old standby as the lowest-sugar cereal, has honey nut and apple cinnamon versions.

Why do innovators lose their initial consumer loyalty so quickly? The problem occurs when an innovator becomes enamored of his new formulation or technology and builds his entire marketing premise on this new idea. By focusing too heavily on the product, without developing a relationship between the consumer and the brand name that results in brand equity development, the innovator becomes vulnerable. Major brands with loyal consumer franchises and strong brand equities can easily reproduce the technology or formulation and have the new product plus the trusted brand name. As a parent, would you feed your child Kid's Cuisine brand single-serve meals or Gerber brand single-serve meals? While Kid's Cuisine can be credited with opening a new segment of the frozen food category, Gerber's baby expertise is likely to be preferred.

The original manufacturer's innovation is preempted, and he's left out in the cold (or bought out, if he's one of the lucky few). For the consumer, the result is confusion. After each major brand has added a line extension to compete in each new niche, the consumer is faced with a new market segment and many more products. And all of these products now offer similar—if not identical—benefits to the same consumer. In fact, line extensions accounted for 80 percent of the 12,055 new product introductions in 1989, and are expected to account for 90 percent of new product introductions over the next five years.

The only winner is the market leader who extends his line, advertises heavily, and captures a few extra share points while expanding his franchise. All without the expense of a test market, since the innovator company's success was experienced enough to validate entering the niche. The message: Mesh your point of difference with a consumer bond that goes beyond simply the innovation.

UPROOTING THE PROBLEMS

Is niche marketing possible without creating confusion? Yes, but marketers must be aware of the causes and effects of consumer confusion in order to manage it. Confusion goes deep and a complete understanding of the consumer is critical to achieving effective niche marketing.

The manufacturer's point of greatest consumer contact is the retail outlet. Organizationally, stores are a key source of consumer bewilderment, as retailers arrange store shelves by category and company. Although that helps a brand manager doing store shelf checks and creates a leadership "billboard effect" for companies, it does nothing for the consumer. Consumers know little of manufacturers; they think of products in terms of brand.

A cereal shopper looking for his favorite brand of fruit-added cereal might never get that far. Although the shopper may discover an enclave of fruit-added products in one area, his brand is often not there. Because the shopper does not know his favorite is made by another manufacturer, and shelved separately, he has the following options: default to the fruit-added cereal in front of him; spend precious time searching; or select another familiar brand name, even if it is another type of cereal. This process is extremely dangerous for marketers as it undermines any perception of difference between brands, Marketing budgets can be rendered entirely useless by shelving that is not friendly to the consumer.

Additionally, store shelves contain so many brands that the consumer is often confronted with "overchoice"—too many packages on the shelves. In the hair care category alone there are over 200 brands. When the variety of sizes, formulas, delivery systems, and scents are added, consumers start to short-circuit in the store.

How do consumers handle this confusion? Often they bring a friend to the store. In addition to making the experience a bit more pleasant, family and friends provide advice on purchases. One of our observers noticed two women taking almost 30 minutes to engage in a debate about the pros and cons of a cough medicine one needed for her child. "How can something be a cough suppressant and an expectorant at the same time?" they wondered.

These reactions reduce brand names to the sum of their parts. As such, brands are forced to compete on a highly technical level where perceived product innovation is king. In that environment, consumers choose products by specific information, ingredients, or other label notation.

CONSUMER-FRIENDLY NICHING

So how can marketers improve the situation? How does a company ensure the continued growth of current brand names and the successful introduction of new products in the future? The answer lies in our ability to select the appropriate consumer group and develop a bond with that group that is strong enough to withstand the in-store experience. Success in the next decade depends on our ability to put the consumer first. The niches we develop now should not be product niches at all; the profitable niche of this decade should be "consumer friendly."

If done correctly, consumer-friendly niching will establish a bond with the consumer that will be capable of cutting through information overload and product clutter. That bond will create loyal customers who identify with what your product stands for and look to include it in their lives. In today's environment this kind of consumer relationship will override changes in form, function, or price.

Adopting a consumer-friendly niche involves much more than changing your perspective. It means committing yourself to a certain group of people. It means considering everything from their point of view, and being clear and consistent in your communication. Anyone who has been a salesperson knows the importance of "mirroring" their customer: behave like they behave, put them at ease, and help them feel comfortable with you. Only then will your customer really hear your pitch.

Today's consumer is trying to make sense of a complicated world that marketers created. In the next decade success will depend on our ability to translate the retail world for consumers. That means understanding who they are, what they need, and how they feel about their purchasing decisions. Brands that can do this will win the loyalty and respect of consumers. In other words, they will have found their success in a consumer-friendly marketplace.

Wilder Baker is president and CEO of Warwick Baker & Fiore, a New York-based mid-sized advertising agency.

Robert Fiore is the company's vice chairman and chief operating officer.

Introducing New Products During Tough Times

Hunter Hastings
Chief Executive
Ryan Management Group

Consumer product debuts increasingly rely on a mix of promotional techniques in which advertising plays a nontraditional role.

C hief executives must remain open-minded about change and the opportunities and challenges it presents. We're living in an era when oat bran can be good for you one moment, and then suddenly it's no longer so good for you as it was yesterday and tomorrow it may well turn out that it's downright unhealthy. One can never be certain of the lasting status of anything in our world. This is especially true of marketing, where change is our currency and our opportunity to find and grab a competitive advantage.

The role that advertising plays in marketing, and particularly in product introductions, has changed dramatically in the past decade. Advertising can no longer play the role traditionally assigned to it in new product introductions. But advertising continues to be allotted a major percentage of virtually every introductory plan budget because marketers look to the past rather than to the future. In the 1990s other forms of direct, creative communication with the consumer will replace advertising in successful product introductions.

Advertising was once the *sine qua non* of marketing, the silver bullet. Good advertising would not only create consumer awareness, but would also help build distribution, support pricing strategy, and achieve trial and repeat volume. In fact, a great advertising campaign was the single answer to all marketing problems.

But virtually every assumption on which this view is based has changed. Advertising is, at best, only a partial answer to the questions posed by the new marketing dynamics of the 1990s. Advertising still has a role to play as part of a bigger, more flexible ensemble of marketing strategies, particularly in business-to-business marketing, but in consumer marketing, it will deliver its best performance in a supporting role.

Advertising cannot do what it once could. The most important aspect of this change is in the area we used to call "making copy points." Once, advertising could provide detail. Today, audiences have segmented and they continue to do so at an exponential rate. It is virtually impossible to reach many of the new target niche audiences efficiently or effectively. One either runs into the problem that the new media choices are so fragmented that no combination of market slivers make up a decent pie, or worse, media fragmentation flies in the opposite direction to market segmentation. Because of shortened spots (nearly 50 percent of TV commercials run for only 15 seconds) and magazine advertising clutter, it has become reckless to attempt to convey more information than the brand name and the product category. This fact is particularly damning for an introductory product that almost by definition needs to tell prospective consumers something more about itself.

FOUR NEW WAYS WITH NEW PRODUCTS

How can chief executives best respond to the formidable challenge of the consumer dynamics of the 1990s? Alternative forms of marketing have grown substantially. Marketers are now using sales promotion, public relations, special events, licensing, trade allowances, and merchandising. By examining the changes taking place in the marketing environment, we can predict the four key forms new product introductions will take.

Promotion-driven introductions

Sales promotion is now a major force in consumer marketing communications. If, for example, promotion is utilized to increase shelf space and create displays in store, it eloquently communicates that a new product is important, is worthy of consumers' attention, and merits trial. If the trial message is reinforced with a sample or coupon, the consumer's receptivity is heightened. You can easily envision how a multi-layered promotion campaign can be structured.

The ingenious marketer with limited resources can confidently decide in favor of a promotion-driven new product introduction. Those who have often have achieved spectacular success. One excellent example is Smartfood popcorn, whose president, Ken Meyers, based his product introduction entirely on samples and the use of the packaging itself as a visual symbol to achieve awareness and word-of-mouth recommendation. "There was really nothing else we could have done with our money that could have given us any value. We decided that our product and our packaging were our best advertising tools," says Meyers. It is better to be single minded in pursuing unique communications goals than to make a small budget even less effective by splitting it up among the conventional mix of marketing tools. Smartfood quickly became a $20 million regional brand and continues to grow under the new ownership of Frito-Lay, which has not tampered with the winning marketing formula.

Distribution-driven introductions

There are certain categories and brands for which distribution itself can do a better job of communication than either advertising or promotion. In this case the entire communication with the consumer can be conducted at the point of purchase. One set of consumers will develop a positive perception of a brand simply because it is available in the "right" outlets. The choice of distributor implies a validation of the brand by those outlets.

The beverage category provides us with some recent examples of building a brand using the distribution process. Perrier was first introduced in the United States in carefully selected locations—

restaurants and what are called "thought leader" locations, where trendsetters congregate and are seen by trend followers. Perrier's adoption by the "right" group in the right locations assured its initial success. Later, Perrier changed its distribution system as it emerged from introductory status to broader acceptance. Now, it is a supermarket and liquor store staple as well as an on-premise brand.

Many hair care brands have won recognition by using the salon distribution channel. Once validated by the acceptance of salon professionals, Jhirmak, Redken, Paul Mitchell Systems, and Nexus went on to successful broader retail distribution. But initial communication methods, including professional seminars, providing ideas and news to salon customers, and a generally supportive and exclusive relationship with the channel (including appropriately high profit margins) helped the manufacturers launch $100 million brands. At the same time, this form of new product introduction erected powerful barriers against further entry to the exclusive salon channel by conventionally advertised retail store brands.

Public relations-driven introductions

New public relations (PR) systems provide marketers with a complex and sophisticated set of tools for marketing products or services that do not lend themselves readily to advertising and might otherwise go largely unnoticed. Think, for example, of the products and brands that have emerged from the world of auto racing: performance tires like Goodrich T/A radials, motor oil brands like Quaker State and Pennzoil, and even esoterica such as STP gas treatment have become prominent names and have gained wide usage because of their association with auto racing and their visibility on the track. This association was initially brought home to its target audience primarily by PR. Public relations has more credibility in making these connections than does advertising, even though advertising is often used to secure the ground once PR has helped the product with the initial breakthrough to the broad market.

Sports shoe brands like Adidas and Nike built their market base by contracting with star athletes to wear their products and by publicizing endorsements to target consumer groups. A presence among "high visibility" people or activities—professional athletes, entertainers, prominent businessmen—can be worth more than all the advertising in the world. Sometimes, advertising-oriented marketers choose to create the connection artificially and then advertise it—as in the Pepsi/Michael Jackson ads or the K mart/ Martha Stewart ads. Increasingly, this will become the wrong way to seize the opportunity. Not only can the advertising spending be matched by competitors, but the association with the personality loses credibility with the audience simply because it is advertised.

On a slightly more whimsical note, we can place the introduction of Paul Newman's "Newman's Own" brand in the PR-driven category, even though Newman has recently succumbed to the temptation of advertising. His "funky" pasta sauce concoctions, salad dressings, popcorn, and lemonade were based entirely on borrowed recipes, but the PR opportunities inherent in the marketing were strong enough to carry the brand through introduction to the point of being self-sustaining. The fact that charities are the beneficiaries of Newman's Own sales gives the brand a "green" character perfectly suited for the 1990s, which is again effectively communicated through PR. Advertising might have been incompatible with the launch of this venture—it would have been seen as too blunt, too self-serving.

New products from umbrella propositions

The technique for introducing brands without advertising, which I believe will have the most currency in the coming decade, uses all of the aforementioned strands. That technique may be termed brand "equity" expansion. The basic idea is that advertising will come to communicate, not the individual character and benefits of single products and services, but the more general value and appeal—the built-up equity—of an umbrella proposition stated through a brand name. Individual new products will emerge from beneath such an umbrella and establish their market base exclusively via promotion and merchandising techniques.

The nearest example today of marketing expansion using the umbrella technique is involved with the Weight Watchers brand. Weight Watchers is a system by which consumers can lose weight and regain the fitness, shape, and healthy lifestyle they desire. The system includes clinics and courses, and all kinds of foods, snacks, beverages, and condiments. Currently, Weight Watchers advertises its clinics and frozen entrees. Yet the whole franchise is growing in many more directions than the segments that are advertised. Weight Watchers can introduce new products and variations without additional advertising support because the system legitimizes all new entries. All Weight Watchers must be concerned with is managing the business, providing in-store merchandising, which will take care of awareness, and in certain cases, providing trial incentives.

Brand franchise expansion is the most eloquent expression of the new marketing dynamics at work. It represents a whole new way of thinking about what a brand is, and the role it plays vis-à-vis consumers. With this new thinking comes a new appreciation for what advertising can and can't do in a new product introduction context. If the corporation owns a brand asset that already has meaning for consumers, and that meaning can extend to cover the new product being considered for launch, it is redundant to tell the consumer a second time about the equities of the brand. In many cases it will be sufficient to invite the consumer who is already familiar with the brand, and trusts it, simply to try its new form, using trial incentives rather than advertising to reinforce the message.

Porsche has licensed its name for a line of Porsche design products, which range from expensive sunglasses to cigarette lighters. Since design, engineering, functionality, and aesthetics are all highly consistent with existing brand imagery, the brand expansion increases marketing desirability. Mars and Three Musketeers candy bars are now available in ice cream form. This represents more than just the use of the brand name in a broader context. The brand owners have been careful to duplicate the unique tastes and textures of their products in the new form so that existing consumers receive an equally pleasurable and distinctive taste experience when they choose the ice cream form of the brand. Remington, with a solid reputation in shavers, has expanded its franchise to include women's shavers and nail polishers. It announces itself as a grooming or personal care company, clearly positioning itself for further focused brand equity expansion in the future, when more new products will emerge from beneath this umbrella brand identity.

THE BEST MIX FOR THE MONEY

Building brands and introducing new products will be a much different proposition in the 1990s than it has been to date. There is no road map, but we have been able to identify some signposts. From popcorn to shampoo to tires to diet food, one sees our key principles at work, demonstrating the power of creative consumer communication tools other than advertising. Sales promotion, PR, endorsement, distribution techniques, and other new tools have taken on many of the aspects of advertising. They have superior powers to create informed awareness and trial and repeat purchases.

Given the right picture of our target audience and its attitudes, habits, and practices—the kind of picture that the new, emerging market research tools are beginning to draw—we can classify the way in which the audience can be most effectively reached. Given an understanding of our product or service and its role in the target audience's lifestyle, we can classify the most likely ways of achieving awareness and trial. Combining the two, we can develop an introductory marketing plan that is truly tailored—not just to a target audience by demographics in a specialized media plan, but to target attitudes, situations, and susceptibilities—to optimal receptivity on the part of consumers.

We need to be realistic in assessing when it is better to allocate dollars single-mindedly to the most powerful weapon in our marketing armory. One can certainly test different combinations of spending, ranging from zero advertising dollars upward, and then measure which marketing mix works best. As a result, we can identify, over time, those new products and categories where promotion and other non-advertising devices should carry the entire introductory cost. These will be categories in which trial is an absolute must and doesn't follow automatically from advertising-induced awareness. An objective analysis will reveal several such categories in which introductory plans should be driven exclusively by non-advertising dollars. Selling such a bold plan may still require the fortitude of a pioneer in the face of strongly entrenched disbelief. But in many cases, advertising will be completely irrelevant to the decision-making process involved with new product introduction.

Hunter Hastings is chief executive of the Ryan Management Group, a division of the D.L. Ryan companies, a marketing services organization.

A Dance with the Devil

Hunter Hastings
Chief Executive
Ryan Management Group

Before being swept away by the green marketing tide, you better learn how much is based on consumer wants versus agitprop.

M arketing departments the world over have reacted enthusiastically to the apparent opportunity presented by the environmental or "green" movement. It appears on the surface to be one of those long-term trends that if properly interpreted can create the conditions favorable to significant changes in market share and competitive relationships in a number of industries. "Green" could become what "light" is to beer and what "fat free" is to mayonnaise.

Hence, we have witnessed the unveiling of "degradable" trash bags, the switch by McDonald's from polystyrene to (partially) recycled cardboard for its burger packaging, and the arrival of concentrated detergents and dolphin-safe tuna.

ENVIRONMENTAL AVALANCHE

Conventional thinking about environmental marketing sees it as both aggressive and defensive. The aggressive mode purports to build business by staking out a leading edge position at the forefront of a great consumer surge. The defensive mode holds that those brands and businesses that don't respond will be left behind and made redundant by those that do. Either way, this is an entirely passive view of the role of marketing: Find these occasional avalanches and either stand in front and be carried along or miss the moment and risk being engulfed.

To borrow another metaphor, environmental marketing is becoming what that disreputable duo Trout and Reis call, "A Horse to Ride." They advise us not to worry about strategy or the long-term consequences of immediate actions, but simply to find (largely by accident) something that "works" (i.e., increases short-term sales) and continue to do it until it stops working.

LONG-TERM MARKETING

This kind of advice is not only empty and pathetic, it is dangerous. It rejects any concept of strategy based on long-term goals and the influence of any framework of brand equity in favor of opportunism. CEOs must prepare to marshal their arguments against this insidious tide, since they can reasonably expect a torrent of "green" marketing proposals from their brand managers and directors.

Here are some thoughts from the other side of the debate:

• Consider the source of the green movement. It lies in politics, not consumer marketing. Environmentalists are fundamentally antibusiness. They accuse business of selfish and destructive practices that sacrifice the good of the planet to the depredations of untrammeled commercialism. Their response is to trammel it; they are rigid regulators and would like nothing better than to lay down a comprehensive set of laws to further their own agenda. The free market is furthest from their mind.

• The movement is poorly established, and it swirls and swells and changes in a maelstrom of half-formed ideas and temporary alliances. Often, it is internally contradictory; the goals of the rain forest preservers are not always compatible with those of the antipollutionists or the global energy optimizers. Often, this means that a company trying to respond to one of these groups merely succeeds in offending several others. It is impossible to plan a marketing effort based on politics du jour.

• Environmentalism is not scientifically well grounded even when it purports to be. (It's been pointed out that one group of environmental rabble rousers, the Center for Science in the Public Interest, is neither central nor scientific, and certainly not in the public interest!) Many of its tenets are whims, hunches, and ideological sound bites. As such, they are fragile and insubstantial.

It is worthwhile to contrast this with the health movement in food, beverage, and tobacco products. While there are still twists and turns and new discoveries and interpretations from time to time, there is an eminent and irrefutable body of science linking longevity and better health to revised habits of food, beverage, and tobacco consumption.

• The pace of technology can quickly make obsolete a lot of the major symbols of the environmentalist movement. Incineration technology can rapidly replace landfills (notwithstanding the irony that it is environmentalists who stand in the way of this progress). Advances in recycling will make it a cost-effective and broadscale process, and then free-market forces will ensure efficient collection procedures. It will be important for marketers not to paint themselves into a corner they can't escape from when a technology advance reverses the field.

• We must be sure we are listening to the consumer and the customer and not to self-styled and unelected spokespeople. Environmentalism as we hear it expressed most audibly is the creed of a highly vocal and very narrow minority amplified by supportive journalists. Marketing is the science of identifying customer/ consumer needs and meeting them, and the "needs" met by environmental marketing are seldom obvious, and often nonexistent.

There may be legitimate niche businesses available in return for meeting the agenda of the "greens" (the "cruelty-free" cosmetics of The Body Shop is one that comes to mind), but marketers who are responsible for sustaining bigger businesses must tie themselves to the mast of reason and consistency in the face of such siren calls.

GREEN REASONING

Having deconstructed environmentalism in this way, what should the CEO look for when seeking to sort the precious metal from the base. There are five tests of reason:

1. *Is there a genuine consumer benefit?* Theoretical advances in the management of the ecostructure will not persuade many consumers to spend their hard-earned dollars on your product rather than

an alternative that is superior in function, price value, or some other real benefit. Can you demonstrate a real need, either in legitimate research or in the marketplace? If not, don't approve the idea.

In some cases, the need may be emotional rather than functional, but it must be nonetheless real for all that. For example, kids who are influenced by the "Save the Planet" talk coming from their teachers, pop music icons, or Saturday morning cartoon characters may have a genuine need to follow their lead, and they may be able to do so by using a "green" product. The demand will transfer to parents who seek to satisfy these needs in their children. It is perfectly legitimate for marketers to respond.

For adults, however, different emotions or more rational needs may quickly take precedence. Then it is important to ask:

2. *Is there a hidden violation of any fundamental marketing principles?* Many food companies, responding hastily to the early but rapidly emerging trend toward "healthier" foods, stubbed their toe on the rock of good taste. While consumers said they would sacrifice taste for a healthier ingredient list, the fact is that they refused to do so in practice. Many of the early "healthier" foods were expensive failures because they didn't taste good. Others were rapidly eclipsed because scientific advances improved the taste of healthy formulations. Aspartame tastes good, saccharine doesn't, and therein lies the difference between original Tab and Diet Coke.

Green products and propositions must be rigorously examined to make sure they don't run foul of analogous marketing principles of simple functionality. If you're greener but you don't wash whiter, you won't get far.

3. *Is your approach holistic?* When McDonald's made the switch from polystyrene to cardboard clamshells for its burger packaging, one pressure group argued that the total energy usage and associated pollution output for the cardboard package was greater than that for the polystyrene package.

Whichever it is true, it illustrates the Scylla and Charybdis nature of the problem: Avoid one pressure group and you fall into the clutches of another.

It is crucial, therefore, to take a holistic approach that orchestrates counterpollution actions with original resource preservation actions and balances animal and plant concerns with human concerns. Where you recognize politics in the guise of consumerism, it would be wise to embrace more positions than the environmentalists can assault at once, including preservation of jobs and maintenance of international competitiveness. Marketing seeks needs to fill; politics seeks alliances.

4. *Is the proposition capable of evolving and growing?* A short-term success may quickly turn into a blind alley if technology or learning or evolving consumer needs change the rules of the game. It is unwise to make irrevocable commitments in the chimerical light of the environmentalists' green lamp. The best propositions in these circumstances are responsive but flexible. Using the McDonald's example previously mentioned, it could reasonably be argued that they can easily make a second-generation packaging change if appropriate, and that they haven't left themselves open to massively damaging assaults by pressure groups or the competition. Nimbleness will be an increasingly valuable corporate attribute in the shifting environmental stands.

5. *Does the proposed action fit with the long-term strategy of the business?* If your marketing department has a well-grounded idea of what your product or service stands for, it will be easy to decide whether or not a particular environmentally responsive marketing proposition will help or hinder. This is the basic idea behind brand equity: tactics come and go but brand equity can last forever. One of the best examples is Tide detergent from Procter and Gamble. It is and always will be "the washday miracle"—the product that employs the latest technology in the service of the cleaning needs of the consumer. This equity has enabled Tide to sail through the phosphates controversy (remember that?), the enzyme controversy, and to make a seemingly effortless transition from powder to liquid to concentrated powder.

Check to make sure you have a good idea of the lasting equities in your brand or business, and then ask whether or not making it greener makes sense in that context.

Environmentally responsive marketing may be good business under certain carefully examined circumstances. If taken lightly, however, it's a dance with the devil, and the consequences may turn out to be black rather than merely green.

Hunter Hastings is chief executive of the Westport, Connecticut-based Ryan Management Group, a division of the D. Ryan companies, a marketing services organization.

Lean, Mean, & Green

K. Grahame Walker
President and Chief Executive
Dexter

Staying competitive in the environmental era isn't simple, but there's no other choice.

I f Seth Dexter could defy the laws of life and death, I'd invite him to Windsor Locks, Connecticut, to visit the company bearing his family's name. On one hand, he would marvel at the size and applaud the industrial success that has blossomed from his entrepreneurial seeds. However, he also might wonder if it was going to scare away the fish.

For many manufacturing executives today—especially those in industries as highly exposed and regulated as the chemical and specialty materials business—Seth Dexter's qualified approval translates over the centuries into a dilemma: Can you be green and competitive? What are the economic, social, and personal tradeoffs?

Well, there aren't any. Manufacturers no longer have the luxury of the environmental naivete and innocence prevalent two centuries ago. Beyond the possible question of whether or not the striped bass and rainbow trout would be biting after the first cargo-laden steamboats churned up the river, little thought seems to have been given to the effects of growth and expansion. With all due respect to my predecessors who nurtured Seth Dexter's mill into a full-fledged papermaking operation, I suspect that new products and new markets were all that mattered.

TRIMMING YOUR WASTE

In the 1990s and beyond, the real question for U.S. manufacturers will be whether or not we can be competitive if we aren't green. An odd and costly proposition from one whose job description includes a primary obligation to shareholders? Not in the least. As in many aspects of business, through simple analysis we can demonstrate that industry must be green—truly green—to be competitive.

Let's first consider cost arguments against positive environmental behavior—whether it's merely compliance-oriented or if it's pro-active. Critics might select statistics that depict the enormous expenses associated with environmental legislation. Industry estimates, for example, conclude that the Clean Air Act passed on October 27, 1990, will cost American manufacturers $50 billion a year. That estimate, which at one point ranged as high as $100 billion, looks at real outlays such as the cost of equipment to control toxins or filter ozone pollutants. It does not even attempt to address societal costs such as unemployment compensation, education, and retraining for displaced workers (assuming new jobs exist), and the economic effects on communities that lose industries because the high cost of compliance drives them to close, be absorbed elsewhere, or even relocate offshore.

I myself have argued that the regulatory administrative burden alone is becoming excessive by pointing out that Dexter's environmental managers and regulatory staff receive more than 1,000 notices annually of new regulations or amendments to existing regulations—a notice approximately every two working hours. Many other costs exist, of course, that lend credence to the concept of tradeoffs. Updating and training in the ever-evolving field of environmental advice has a strong tendency to run up high tabs for consultants, attorneys, and eco-spin doctors. And one might be able to craft a convincing argument that regulatory overkill diverts capital from the development and funding of real solutions.

But massive numbers, real and imagined, cannot mask a specious argument. Just consider the costs of not acting in an environmentally responsible way. Not least, of course, are the

TABLE 2-3
Total Annualized Costs for All Pollution Control Activities

				2000	
	1972	1987	1990	Present	Full
In Billions of 1986 Dollars	26	85	100	148	160
In Billions of Estimated 1990 Dollars	30	98	115	171	185
As Percent of GNP	0.9	1.9	2.1	2.6	2.8

1. Annualized costs are defined as the sum of the operating costs for the year in question plus annualized capital costs, which include interest and depreciation associated with accumulated capital investment. In other words, annualized costs represent the real resource costs of tying up funds in the purchase and installation of antipollution equipment.

2. The present option assumes that present levels of implementation of existing programs remain the same as in 1987. The full implementation option assumes that the investments needed to bring about nationwide attainment of the national ambient air quality standard for ozone and the fishable/swimmable goals of the Clean Water Act for municipal systems are made by the year 2000.

Source: American Council for Capital Formation, EPA.

direct, easily quantified expenses of litigation and penalties that will come as regulatory authorities react in a blunt manner that undoubtedly will involve very serious amounts of money, and increasingly, criminal prosecutions. Any executive—no matter how isolated, insulated, or invisible he believes his company to be—must accept the fact that anything less than environmental responsibility will mean facing such expenses.

Many other immediate and long-range costs will be exacted as well. The toll will include the productivity of disillusioned employees whose pride is replaced by cynicism, and it will be weighted by defections of talented workers who envy companies that not only comply, but strive to remain a step ahead. The confidence and loyalty of customers, suppliers, and other business partners will erode as rapidly as do corporate images battered by the negative, relentless coverage heaped on environmental errants and villains alike by our media culture. The allegiance of shareholders will evaporate, especially as green strategies sway huge blocks of institutional investors.

See Table 2-3 to put a price tag on all that.

But we need to go further. Given that noncompliance is not a viable choice for a responsible company, we have to change the short-term and short-sighted "end-of-the-pipe" mentality that clogs the otherwise clear thinking of too many industrial executives—which in turn alters the understanding and behavior of the managers and technicians they lead. That mentality is short-term because of the tendency to limit cost and risk analyses to treating symptoms—for example, neutralizing effluent at the point of discharge. It is short-sighted because it does not provide a cure—for example, by addressing the creation of the undesirable effluent in the first place. Where is the wisdom in funding an environmentally unfriendly process whose eventual demise will be mandated by future regulations? Would it not be more responsible to shareholders to invest perhaps a greater sum to change and improve the product and manufacturing process to ensure purity before the "end of the pipe" is reached?

THE BOTTOM LINE IS GREEN

The environmental pressure that sometimes seems so staggering for industry, and particularly for manufacturers in the chemical business, should be viewed as a catalyst for becoming more competitive. Why? Because a pro-active approach to environmentally acceptable products and processes will ultimately reduce costs, increase gross margins, and positively position a manufacturer. The driving force behind such increases, of course, is the quest for new proprietary, patentable technology. Proprietary technology is the lifeblood of the specialty materials business and clearly gives manufacturers a sustainable competitive advantage in global markets. (Table 2–4 provides a global perspective.) Examples from my company clearly illustrate the point.

One of our largest markets is for coatings that protect beer and beverage cans and their contents from each other. Traditionally, the production of such coatings has relied on the use of volatile solvents. A competitor broke ahead of us in producing coatings that minimized solvent use. Finding ourselves in second place was embarrassing and frustrating because we had invested a great deal of time and energy to produce our own water-based and

TABLE 2-4
International Comparison of Pollution Control Expenditures (Percent of GDP)

Country	1975	1976	1977	1978	1979	1980	1981	1982	1983	1984	1985	1986
United States												
Nonhousehold	1.60	1.59	1.59	1.51	1.57	1.60	1.53	1.50	1.45	1.42	1.44	1.50
Incl. Households	1.87	1.85	1.86	1.77	1.81	1.83	1.74	1.70	1.67	1.66	1.67	1.74
Austria		1.09		1.16								
Finland						1.31	1.19	1.24	1.12	1.10	1.32	1.16
France												
Nonhousehold							0.87	0.86	0.85	0.84	0.85	0.89
Incl. Households											1.10	1.15
West Germany	1.37	1.36	1.29	1.33	1.37	1.45	1.45	1.45	1.41	1.37	1.52	
Netherlands						1.11		1.18			1.26	
Norway		1.66									0.82	
United Kingdom							1.57				1.25	

Note: Data reflect capital plus operating expenditures for pollution control as a percentage of gross domestic product (GDP). Comparable estimates of pollution control costs in other developed countries are available for certain Western European nations only as a result of data collected by the Organization for Economic Cooperation and Development (OECD). The OECD largely used a total nonhousehold expenditures measure of costs and the GDP measure of national income to make the estimates comparable between countries. In order to make the U.S. expenditure estimates presented in the EPA study comparable to these OECD estimates, U.S. nonhousehold expenditures must be shown.

Source: American Council for Capital Formation, EPA.

therefore more environmentally acceptable coating. Driven by the ignominy of running in our competitor's shadow, we developed what we believe to be a superior water-based coating, a belief supported by the subsequent steady gain in market share.

Another example that stands out occurred in our aerospace adhesive business. A customer facing environmental pressures wished to eliminate the use of solvents in primers used to prepare surfaces for the application of high-performance adhesives. Customers desired a water-based primer—and an adhesive bond with the same performance characteristics. With the incentive of satisfying customer needs, we were able to achieve these objectives. We also realized the enormous secondary benefit of reduced product-development cycle time, thanks to water-based resin technology being transferred from one division to another, even though it served an entirely different market, with consequent elimination of duplicate development costs.

GREEN GROWTH

In a larger sense we did much more than stay abreast with the marketplace or fill an order. We helped customers fulfill their own environmental responsibilities, and we made a real contribution toward the reduction of solvent use in our own business. These reductions not only benefit the environment, but allow our business to achieve compliance at a lower cost than by "end-of-pipe" treatment of solvent emissions. In addition, these successes have spurred more ambitious solvent-reduction objectives. One division, for example, has a goal of zero-solvent use in a specific time frame. Pro-active environmental programs and the competition they generate clearly have benefits to customers and the general public ranging far beyond the competitive advantages they provide for individual companies. Management, however, must take several immediate and direct steps to enlarge environmental goals:

• Make the environmental commitment, and make it loudly enough and clearly enough and frequently enough that every manager and employee hears it. Without genuine and continuing commitment from the top down, environmental pro-activity has little chance of flourishing and delivering real results.

• Develop a comprehensive policy statement. Don't be overwhelmed. Start simply with a statement of environmental principles, and then distribute them companywide.

• Work to contribute to regulatory common sense by cooperatively seeking balanced perspectives and reasonable solutions.

• Make a commitment to increase R&D expenditures. Set demanding goals and schedules.

• Eliminate expenditures for green promotion that is nothing more than window dressing. Forget gimmickry.

• Take a walk through your plants. Talk to employees. Take in-plant training. Become aware of how your employees are exposed to your commitment. Ask people how they feel about the environmental consciousness of the company.

• Hire a director of environmental affairs if you do not have one. My preference is for one with "lawyer" on the resume, because the considerable and rapidly growing amount of legislation, directives, and changes that regulate our activities are couched in fine print and terms that only a lawyer has the disposition to tolerate.

• Give your environmental affairs direct access—if not reporting responsibility—to you and your board. Ask him or her what the greatest concerns are.

DEFENDING THE HOME FRONT

Finally, realize that being green and competitive means accepting some conflicts, contradictions, and judgment calls. As I mull over my own motivations for committing the resources of a $900 million global company to environmental pro-activity, I invariably reflect on how my home gardening mirrors the complex strategies of industrialists who must balance ecology and the environment against productivity and progress. Whether in my backyard or the world at large, vital human interests must be weighed against their potential impact on the environment.

K. Grahame Walker is president and CEO of Dexter, a $1 billion specialty materials maker, and oldest continuously listed company on the New York Stock Exchange.

Communicating with the Corner Office

Peter J. Velardi
Chairman and Chief Executive
Vanity Fair

Memos, brochures, slide shows, and sales incentives are not enough. Here's what it takes to get through.

Marketing is in the midst of a fast and bumpy change. Evidence shows that despite the increase in time and money spent on advertising and marketing, the important corporate buying decision makers have become more remote and inaccessible than they have ever been. CEOs have come to realize that delivering their company's marketing messages to senior executive customers is one of the biggest challenges they'll face in the 1990s.

Numerous factors have contributed to this dramatic change in business: mergers, acquisitions, trade advertising, direct mail, and senior-level sales relationships, to name just a few.

In the past 10 years alone there have been more than 23,000 mergers and acquisitions. As a result, merchandising decisions have been consolidated, and are now made by a few high-ranking, well-protected executives. The Macy's buyout and the May Company's acquisitions are a few examples of consolidations that have greatly changed the industry. About 20 percent of a company's customers account for 80 percent of its business—and that's never been truer than today.

Trade advertising, effective in reaching buyers, has had only a minor impact on the person in the corner office who is busy with five-year plans, budgets, and meetings.

Direct mail is also ineffective because it has reached such volume today that it cancels itself out. It is reported that 9 million companies spent $3 billion sending mail to each other in 1988. Unfortunately, direct mail doesn't often make it past the CEO's gatekeeper.

Senior-level sales connections are not totally effective either. Young salespeople view those positions simply as a rung on the corporate ladder.

As a result of these factors, selling has lost much of its personal touch and many companies have lost their personality. It has been harder to communicate about the intangibles of a product or service —things like quality, dependability, and profitability—which are the most important concerns to the chief executive. Since most sales take place at the junior level, buying decisions are too often based on who offers the lowest price.

In the 1990s it will be important for CEOs to find new ways to recreate the relationships that may have diminished between career salespeople and senior management.

THE CEO's ROLE

An important priority for the 1990s is for the CEO to take a more active role in the marketing process. The CEO has the opportunity to reach out to important customers and establish a dialogue that will overcome the current failings of the marketing system.

The corner office of the CEO is a powerful one that can be leveraged to aid the company's marketing efforts.

At Vanity Fair, for example, we have salespeople who communicate with buyers, and regional managers who work with merchandising managers. I must communicate with the 250 or more key customer CEOs and prospects. They are my blue chip list.

Having a personal rapport with the customer's corner office is invaluable. If there's a problem, the CEO needs to know about it. If there's a particularly favorable situation that needs nurturing, the CEO should nurture it. The best way to do that is to establish an ongoing rapport with the customer CEO—use the impact of personal dialogue to build a mutually advantageous and lasting relationship with the target audience.

At Vanity Fair, we witnessed the importance of having good relationships. A major retailer we have done business with for several years suddenly stopped buying from us. We eventually learned that a minor problem had reverberated up the chain of command until it reached a senior executive. The executive gave the order to stop doing business with us. We had no way of understanding what happened because we had no access to this executive. It took us two years to reestablish contact with that retailer and get them back on our customer list.

Personal relationships are the single most valued part of selling. People tend to do business with people they want to do business with. This personal rapport can set you and your company up to be perceived as different—and it is a short stride from this perception to being perceived as better.

COMMUNICATING BY NETWORKING

How can a CEO find time to communicate with 250 senior-level executives? A technique is needed that allows CEOs to communicate who they are and what they stand for—one that makes an impact. It must be more than a four-color brochure; you can't create emotion with that. One way is through networking. In my own networking, I meet with 20 or 30 executives a year through various interactions. To reach more is not possible.

A CEO must use a technique that communicates the language of the corner office. Existing marketing communications programs do not treat different levels of executives any differently. Yet there is a different language spoken as you get onto the higher floors.

At lower levels of management the conversation usually gets into areas of price and logistics. The clothing buyer, for instance, wants to get the best possible price and delivery schedule. This neutralizes the leverage companies have in their selling efforts and facilitates the development of a perceived parity with lesser competition.

The higher the level of management drawn into the conversation, the more the intangibles such as a vendor's commitment, tradition, and quality come into play. A common error is to extend the selling language directed to the lower executive (both in content and in format) to the senior management level.

What should be happening at the senior management level is a form of communication that is formulated to intrigue and impress. What is needed is sophistication and a level of meaning and creativity that will attract and hold senior-level attention.

THE TACTILE SENSE

It was while I was struggling with this challenge at my own company that an interesting sales message made its way past my gatekeeper and landed in the middle of my desk. It intrigued me. It was witty, sophisticated, innovative, and got its message across to me in a dramatic, memorable way.

My secretary brought me a large, long box—the type used to deliver roses. Inside on a sheet of paper was written: "When you've got a lot on the line. . . ." Under that was a wooden apple with a real arrow through its center and written on another piece of paper was: "You've got to be right on target."

I read the sales message—something which I never do—that was the crux of the communication. It explained an exciting marketing philosophy that delivered with impact a tightly focused message to a select list of key decision makers. The entire package demonstrated to me how a blue chip list of people can be reached effectively.

Two weeks later another message arrived and was brought to me by my secretary with great interest. By now this Dimensional Marketing program, as it is called, had become an "event" in my office. My own secretary had been enlisted on the sender's behalf. I realized that this could be the answer to my own marketing communications problem. If this medium worked on me, got past my own gatekeeper and effectively spoke my language, why couldn't I adopt it to communicate to my peers?

The people who designed these marketing tools, The Blue Chip Marketing Group of Stamford, Connecticut, effectively communicated an employee benefits program from Travelers insurance. One of the concepts in the three-part program featured the headline "To add an extension to your employee relations program . . . give us a call . . . we're as close as the nearest phone" and was illustrated with an actual telephone.

The vice president of sales at Travelers explained that this marketing technique had established relationships with key top-level people. He credited the innovative marketing with opening many doors; so his salespeople could give presentations and subsequently book business from some Fortune 500 corporations.

This form of marketing, "Dimensional Marketing," as practiced by Travelers and many other companies, is based on the premise that the sense of touch—the tactile sense—is the greatest, most communicative sense in our bodies. This type of marketing is a form of communications that delivers a message in dimension.

DIMENSIONAL MARKETING

The Phoenix Mutual Life Insurance Company used dimensional marketing to reach pension fund managers. They wanted to convey an innovative, friendly feeling of service. "When it comes to service, we respond in a big way," was the headline for copy that was illustrated with an oversized, working service bell, one of three concepts they used. The program worked so well that the company got calls from prospective clients even before the sales force could contact them. Among the business brought in by the program was a $10 million pension fund landed in record time.

We investigated and discovered that a definite trend was developing with other companies using dimensional marketing. Other companies that have used the dimensional marketing technique to effectively reach small groups of top-level people are Champion, Mobil Oil, and Mattel. Some newspaper publishers wrote letters to Champion commenting on its dimensional marketing program for newsprint. Since when do top executives take the time to write compliments to you on your efforts to sell them?

This technique of dimensional marketing can be effectively used by the CEO in communicating with the corner offices of customers providing the bulk of their business.

Working with Blue Chip Marketing, we tested this marketing technique at Vanity Fair. First, we wanted to communicate what Vanity Fair is and what it stands for. This is a specific task of the CEO. We had a specific corporate culture we wanted to communicate; one of a responsive, progressive marketer. Some of our key customers perceived us as being a "sleepy, predictable" manufacturer. The challenge to us was to alter that inaccurate perception.

Then we had to case our message in the language of the corner office. I feel that the most important issue in communicating with top executives is the fact that they know I value their business and their opinion. My dialogue with them doesn't include the mechanics of selling—that's for other individuals within our respective organizations to cover. Since we needed to reinforce our perception as a responsive, progressive marketer, we selected three basic issues to communicate with our blue chip audience: quality, profitability, and service.

The headline, "Our stamp of quality. . . ." sets up a premise illustrated by a giant rubber desk stamp of the word "Quality." The copy points discuss Vanity Fair's long-term dedication to quality products, service, and customer support.

The headline, "Here's one way to have four big quarters in a row . . .," sets up a premise illustrated by four oversized coins. The copy talks about the value of Vanity Fair's introductions and price policies that went into effect in the four quarters of 1988.

Another headline, "When it comes to service . . . ," sets up a premise illustrated by an oversized address book. The copy discusses how Vanity Fair is the "big name" in service to the intimate apparel industry. On the "V" page is my name and phone number.

THE CORNER OFFICE RESPONDS

Before beginning a corner office dimensional marketing program, you should conduct a retail perception benchmark study across your prospective audience.

After our program was completed, we conducted another study with the same group of people. The results were exceptional. Our service was perceived to be at the highest level in the industry and our advertising and marketing support was perceived to have improved dramatically. Our overall image of being a marketer of fashionable products improved tremendously, and our image of being a responsive "industry communicator" increased substantially.

I've received many letters and phone calls from my blue chip audience in response to my program. That response has allowed me to reinforce my relationships, and in some cases, to begin a dialogue with key individuals that simply would not have happened otherwise.

Many of my current key customers interpreted the program as a personal "thanks for the business," and that proved very rewarding. Finally, a number of my salespeople and regional managers have indicated how the impact of this program has "trickled down" to their buying levels in a positive way.

Done properly, a corner office communications program has precisely the right effect on the audience of senior executives with whom the CEO must communicate. CEOs have important marketing assets they can leverage on their company's behalf. But the most important asset is their ability to speak the language of the corner office.

Peter J. Velardi is chairman and CEO of Vanity Fair, the Monroeville, Alabama-based manufacturer of ladies intimate apparel. Velardi joined the firm after graduation from high school at age 17. Beginning in the mail room, he then held positions in sales, marketing, and executive management before becoming president in 1983 and chairman and CEO in 1988.

No Strings Attached

Michael D. Rose
Chairman, President, and Chief Executive
The Promus Companies

Unconditional service guarantees make customers happy, but they play an equally important role in improving service sector productivity.

S everal years ago a European tourist was asked by an American friend what he thought of the service he had been receiving on his visit to the United States. The visitor slowly cast his eyes upward, stroked his beard, and recalled a line from a 19th-century London play.

"My friend," he punned, "service hasn't been practiced in America in years."

Many of us would agree. Who hasn't suffered at the hands of the airlines, been rudely treated by a waiter, or had to search in a department store for a salesperson to take our money?

These experiences are now so universal that both *Time* and *Business Week* have run cover stories depicting the quality of service in America. Clearly, during this decade, service providers must improve their offerings if they wish to remain competitive in increasingly mature markets. My own view is that an unconditional money-back guarantee of service satisfaction will be the tool by which this will be accomplished.

AIMING TO PLEASE

Early signs of a move toward unconditional service guarantees are already apparent. Ron Zemke, author of *The Service Edge*, for example, notes that service is generally improving today because service companies are finding the trend profitable. Zemke identifies 101 service companies that he believes are doing things right. Each of these companies maintains high levels of customer satisfaction, a healthy growth rate, and enviable profits—all because of superior service. Management aims to please and to profit.

Richard J. Schonberger, author of *Building a Chain of Customers*, claims that customer satisfaction goes far beyond the person who buys the product or service. Performance is no longer measured internally, he says, but instead is judged by what is good for the customer and the next customer too.

The emergence of the unconditional money-back guarantee in the service industry—"If you don't like the service you've been given, you get your money back. No ands, no ifs, no buts"—is a logical response to a changing market. There is a clear trend in the product arena to longer and more extensive warranties, in part as an attempt to emulate and compete with the superior quality records of foreign-made products. Some CEOs are accustomed to unconditional product guarantees, usually those in highly controllable product environments, but limited product warranties are still in the majority.

CUSTOMERS AS INSPECTORS

For many companies, the very thought of an unconditional guarantee of service satisfaction is frightening. Human service providers are less predictable than machines, and services are consumed as quickly as they are given. The reality, though, is that if you are doing your job well, the unconditional service guarantee becomes the ultimate point of differentiation in the service industry. You can set standards of excellence and train your people to meet them. Your customers become your quality inspection system. Thus, the unconditional service guarantee becomes the ultimate tool by which you can mold a service culture in your organization and measure your own success on a daily basis.

At Promus, spun off from the former Holiday Corporation when the Holiday Inns brand was sold to the U.K.'s Bass Group, our experience with unconditional service guarantees has been positive. The Hampton Inn hotels and Homewood Suites hotels stand fully behind an unconditional service guarantee. We plan to implement an unconditional guarantee soon within our Embassy Suites hotel brand and with the key guest service areas of Harrah's, our casino gaming business. In fact, our commitment to unconditional service guarantees led us to change our name to The Promus Companies. "Promus," derived from the Latin "to serve" and pronounced as "promise," defines our commitment to service.

A handful of other service companies have been living the guarantee concept for years. Nordstrom's is deservedly famous for its service as a department store; L.L. Bean for dependable, high-quality mail order goods; and Federal Express for getting it there "absolutely, positively overnight." Even Domino's Pizza promises that it will deliver its pizza to you in 30 minutes or less, or your money back.

Chris Hart, a professor at Harvard Business School, picked up on what he perceived as a small but developing trend toward unconditional service guarantees in the mid-1980s. His research on the issue later led to a seminal article on the role of unconditional service guarantees published in the *Harvard Business Review* in the summer of 1988. (See Box 2–1.)

Professor Hart's article on unconditional service guarantees came as an eye-opener. It was the practical hook on which we could hang a new corporate culture and create a pragmatic, customer-oriented point of differentiation. An unconditional service guarantee was the cornerstone we had been looking for in the process of service industry corporate reformation already under way.

REDEFINING ROOM SERVICE

We knew as a practical matter we could not implement an unconditional service guarantee within the Holiday Inns brands because of the diversity of both our product offering and the

---

Box 2–1

Smart Service

Although he shares Mike Rose's conviction that service guarantees will become more commonplace in U.S. business, professor Christopher W. L. Hart is worried that many companies will implement service guarantees only as "marketing gimmicks," thus creating widespread consumer confusion about what the concept really means.

"There are really two trends under way with respect to service guarantees," says Hart, who will soon be leaving academia to head the TQM Group, a Cambridge, Massachusetts, consulting firm, which he recently founded.

"On the one hand, there are a large number of service companies that are looking at a service guarantee strictly as a competitive tool; on the other, there are a more limited but highly enlightened group of service providers who believe they have an ethical responsibility to give customers what they pay for and are willing to put systems into place to ensure the customers are satisfied."

"There is nothing like increased variable costs to get management's attention and that attention is needed to convince employees that management is serious," notes Hart. He also points out, however, that the single greatest barrier to implementing an unconditional service guarantee is employee skepticism. "Every company has gone through a flavor of the month campaign so often that employees are genuinely skeptical of anything new."

---

operating skills of our franchisees. Our new hotel brands, however, looked promising for such innovation. As a consultant, Professor Hart helped us map out our strategy for implementing the guarantee in the Hampton Inn brand. Thus, we were able to add a new and continuing element to the process already under way to refocus ourselves as a service-based, customer-oriented company.

The process had been characterized by five chronological, yet almost simultaneous steps within our hotel brands:

First, we chose the hotel market segments in which we wanted to compete. Second, we established the criteria that would set our brands apart from each other and find a competitive edge. Third, we initiated efforts to build a service-oriented culture of pride and fun. Fourth, we developed new ways to hire, train, and retain employees and to ensure that future franchisees would share and commit to our approval toward customer service. Fifth, we established objective criteria to measure success both in satisfying our customers and in meeting our financial goals. Then we added a sixth step: the creation and implementation of the unconditional service guarantee in each of our hotel brands.

PRODUCTIVITY IS GUARANTEED

The unconditional service guarantee is the single most effective management tool. The mere presence of the guarantee forces a company to do several things better than it ever had to do them before. In interviews with more than 300 Hampton Inn employees—from general managers to housekeepers—the hotel chain's front-line workers expressed a high degree of comfort with the program and believed that it motivates them to work harder and do a better job. Bruce W. Wolff, Marriott vice president for distribution and marketing, says "unconditional service not only makes the customer happy, but gives employees a very clear focus." Our employees see the guarantee as tangible evidence that management believes Hampton Inn employees are the best in the market, and in turn, the employees believe their job is more important than ever before.

An unconditional service guarantee:

• Forces companies to be constantly aware of what customers really want and expect. This is much different from simply providing quality products in particular market segments. It is also more than occasionally doing customer research. It is taking every customer's temperature, every day. By knowing what your customer's wants are and meeting those wants, you create a unity of expectations between customer and employee.

• Forces companies to establish and to maintain clearly defined standards of excellence in customer service. Often it is useful to have these standards printed and distributed to employees, who can use them as the benchmarks to measure their performance. We have published a series of promises of excellence to customers, employees, franchisees, shareholders, and local communities. Publishing them does not make the promises real, but constantly reinforcing them does.

• Gives companies a clear standard to hire and train against. When employees learn that their performance is judged by the customer every minute of every day, the most responsible and service-oriented will be enthused about the opportunity. Plus an unconditional standard of excellence makes training more effective since employees understand that taking care of the customer is their number one job responsibility.

• Forces companies to respond to customer feedback. Only by listening closely and responding immediately can any service provider meet his customer's needs. And if the company fails, for whatever reason, the customer should not have to pay.

• Permits companies to focus their marketing efforts. Marketing can zero in on points that customers say are most important to them. The bottom line result is a product or service that elicits positive response from the customer and profits the shareholder.

Although few service companies today offer unconditional guarantees, I believe that the practice will become increasingly common. Unconditional service guarantees are the wave of the future. Those companies choosing to ignore them or refusing to implement them are doomed to surrender their competitive edge to those who stand fully behind the services they offer.

Michael D. Rose is chairman and CEO of The Promus Companies. Promus is the parent company of Harrah's Casino Hotels and Embassy Suites, Hampton Inn, and Homewood Suites hotels.

WORLD-CLASS MANUFACTURING

A CEO's Odyssey Toward World-Class Manufacturing

Earning the National Quality Award took people, time, and money just when Xerox had little to spare. But taking on that challenge can pay off when one is forced to make the hard calls needed to compete. CEOs just embarking on this journey can learn from David Kearns' own voyage of discovery.

Japanese competition ate up Xerox's share of its bread-and-butter U.S. plain-paper copier market, which hit an all-time low of 8.5 percent back in 1985. But by 1989, Xerox had pushed its market share back up to more than 15 percent. The credit for that amazing competitive feat goes to a commitment to quality that captured every aspect of the extraordinary business reorganization driven by Xerox Chairman David T. Kearns, succeeded as CEO by President Paul Allaire on August 1, 1990.

Kearns saved Xerox by forcing the copier cyclops to look ahead for a way out of the Japanese clone attack. The numbers prove he was right. Revenues rose to $17.6 billion in 1989, sending net income up 82 percent to $704 million and earnings up 88 percent to $6.56 a share. The key point is that Xerox made money by doing it right. Customer satisfaction was up 38 percent in the past four years. A total quality process was used as a weapon in the fiercely competitive global business machine market.

That's how Xerox won the coveted Malcolm Baldrige National Quality Award (NQA), created by Congress in 1987 to recognize that quality products are the best weapons in the trade war. "If you can stand the pain, look at your company through the eyes of your customers," challenges a full-page Xerox advertisement in

The Wall Street Journal, celebrating the company's victory. To win the manufacturing Holy Grail, Xerox had to achieve a gold medal finish in seven key areas: leadership, information, planning, human resources, quality control, quality results, and customer satisfaction.

The last three make customers the ultimate judges. Their votes were earned by a process known as competitive benchmarking, in which every aspect of business at Xerox, from the production floor to the billing department, was rated against the best competitor in any industry. In the billing sector, for example, Xerox's world-class benchmark company is American Express. The two companies are fundamentally different. But benchmarking showed Xerox how to improve its billing process by 35 percent in the past several years.

After a history of missteps, the NQA flag is flying at Xerox world headquarters in Stamford, Connecticut. In copiers, printers, and document processors the company has been performing exceptionally well. But Xerox is really two companies split on a roughly two-to-one basis. The $5 billion financial services sector of the firm has been a disaster whose dismal results have actually masked manufacturing success. Kearns promoted the company's move into financial services in the early 1980s as a cure for a sick copier market, and the sector once seemed destined for an equal role. Prudential-Bache Securities analyst B. Alex Henderson explained, "They got into that business when their backs were against the wall." But the wall has arisen in another part of the playing field.

A Chief Executive of the Year finalist, Kearns is well regarded by his peers, but Xerox's recent reverses cost him the top accolade. Incoming CEO Allaire, a 24-year Xerox veteran, made his name at Rank Xerox in the United Kingdom, and is associated with the brighter business products sector of the firm. But he is no less committed to the quality process, and benchmarking may lead Xerox out of financial services altogether. "There aren't any sacred cows," Allaire told *The Wall Street Journal.*

You have spoken widely about the changes you put Xerox through. What do you have to change before you begin to change a company?
What really got me to change was that we really needed a complete new process. In the early 1980s we had a huge way to go. Productivity was improving by 7 or 8 percent a year, but we needed

gains of 17 percent to catch up. The people we were running after were improving at very high rates. So I really started to look for something else, some process that I now call the quality process. It's a way of giving people the tools they need to compete—that's what the quality process is.

I read *Quality Is Free*, Phil Crosby's book, and was taken with it. We had Crosby come and talk to our managers. I found it invigorating because his thought process wasn't complicated, but I decided that what he wanted was very hard to do. We had a famous meeting around here which is now called the Wet Noodle Meeting. I told our senior managers that when it came to change, I felt like I was pushing a wet noodle. We really weren't making any progress. And they came back and said, well, we're doing this and that and you don't really understand.

But we were forced to change. We knew that we had to change, that we were going to go out of business if we didn't. That was the driving force. I was half right and they were half right, and then we decided, as a team, that we should really go after not a program but a process—and we use that word over and over again—a business process for the 1980s, incorporating the principle on which we were going to run the business. And we started top-down training on the basis that everybody had to change their behavior. It was very controversial. Somebody said to me, why didn't you just tell your people what you wanted, and I said, we tried that and it didn't work. The quality process is different because it gives people the actual tools—training is absolutely critical.

> **What was the most important thing you got out of it? You've said that it's important not just to benchmark your products, but to benchmark every aspect of the organization. What does that really mean?**

A benchmark is a standard—when we benchmark our company we compare it against what other companies are doing. People have been breaking down their competitors' products for years. There's really nothing new about that. An awful lot of people, when they focus on quality, tend to focus on manufacturing only. That's a big mistake. But a more sophisticated understanding—and this is a part of our competitive benchmarking process—seeks to know not just where your competitor is today, but exactly what trajectory your competitor is on. It's not just the hard measure of where someone else is, it's how are they doing it. It's not just understanding unit manufacturing cost, but how the competition engineered the product to lower manufacturing cost. It's peeling the onion to its minute layers. Part of our planning process now is that every functional group has to find the best two or three competitors worldwide in what they're doing.

The key thing was that we determined we would change our behavior, how we operate the business. We've looked at different companies—Florida Power and Light has a quality process that we used as a key benchmark. They've been marvelous about sharing information with us. I went down there, and one of the things that really impressed me about Florida Power and Light was that there wasn't a specific quality section. The quality is just embedded in everything they do. It's just there in all the company's objectives. That experience raised our sights.

You place a great deal of emphasis on training. Just how much does that cost?

We aren't the highest spender on training on a per person basis— I think IBM is higher—but we are higher than most. We spend more than $300 million a year on training. That's a little more than 2.5 percent of our revenue. It means we invest about $2,500 in training per employee per year.

What we really did differently was to start from the top down. Everyone upstairs went to school and then they taught the next level down. Having to teach something is how you test yourself. The whole experience took place in what we call a family group in the actual workplace. That allowed people to work on projects that were real, not hypothetical.

Working on real projects as part of training in not unique. But in the family group people worked on problems that were significant. We substituted quality training for general management training. What we were really doing was embedding the quality process. And we're not all the way through yet, but we really are quite far along now.

That's the system von Steuben used to train George Washington's army. He would train a brighter group and make them corporals and they would train the next group.

I don't know if we train the brighter guys, but we do train the top people first [laughter]. We were really trying to indicate to people that the quality process wasn't going to fade away. Training has been an important part of the company for a long time. We did it differently this time and utilized some of our strengths in the training area to help us.

When you train for a commitment to quality, what stands out as the most important benchmark of all?
Customer satisfaction is number one. We asked ourselves what does quality mean? When we honed in on that we found that it meant meeting customer requirements. And if you're going to meet customer requirements, you have to know what they are, and they change constantly.

Do you continue to take calls from customers? It's been said that you'll interrupt a meeting when a customer calls you.
We divide it up here—each person gets a day a month. On that day you're allowed to interrupt anything. I also get things in the mail all the time. One that really struck me was a very constructive letter. This wasn't an "I want my money back" note. The customer had bought one of our copiers and returned it because he couldn't get it to work. He just indicated a few things he wanted me to know about. So I got an identical machine, brought it in here, and we did our own little test on the thing. Sure enough, he was right, in the opinion of the ladies here in the office, that the instructions weren't clear and there was no service number given. And then we experienced the same mechanical problem he had. We looked into where that particular machine came from, and we learned that it hadn't been purchased through our system. I called the customer and learned a little more from the conversation. That was an interchange with a customer that resulted in our doing things differently.

Now recently I installed one of our facsimile machines in my own house. I called the 800 service number to see if I'd get an answer—this was on a weekend. I did, and I later wrote a note about it back at the office. What bothered me was that we did it with one product and with another product we didn't. What I really learned was that we didn't have any cross-flow in this area of the organization between one product group and another.

After this mishap were you angry with your own organization?

I'm not a particularly patient person, and people can get angry. But we are trying not to do that. We are trying hard not to hit people in the head with a four by four. Instead, we're going back and inspecting the process. Part of the quality process is learning to inspect the process, not the final outcome. That's not just true at the end of the manufacturing line—it's true in the way we manage the business totally. What we learned this time was that we didn't have a very good process for moving information from one product group to another. In this particular case the process didn't work.

If a customer complains and all you do is shout and scream and say you shouldn't have done that, you don't really get very far. It's going back and understanding what went wrong that matters. Some amount of fear helps, but fear has got to be used appropriately. If you use it too much it won't work, but people have to be concerned about the consequences of unhappy customers. And we're trying to get much better about what it is in the process that caused this to happen. We think 100 percent customer satisfaction is now "doable," and that's our target.

As a result of the ever-increasing expectation levels of our customers, we may be setting some goals that are higher and higher and that we'll have to grapple with. Our competitors are getting better and better all the time. I think doing things like this to energize the company is a good idea. Going for the Baldrige Award again might be a good idea.

Did you ever total up the cost to Xerox of pursuing the Baldrige Award?

If all you were going for was just to win the award you wouldn't do it. We put about 17 people on it for a year during a time when huge cost pressures were on us. We put a senior management team above that group because I really did want to win the award. But why go after the award? To rate yourself on a worldwide basis against the very best, and then use that information to build the future. There isn't any question in my mind that it's a highly worthwhile experience.

Two years ago we started to share our experiences with the quality process with our best customers. We found this to be a marvelous marketing tool. We do not talk Xerox products. But we have developed relationships on a much broader scale with many of our customers as a result of the quality process. Now winning the Baldrige Award has strengthened that some, and we've broadened our sharing of information as part of our new responsibility. I would urge everybody—service companies and manufacturing companies—to go after the award, and I wouldn't worry about winning it.

Does the NQA equal Japan's Deming prize for quality?

Yotaro "Tony" Kobayashi runs Fuji Xerox and they won the Deming prize in the early 1980s and said it was an absolutely worthwhile experience. They used it as a symbol indicating the company's sense of purpose and drive. We learned a tremendous amount from Fuji Xerox.

What about the Japanese as competitors?

We compete with the Japanese in a whole set of products, from low-end copiers through mid-range copiers, where from a quality and reliability standpoint we stack up very well. From a cost standpoint, and this varies by product, we are quite close competitors at about 130 yen to the U.S. dollar. At 160 yen to the dollar it gets kind of dicey, but the point is that we've come close.

We compete very effectively inside Japan because we have a joint venture, Fuji Xerox, that works very well. The point is that competition with the Japanese is a cost issue. We have to keep coming down where cost is concerned. We've brought unit manufacturing cost down about 45 percent. Our target for the next four years is to take that down another 50 percent. That's the kind of objective we think is necessary. Remember in the early 1980s the Japanese were selling products in this country for what it cost us to make them.

How close are you to manufacturing in the United States a low-end copier that would compete directly with Japanese machines? Can you beat them at the same game they tried on you?

In the mid-range we're there. In the low end, we do it through a combination of Fuji Xerox and Xerox. We have really utilized our joint venture in Japan. Basically, we can compete very effectively.

You've changed Xerox, but is it where it ought to be to compete and win in the 1990s?

We have two parts of our company. Financial services is having difficulty currently. But even if you ask about business products and systems, the answer is no. We've come a long way and we're on the right trajectory. But we have to use the quality process to help us achieve intensified goals.

Back to Basics for U.S. Manufacturing

Edward L. Hennessy, Jr.
Former Chairman and Chief Executive
Allied-Signal

Numbers-driven executives of the 1980s are now counting their losses for the 1990s.

W e CEOs don't have all the answers. For instance, how can we explain our collective failure to properly manage this nation's once-mighty manufacturing sector? Our failure has left the door wide open for the Japanese and other foreign producers to shoulder U.S. companies aside in a growing number of core industries, including consumer electronics, machine tools, and semiconductors.

What happened? Simply put, the success of America's manufacturing establishment during and after World War II went to our heads. We had produced everything from Liberty Ships to light bulbs with unchallenged superiority. Our domination of world markets in the 1950s and 1960s led to complacency, arrogance, and sloppiness. No one could tell us anything about manufacturing because we had done it all—and were sure we knew how to keep doing it.

About this time, a new breed of executive began taking over the reins at many companies. Its members were tightly focused on finance, marketing, legal, and administrative concerns. Younger managers, myself included, chose these new-fashioned executives as our role models.

Unfortunately, these numbers-driven leaders often showed little interest, or appreciation, for what was occurring in the manufacturing end of the business. Consequently, they failed to properly manage their investment in worker skills, plants, and equipment. And so, in recent years, the U.S. manufacturing base has weakened, gravely threatening our economic stability and future standard of living.

There have been other sobering signs for U.S. industry. For one thing, this nation's manufacturing productivity lagged far behind the average annual increase of our 11 major industrial competitors between 1960 and 1985. In terms of technology, foreign inventors captured nearly 47 percent of U.S. patents in 1988, up from 35 percent in 1975. But perhaps the most dramatic evidence of our manufacturing erosion over the years is the string of record trade deficits. In the last eight years, they have totaled $900 billion, and in 1988 alone, our imports outpaced exports by $120 billion. And while that did represent a 21 percent improvement over 1987, the drop in the value of the dollar drove this improvement, and most economic analysts expect the trade gap to continue to widen this year.

Some say we shouldn't be concerned. They argue that the United States has become a postindustrial economy in which service jobs are all that really matter. For example, in a recent memorandum to his students on career planning, a prominent Harvard professor and economic policy analyst advised that manufacturing jobs are fast disappearing, leaving only two broad categories of work: complex services and person-to-person services. I strongly disagree. This country has not become—and it cannot afford to become—a predominantly service-oriented economy. Instead, we should be working toward the regeneration of a manufacturing sector that will enable us to compete aggressively anywhere in the world.

The Japanese have rushed to fill the void left by the U.S. manufacturing decline. Unlike the Americans, they knew precisely where their money could do the most good—and that was in manufacturing improvements. Even today, Japanese manufacturers spend the equivalent of $2 of their research and development budgets on process innovations for every dollar spent by

U.S. manufacturers. Japanese products also reflect what that country's culture has long revered—economy of design and ease of operation.

It's now time for America to seize the manufacturing high ground once again. Some have suggested that we do this by thinking and acting more like the Japanese. According to this view, Japan's true genius lies in its culture—its ironclad sense of discipline and purpose that enables the country to organize its people for the common good. To compete, they maintain, it is necessary for our culture to become more like the Japanese.

Nonsense. The only way this country can regain its global preeminence is by summoning up the qualities that are natural to us, the qualities that made us great in the first place. Those included individualism, inventiveness, openness, and a tolerance for social change.

America's real strength *is* its culture. We produced a nation of free-thinking individuals, then unleashed the forces of creativity and enterprise on the road to building the mightiest manufacturing machine in the world. It's no accident that the Japanese learned many of their manufacturing techniques from Americans.

But then something happened. Somewhere along the way, we stopped challenging ourselves. We stopped asking the hard questions and demanding thorough answers. This created a vacuum, which the Japanese and other foreign competitors were only too eager to fill.

What we must now change, if we are to restore this country to greatness, is not our culture, but our technique. We must retool our thinking as it relates to quality, design, productivity, participative management, and more. For example, we must never think of product quality as a manufacturing problem—but as the solution to the problem. By managing for quality, we build low cost and high productivity into the manufacturing process. In addition, we must stop thinking in terms of the most sophisticated product or process design, and start thinking in terms of simplified style and ease of assembly. For too many years we've looked to technology to fix what ails us. But today, you don't have to look very far to find companies that have overautomated, creating a whole new set of problems for their owners.

RETHINKING MANUFACTURING

In short, what this country really needs is a new set of principles that challenges the ways we've been conditioned to think about manufacturing for the past 40 years.

We must become better manufacturers, more innovative managers, and, above all, smarter competitors. Too often, these needs are obscured by finger pointing at other countries, or public rantings about the size of the trade deficit. Instead, we should be working hard to erase that gap by making affordable products that the world needs and is willing to buy.

Too often, the United States has failed to turn its scientific excellence into marketplace winners. We must learn once again how to translate great ideas into high-quality products, fast and inexpensively. One way many American companies are facing up to the problem is by forming teams of marketing, manufacturing, and research and development people at the earliest stages of new product development. This collaboration enables them to get products off the drawing board, into production, and out to the marketplace much faster than traditional linear systems.

Hewlett-Packard, for example, sent its people around the world looking for better ways to run its business. It then embarked on a number of new directions, including a total quality management approach in every one of its departments, from shop floor to the engineering and administrative offices. Motorola also launched a commonsense program of improvements—and won the first annual Malcolm Baldrige National Quality Award in the process. Today, Motorola designs products that are easier to manufacture by bringing together design and production engineers from day one. Motorola also teaches employees to inspect their own work and to maintain their own machines.

Within Allied-Signal's $4 billion automotive products group, we've undertaken sweeping changes in the way we manage processes and people. Teamwork is now rampant; functions that used to be separate are now tied together. Our brake plant in Sumter, South Carolina, for example, has adopted the well-known just-in-time approach to control inventories; we now schedule all plant activities based on what our final assembly lines need for that day's production. We've opened up communication lines between upper management and first-line supervisors, and we gave factory workers much greater responsibility for the quality of the products they make.

When it comes to manufacturing rebirths, however, few firms have been a bigger inspiration to us all than Ford Motor Company. Ford, along with the other U.S. automakers, was shaken to its very foundation in the early 1980s by the foreign import explosion. Ford responded with a no-holds-barred drive to improve quality. Among its principal tools were statistical quality control, a technique for spotting defects as cars or trucks were made, rather than in after-the-fact inspections. Ford also gave its workers a much greater voice in decision making, especially as it related to operations, processes, and machines that they used every day.

On the road to enhanced quality, Ford learned another vital lesson: that simpler is better. For example, it redesigned an instrument console for the 1987 Escort with only six parts, compared with 22 in the 1984 model. The results were dramatically reduced material and labor costs—and vastly improved quality. Design simplicity is a lesson that Allied-Signal has also taken to heart. Last year we were selected to supply engines for the new LHX Army helicopter program. Our jet engine design includes 80 major parts that can be replaced or maintained in the field using only six basic hand tools.

MAKING CHANGES

The impetus for such fundamental changes within our nation's factories must come from the top executive ranks. Recently, a Nobel laureate in economics suggested that the catalyst for change in American industry would be U.S. managers' "sheer terror" when faced with aggressive foreign competitors. I have more faith in the strength of our system—and in the resolve of our business leaders. More and more, American executives are looking for new and better ways to manage and manufacture. And American workers are responding creatively and enthusiastically. To be competitive in the 1990s and beyond, American executives must also embrace the long-term versus the short-term view. That is, we must respond to the need for long-term investment in research and development and for risk-taking strategies that position our companies in new markets and technologies—and not be overwhelmed by the cry from the financial community for more short-term profits and dividends. None of us can rest for a second. We must steadfastly work toward an environment where change is recognized and where risk is suitably rewarded; where teamwork across all factory operations is actively encouraged; where continuous improvement is the way of manufacturing life.

We must, in sum, get back to the basics that once made this country the manufacturing marvel of the world.

Edward L. Hennessy, Jr., is former chairman and CEO of Allied-Signal, a $1.7 billion manufacturing company with businesses in aerospace, automotive, and engineered materials.

High-Velocity Manufacturing

William A. Sandras, Jr.
President
Productivity Centers International

Global competition is both fast paced and high quality. Catching up means greater production velocity with superior quality control.

S tandards of performance that were once acceptable are just not competitive today. Quality, for example, is expected— even taken for granted—but quality is only one element necessary for success in an increasingly competitive global marketplace. The new competitive edge lies in responsiveness and the ability to achieve high-velocity performance. Just-in-time (JIT) and total quality control (TQC) are the processes—or the tools—that can make high-velocity performance a reality.

An excellent way to understand the capabilities of JIT/TQC is to picture a pipeline running through the factory or operation. At one end we pay our suppliers for material entering the pipeline. At the other end our customers pay us for the products we ship. Our goal is to reduce the time between payment on one end and receipt on the other. Therefore, we need to move material through the pipeline more quickly. A fat pipeline will allow us to make shipments, but sluggishly. With a narrower pipeline, we can make the same rate of shipments if we accelerate the velocity of the flow through the pipeline. A faster throughput time will also allow us to be more responsive to changes in the marketplace.

The Ford Motor Company knew about the effectiveness of high velocity through a manufacturing pipeline as far back as 1926, when its River Rouge factory was able to go from raw ore to a car engine to cash in 41 hours. Years later, Taiichi Ohno, at Toyota in Japan, built on Ford's philosophy and processes and developed the Toyota Production System. Today's version of the Ford and Toyota systems is called Just-in-Time/Total Quality Control.

We must realize, however, that in reducing the diameter of the pipeline and increasing velocities, we invariably uncover constraints that can have a negative effect on quality, cost, or delivery and, subsequently, our competitive standing. JIT exposes these constraints in a priority order and then forces us to act upon them. Its purpose is to improve a company's ability to respond economically to change. The desired action is to form a team of people that can focus on the prioritized problem, determine the root cause, and implement and monitor countermeasures. This process requires the effective problem-solving skills found in the TQC process. In other words, JIT exposes the problem and stimulates action; TQC is used to solve the problem. JIT and TQC are two sides of the same coin.

After a method is discovered and implemented to deal with the first constraint, we can continue until we encounter the next constraint. These constraints fall under the definition of waste. In a JIT/TQC environment, waste is defined as an activity that does not add value for the customer. Waste can be part of excess inventory, setup times, inspection, material movement, transactions, or rejects. Essentially, any resource that is not actively involved in a process that adds value is a waste.

When viewed through JIT glasses, waste is rampant. One factory in South Carolina determined that to produce its product it was moving materials a total of 3.7 miles. A semiconductor manufacturer discovered a costly series of processes that added no value: the work of one person was checked by a production inspector, then by a quality control inspector, and finally, by a government inspector. A Japanese visitor, touring a California factory, saw inventory sitting in a locked stockroom on his left, and "work in process" inventory sitting on the production floor on his right. Puzzled, he asked, "What is the difference between the inventory stored on my left and that stored on my right?" The answer to his question would be "Not much." Although the two were called different names, they were both just sitting there and velocity was approaching zero on both sides.

JIT/TQC should not be mistaken for a waste reduction program. Its purpose is to raise the question of how traditional approaches can be changed to eliminate the need for non–value-adding activity. JIT/TQC is a process designed to prioritize a never-ending list of factors that lead to the achievement of higher velocities. It is a process structured to make opportunities visible, to stimulate people to action, to give feedback on progress, and to develop people into effective problem solvers.

The development of people is, in fact, the key to JIT/TQC. No machine exists today that can visualize opportunities for improvement, determine the actions to take, implement the ideas, and then verify the results. Unfortunately, most people have not been well-trained in observing or problem solving. But with JIT/TQC, problems translate into opportunities. The "thinking worker" becomes essential.

Inefficient use of people is one of the greatest examples of waste. We tend to hire hands—and then fail to use the heads that go with them. JIT/TQC stresses the importance of everyone involved in the process, from top-ranking executives to the workers on the floor. Each is viewed as a potential problem solver. Communication lines open as all levels of a company are forced to join together to develop solutions.

The pervasive team spirit that should exist within a company, if solutions are to be developed effectively, must be fostered by creating an environment that is conducive to change. This responsibility lies with the upper echelons of the organization. If top management can show that it is willing to dedicate time to the implementation of JIT/TQC, the message will travel down to the other levels of the company.

Beckman Instruments, a medical instruments maker, was successful in demonstrating commitment when the company first began discussions on implementing JIT/TQC. A meeting, which included a continuous chain of workers from top to bottom, was arranged at a local hotel. The president, upper management, supervisors, and personnel from the proposed pilot area were all in attendance. It was the first time so many elements of the organization had come together. The dedication that was obvious from the start was bolstered as the company went on to eliminate the problems that were threatening its competitive position.

ONE LESS AT A TIME

JIT/TQC is not simply a continuous improvement philosophy with a respect for people. There is a simple, yet highly effective process that makes the philosophy practical. The process of JIT/TQC is what sets it apart from other "efficiency projects" of the past. To meet the goal of zero waste, we must learn how to manufacture (or service) economically "one less at a time."

The first question to ask is if there is any non–value-adding activity occurring in the pipeline. If the answer is yes, we must then determine if the process is still economical. If it is, one unit (whether it be of an order quantity, lot size, distance of travel) is removed and the steps are repeated. This continues until a constraint appears that no longer makes the process economical. We are then forced to change the process before we can continue to manufacture.

Unfortunately, we have been programmed over the years with cliches. "If it ain't broke, don't fix it." "Don't rock the boat." We ask ourselves why we should change an operation if in essence it is economical. Such attitudes are programs for failure in today's competitive society. They reflect an unwillingness to change that could prove disastrous. Even efficient, and economic operations have room for improvement. Removing one unit from the pipeline will automatically increase velocity. If there are 500 units in the pipeline, removing one will accelerate the flow by 1/500.

THE KANBAN TECHNIQUE

Kanban (rhymes with bonbon) is the technique that makes the "one less at a time" process practical. It is JIT's control mechanism. Loosely translated from the Japanese, kanban means "card" or "visual record," but in fact, it has no adequate English translation. A kanban limits the amount of inventory in the pipeline by serving as an authorization to produce or move inventory.

Kanbans and empty milk bottles have similar functions. Back when we had home milk deliveries, an empty milk bottle on the front porch authorized the driver to deliver another full bottle. The number of bottles limited the amount of milk inventory at a customer's home. If there was no consumption, no replenishment occurred. A kanban works the same way, as a signal to replace what has been used.

Kanbans can come in many forms, from squares taped to the floor to actual cards or returnable containers. They provide the visual control that is essential to the "one less at a time" process. The current sum of kanbans represents the level at which the factory is known to run effectively. Only when we have a clear ceiling established by the sum of the kanbans are we able to take one away and identify the constraint that surfaces.

There are two difficulties with the kanban technique. The first is our own experience. We have been conditioned to believe that if it isn't more "sophisticated," it isn't better. Kanban represents a giant step toward simplicity. The second problem is the fact that the "one less at a time" process using kanban is very effective in making us aware of constraints. Unfortunately, that makes us uncomfortable, but that is precisely the purpose of JIT/TQC. It wants us to be acutely aware of each constraint that we uncover. If we experience discomfort, we are apt to do something about it. JIT/TQC forces us to ask questions. As the manufacturing process itself is simplified, we soon become aware that constraints to higher velocity may also lie elsewhere in the company—with the suppliers or even with the customers. JIT/TQC can drive the changes in these areas that will further accelerate the flow through the pipeline.

A FULL SPECTRUM OF APPLICATIONS

As other earlier constraints are eliminated, product design frequently emerges as an opportunity. JIT leads us directly into design for manufacturing (DFM).

In the 1980s Hewlett-Packard consolidated low-cost terminal production in Roseville, California. The new managers found themselves in danger of losing a $200 million business. Customers praised the quality of the terminals but were not enthusiastic about their high price. Fortunately, the new management team had previous experience with JIT/TQC. First, they simplified the factory processes as much as they practically could. It then became apparent that the current product was not designed to be cost-competitive. They formed a new product design team, made easier because JIT/TQC efforts had developed their people and promoted teamwork. They surveyed customers and performed value analysis. In a few short years they had simplified existing processes and then leveraged that knowledge by introducing a new terminal design. The result was the lowest cost computer terminal manufactured anywhere in the world.

Similarly, JIT/TQC also provides a fertile environment for automation. Money spent on automation prior to JIT/TQC implementation tends to go to non–value-adding activities. Companies that decide to automate after introducing JIT/TQC have eliminated many wasteful activities and are better equipped to determine where automation would be most valuable.

Computer-integrated manufacturing (CIM) follows the same path as DFM and automation. CIM deals with traditional information processes. After JIT/TQC is in effect for a short time, the manufacturing process tends to become faster than other processes such as replanning and order entry. JIT/TQC can then make it apparent where information system improvements and integration are needed.

JIT/TQC also has significant impact on cost accounting. Traditional costing is designed to value inventory, but it is ineffective at helping us manage processes. JIT/TQC practitioners have been leading others in the implementation of activity-based costing (ABC), which focuses on costing the processes as well as the material.

A U.S. manufacturer of circuit boards is one of the country's most advanced facilities in JIT, TQC, and ABC. Through the use of JIT/TQC, maximum lot sizes have dropped by a factor of 10. Now that production output is becoming more linear, the company recognizes the inefficiencies large onetime orders can cause. As a result, discounts will soon be offered on small orders. The company would rather have a long-term customer-supplier relationship with frequent small orders than the adversarial customer-supplier relationship with large quantity discounts. This proves to be economical for all parties.

As velocities accelerate within the company, JIT/TQC expands our vision to the supply and distribution pipeline. Suppliers should be seeking to accelerate their flow as well. The supplier's objective should be to crush lead time. As transportation constraints are also resolved, deliveries will become more frequent. More frequent deliveries will then lead to changes in the accounts payable and accounts receivable departments.

JIT/TQC will also drive significant changes in human resources. The flexibility of people, not only equipment, is important. Increased flexibility translates into fewer labor grades, which in turn affect compensation. Asking people to help you become more productive carries with it the moral, ethical, and practical obligation to sincerely try to maintain their employment. This means policy changes and a real commitment to training and retraining. It implies obligation on both the part of the company and that of the employee. Just as the company must keep itself competitive, so must the employee. Thus, the company must dedicate itself to educating the employees and the employees must dedicate themselves to learning.

OVERCOMING OBSTACLES PAYS OFF

JIT/TQC has been proved to be practical. However, implementation is not easy and cannot be done casually. It requires a vision, a competitive attitude, and an environment conducive to change. These elements for success must be established at the upper ranks of a company if they are to spread throughout the company. The biggest obstacle to JIT/TQC success is mental rather than physical. The cost of converting a facility to JIT/TQC is conspicuously low. The only expense in getting started is for education and consulting.

Impressive results are evident in a wide range of industries. Beckman Instruments cut throughput times from 60 days to 6 and then to 2. Hallmark Cards took production of telecommunications equipment from 20 days to 2. Both of these companies were willing to take a chance and accept change. As a result, they all saw at least a tenfold improvement, the kind of improvement that any company that is willing to take the risk should expect.

We offer a lot of excuses for not being able to compete. They range from culture to labor rates. The fact is we can compete—but not by simply maintaining the status quo. As one general manager told his people as they were embarking on a JIT/TQC implementation, "You can either fight or go hide in the corner. There is no middle ground." One thing is clear. We will change. We do not have the ability to stop change. We can only decide if we want to control the change or have our competitors do it for us.

William A. Sandras, Jr., author of *Just-In-Time: Making It Happen*, is a principal of the Oliver Wight Education Associates and president of Productivity Centers International of Johnstown, Colorado.

Fighting "The Attitude"

Dr. Sheldon Weinig
Chairman and Chief Executive
Materials Research Corporation

ROI analyses have killed more product lines than overseas competition.

W hat if they gave a seminar on advanced manufacturing techniques and nobody came?

That's not entirely an idle question. The Society of Manufacturing Engineers scheduled a three-day seminar called "Semiconductor Manufacturing: Building a Competitive Edge for the 1990s."

It was canceled for lack of interest.

All right. The seminar was in Tempe, Arizona, which isn't exactly the center of the universe. But I can't believe geography was that big an obstacle. Not when the American semiconductor industry is treading water as it tries to match the manufacturing advances of its overseas rivals. (That's the polite way of saying the Japanese.)

The fact is, when it comes to manufacturing, most Americans suffer from what many schoolteachers like to call "an attitude."

To be sure, manufacturing is making a comeback in the consciousness of American CEOs, although precious few of them have ever worked in a manufacturing plant. The facile cliches about the "twilight of the industrial age" and the "dawning of the service economy" lost their currency as American business woke up to the fact that we were being beaten up by foreign companies because they could make things better and more economically than we could.

ENCOURAGING A MANUFACTURING REVIVAL

We must realize what a critical choice we now face. The United States can evolve into just a service society, or it can become a fully integrated industrial society. The path we ultimately take depends on whether or not we can evolve meaningful domestic manufacturing capabilities. And that, in turn, is a function of the number and quality of engineers and scientists that we produce who are interested in manufacturing as a career.

Indeed, the beginning of a manufacturing revival is underway in this country. If that revival is going to blossom into a full-scale renaissance, we have to do something about the attitude problem. It takes many forms. One of the most common is the reluctance of our best and brightest educated Americans to make a career in manufacturing.

Career paths of engineers are almost definable by their academic standing. The top third go on to graduate school and pursue research and development careers. The middle third, confronting economic reality, either seek MBAs or enter sales, leaving the bottom third to become practicing engineers and the backbone of our faltering manufacturing operations. (I have exaggerated the numbers to highlight the seriousness of the problem, not to discourage or insult those few who have chosen careers in manufacturing.)

This distribution of career choices is a result of the "clean hands syndrome," economic reality, and the anachronistic image of manufacturing executives as cigar-chomping businessmen with ample bellies, coffee breath, and a vocabulary restricted to four-letter words used to supervise manufacturing operations. (If only it were true.)

Consider this. Eleven major corporations concerned about developing manufacturing talent sponsored a two-year graduate program in manufacturing science at MIT, at a cost of $46 million. That program graduated its first class this fall, and over a third of the graduates chose jobs outside of manufacturing.

Is it any surprise that when equivalent production machines are delivered to a Japanese manufacturer and a U.S.-based manufacturer of similar products, the uptime (which is the time that equipment is ready for production) in the Japanese plant is nearly

15 percent greater than in the U.S. plant? In Japan many of the operators are engineers learning their trade, whereas in the U.S. plant many are former farmers who can't even spell "technology."

Why do the best and the brightest flinch at opening the factory door? Part of it is the legacy of the indulgent 1980s, when every other 23-year-old coming out of business school aspired to be the next Michael Milken (pre-sentencing). We also can't discount the fact that the generation entering the workforce today grew up in an era when the so-called experts were telling us that manufacturing was an anachronism in highly developed countries like the United States. Robots controlled by computers would replace production personnel in factories of the future. Unfortunately, someone forgot to tell them that highly trained technical people are required to design, install, and maintain these factories. Should we be surprised that students got the idea that manufacturing is a dead end for their careers?

AN ALL-BLUE-COLLAR WORKFORCE

To correct this, we need to do a much better teaching job, especially in engineering schools. We need to make a quantum leap in the quality of science and engineering education. We need to strive toward the concept of an all-blue-collar workforce instead of an all-white-collar workforce. We need engineers and managers who know where the shop floor is and what to do if they ever get there.

Before I founded Materials Research Corp., I taught materials science for five years at the Columbia University and New York University engineering schools. It was always understood that there would be some attrition during the first year, but today this erosion rate has been institutionalized. Forty percent of the freshmen who enroll in engineering or science programs change their majors or leave school before the end of the first year. Twenty-three percent desert during their remaining undergraduate years. An important factor is that academicians think that one of their primary functions is to weed out students rather than stimulate the interest of aspiring engineers.

Follow-up studies of students who dropped out of technical courses revealed that many could handle the academic demands of science or engineering, but could not handle the unimaginative, anachronistic manner in which these subjects are taught in most schools. Even those students who stick it out and become scientists and engineers tend to see manufacturing as a job of last resort.

RAIDERS ON YOUR PAYROLL

This problem takes on still other forms inside our corporations. Corporate leadership is desperately trying to adjust to a longer time horizon in its decision making, especially for manufacturing investment. Unfortunately, control is still in the hands of people with little understanding of the manufacturing process—and even less appreciation for the long-term potential of market share.

The bean counters are very much alive in corporate America. Return on investment analyses have killed more product lines than overseas competition. They don't fracture and dismember companies from the outside like their merge and acquisition cousins of 1980s, but they can choke off growth from within. Over the long run, the business school–bred bean counters who believe that a little knowledge of finances, human resources, and marketing gives them the tools of management are probably a bigger threat than the corporate raiders and disaggregators. At least you can see that gang coming. The former, on the other hand, are already on your payroll.

Still, nonmanufacturing people aren't the only source of "the attitude" in manufacturing. I see a very troubling form of the problem in the short-term career horizons of the skilled engineers and other technical people that manufacturing desperately needs.

The values of the youth culture notwithstanding, time and experience are precious assets in manufacturing—especially in dynamic, changing industries. Windows of opportunity are narrow, and a skilled team needs to be in place to take advantage of them. When a company is racing to translate new technology into a marketable product, there is an immense value in having such a team in place. There's no substitute for experienced people immersed in the technological history of the industry in which they're working.

Assembling and holding a team like that is difficult for most manufacturing companies. That's because the job market of the last

20 years has created a generation of technical vagabonds. They've developed the attitude that earnings and promotions are a direct function of job switches. (Unfortunately, for many industries employing engineers there is a fair amount of truth in that proposition.)

They have no goals for where they want to take the company. They have a clear goal for where they want to take themselves. It's usually out the door and to another company. I have nothing against personal advancement, but this "love 'em and leave 'em" behavior is something we can't afford to indulge any longer. To compete effectively with world-class international companies will require long-term commitments by both the company and its technical personnel. Manufacturing success will be particularly sensitive to the solution of the long-term personnel commitment problems.

In finding solutions we must address both attitude and technology. Attitude problems are, by definition, people problems. However—except for our well-founded worries about the public school system (which is a subject for another time)—most discussions of manufacturing competitiveness usually center on technology. I've spent my life working with technology. I run a business that provides advanced manufacturing technology to the semiconductor industry. So I don't question the importance of manufacturing technology, and I don't question the contributions it has made to America's nascent comeback in manufacturing.

I am equally convinced that statistical analysis, cluster manufacturing, just-in-time delivery, and all the other advances in production technology are necessary to improve American manufacturing, but they are not sufficient to make us world class. We must address the people problems, and this comes down to changing drastically the attitude of our technically trained men and women about careers in manufacturing.

Society and industry must similarly change their attitudes if we are to attract some of our talented young people to manufacturing. American industry can start by according greater recognition and compensation to our blue-collar technologists. "The attitude" will not change rapidly, but a good time to start working on the problem is now.

Dr. Sheldon Weinig is chairman and CEO of Materials Research Corp., a wholly owned subsidiary of Sony USA.

The Automation Imperative

William J. Fife
Chairman and Chief Executive
Giddings & Lewis

What does the next manufacturing renaissance call for?
Cost-conscious machines that operate at high tolerance and totally
integrated automated production.

T he manufacturing world of the 1990s has taken on a far different character than the one most of us knew just a few short years ago. What once was the province of foremen and machine operators has become the focal point for many corporate long-term strategic concerns. No longer is the factory floor merely regarded as a cost center, but as an opportunity to gain a competitive edge in the global marketplace.

More and more managements are being converted to the doctrine that the renaissance of their manufacturing operations is the first step on the road to achieving leadership positions. For most, there is no longer any question about whether to automate—only when. Demographic trends at work in the world today certainly represent one factor contributing to the automation imperative. Because of lower birth rates in the 1960s and 1970s, the overall labor pool is shrinking. Roughly 75 percent of Americans who will be in the workforce in the year 2000 are already employed today. In 1995 we expect to have 50 percent fewer high school graduates than we did in 1971, according to one college dean who was quoted in *American Machinist* magazine recently. Over the decade of the 1990s, that translates to a shortfall of 20,000 to 25,000 engineers each year.

These demographic trends are not confined to the United States. The president of Yamasaki Mazak, Teruyuki Yamasaki, stressed this same point recently in the *Japan Economic Journal*. "To survive international competition and solve the labor shortage," he said, "every plant has to introduce the flexible manufacturing system sooner or later." Similar views were expressed in the United Kingdom at a series of manufacturing roundtable discussions sponsored by our company. The shortage of skilled people was at the top of the list of concerns for the future of manufacturing operations. And along with the shrinkage in the skilled workforce, many of those who are newly available simply do not choose to enter industrial manufacturing work because of its perceived low social status.

Even if skilled manufacturing people were plentiful during the 1990s, companies in the industrialized nations will be at a severe disadvantage in world markets unless they adopt advanced automation technologies. The manufacturing methods of the 1960s and 1970s, and even the 1980s, are available everywhere in the world today. In Eastern Europe, in South America, and certainly in the developing "tigers" of Southeast Asia, there are large pools of semi-skilled labor available who can put the older methods and technology to work. So if manufacturing firms in advanced countries are going to compete globally, or even in their own backyards, their manufacturing methods must literally be on the cutting edge of technology. And that simply means more investment in productivity-improving automation equipment. A workforce trained in these technologies is needed too.

COST-CONSCIOUS MACHINES

Cost savings and quality improvement are two of the primary benefits behind automation projects. For some companies, automating their metal-cutting operations may mean remanufacturing old machine tools to bring them in line with today's technology. For others, it may mean installing new standalone machine tools with pallet pools for setting up parts to be machined offline, so that the only downtime for the machine tool occurs when parts are shuttled in and out. For still other companies, we may be looking at cellular systems or more complex flexible automation systems. Similarly, in assembly automation, some companies may be in a position to start slowly on a modular basis with automated conveyors, whereas others may be able to utilize a more complex, fully automated project where products are assembled in seconds.

While we may not yet be ready for much-publicized "lights-out" factories, most far-sighted companies are taking the automation steps that are appropriate for their own situations. Giddings & Lewis developed, for example, a two-machine cellular manufacturing system for automated machining of split case pumps. The former process machined the pumps as individual halves, which were then mated together in final assembly. Working as a concurrent engineering team, our people and the customer's people developed a joint process to machine the two halves as one part, using spacers to allow the tools to reach inside the casting for the internal machining operations. Because the design team was committed to flexibility, the product designers agreed to redesign the product slightly to allow for easier manufacturability. The result was a 15 to 1 improvement in productivity. Production was increased from one finished pump in three 8-hour shifts, to five finished pumps in one 8-hour shift.

Our work with Caterpillar involves a cellular manufacturing system for automated production of brake and axle housings. Their people and our people, working as a single team, designed a new process that greatly reduced the number of times parts had to be "fixtured" for machining operations. The team added in-process gauging and compensations to the process so the parts could be automatically measured and the tooling adjusted accordingly. And, very importantly, the process was fully simulated and completely maximized before the machine tools were built.

QUALITY IS TIGHTER TOLERANCE

Quality improvements can also be dramatic with new automation technology. Whenever human intervention can be reduced or eliminated, the chance for error is, of course, reduced accordingly.

All of the critical surfaces on the Caterpillar parts are now machined in just one setup using a special back face bar so the part does not have to be removed from its fixture, turned over, and repositioned—all of which takes time and manpower, and can, of course, impact quality. Tolerances in the operating system are held to six-sigma standards, and the just-in-time inventory capability of the system permits machining through final assembly in only 24 hours, compared to two months with the previous methods. In another system for a pump manufacturer, scrap parts were reduced to zero after a two-machine cellular system was installed. The system consistently maintained very tight tolerances of plus-or-minus one thousandth of an inch on the pump bore alignments, providing the quality called for.

The new Saturn plant in Spring Hill, Tennessee, has received a great deal of media attention recently. Working together, Giddings & Lewis and the Saturn people developed a new body-framing system that produces two models of the Saturn at a rate of 72 body frames per hour, and has the flexibility to be able to incorporate new models as needed, with only software changes, rather than a complete retooling. A total of 102 robots are used in the system. For a manufacturer of aircraft engine components, a two-machine cellular system was installed with advanced software and adaptive controls. Probing cycles are used to determine tool wear and part-processing quality, and the machines are programmed to react accordingly. Manual inspection is eliminated entirely, and the parts are repeatedly machined with accuracies of plus-or-minus two thousandths of an inch. It is important to point out that the advantages of reduced maintenance time, substantial flexibility, and almost instant changeover for new models were only possible because of the willingness of designers from both the customer and the supplier to start with a blank sheet.

A CHALLENGE BEYOND SURVIVAL

Several factors lie behind these successful automation projects. One is certainly a growing sense of confidence by both customers and suppliers in their ability to develop and successfully operate such systems. Many companies have adopted a step-by-step, modular approach, in which systems are installed in phases. As operators involved in changing their manufacturing methods become more comfortable with the new technology, second and third phases of the planned systems can be brought on line.

A second factor contributing to successful implementation is the increasing cooperation between customers and suppliers. The sealed bid mentality that formerly governed many industrial purchases has given way to a realization that the best minds from both sides can be melded into a single team that has as its goal the successful start-up and continuing operation of the automated system. Concurrent engineering (or simultaneous engineering) teams become the rule rather than the exception for many purchases of automation projects, particularly in the automotive industry.

The third element that is contributing so much to success of automation investments is the onset of what we call "The New Age of Manufacturing Creativity." Usually, when we think about the word "creativity," we think of an interesting new television commercial, or something associated with advertising. But creativity is really about "coloring outside the lines"—about new ways of doing things. In many cases, the innovators are long-time employees who are excited to be able to approach old problems from new directions. In other situations, they are young people who do not understand the old argument that says, "We have never done it that way before," or "I do not think that will work." It is this change in attitudes—this fresh thinking—that is fueling the turnaround in manufacturing in companies all over the world, and particularly in this country.

For example, an aerospace company was looking for new ways to speed up the manufacturing of aluminum skin panels for large booster rockets. They wanted to be more competitive in serving their traditional customer—the U.S. Air Force. However, they also wanted to be in a better cost position so they could compete for private commercial aerospace projects. A cooperative, simultaneous engineering effort between their people and Giddings & Lewis resulted in an automated cellular system that has the capability to mill a complete rocket skin every 24 hours, compared to one or two per week with the previous method. The manufacturing people at the aerospace company could have continued to mill these large aluminum skins the same way they had always been done before—laid down flat in a horizontal position. But instead, the new system lifts them up into a vertical position so that large amounts of aluminum chips can be removed quickly. None of the equipment in this situation was new or revolutionary—it was the way it was applied that was innovative and creative and different.

AUTOMATION IS GLOBAL

We can, of course, continue to manufacture the same products the same way we have always done it. There may seem to be few risks in using proven techniques that we have come to trust over time. But that is a dangerous strategy in today's rapidly changing manufacturing world. The only strategy we can trust, in fact, is that if new automation techniques are available, a competitor may well be adopting them. U.S. manufacturing companies, in particular, have no other choice but to respond to the automation imperative. Most are playing a gigantic game of automation catch-up, left over from the difficult days of the mid-1980s. Our traditional reaction as a nation, when we get pushed into a corner, is to roll up our sleeves and get with it.

Today's renewed emphasis on manufacturing is being driven by the advent of a truly global economy, with all of the changes for business people that this implies. The global economy of the 1990s will be characterized by instant global communications. We have already seen the fax machine and teleconferences take over international business. It now takes only as long to get from New Delhi to New York, or from La Paz to Los Angeles as it takes a fax machine to transmit a quotation or receive an order. What new communications systems we will be using in the global economy by the end of this decade we can only guess at right now, but we can be sure they will have a major impact on business, literally knitting the world closer and closer.

As transportation and communications advances shrink the distances between markets and production sources, those who do not learn how to do business internationally may not be in much of a position to do business within their own borders. We will see successful companies operating with truly world-class sales and marketing organizations. As trade barriers continue to fall, as they inevitably will, we will all find ourselves with emerging market opportunities in places that many companies may not even think about today. And we must have the contacts and be able to provide the service required so that we can build the relationships that lead to lasting customer-supplier partnerships and improved corporate revenues all over the world.

We must be able to deliver products and services from global manufacturing and distribution points that are dictated not by where we have always operated from in the past, but where we can find the available skills and resources to best serve our new business partners. This strategy may mean joint ventures or wholly owned facilities, or merely leased space in a dockside warehouse. In a similar fashion, many U.S. companies are exporting their components—including finished castings—to overseas customers for final assembly there. Whatever the final structure may be that makes sense for a particular company, it must be dictated by the ability to serve customers on a global basis. More and more companies are using global sourcing, where components and raw materials are obtained anywhere in the world where the right combination of quality, delivery, and pricing makes sense. Even such items as heavy castings, with fairly expensive shipping costs, are being sourced for American firms in such unlikely locations as Spain and Brazil.

In the dynamic environment of the 1990s, with its global sourcing, global sales and marketing, and global communications networks, those companies that are prepared to offer quality-based, value-oriented products and services will be the ones who stake out and hold world-class leadership positions. And if there is any key to building those leadership positions, it may well lie in taking advantage of the proven manufacturing automation opportunities that are now available everywhere in the world today.

William J. Fife, Jr., is chairman and CEO of Giddings & Lewis, a world class manufacturer of factory automation systems with headquarters in Fond du Lac, Wisconsin, and 2,200 employees worldwide.

Accounting for CIM

Scott S. Cowen

Dean
Weatherhead School of Management
Case Western Reserve University

Accountability for high-tech production means more than a final tally. Getting the numbers on cost-integrated manufacturing takes just-in-time accounting.

D uring the last two decades—the 1980s in particular—U.S. manufacturing companies have made significant investments in advanced technology in order to gain a competitive advantage in a global marketplace and enhance profitability. Computer-integrated manufacturing (CIM), just-in-time (JIT), robotics, and flexible manufacturing systems are just a few of the wide array of technologies available to companies that are looking to transform their operations. But despite the increasing financial commitments by senior management to these technologies, executives often are plagued with doubts as to whether or not they are getting the full expected benefits from these investments, especially in light of the substantial amounts of dollars and time required to install and effectively implement these systems throughout the workplace.

As one CEO put it: "We are in the process of making a multimillion dollar investment in computer-integrated manufacturing, but I can't seem to get any reliable, objective financial and operating numbers to help me make an informed decision." Another reported: "I don't understand how our product costs can be increasing at such a rapid rate, given the significant investments we've made in 'cost-saving' technologies such as robotics."

Moreover, these executives realize that an incorrect decision can have a significant long-term impact on a company's global competitiveness, accountability, and overall profitability.

One particularly difficult and frustrating aspect of the movement toward advanced manufacturing has been the slow pace of investment analysis and cost management systems—for example, project analysis, product costing, and performance evaluation—in adapting to the requirements or characteristics of these new technologies. The dilemma was expressed by a third CEO, who commented: "We have no confidence in the product cost data we are receiving because we are still allocating overhead to products based on direct labor hours, despite our success in virtually eliminating direct labor dollars from product cost."

Change, as always, has come at a slower pace than is desirable. If U.S. companies are to be successful in integrating advanced manufacturing technology into the workplace and, in particular, aligning investment analysis and cost management systems to these manufacturing systems, there are certain commitments that will be required from senior executives and their organizations. The traditional investment analysis process in most companies involves a "bottoms-up" approach, in which investments are justified on the basis of anticipated cash inflows and outflows. Frequently, the company generates the necessary cash flow data based on its prior experiences, engineering specifications, vendor data, or the experiences of others with similar types of projects. This data is then put to work to provide cost estimates and investment measures.

Theoretically, investments in advanced manufacturing technology should follow a process similar to the one described here; practically, however, such an approach would be impractical for at least three reasons. First, many of these technologies are in the early stages of use and the necessary data for an investment analysis is simply unavailable or not readily accessible. Second, investment in these technologies can be a transforming act for a company; that is, it has the potential to have a significant effect throughout the organization that may not have been anticipated when the initial analysis was conducted. And finally, these technologies often carry "learning effect" costs that are much higher than more traditional approaches to manufacturing and automation. Therefore, executives will have to rethink their usual approaches to investment analysis with regard to advanced manufacturing technology.

OVERCOMING ACCOUNTING LAG

Most accounting systems are designed primarily to meet the external reporting needs of an organization and secondarily to support managerial decision making. Accounting systems focused on the former function are a necessity because of legal and reporting requirements, whereas systems focused on managerial decision making typically lag behind changes in an organization's external and internal environments. This lag time occurs because such management accounting systems—for example, budgeting, cost accounting, and transfer pricing—are often seen as discretionary and requiring a large investment of time and dollars, while producing no identifiable and quantifiable benefits for the corporation and its bottom line.

Significant changes in management accounting systems usually are prompted by a "crisis" such as loss of profitability, reductions in market share, continual surprises, or a loss of control. But by the time such a crisis occurs, it is too late for a systems change to make much of a difference. A key to sustaining long-term success is the ability to anticipate when and how an organization's management accounting systems should be changed and to commit the necessary resources. This ability is particularly important as an organization invests in advanced manufacturing technology, because to fully measure the actual costs and benefits of such investments, the organization's cost management systems must be designed to be consistent with the new information requirements. But this is unfortunately not the case in most organizations.

As investments in advanced technology are made, a business organization will have to change its cost management systems in at least two significant ways. First, it must broaden and reorient its perspective on why and for what purpose cost data are needed. Advanced manufacturing technologies often are adopted to improve competitiveness throughout an organization and ultimately increase profitability.

Traditional cost systems typically have been designed to determine product costs for inventory valuation purposes, using a combination of job order and process costing in conjunction with full absorption costing. However, investments in advanced technology often require that the organization adopt a different perspective on how costs are accumulated. That is, such investments necessitate a focus on all costs—non-manufacturing as well as manufacturing—and, in particular, require cost data relating to the activities that are tied directly to the reasons for the acquisition of the technology (e.g., quality, customer service, cost reduction).

To help ensure that cost management systems are designed to meet the needs of management as well as the requirements of the technology, these systems must be aligned with an organization's value chain. A value chain comprises all of the critical activities required to efficiently and effectively move a product from customer awareness to order to delivery and thus enable the organization to gain competitive advantage. Components of the value chain include the gamut of manufacturing and non-manufacturing functions, from order taking to customer follow-up, from packaging to shipment. Typically, these activities account for the larger percentages of product and operating costs in a business and often are viewed as the key factors in a company's ability to sustain a competitive advantage. Cost management systems must be designed so that they can identify costs and assets—and, therefore, performance—with regard to each component of the value chain.

THE VALUE CHAIN PERSPECTIVE

The second critical shift required by accounting for CIM means rethinking how overhead is allocated to the various components of the value chain, including products. Investments in advanced manufacturing technology have significantly reduced the percentage of direct labor cost to total product cost, often leading to a corresponding increase in overhead cost as a percentage of total product cost. Despite this shift, many firms still allocate overhead cost to products on the basis of direct labor dollars or hours. This method of allocation can seriously distort product cost because the cause of the overhead cost is not related to direct labor. A decision to implement advanced technology requires that a manufacturing company reexamine its method for allocating overhead, the size and type of overhead pools employed, and the organizational level at which overhead is allocated (e.g., plant, department, manufacturing cell).

The value chain perspective described here suggests the use of multiple bases for allocation, depending on the nature of the activity under analysis within the chain, the adoption of more and smaller overhead pools since the value chain will focus the organization's attention on a greater number of activities, and the allocation of overhead cost at lower levels in the organization. Such a reallocation of overhead early in an organization's planning process should minimize the possibility of distorting product cost and provide strategic information that will help it to gain and sustain a competitive advantage.

NEW NUMBERS FOR NEW TECHNOLOGY

Recent field studies examining the investment decision-making processes in companies with advanced technology point to several recommendations that have significantly improved the investment analysis process in this area:

Evaluate the total impact of the technology throughout the workplace in the early stages of the investment analysis process

A significant investment in advanced technology will ultimately have an impact on all of the business functions of an organization, from human resource management to cost accounting to product marketing. How often have you heard an executive complain that the skill base of the company's workforce was not adequately prepared for a new technology? Or that although the intended purpose of the technology was to enhance product quality, the existing accounting and operating systems were not in place to measure the cost of quality? One way to anticipate the possible impact of a technology investment and to have this understanding reflected early in the decision-making process is to form project teams with representatives from all major functional areas of the company to analyze and evaluate the potential investment. This team should consider the proposed investment in terms of its financial as well as nonfinancial implications in all areas.

Prepare the organization to receive the technology and build these costs into the investment analysis

Part of the planning process for investing in an advanced technology should be devoted to analyzing how the technology will be implemented in the workplace as well as to properly preparing the workforce to make the maximal use of the investment and, hopefully, realize the benefits originally intended in the project's justification. For example, if one justification for an investment in technology is that it will improve product quality, this expectation must be communicated throughout the organization so that executives in all functional areas are prepared to help achieve and capitalize on this objective. I recently observed the efforts of a large manufacturer with retail operations to implement point-of-sale equipment throughout the retail chain, a move that would require a substantial multiyear investment. The firm's MIS department served as the catalyst for change with the blessing of top management. During the final review of the proposal, it became evident that most of the heads of the functional areas, though aware of the project, had not been challenged to think through in detail how the technology would affect their respective areas. Subsequent study indicated that the project would have much larger cost and workplace implications than originally planned.

Develop a strategic perspective with regard to all investments in advanced technology

Whenever an organization invests in an advanced technology such as cellular manufacturing, CIM, or JIT, it is making a strategic statement in the sense that these types of large investments are usually motivated by a desire to enhance competitiveness. Therefore, all such investments must be evaluated in terms of the overall strategy of the organization and its business units. This approach minimizes the possibility of an organization establishing isolated and possibly unconnected "pockets" of technology as opposed to a total strategic approach to this type of investment.

Take the long view

Most investments in advanced technology cannot easily be justified using payback criteria. In most cases, the costs are immediate and more definite, whereas the benefits are longer-term, more difficult to quantify, and more far-reaching. It is not uncommon for executives to significantly underestimate the cash outflows for these projects while overestimating the cash inflows. Benefits tied to product quality, customer service, and product enhancement are often difficult to quantify in practice. At the same time, these represent some of the potentially largest benefits to the organization from technology investments, in addition to promoting cost reduction, efficiency, and a ripple effect throughout the organization that ultimately leads to additional significant benefits. This type of investment requires that an executive have the patience and courage to forego investing in a less risky, shorter-term payback project in favor of a strategic investment that cannot readily be justified using traditional capital-budgeting techniques and processes. In addition, senior executives should challenge their financial operations to develop more innovative ways to analyze these projects, so as to have a balanced long-term view of the financial and nonfinancial aspects of an investment.

Conduct postaudits of investment in advanced technology

One of the most positive and helpful ways to improve the investment analysis process for advanced technology is to periodically conduct postaudits of the firm's investments. Through such audits, the organization should develop valuable insights into how to improve its investment processes and realize the maximum value of its technology throughout the organization.

The aforementioned observations merely touch the surface in addressing the kinds of changes in an organization's investment analysis and cost management systems processes that are necessitated by the decision to implement advanced manufacturing technology. The most important of these observations is that such a decision often represents a critical strategic initiative that is likely to set off a chain reaction throughout the organization and result in a much more intense and broader experience than executives may have anticipated. The ripple effect is likely to be felt most strongly in the management accounting systems area because the responsibility for "keeping score" for executives and aiding them in decision making rests with that functional area.

Scott S. Cowen is Dean of the Weatherhead School of Management of Case Western Reserve University, and Professor of Accountancy. He serves on the board of directors of a number of U.S. corporations.

Reducing Inventory Through Logistics

William M. Clifford
Chairman and Chief Executive
St. Johnsbury Trucking Co.

Line managers think a large inventory gives them a security blanket, but CEOs are finding that this blanket may be too much for their balance sheets.

T he cost of storage space for surplus inventory can be a black hole on manufacturers' balance sheets. Preferring to err on the oversupply side, many companies waste money and space that could be used to generate profits. Some firms, however, have developed management systems to reduce cycle times without disrupting production. They have reviewed linkages up and down the distribution chain and replaced massive warehouses and departmental safety stocks with integrated information and transportation systems. Instead of shipping materials to a distribution center and then by truckload to the factory, they have instituted just-in-time (JIT) logistics systems with daily "milk runs" from suppliers. Similarly, they are meeting the demands of retail and wholesale customers for time-definite shipments.

Yet attempts to implement JIT are usually met with contention by department and line managers. From their perspective, surplus inventory is a comforting security blanket. Since their performance would depend on suppliers and transportation carriers, they perceive JIT as hazardous. CEOs and financial executives may view warehouses and work in progress inventory as costly bottlenecks and a JIT pipeline as cost-efficient work flow, but production and inventory managers see JIT replacing their safety stocks with computers and promises.

It is true that inventory reduction and the resulting savings require controlling distribution and communications; one snag in transportation or communication and the production schedule can be suspended. Therefore, the linchpins of a JIT program are reliable, time-definite deliveries and a real-time, shipment-tracking system. Although there are varying methods for establishing carrier relationships and setting up information networks, some basic criteria exist. A company can provide the foundation for an effective JIT logistics program by removing seams in the material flow process caused by multiple handling, linking distribution, production, inventory, and customer service functions, and reducing the number of product and service suppliers in order to work closely with each one.

ELIMINATING BUFFERS

The progression from materials at a vendor's site to finished products at retail and wholesale outlets is a series of processes, with a seam occurring at each transition point: from supplier, to carrier, to warehouse, to production line, to inventory, to carrier, and finally to wholesaler. The conventional method of smoothing these seams is to build safety stocks over them. JIT proposes to eliminate them. Some seams may be unavoidable—even desirable—yet most can be eliminated.

In process, safety stocks can hide a number of serious flaws, such as inflexible production schedules, inaccurate or missing shipping information, and poor material planning and marketing projections. These flaws are logistics defects and result in excess inventory and multiple handling. JIT removes them through time-definite and point-of-use delivery of materials. While identifying and eliminating logistics defects requires different procedures than product defects, it is no less important to the bottom line. Companies consider product defects critical because there are no alternatives or buffers: they lead directly to dissatisfied customers. However, delivery defects occur all the time—especially across seams—yet they go undetected because of buffer stocks. But, like product defects, they erode corporate profits.

JIT distribution is a process of continuous improvement. A company cannot be expected to instantaneously switch to a fully operational JIT system. However, the benefits of eliminating some excess inventory can still be substantial.

For example, Hewlett-Packard's analytical instruments plant in Avondale, Pennsylvania, reduced some in-process inventories through daily, point-of-use deliveries for locally sourced materials. Their JIT system includes a dedicated truck and driver on a daily scheduled route and a material handling system that uses specially designed reusable carts. The driver picks up materials from eight vendors—all within a 50 mile radius of the plant—and drops off empty carts for the next day's shipments. The following morning, he stages the loaded carts at workstations on the production line, loads the empty carts, and begins the loop again.

JIT deliveries can also be employed for outbound distribution. 3M was able to close a distribution center in Needham, Massachusetts, yet still maintain overnight standards to New England and upstate New York retailers. Through a program called "Partners in Quality," 3M has a partnership with its regional carrier, which provides next-day delivery to customers on dedicated truck routes from 3M's New Jersey distribution center.

Along with cost savings, establishing inbound and/or outbound JIT logistics will uncover distribution flaws. Unfortunately, by exposing defects, the JIT system is often cited as the source of them. Previously unnoticed problems will obstruct transportation flow and have production and warehouse managers clamoring for inventory stockpiles. Production managers must be assured that their station will not be idled because a component did not arrive on time. This is not just the transportation or inventory manager's responsibility; department managers that used to be unconcerned with shipping information will become very involved. Production will communicate with inventory and traffic departments, because, in essence, their parts and materials are in motion. Purchasing managers may incur increased costs for smaller lot orders, but the effect will be reduced inventory carrying costs. Each department must understand its role in the material flow process.

LINKAGE OF TRAFFIC, PRODUCTION, INVENTORY, AND CUSTOMER SERVICE FUNCTIONS

In many companies individual departments operate independently with isolated controls, divergent goals, and little communication. Consider how each department is evaluated.

Production managers are judged on cost per unit to produce, and quality control. All they want to know from the front of the pipeline is, "Do we have enough parts and materials to keep the line busy?", and on the back end, "Do we need to produce more or less units?"

Inventory managers are usually encouraged to stockpile. Production wants spare parts in case demand increases, and more room for finished products if demand goes down. Sales and marketing want to ensure products are available when the customer wants them. The prime function for most inventory, therefore, is just in case, with the manager's performance only noticeable when a shortage occurs.

Transportation managers are judged on cost per unit. They ship with carriers that provide volume discounts, working with as many as possible to price-shop. In the JIT environment, however, the emphasis on transportation control moves from costs to quality. Compounding this problem is the penchant among purchasing managers to order large quantities because their performance is also measured on unit price.

Customer service managers are judged on customer satisfaction, which is consistent with JIT goals. They know if order times are compressed, they become better suppliers; it is a competitive advantage based on improved customer responsiveness. However, their efforts are often compromised by inventory, production, and transportation priorities.

Aligning departmental goals with a focused, corporate goal can lead to turf wars. Problems occur when the productivity of one department is given higher priority than the overall goal. For example, manufacturing is a sacred cow in many companies, with production performance increased at the expense of other departments. The larger issue of total quality management—of product and service—is muddled, and inventory (both materials and finished products) simply expands to allow for steady production.

Consider the auto industry, widely acknowledged for its innovator role in JIT systems. While vendors provide time-definite deliveries to specified point-of-use locations—eliminating most material inventories—outbound logistics are still based on the stockpile theory. Because production is the focal point of the auto industry, 60-day inventories become 90-day inventories, and the carrying costs rise proportionately. Auto manufacturers attempt to artificially increase customer demand to meet production, then stockpile and discount excess vehicles so production does not back up.

It is understandable that the primary focus of most manufacturers is production; corporate functions such as marketing and distribution are meaningless without a high-quality product that is efficiently produced. Manufacturers may think their companies are service-oriented, yet it's easy to underestimate the importance of elements that may be vital to retail customers, such as delivery schedules. For many retailers, next day delivery is an essential part of inventory control. Quality products mean little to retailers if they can't secure prompt delivery.

Many JIT theorists claim time-definite deliveries require stable production schedules. While they may make the purchasing manager's job easier, they unbalance the overall distribution system. Inflexible production leads to the major failing of some JIT programs: inventories are not eliminated, merely moved to suppliers (and transferred to manufacturers as higher materials prices) or to postproduction inventories. It is important to note this relationship to inbound and outbound inventories, and how they are often treated independently because of production. Yet in a study by Northeastern University, nearly two-thirds of the surveyed companies with their own JIT programs are also JIT suppliers. The notable exception, of course, is the auto industry.

WORKING CLOSELY WITH SUPPLIERS OF PRODUCTS AND SERVICES

The concept of linkage should not be confined to in-house departments. JIT dictates that companies develop closer ties with suppliers of products and services. Manufacturers purchasing more goods from fewer vendors are in a position to influence supplier quality control programs and reduce purchase lead times. They are also more interdependent with these suppliers, which motivates both companies to engage in a more cooperative joint venture relationship.

Just as JIT requires manufacturers to work more closely with suppliers, they must also develop partnerships with their suppliers of distribution—carriers. Quality and timeliness hinge upon carrier performance. One of the main problems with JIT deliveries is a company's inability to control the freight until it reaches the customer. They turn freight over to a common carrier with little or no information support. Common carriers not linked to the supplier-manufacturer communication system operate in a black box. Suppliers put the product into the box, but cannot tell exactly when it will come out. Correspondingly, carriers are not provided service requirements and expectations. Manufacturers need to know the exact status of their materials at all times; carriers need information on shipping volumes, transit time requirements, special service needs, traffic flow patterns, equipment requirements, performance goals, operating procedures, and shipment-tracking abilities.

Interestingly, companies will share information with their suppliers and customers that they would not think of sharing with carriers. According to the Northeastern University study, while 45 percent of JIT companies use electronic data interchange with their customers, and 33 percent with their suppliers, only 26 percent share this resource with their carriers. There should be a partnership with the carrier. Linking the carrier into the computer loop will cut administrative costs by moving closer to the paper-less transaction. More importantly, it can improve efficiency by allowing the trucker to plan in advance. Carriers do offer volume discounts, but they also discount for predictable service runs.

Another important aspect of computer linking is the ability to track shipments throughout the distribution process. This feature is extraneous for the 95 to 98 percent of shipments that proceed smoothly and arrive on time, but for the other 2 to 5 percent, the ability to access shipment information—where it is, when the customer needs it, how long it will take to get it there—is critical. A real-time automatic identification system—part of an overall EDI system—is necessary because there is virtually no time in JIT systems to track missing materials or to correct delivery errors. This shared information can be used to solve problems quickly.

A strategic alliance must develop between all JIT participants. Moreover, the carrier should be linked with all parts of the company directly, as well as suppliers and customers. Often, other than the sales force, truck drivers are the company's only contact with clients. Therefore, they need to communicate with customer service people. How can a customer service representative promise a service to a client without knowledge of how and when it will get to him? It can create the same frustration as telling a supplier "the check's in the mail" and blaming the delay on the post office.

PATIENCE

Forming a distribution pipeline takes patience, and must be done cautiously, as manufacturers will be operating with reduced margins for error. However, as manufacturers become more service-oriented—and have the ability to quickly register customer demand through cash register scanners and computerized purchase orders—products are more likely to be built as needed rather than made to stockpile. In this environment inbound and outbound inventory reductions are possible without jeopardizing operations. The ideal flow becomes a narrow pipeline from suppliers through retailers.

William M. Clifford is chairman and CEO of St. Johnsbury Trucking Company, headquartered in Holliston, Massachusetts. St. Johnsbury was named Regional Carrier of the Year for the previous two years by the National Small Shipments Traffic Conference (NASSTRAC).

The True Cost of Recycling

Carl C. Landegger

Chairman
Black Clawson Company

The call for industrial recycling has never been louder, but the real social and economic costs may be falling on deaf ears.

W e have recently witnessed McDonald's, one of the most successful consumer products the world has ever seen, switch from the ubiquitous white plastic container to a multilayer paper sheet for its hamburgers. Proctor & Gamble, Kimberly-Clark, and Scott are all redesigning the material in their baby diapers to make them environmentally friendly. Laws have been passed in more than 20 states mandating that newspaper publishers use paper consisting of at least 40 percent recycled fiber or they will be forced to pay a punitive $50.00-per-ton fine. All three of these developments are the results of consumer pressures to recycle. All three ignore the social and economic costs involved.

The "why" of recycling quickly becomes all things to all people. Some believe it is to preserve materials perceived to be in finite supply on this earth. Others recycle in order to preserve the environment. Still others advocate recycling to reduce the amount of material ultimately going to our landfills. A survey points out the strong public support for protecting the environment and making improvements. In all cases, the vast majority of citizens perceive recycling to be a good and necessary endeavor despite the cost. I believe, however, that we must seriously question whether or not the costs involved should continue to be ignored.

In the case of McDonald's polystyrene plastic box versus its composite paper sheet, we have seen the recent advertisements put out by the plastics producers in which they claim that the plastic box requires less energy to produce than the composite paper sheet. It is also a fact that the plastic container can be recycled whereas the composite sheet cannot.

Plastics can be recycled. What is not generally known is that as a practical matter, mixed plastics cannot be recycled. Plastics can only be recycled if they are all of essentially the same chemical composition. This is known as "single resin source" recycling.

PLASTIC LUMBERJACKS

A thousand-pound-per-hour plant for postconsumer plastics—quite a large plant—can be installed for around $5 million and can produce pellets that could once again be extruded into similar plastics, or alternatively, into so-called "plastic lumber." However, there is a very real limit on the amount of plastic lumber that can be used because its cost is many times the cost of conventional lumber. In other words, it takes a very special and very limited application to be able to use plastic lumber economically. Plastic lumber is far from becoming a viable lumber alternative anytime soon.

Recycling in the paper industry is another case in point. Contrary to general public opinion, paper recycling is not something new. For at least the last 30 years, 30 percent of all paper and board that has been produced and marketed in the United States has been recycled.

A large percentage of corrugated boxes—the type of box used for cases of beer or other canned products—has always been made out of recycled postconsumer wastepaper. Up until now, postconsumer wastepaper has been a less expensive source of fiber than the "virgin fibers" that are created by turning trees into corrugated boxes.

About two years ago, approximately 20 states began passing legislation mandating that newspaper publishers use only newsprint containing 40 percent or more of recycled paper for the production of newspapers. Basically, the law now requires the publishers to use 40 percent recycled content in paper by 1995 or to pay an environmental tax of $50.00 per ton, an amount roughly equivalent to 10 percent of the value of the newsprint they buy.

The economics are a disaster for several reasons:

1. A 300-to-400-ton-per-day wastepaper recycling plant costs in the order of $60 million.

2. In most cases, these plants are being bought by companies already in the newsprint business who are not increasing their production. Quite the contrary, they are having to shut down parts of a perfectly good manufacturing plant in order to utilize the fiber being produced by the newly purchased recycling plant.

3. This means that they are required to continue to carry the depreciation of the old plant, and, at the same time, absorb an additional cost of between $30.00 and $50.00 per ton to repay the capital they borrowed to build the recycling plant.

4. This $30.00 to $50.00 per ton, when added to the cost of the wastepaper, plus the transportation of that wastepaper to their paper mill, plus the operational cost of cleaning the wastepaper with their newly purchased systems, means that in most cases the resulting cost of the newsprint produced is higher than the newsprint they had been producing directly from trees.

5. It goes without saying that the newspaper publishers, while demanding that they receive newsprint with 40 percent recycled fibers, are not in a position to pay more for this product than they have been paying for their standard newsprint.

Under these conditions, it is not surprising that many newsprint producers are less than enamored at the thought of using wastepaper as part of their raw material base. On the other hand, since the publishers are forced by the laws to demand recycled papers, the newsprint producers have no choice but to swallow hard and absorb the extra costs in order to be able to stay in business.

PULP FICTION

I have been associated with the pulp and paper industry all of my adult life and have seen the industry absorb billions of capital expenditures and operating costs for both air and water pollution control. I have never heard a chief executive seriously question the need or propriety of such expenses. However, the need and propriety of requiring the capital expenditures and operating expenses associated with this 40 percent recycled fibers program are being questioned by virtually all chief executives on a daily basis. They see a great number of problems.

1. The mandated recycling of paper changes the basic economics of the industry. Historically, the industry has been near the source of supply, that is, near the woods. Suddenly, by political mandate, 40 percent of the source of supply has moved into the urban areas with a tremendously increased cost for freight.

2. All of the large newsprint producers have wood holdings. These wood holdings have now in many cases become only marginally economic because:

• They cannot be converted to lumber without totally flooding and ruining the lumber market.

• In Canada, the very suddenly unneeded, unusable wood must be returned to the province. This means the province will lose the income that they have drawn from these wood holdings, which in turn brings with it a host of other problems, including a lower tax base for the province and substantial unemployment in sparsely populated forest areas.

• In the United States, the small wood lot owner who has been selling his surplus wood to the pulp mills and the newsprint mills will find that his market has disappeared, which brings with it a host of social problems.

3. The newsprint industry and parts of the paper industry are either heading into or already are in a recession. Their executives feel that this is not the time to force them into large capital expenditures that result in increased costs, rather than allowing them to use their capital expenditures as they have traditionally used them to decrease costs.

The magazine publishers are watching what is going on with the newspapers very carefully. They clearly recognize the social and political pressures driving this recycling movement and through their association are trying to come to grips with the problems that they will face when the law mandates that they use a certain percentage of recycled fibers in their products.

Since recycling has already been mandated for the newspapers, and since the federal government has mandated that the paper and board that it buys should contain 40 percent recycled fibers, the magazines know it is only a matter of time before laws are passed mandating recycling for them. The government has naturally left itself a very large loophole by requiring its purchasing agents to buy paper and board containing recycled fiber "only if it is available," and the reality is that it is not available.

In Charles Dickens' time, the law was an ass. Some things have improved since then, others have not.

RECYCLING AND REALITY

While the public thinks more corporate participation is important to champion recycling and other environmental causes, we continue to debate the very definition of what recycled paper is. The question has been posed as to whether any paper or board, regardless of its use, can be determined to be "recycled" or whether only so-called "postconsumer papers" should be considered recycled. The second major debate is how much recycled fiber a new paper product must contain before it can be considered recycled.

For example, my company is by far the largest producer of machinery for paper recycling, and as such we are proud to be using recycled paper as our basic stationery. It is with some considerable embarrassment that we discovered the paper that we have proudly labeled "recycled paper" contains less than 10 percent recycled fiber.

Another example is in the 40 percent of magazines distributed to newsstands that are returned to the publishers; they are not considered postconsumer recycled waste. This would be the largest single source of wastepaper available to the magazines for recycling. As another example, there are stories floating around, which I believe to be true, that some mills are exchanging rolls of unused newly produced papers, which they are then cutting up and putting back into their papermaking stream so that they can claim the resulting papers produced are "recycled." It is evident that a great deal of work must still be done in even defining what recycled paper means.

In Europe, the Germans and a number of others have established very definite standards on the minimum requirements to be able to use the designation "recycled." The United States is very far from this definition because of the many varied pressure groups, all of which think their particular definition is not only technically accurate, but perhaps much more important, morally accurate.

What we as a nation are doing is deciding that anything that falls under the heading of "recycling" is more than good; it is sacred and cannot be challenged. The reality is quite different.

McDonald's plastic box was recyclable. The composite paper sheet that replaces it will most probably not be.

A LANDFILL OF LEGISLATION

It is easy for the state and federal legislators to pass a law mandating a high percentage of recycled fiber in newsprint for the newspapers, magazines, and for those papers purchased by the government. The reality is within a few years there will not be enough wastepaper to enable all of these laws to be implemented.

Plastic trash bags that are advertised as decomposing will do so in bright sunlight and rain. They will not, however, decompose if buried deep in a landfill.

If we really wish to reduce the amount of material going to a landfill, we must recognize that all of the wastepaper going to landfills is equaled by the tonnage of dead leaves and grass cuttings sent to that same landfill. The latter can be turned into compost or animal feed for a fraction of what it costs to recycle paper.

The proper allocation and use of resources must distinguish between renewable resources, such as trees, and nonrenewable resources, such as petrochemicals and metallic ores. Logic requires us to establish sensible and well thought out policies to implement the goals we are trying to reach. The present trend of accepting any program under the emotional code name of recycling is both socially and economically short-sighted and wrong.

Carl C. Landegger is chairman of Black Clawson Company, a New York-based privately held manufacturer of papermaking machinery and systems.

4

THE IMPACT OF TECHNOLOGY

Will the Alliance Bear Fruit?

Apple's John Sculley is betting the orchard on it. As the PC revolution enters its second decade, his link-up with archrival IBM and emphasis on object-oriented technology should bring Apple's products out of the classroom and into the boardroom.

W hen Ronald Reagan opined that we may witness the Apocalypse in our lifetimes, he might not have been entirely off the mark. So far, the 1990s have seen the lions and the lambs lie down together in record numbers. James Baker brought the Israelis and the Arabs to the table. Former communist powers are teaming up with Western business interests as they embrace capitalism. David Duke went stumping on Jesse Jackson's talk show. But pound for pound, one of the strangest revelations has to be the joint venture between Apple Computer and IBM. Wasn't it only yesterday, after all, that Apple founder Steve Jobs was comparing Big Blue to Big Brother?

All that has changed under the stewardship of John Sculley. As chairman and CEO, the former PepsiCo marketing wiz has revamped Apple in ways that had appeared previously only in Jobs' worst nightmares. In addition to the IBM venture—by far the most ambitious of Sculley's projects—Apple announced a deal with Sony this past October to build the PowerBook 100, which Sculley says will allow customers to use laptops "in the same easy, empowered way that they had become accustomed to with Macintosh." Also, Apple will continue its long-time alliance with Motorola, which manufactures Apple's microprocessors. The IBM and Sony deals represent a major shift in strategy for Apple. Walter Winnitzki, deputy manager of Brown Brothers, says, "Apple is finally delivering what its customers want. Its previous policy had been to dictate to its customers what they should be buying."

There are four main goals Apple and IBM hope to realize through their collaboration. The big one is the plan to develop "object-oriented" software, which will break down the format barriers that currently prevent large networks of equipment from interacting. Second, they will make it easier for Macintosh and IBM PCs to work together and share software. Third, IBM will license to Motorola the right to manufacture and market its RISC chip for the new desktops. (That's bad news for Intel Corp., which had a virtual monopoly on the microprocessor market for IBM and other PC manufacturers.) Fourth, Apple and IBM will create a "multimedia" system that will allow PC users to send and receive video and audio programs.

With the alliance, Sculley hopes to move Apple out of the realm of hobbyists and educators and into the corporate world. But will it work? Patty Seybold, publisher of *Paradigm Shift* and president of Office Computing Group, told *Chief Executive*, "Sculley seems to be making the right marketing and political moves. Whether he's making the right technical moves is hard to say."

While both IBM and Apple stand to reap huge benefits if the partnership succeeds, it's definitely a "must-win" situation for the latter. Sculley's greatest task has been the transition to corporate computing, which has not gone without snags. In his quest to expand market share, Sculley cut prices 30 to 40 percent across the board last year, thereby slicing Apple's margins to the core. In May 1990 the company reduced its workforce by 10 percent. And just when it seemed that things were turning around, Apple posted an 18 percent decline in earnings for its fiscal fourth quarter. Sculley is putting his faith in the joint ventures, new technology, and his own marketing savvy.

HARVEST TIME

Once the alliance between Apple and IBM establishes a uniform information highway, what can we expect?
What makes this alliance different than others in the industry is that it really starts with what's in it for the customer. The most important thing for our customers in the 1990s is going to be the reorganization of work. How do you get people to change their behavior so they'll work more productively? It's going to require that computers become a part of the workplace in a far more per-

vasive way than we saw in the 1980s, which means that the computers have got to be easy to use, which is Apple's great strength, and computers have got to communicate over large enterprise systems, which is IBM's great strength.

What we're doing is bringing together Apple's core competence with IBM's core competence, and creating a series of foundation technologies that can dramatically improve the ability of technology to deliver on the productivity promises made in the 1980s, but which in many cases were never realized.

> **Isn't Apple's alliance with IBM a bit lopsided given IBM has nothing like the same need as Apple to make the venture a success?**

The reason why IBM and Apple joined together was that both of us are systems companies. We're both capable of creating new technologies, but if we can't get them to market and get them adopted by the application developers, then the customer will never see the end user value of it. And in order to counterweight the drift that the industry has had toward commoditization, we didn't think any one company alone, even IBM, could achieve success. That's why the two companies who had traditionally been vigorous competitors joined together for the common goal, to create new foundation technologies.

Now, at the same time that we're working closely together, we said we are willing to continue to share technologies, even though we know, as vigorous competitors, that we run the risk of taking sales away from each other. But we would rather take sales away from each other in an expanding, exciting industry that's driven by innovative technology, than in an industry that's drifting toward commoditization.

STILL WAITING FOR THE PAYOFF

> **After all that's been said and done about office productivity, why hasn't the PC really changed anything?**

If you look at the statistics on productivity in the office, you're correct that there has been no substantial increase in productivity over the last 10 or 20 years. But it's not that the technology doesn't enable people to be more productive. The problem is that we have taken very expensive technology, and we have forced it onto the old way of working. What it really requires is a systemic change in the way the people do their jobs, which means they have to think differently, communicate differently, and work differently.

So the big revolution of the 1990s isn't just technology, though that's a part of it, but it's how people use technology. The problem with the 1980s computers was that they just weren't easy enough for normal people, nonexperts, to use. They didn't do enough for people when they had to work together over networks.

How do you bring people closer to how the software should be used?

That's the central theme of what interests Apple the most in the 1990s. It isn't just about processing data now, it's about enabling people to work differently than they have in the past. You've got to make the tools that we put in front of people so obviously better than what they had that they'll want to adopt the new behavior. That's a marvelous opportunity for Apple, because what we care about passionately is making technology easy to use.

What tool or process do you presently have or will have that directly addresses that?

One of the best examples we have is the new line of PowerBooks that we just introduced. Apple was late to market with laptop computers, but when we finally came, it was with a very different concept of what a notebook computer should be. Other computer companies said that the notebook was an opportunity to make big machines smaller so you can carry them around with you. We said that it should be more than a computer, because when people are walking around they want to do more than just run spreadsheets. They want to access information, send information, carry out transactions, and be able to do it in the same easy, empowered way that they had become accustomed to with Macintosh.

What we did was to design a notebook computer that integrated communications into the user interface as successfully as we had integrated the ease of use of computation into our desktop machines. It's a radical point of departure, but it's one that is already starting to validate the idea that people will change their culture and behaviors if you give them tools that do things that they find to be really useful. It's not just about computation.

FROM PEPSI TO PCs

Since coming to Apple from Pepsi, what cultural changes have you had to make?

One of the things that really struck me when I first joined Apple and had been out here five or six months was my first trip back to the East Coast. I saw some of my old colleagues, and they said, "Tell us what it's really like out there in Silicon Valley." I said, "They've got this really strange idea that work ought to be fun." And they said, "Oh, you've got to be kidding. You've been out in the sun too long."

The idea that work ought to be fun is incredibly powerful, because people are more likely to be productive, get involved, and be creative if they're enjoying what they're doing. The old idea was that if somebody was having fun at their job, they were probably goofing off.

It just shows you how quickly our ideas of success change in about a decade. It isn't just my change from one industry to another. The whole world has changed a lot as well over the last decade.

How have these cultural changes affected the way you do your job?

The world I came from was very hierarchical. I've been at Apple for almost nine years, and when I left corporate America it was still in the command and control concept of management. It's really only in the last decade that we started to see real decentralizing going on in corporations.

Since I don't have a large staff, when I have to work on a project that I'm interested in, because I'm also the chief technology officer of Apple as well as the CEO, I do it over electronic mail. I assemble a small team of people electronically to work on a particular project. We may all be in different time zones and working at different times of the day where we are, but we are able to focus on a project until it's completed. Then this group is dissolved, and the human resources department never knew that organization existed, much less that it was disbanded, because it's an organization that exists as required over a network.

What makes Apple unique is that we are all tremendous users of our own technology, starting with the CEO and moving right up through the factory workers or the people out in the field. We have a common denominator, typically on our electronic mail systems, which allows us to use it as easily and as intuitively as other people may use telephones.

**Do you use a proprietary information bank that is
shared only within top management, or does
information truly flow outside this circle?**
No, information truly flows. Obviously, there is some sensitive financial information that we cannot share because of SEC disclosure rules. For the most part, however, it's a dramatic change from the soft drink industry, where information was guarded almost religiously. In this industry, information is a perishable commodity; it's out of date literally in days. There's far more advantage to making it available to the people who need to use it than to keep it away from people because it's proprietary.

THE OBJECT OF HIS AFFECTION

**Take us into the future when object-oriented software
is up and running. How would CEOs use this in their
businesses, and how would it change what they're doing?**
The first hurdle that management must cross is not what technology to choose, but what business process to install that will give it a competitive advantage in the global marketplace. More and more, before we even get to the question of technology choice, those business decisions are going to center around the ability to move information rapidly to the right levels of management, where decisions can be made and then implemented successfully.

In the case of the snack food industry, for example, the name of the game is to have the freshest products on the shelf and to be able to manage the shelf space so that your bestselling products are always in stock, because if you run out of stock, it's a lost sale. It goes to the competition.

You need to be able to respond to something that your competitor does almost immediately. In the 1970s we were more than willing to settle for information every two months that would tell us how our market share was doing in soft drinks or snack foods, and that information was not very detailed. In the 1990s, however, you have to have that information by store, by product, and you've got to be able to have that information usually on a daily basis.

That's an incredible change in the business process, to allow you to have that level of detail of information. Clearly you don't want that detailed information flowing all the way up through the hierarchy of a system that goes up to a command and control executive management in headquarters. It would sink from its own weight. You've got to find a way to get very timely information to the appropriate levels of management, which is why so many corporations are leaning toward more and more decentralization. But you've got to get the information in the right form to that decentralized management so they can quickly make decisions, and those decisions can get quickly implemented.

It's not that the things we're talking about are always new problems. It's just that we have to have new solutions to these problems, and the big difference in the 1990s is the ability to get far more productivity from people working together as opposed to people working by themselves.

Do you have any plans for products that will make so-called dumb objects such as telephones, automobiles, kitchen appliances, or beepers into smart products?
Absolutely. Every successful computer company today is rethinking its core competence for the 1990s. In our case, we think our greatest core competence is ease of use. That's what we're really good at. So why should we just be making easy-to-use desktop computers? We know that the consumer electronics industry is going from analog technology to digital technology. We know that there is a need for a software architecture that enables new kinds of products, whether it's digital TV or electronic books.

We also know that there are going to be revolutionary new products that will be used in business that are going to be highly miniaturized. That in many ways will include the component know-how and miniaturization skills that the Japanese have learned.

**Will we see more alliances with companies such as
Sony to go into these other products?**

Alliances are really going to be required in the information
systems and technology industry of the 1990s, because no one
company can afford to do everything by itself. We will be known
by the company that we keep. In the systems world we have a
seminal relationship with IBM. It gives us entry into the corporate
computing environment with a stamp of approval from the
world's largest and most successful enterprise systems company.
In the consumer field we've had a long relationship with Sony,
and you shouldn't be surprised to see Apple work with several
different Japanese companies, not just a single company. And in
the communications field, we'll continue our long-standing relationship with Motorola.

**How do you answer those who argue that Apple seems
to have lurched from strategy to strategy between
various shake-ups? How long will you hold your
present course?**

Apple's vision of empowering individuals with computers that are
very easy to use hasn't changed at all. What has changed at Apple
was that we tried to move into the business market and not sell
just to enthusiasts and schools, and we've had some success
with that.

Today, Apple accounts for all of the growth in the personal
computer industry. All the worldwide growth is coming from
Apple's products. If we weren't getting the kind of growth we are
from our new products, then we never could have survived in an
industry that is going through a slump. You're rewarded on your
ability to quickly adapt to the changing industry conditions. If you
don't adapt, you don't survive. But what hasn't changed is we
have not abandoned Apple's original vision, nor do we intend to
abandon it during this decade.

The Seduction of Technology

Fred G. Steingraber
Chairman and Chief Executive
A.T. Kearney

Does technology provide a competitive advantage? In the past, U.S. executives said "yes." Recent horror stories have made some lose their faith in its sublime. But others use it judiciously as part of a multidimensional competitive arsenal.

R obotics and sensors. Cellular manufacturing. The factory of the future. Computer-integrated manufacturing expert systems. (Computers that have the capability to simulate expert reasoning). Each of these expert systems represents a major capital investment— and a vision of manufacturing superiority that rarely becomes reality.

This may be oversimplifying the complex question of competitiveness. However, far too many manufacturers have made the decision to invest in automation; they've done so with a limited vision of how the investment relates to their business strategy, how it will help beat the competition, and how it should be implemented—or, even what the alternatives might be.

NEITHER SAVIOR NOR SATAN

Is technology the silver bullet? Or the loaded chamber in a game of Russian roulette? Realistically, technology is neither savior nor satan; its significance has been overemphasized. It is just one of the many tools that can help improve competitiveness. Some companies can even succeed without it.

Our obsession with technology is not new. Americans have always been easily charmed by new gizmos and better mouse-traps. Furthermore, the massive changes wrought in our business and personal lives in the last century by the automobile, the telephone, television, xerography, and facsimile are enough to make one believe in magic. We sometimes have a naive faith in technology as a change agent—in the ability of "something new" to improve our lives. The sight of an electronic product in a mail-order catalog gives us a twinge of Christmas-morning excitement. And so does the potential of a robot that could save 30 percent of direct labor costs.

"Americans tend to believe you can replace people with capital and therefore become more productive," says a retired colleague who has helped clients implement automation. "The Japanese know that when you decide to make a technology investment, you need trained and motivated people to make it pay off," he says.

THE SETTING FOR SEDUCTION

The damage inflicted by foreign competitors in domestic and global markets has made executives seek quick answers. Countless competitors, disappearing market share, and reduced profits scared manufacturers into attempting revolution on the plant floor.

During the last 20 years, worldwide market share for U.S. manufacturers has dropped by two-thirds in electronics, by half in auto production, and by one-third in steel. Two-thirds of the 100 largest public corporations now have foreign ownership. Senior management in most U.S. corporations neglected the factory as an opportunity to secure a competitive advantage.

Since the early 1980s, when U.S. manufacturers became aware that they were no longer kings of the industrial hill, they have tried one solution after another—frequently involving investment in automation. U.S. manufacturers have spent billions on automation: 1987 and 1988 investments in computers and process-control equipment alone totaled about $38 billion. Yet, U.S. durable goods producers still lag far behind Japan in several important measures of competitiveness: work-in-process, inventory lead times, quality defects, equipment age, and annual automation investment per worker. According to the Department of Defense, the United States is behind Japan in private investment in plant and equipment as a percent of GNP—10.2 percent versus 17 percent for Japan.

TECHNOLOGY AS A COMPETITIVE MILLSTONE

A.T. Kearney Technology studied more than 100 cases of corporate technology shortfalls that occurred during the last decade. In more than two-thirds of these situations, one or more of 10 fundamental errors lay at the heart of the technology problem. Not one of the 10 errors was a technology problem; all were management problems.

So much has been written about the dangers of the wrong technology investment that many executives have become skittish about making any commitment. The business press has been full of horror stories about the failure of technology. *Business Week's* June 1988 cover story dealt with "The Productivity Paradox: Why the payoff from automation is so elusive—and what corporate America can do about it." Tom Peters' syndicated column warned, "Robots and automation aren't the real cure for ailing industry." *Boardroom Reports* offered us "Lessons for all to learn from GM and its problems." *Harvard Business Review* published Timothy Warner's article on "Information Technology as a Competitive Burden." *The Chicago Tribune* explored the problem in a series entitled "Technology in America." The article quotes a Purdue University professor and manufacturing expert: "I think there has been a great turning away from technology in manufacturing. A lot of people invested in robots and machines . . . and felt that they got burned. They tried to buy a fix."

Publicity of this sort and industry gossip among suppliers, competitors, and customers have made many executives feel insecure. Results have been disappointing for many companies, but some spectacular and well-publicized horror stories—such as the GM and John Deere experiences—probably were the most damaging. Observers have said that GM's investment of $40 billion over an eight-year period was made without adequate preparation of employees or systems. They continued to lose market share and profits. John Deere's investment in flexible automation for a farm tractor plant was made just before the bottom dropped out of farm prices. Farmers no longer could buy new equipment every two or three years, so Deere was forced to scale back capacity.

There are two dangers in considering the use of technology. One is the possibility of acting precipitously and doing it wrong. The other is the danger of being paralyzed by fear of failure and not acting at all.

Joseph E. Izzo, head of A.T. Kearney's information technology practice, discusses technology strategy in his book, *The Embattled Fortress*. Izzo points out that the enemy is not the technology, nor its user, nor its manufacturer. "The enemy is the status quo—continuing to accept yesterday's solutions to support tomorrow's organization." The worst damage that could be inflicted by the technology millstone would be to make U.S. manufacturers accept the status quo.

Technology has failed to fulfill its promise for several reasons:

The technology bypass

The technology bypass often seems like a shorter route than paying attention to the improvements that should be made instead of, before, or beyond technology. Technology is one of many improvement tools; it is not a panacea for corporate ills. Indeed, some companies have brought about change successfully with little or no technology.

The manufacturer of a well-known gas grill used the less-is-more approach to customer product assembly. Declining sales were at least partly explained by frequent complaints from dealers and consumers about complicated and time-consuming product assembly. The company used value analysis to determine the need to minimize the number of parts and develop interchangeable parts; they also designed a snap-on rather than bolt-on assembly, and rewrote and redesigned an unintelligible instruction manual. These improvements reduced field assembly time to less than 30 minutes, reduced cost of goods by one-third, improved product quality, and doubled sales. Within one year from the date the redesigned product line was introduced, operating profits increased by 300 percent.

In contrast to the GM experience, Ford and Chrysler made modest technology investments but put emphasis on "soft technology"—people involvement, quality improvement, competitive benchmarking, and making better use of existing equipment. Ford's "Quality Is Job One" program was not only effective in achieving manufacturing improvement, but an important marketing advantage as well. Certainly Ford and Chrysler will have to make major technology investments in time to keep up with their U.S. and foreign competition. When they do, they will have created a better environment for the introduction of technology.

Toyota's No.9 Kamigo engine plant was made famous in Richard J. Schonberger's book, *World Class Manufacturing*. It became known as the most efficient engine plant in the world, not by investing billions in new technology, but by taking advantage of equipment already owned. Kamigo's 20-year-old equipment has been retrofitted with improvements such as automatic loaders and checkers. Machines can be set up quickly, eliminating the need to run large batches. There are no large storage areas or storage and handling equipment, so machinery can be laid out in a small space. One operator can handle several machines at once. Engines are made and delivered hourly to the nearby assembly plant.

When Kamigo's output is compared with Chrysler and Ford's engine plants, the differences are startling. The American plants are more than three times larger with inventories measured in days (2.5 to 5 days for Chrysler, 9.3 for Ford), whereas Kamigo's inventory is 4 to 5 hours. Kamigo's labor per engine is less than 1 hour, versus 5.5 hours for the Chrysler and Ford plants. The final surprise: This is Toyota's oldest plant.

Strategic advantage

Too many U.S. manufacturers seem unable to evaluate technology's contribution to strategic advantage—how it can enhance efforts to improve quality, customer value, responsiveness, and cycle time or increase product offerings. U.S. executives are good at evaluating capital investment in terms of productivity, ROI, direct labor, and other cost-reduction implications and creative applications.

Waterloo Industries, a manufacturer of professional tool cabinets, is a good example of technology used for strategic advantage. The company found its high-end market threatened by competitors from the Far East who brought the price down to 40 percent below the current market. The company knew incremental cost-cutting would no longer protect its share of the high-end industrial market and meet the competition head-on in the consumer market. Moreover, offshore relocation or outsourcing were not appropriate answers to closing the major cost differential.

After thoroughly studying the direct labor portion of the value-added cost chain, the company made design changes to improve manufacturability, and proposed plans to adopt computer-assisted design and manufacturing. This resulted in lowering direct labor costs by 90 percent. But more importantly, management explored options for making greater use of the larger capacity that the changes would provide. They concluded that they could successfully enter new markets with new products by supplying components to manufacturers of office and hospital storage cabinets. The introduction of technology protected their current product and provided them with a competitive cost advantage for new markets.

Honda Motors provides yet another example of business strategy successfully driving manufacturing strategy. Honda North America is known for flexible manufacturing systems that can easily switch from Civic to Accord production. In fact, Honda threatens to replace Chrysler as No. 3 among U.S. auto manufacturers. When the Honda Civic was first introduced in the U.S. market, Japanese manufacturing technology enabled Honda to lure American consumers to their unknown car with a price tag of $2,000. Honda's technology delivered the low unit cost, quality, and value that accomplished Honda's strategy of endearing the car to American drivers. Now Honda could diversify models and move into higher value-added products. Their strategy was aided by their ability to switch from one product and feature to another.

A modest investment in computer-integrated manufacturing made it possible for Allen Bradley (AB), a manufacturer of electric motor starters, to increase its responsiveness to customers. The technology allowed AB to operate as if its factory were many minifactories. A total investment of $15 million enabled the company to cut costs by almost 40 percent and gain flexibility. Their new operation could quickly switch production from one product to another in lots as small as one unit—with 125 variations on motor starters. The AB plant blended product design, manufacturing systems, and computer controls with strategic management.

Frito-Lay, the Dallas-based snack-food company, has many products and a manufacturing and store-delivery system that must quickly move materials from farm to grocery shelf. The operation consists of 100 products in 240 package size variations, produced in 38 plants and sent to 1,650 distribution centers. That totals thousands of possible order configurations.

The growth in new products, spurred by the need to remain competitive in the snack-food industry, meant that route sales staff were buried in paper and the company was printing new order forms on a weekly basis. Frito-Lay spent four years evaluating strategy before deciding to equip its 10,000-person route sales force with handheld computers. The company estimates they save each salesperson about an hour in paperwork per day and provide better cash control. Most of all, the equipment helps the salesperson respond to customer needs and demands. By providing superior service, Frito-Lay justifies its share of shelf space in grocers' snack-food sections.

Preparatory work

Unrealistic expectations about the preparation necessary to introduce technology may doom the project. Management often feels the hard work is done in the boardroom where capital expenditures are rigorously reviewed and approved. While anticipating that a class or self-teaching manual will be needed to prepare workers for a revolution in work practices, the preparation effort is often underestimated by a factor of at least three to five times. A substantial amount of time and funds is needed for retraining, development of new skills, and sufficient practice in using them before the changeover to new technology can be successful.

Xerox Corporation did its preparatory work right. Xerox wrote one of the most successful product innovation stories in history with its first plain paper copier in the 1960s. Although in the late 1970s, half its market share disappeared, Xerox ignored emerging competition from home and abroad for a long time. But after studying Japanese manufacturing techniques, they made major changes, driven by business strategy. Xerox concentrated on enabling their people to succeed in the new environment. They trained design engineers as generalists so they could design for cost, manufacturability, and serviceability. They initiated a "team-work day," where employees demonstrate business improvement ideas. In 1982 there were 500 entries; in 1986, some 6,000 Xerox employees demonstrated ways to improve quality.

Xerox also radically changed the way they worked with suppliers. Suppliers were consulted much earlier in the cycle, so they could contribute to the design and manufacturing process. The number of vendors was cut from 5,000 to 300. Quality and reliability became priorities; quality problems were cut by two-thirds in two years. Computer-aided design systems shortened development time and reduced development costs. Xerox reduced the labor content of its products, as well as the number of parts. It cut new product introduction time in half. The results were stunning: sales and profits both increased, despite falling prices in the marketplace.

Measurement systems

As technology helps move plants, offices, and warehouses to a less labor-intensive environment, new measures are needed of employee performance and pay, including cost per unit produced, quality or rework, and capacity utilization. Management needs new methods to make decisions and evaluate the success of technology investments.

Traditional methods contribute to the "measuring-the-wrong-thing" problem. Most current cost-accounting systems were developed when direct labor was a major component of manufacturing costs. Today, direct labor is typically a small component of the value-added chain. In addition, actual costs per product may be difficult to obtain since costs are usually allocated horizontally across plant or division, rather than vertically by product. Also, management needs to continually adjust to more ambitious targets to improve productivity, net quality, and customer responsiveness.

In the case of a Fortune 100 durable goods manufacturer, missing and misplaced measurements were resulting in costly state-of-the-art technology operating at one-quarter to one-third the uptime levels of competition. Functional units produced optimal results within their traditional measures of accountability. Maintenance, for instance, continued to minimize spare parts inventory to the detriment of uptime. Production supervisors maximized direct labor efficiency, but didn't staff the transfer lines to avoid downtime. On top of this, key integrating measures, such as cost per unit and uptime, were missing altogether. Then management began to measure machine uptime, find sources of downtime, and change its organization and measurement methods. Uptime on the plant's transfer lines increased an average of 52 percent and cost per unit declined about 21 percent. Long-term results are expected to be even better.

Jos. A. Bank Clothiers manufactures every item of clothing in its own plants and sells directly to the consumer in its 34 stores and by catalog. A privately held business, Bank utilizes some of the latest technology available in the clothing industry—yet still manufactures clothing by hand the way it was done when the company was founded early in the century. The new technology is found primarily in the distribution center, where computers and conveyor grids move the merchandise out.

Measurement systems were adapted to new equipment and procedures. Now the firm uses a flexible pay-for-performance plan for manufacturing and distribution workers, based on a definition of 100 percent performance for each job. When new equipment is introduced, the 100 percent rate is set after workers have used the equipment for a break-in period, not on the basis of theory or past practices. Jos. A. Bank's management attributes its success to its ownership from 1981 to 1986 by the Quaker Oats Company, as well as by its careful management. Today, the 1,900-employee firm's annual sales are more than 20 times what they were in the early 1970s.

KEYS TO SUCCESSFUL IMPLEMENTATION

Technology by itself is rigid. It offers no solutions, often creates more problems than it solves, and deludes management into thinking it has taken care of manufacturing problems by signing a purchase order. But there are ways for both high-tech and low-tech executives to sail around the tempting sirens of technology without crashing against the rocks.

Consider whether new technology is needed

Does the company have the culture, skills, and resources to absorb technology now? View automation as one of many tools to nurture productivity and improve competitiveness and, of course, profits. If existing technology hasn't been managed well, new technology may be doomed before it arrives.

Understand overall competitive strategy

Before you invest in new manufacturing technology, you must consider your overall competitive strategy, including customer demand and market potential. How will the addition of new technology add value to your product? How can new technology improve customer responsiveness and make customers more dependent upon your product? Can new technology tie into your customer's needs or even your customer's systems so that your products and services are invaluable to the customer?

Your new technology should enable you to invite your customer in to see the changes and perceive the benefits to his business. If your technology does not help the customer attain his goals, then it may not provide a strategic advantage for you.

Prepare comprehensively

Take a careful and thorough look at preparatory work necessary to introduce automation. Don't underestimate the time required for full implementation at all levels. Be sure all the interfaces are in place before making any investments. Be aware of implications for maintenance, scheduling, and inventory practices. Review all measurement systems—especially performance and quality—because they may have to change. Check out training programs and packages to make sure they can be adapted to your needs.

Execute carefully

Encourage participation of the total organization during the implementation period to share successes and learn from unsuccessful experiences. Careful and thorough communication is necessary, especially the opportunity of two-way communication with line workers using the equipment.

While the goal is the immediate improvement of the competitive position, a critical by-product is technological literacy and enthusiasm for technology's potential, in order to create an environment where technology is continually upgraded to help sustain competitive advantage.

Technology must be integrated throughout your organization. Get people in different functions and departments talking to each other. Use research and development or information technology staffs as resources on equipment recommendations and capabilities of different systems. But charge all managers with exploring whether and how technology can improve the productivity of their functions and the competitiveness of the business. The addition of technology then becomes not an event, but part of an ongoing process. The question is not "technology, yes or no?" but using different degrees and types of technology at different times.

BACK TO KAIZEN

The Japanese word *kaizen* expresses this approach to manufacturing competitiveness: constant improvement. No single management decision will bring about the ultimate improvement from which the company can continually reap benefits. No matter how major the change made today, it is just another step in a continuing process. Good is never good enough if a company is to gain and retain a competitive advantage.

Those who express reservations about technology are not modern-day Luddites. At the very least, we should all look at new technology with some hesitation. Far too many U.S. manufacturers have unused or misused technology. If we have not succeeded in managing what we have, how will more bells and whistles help? As the poster in a food-processing plant says: "Life is like a ten-speed bike. Most of us have gears we never use." How many of us own ten-speeds, but never shift into more than three gears?

In the long run, companies in the high-cost industrial countries will have to seek competitive advantage through technology. Management has to ask the questions: not *why* or *if*, but *when* and *how*. How is the important question and the hardest one to answer.

Kaizen does not allow basking in yesterday's successes. It does not require spectacular and meteoric improvement. Kaizen requires acting, rather than paralysis. If you seek kaizen, you will use technology as one method to alleviate a perpetual itch for change.

Fred G. Steingraber is chairman and CEO of A.T. Kearney, Inc. During his 24-year career with the firm, he has been instrumental in launching many of its foreign offices and has served in a variety of positions in the United States and Europe. He is an expert on strategy and competitive challenges, frequently speaking on the subject in print and broadcast forums and to audiences in the United States and abroad.

The Information Edge

Alexander D. Jacobson
Chairman
Inference Corporation

Chief executives will need to rethink what information—the data endowed with relevance and purpose—means for them. In information-based companies, "endowed" knowledge may well come from the bottom.

U sing information technology (IT) to gain a competitive edge has become a necessity for corporations worldwide. In the past, IT was used to gain a competitive edge by only a few U.S. companies (for example, the SABRE airline reservation system at American Airlines, the package-tracking system at Federal Express, ATMs at Citicorp, and on-line ordering at American Hospital Supply). There were other ways to win.

Now, driven by the increasing power of computers, the world has changed. Markets are becoming global, first-tier companies are becoming unmanageably large, back-office computers are deluging front-office workers with undigestible amounts of data, and telecommunications are increasing the speed of business transactions beyond human reaction times. To compete successfully in this environment, corporations must use the leverage provided by IT.

THE UNITED STATES AT THE CROSSROADS

On the surface this situation appears to be advantageous to U.S. companies. America has led the world in both the innovation and the exploitation of IT. American computer companies dominate world computer markets, and our businesses are heavily computerized. However, the need to use IT competitively poses a major new challenge to our leadership position. The majority of information systems operating in U.S. companies are dedicated to back-office business functions, (e.g., accounting systems, inventory systems, personnel records). To compete using information, we must redirect IT programs away from the automation of back-office tasks toward the automation of front-office business operations (e.g., marketing, sales, customer service, credit authorization) where they can be used in applications designed to gain competitive advantage. The timing is right to make this transition for two reasons: First, the task of automating the back office is largely completed, so resources once dedicated to that task are now available to be used elsewhere; and second, recent advances in computer technology have made it economically and technically practical to automate the front office.

Shifting the focus of IT to front-office applications represents a major change in the way IT is used by American businesses, and transitions in technology exploitation are always threatening—particularly for the leaders. Entrenched interests, established in the process of creating the lead, are usually substantial and are always strongly resistant to change. Large investments made to create assets that helped build the lead must be protected, which leads to problems of obsolescence. The exploitation of technology by business is an intrinsically difficult and demanding process, and managing this process through a period of change is doubly difficult.

American companies are not adequately prepared to manage this transition. There is a deep schism in most U.S. corporations that separates the employees who manage and do the company's business from those who are responsible for and build the company's IT. This schism is caused by a culture gap between the business and the technology sides of the company. It turns routine IT initiatives into difficult technology transfer processes rather than simple business development tasks. One consequence is ragged exploitation of IT that blunts the competitive edge that U.S. companies need as our markets go global.

The management of the transition must be led by the CEO. Delegation of this leadership role to a chief information officer or to a functional equivalent will not work. The CEO is the only person in most corporations who has the position and the authority to manage cultural issues effectively. If the CEO is not committed to a policy of aggressively using IT, internal barriers will prevent it from being practiced with the vigor and at the level of excellence required to compete with a company that has made the top-level commitment.

BUSINESS OPERATIONS, TECHNOLOGY, AND THE CULTURE GAP

There are two major subcultures within our society as well as within our corporations: technologists or tool makers and business people or wealth-makers. These two subcultures co-exist and are interdependent, but they are not naturally sympathetic to the needs and interests of each other. It is rare that the successful businessperson is versed in the culture of tools. It is also rare that a capable technologist has a highly developed feeling for business.

For example, the basic period whereby business is measured in America is the quarter; the next, and only other important business period, is the business year. On the other hand, there are few significant IT initiatives that can be developed, deployed, evaluated, and assimilated in less than several years. This mismatch in natural periods is one of the major obstacles to integrating technology programs into business practice. Another example is that the introduction of technology implies change. Again, a fundamental property of technology—to cause change—is at odds with a basic need of business—to minimize risk. So the gap between the culture of business and the culture of technology is a natural phenomenon. It is not the result of poor organization, nor of mismanagement, nor of any other failing on the part of people.

In most corporations, there is not only a culture gap between business operations and systems regarding IT, but there are organizational and political gaps as well. Historically, IT has reported up the management chain through finance rather than through business operations. This is because the initial applications of IT were designed and built for the financial side of the business (e.g., payroll, accounting, inventory control). In addition, the equipment was usually purchased from capital budgets administered by finance. As a result, systems organizations nucleated and grew in the back office, separate from the operating divisions that generated the revenues and served the company's customers.

The consequence of these gaps has been to force even routine IT initiatives to overcome formidable institutional barriers in order to achieve success—barriers that have little or nothing to do with the nature or value of the technology project itself. If IT is to be used competitively, these barriers must be eliminated. The process of bringing IT into the front office must be systematic, manageable, and practical for the business people who require the use of the technology. Otherwise, IT will remain a back-office asset and a front-office burden.

To become efficient at integrating IT into business operations requires fundamental changes in the way IT is practiced. These changes can only be made if the CEO insists upon and leads the process of change.

U.S. SUCCESS STORIES

Several visionary companies have made this executive commitment to change, including American Airlines, American Express, American Hospital Supply, American President Companies, Citicorp, Federal Express, and Ford Motor Company. Some of these companies have already reaped major competitive advantages. American Airlines, with its famous SABRE travel reservation system; American Hospital Supply, with its on-line ordering system; Citicorp and American Express, with their general use of computers to support front-office operations; and Federal Express, a company that built its entire business operations on an information system foundation: all are well-known success stories. Each of these programs was driven by the CEO.

Bob Crandall, CEO of American Airlines; John Reed, CEO of Citicorp New York; Lou Gerstner, president of American Express; Fred Smith, CEO of Federal Express; and Karl D. Bays, CEO of American Hospital Supply, all played critical roles in the IT successes of their companies. For example, at American President Companies (APC), CEO Bruce Seaton implemented innovative organizational structures designed to accelerate the use of IT by the company's service workers around the globe. The new structure is designed to make this shipping container company more responsive to the constantly changing needs of its customers. At Ford, CEO Donald E. Petersen has committed his company to the strategic initiative of using IT to dramatically reduce the time required by Ford's designers and engineers to take a new car from concept to customer.

A CASE HISTORY

In a carefully orchestrated process of organizational and cultural change, APC's Seaton is infusing IT into the business operations of his company. To make APC more competitive, Seaton is extending the company's use of computers beyond data management to direct participation in on-line decision making throughout its business operations. His goal: use decision automation to provide more reliable customer service. To make this change, Seaton undertook two major initiatives. He radically changed the organization and practice of APC's information resources division and he implemented several IT initiatives designed to alter the corporate culture so it would become compatible with IT solutions. His intent was to move IT into business operations quickly and permanently.

The most important organizational change he made was in breaking down the barriers between systems and operations by creating a new information resources organization staffed equally from the corporate systems organization and from business operation units. Seaton carefully chose people for this new organization who had already demonstrated strong interest in the type of work done by the other group; that is, he chose business people who were interested in computers and systems people who were interested in business practice. The managers in this new organization report directly to business operations management; in addition, they report dotted line to the management of the corporate systems organization. This change created a new information resources organization that is driven directly by the business side of the company that has an internal culture formed from an

intermingling of business and technology, and that is answerable to systems professionals on technical issues. Seaton personally works with this new organization on a routine basis to formulate and implement specific projects that:
- Automate APC's front-office operations;
- Set APC technology and systems quality standards; and
- Support new technology initiatives until they are fully operational.

Seaton changed the corporate culture with regard to IT first by installing a worldwide telecommunications system that puts all of APC's far-flung offices on the same network, then by buying and dedicating an IBM mainframe to create a network-wide electronic mail system with which to establish "screen consciousness" in APC's army of field service agents. He also increased the number of PCs on the desks of his business operations people from six in 1983 to 1,300 at present. These programs, combined with the radical change Seaton instituted in his information resources organization, have created an appetite for increased automation on the part of his front-office work force. Furthermore, his programs created an atmosphere that facilitates, rather than resists, the rollout of new computer capabilities as they emerge from the information resources group. Finally, they have reduced the burden and risk of generating and implementing the IT projects that bring automation support to the front-office workers. Since the program is new, it is too early to judge its overall impact on the company. But one thing is clear: without Seaton's sponsorship and guidance, the program would not exist.

ELIMINATING THE CULTURE GAP—A SYSTEMATIC APPROACH

Information technology, unlike all other technologies, is concerned with automating what people *know* rather than what they *do*. As a consequence, to practice IT correctly, the employees who will use the technology must be active participants in developing, installing, and maintaining it. Current IT practice does include the users in this process. However, user involvement must increase as business practices close to the company's customers become automated. The more the function impacts customers, the more complex, ambiguous, and changeable are the associated information and business knowledge. So those who use the technology need to participate in determining how the system employs and applies this information.

As computer systems progress from manipulating data to providing true decision automation (making business decisions by computer in concert with human decision-makers), their development must move from being largely in the hands of the systems organization to being shared in a partnership between business operations and systems. These partnerships must be established at the level of the individual piece of application software being built.

Many of these observations have come from my company's experiences in spearheading the introduction of expert systems technology into more than 150 of America's largest corporations. This new software technology, created to bring automation to the front-office work force, can contain and automatically apply far greater quantities of business knowledge than equivalent conventional software technologies. This new type of software requires that those who use and manage the expert system work together throughout the development process with those who program it. This departure from conventional software practice is caused by the focus of the expert system development process on the business practice it supports. In the past, the practice of IT so heavily focused on the computer itself, has been poorly related to business. The new, more powerful information technologies, due to their requirements, offer, for the first time, the opportunity to integrate business operations and systems.

To facilitate that integration, the traditional ROI analysis of expense-reduction benefits for justifying IT projects should be abandoned. Systems that enhance customer relations, implement new marketing strategies, improve morale, or facilitate interdepartmental cooperation may not survive conventional ROI analysis, which usually focuses on expense reduction and ignores intangible or unproven benefits. New methodologies based on marketing and business opportunity analysis must replace ROI in judging the value of front-office automation projects. All of these changes are directly opposed by the institutional barriers that arise from the current practice of IT. These changes cannot be implemented effectively bottom-up; they must be implemented top-down through the authority, enthusiasm, and earnest commitment of the CEO. Specifically, the CEO must:

• Create a strategic-IT plan that defines specific IT initiatives within the context of the company's overall strategic plan;

• Include projects in the strategic IT plan that specifically require deeply integrated participation of business operations and systems (i.e., projects that bring automation to the front-office workers of the company);

• Ensure that the requisite partnerships between systems and operations become a working reality;

• Renovate the review process to focus IT projects on marketing and business opportunity benefits rather than on expense reduction considerations;

• Serve as the rallying point and symbol of the company's commitment to move IT into the front office.

Recent revolutionary advances within the computer industry have led to the emergence of "expert systems," software technology that can leverage the process of change required to move IT more aggressively into business operations. Expert systems are software applications that contain expert-level competence about specific business tasks. This technology uses humanlike reasoning processes to arrive automatically at solutions to the business problems for which it is designed. Expert systems were created to provide decision automation for the first- and second-tier decision makers who make the vast number of routine business decisions every day as they carry out front-office business operations.

In order to build an expert system successfully, the company must first address and bridge the cultural, political, and organizational gaps that separate the business people involved in the project from their technical and systems counterparts.

Expert systems embody substantially larger amounts of pure business knowledge than conventional programs. In order to acquire and program this knowledge, those who have the knowledge and the technologists who program the knowledge must work in a partnership throughout the life cycle of the system. Using expert systems can help to effect general change in the practice of IT in the company.

One of the most significant uses of expert systems has been implemented jointly by American Express (AMEX) and Inference Corporation to assist AMEX credit authorizers in deciding about the acceptability of credit transactions made with AMEX credit cards. This project arose from a technology initiative created several years ago by Lou Gerstner, president of AMEX, to seek and master new information technologies with which to build the foundation for AMEX' next generation of information systems. Although the initiative was not formulated to bridge the operations/systems gap, it did, in fact, forge a working partnership between systems and operations during the three years the system was in development. Gerstner's staff, having selected expert systems as one of the new technologies to be considered, created a specific systems project targeted to support business-operations decision makers— specifically, the credit authorizers. If technically successful, the expert system would be deployed as a production decision-automation system. The project was carried out in three phases. First, the development of a pilot version of the expert system was funded as a research and development project to establish and validate the technical performance of the system. Secondly, a business analysis was performed to forecast the system's economic payback. Finally, the expert system was integrated into the existing production environment that supports the American Express credit authorization process.

Three groups worked in partnership throughout the project: AMEX credit authorization operations personnel (the users/experts), AMEX systems people (the database and application software professionals), and Inference expert system development professionals (the expert systems builders/integrators).

Throughout the first phase—which took 15 calendar months to complete—all three groups worked routinely as a single development team. For example, during the second half of Phase I, weekly teleconferences were held, often involving more than 20 participants from around the United States, for the purpose of coordinating the work of these groups. The transition from the first phase to the second phase was an internal handoff of the project within AMEX from corporate research and development to credit card business operations. The second phase was primarily a business operations function that relied upon the AMEX systems organization to perform data analysis and provide technical advice. The decision to proceed from pilot to production system was made by the executive in charge of AMEX card businesses.

The transition from Phase II to Phase III was a handoff from card operations to systems to integrate the completed expert system into the production environment of the credit-authorization computer system. This phase was, once again, implemented by all three groups—AMEX credit operations and systems organizations and Inference—working together.

The Authorizer's Assistant expert system, as AMEX dubbed the application, was installed as a production system and is in daily use in the United States by all AMEX domestic credit authorizers. The joint efforts of AMEX' systems and business operations people have produced a successful production expert system that now supports an important front-office business function of their company. The system has successfully challenged the institutional barriers between business operations and systems, and has overcome the resistance that typically opposes the introduction of new technology into business—proving that expert systems technology can be used to overcome the intrinsic schisms and impediments that threaten front-office IT programs.

The conventional wisdom in business is to be cautious in bringing a new way of doing business into practice. But in the case of IT, change in business practice—driven by aggressive use of IT—should be encouraged, not avoided. The issue is not whether or not to change, but how to *manage* change so that it happens quickly, efficiently, and successfully, with minimal disruption. Proper implementation of a strategic IT program that aggressively automates the company's business operations will move that company to the forefront in its markets.

Alexander D. Jacobson is founder, and chairman of Inference Corporation, a Los Angeles-based firm that develops and markets advanced expert systems for business, industry, and government.

Are You Unhappy with Your Company's IT Payback?

Robert Bittlestone
President and Chief Executive
Metapraxis

The honeymoon is over.

It's running at several hundred billion annually, with a double-digit growth rate. It dwarfs the federal budget deficit, the defense department allocation, and total annual education spending. In terms of national expenditure, it's one of the 50 largest countries in the world. It permeates every facet of corporate life and affects every decision that we make. It is arguably the single most crucial weapon in the race to win the international business olympics. It is, of course, our annual expenditure on computerization—and it is dangerously out of control.

Over the last few years, I've listened to over a hundred CEOs of major international corporations and government agencies who expressed their views on information technology (IT). Less than 15 percent believe that they are getting their money's worth from their IT investments. Less than 12 percent consider their IT projects to be under proper control, and less than 10 percent regard it as acceptable for their IT projects to be so time-consuming and expensive. Remarkably, less than 5 percent can recall any IT project ever delivering the promised results on time and within budget, or believe that these problems will no longer recur.

Inflationary IT expenditure, coupled with a dubious payback, is now a major concern of CEOs. Other problems may be tough, but a good CEO can solve them. Mergers and acquisitions policy, market share, price performance, labor relations, product research, competitive response, just-in-time, quality circles—none of these are straightforward, but they all fall into the bag of business challenges that a CEO is equipped to tackle.

IT problems are different. They are presented in a language that seems to bear no relation to business goals. When we're asked for our verdict on a $25 million development program for product research and development, we don't expect the text of the proposal to dwell on the detailed physics of superconductivity. When we're hit with an IT project proposal of similar size, the wording makes our eyes glaze before the foot of the first page. The terminology is alien, while the technology is the prime focus. The business has been relegated to the sidelines and the cost-justification doesn't jell. It's no wonder that a CEO I know in the oil business says, "When I hear the word computer, I reach for my capital expenditure veto."

Some CEOs are attempting to solve the problem by pouring more dollars into IT. One technique is to appoint a Chief Information Officer (CIO) at the executive committee or board level. The short-term advantage is that you can off-load your new CIO with all the IT paperwork that's been collecting dust in your in-box. The risk is that your CIO then starts to build an empire, and subsequently finds it hard to understand that your sanity and survival depend on pushing profit responsibility down the chart. The one thing a CEO cannot live with is a high-level, major cost center. Even the CFO usually has dotted-line, not solid-line, reporting relationships with divisional financial staff. A CIO needs to be both saint and master of diplomacy if he is to avoid creating major tensions with divisional chief executives.

Another approach is to engage consultants, not just to advise on a solution, but to operate some or all of the data processing activity on a permanent basis. The immediate effect is gratifying: tough professionalism on project specifications; internal "clients" signing-off on measured benefits; impressive (albeit inscrutable) methodologies; an end to programmers, and the arrival of programs that write other programs. However, the fees tend to escalate rather rapidly, sometimes exponentially, especially when the consultants regularly present you with the compelling logic of keeping up with the standards of the rest of the industry. The consultants seem to know much more about this than your previous in-house IT people did, and it's uncomfortable to ignore their advice, even though your CFO is starting to appear a bit ragged as the fees arrive.

Conversations about IT expenditure seem to revolve around the need for more and more mainframes. The old ones could be enhanced, but not nearly enough for the daunting complexity and uniquely insatiable data appetite of your business. Also extolled are the benefits of distributed processing, which you thought would replace the mainframes, but it turns out that you need them both. This also includes each employee's PC—yet another indispensible tool—which you might have thought was the same as distributed processing, but it is not. Since PCs are becoming more and more complex, it won't be long before corporate profitability is deemed to be conditional on the next gadget—no doubt a solar-powered, aurally implanted picocomputer, with a built-in cellular telephone and fax unit that prints out data from under your hat.

There's also a great enthusiasm for electronic mail, which helps us to send more internal memos—although it's not much use for communicating with customers, which some of us used to think was a nice idea. It looks like we were wrong, because the IT department has now introduced a voice-mail system that allows you to avoid direct phone contact with customers altogether. This time-saving system will enable us to improve our administrative efficiency with desktop publishing, which is turning every employee into a latter-day Gutenberg. Requests to take vacations already startle us by arriving at our desks resembling the front page of *The Wall Street Journal*.

The real turning point will occur with a project called relational database. We can now access the answers—in real time, to the nearest decimal point—to numerous questions, which include once unsolvable corporate conundrums, such as how many left-handed sales representatives we have in Minneapolis who speak Greek.

If you are one of the fortunate few who regard these scenarios as science fiction, there's no need to read on. If, however, these parables look as if they've been plagiarized from your own corporate casebook, the rest of this article is aimed at providing you with a solution.

IN THE BEGINNING

The earliest computers were both expensive and complex, and because of this, we centralized them into a single function. We created a new profession of computer specialists. By contrast, modern computers of comparable power are both inexpensive and simple. Because they are inexpensive and simple, we no longer need to centralize them, nor are we in need of specialists. If we were suddenly presented with the modern computer as a *fait accompli*, we would deploy it in our business in a very different way. There are two reasons why we don't. First, as CEOs, we are conditioned by previous experiences to think of the computer as expensive and complex; therefore, the obvious solutions seem counterintuitive. Our mental processes are not so ossified as to be incapable of any evolution at all, but the microelectronic revolution has been too rapid for this to have occurred. Therefore, we tend to lack the courage of those convictions that we readily apply to other comparable opportunities.

Second, computer specialists have an understandable career interest in guaranteeing and preserving the previous expense and complexity because they have become more interested in the computer than in the business. If this is a conspiracy, it is by no means unique. Our lawyers are more interested in law than in profit; our accountants prefer to certify results than to improve them; our research biochemists would rather grow bacteria than balance sheets, so we should hardly blame IT professionals for promoting ingenious projects that continue to require expensive and complex computers.

The combination of these conditions means that whenever we consider an investment in IT, we should ask ourselves two questions: How would I approach this decision if we had never made any previous investment in IT? And, what would my IT group be proposing if they were more interested in the business than the computer? There are far-reaching ramifications to this type of thinking (See Box 4-1).

Box 4–1

How To Manage In The Land Of IT

1. IT department staff must be drawn from the ranks of business end-users, not career computer professionals.
2. They may spend up to a maximum of two years in the IT department before they return to a business function.
3. They should be on a performance-related bonus inversely proportional to the total that the IT department spends.
4. Each project must be under the line control of an appropriate senior end-user who is not in the IT department.
5. All system development must physically take place in the end-user department for which the project is being developed.
6. All cost-justification for IT projects must be based on end-user commitment to achieving quantified bottom-line benefits.
7. Because computers are getting cheaper, every computer we buy should cost less than the previous one.
8. Because software packages are so universal, in-house development should be the exception rather than the norm.
9. The IT function should be decentralized to the lowest level actively requesting its own capability.
10. The CEO should use a PC to improve his understanding of IT and to develop insight into the business.

At this point, IT should have become a disposable good. Unfortunately, the way in which we attempt to run it at present makes that impossible. Instead of regarding IT as a natural component of any business function, under the "vertical" control of each local line manager we have distorted the corporate structure by "horizontally" pulling IT out of the matrix. In order to understand what this implies, let's look at the most humble of products: the ballpoint pen.

The ballpoint pen was invented in the 1930s to help aircraft pilots write at high altitudes. The first ballpoint pens represented a triumph of precision mechanical engineering, with a close-tolerance machined housing for the tiny ball bearing that rolls on the paper. They cost approximately $75 each—a considerable sum at that time. Because of this, ballpoint pens were kept under lock and key when out of use. Mass production rapidly brought down prices to today's cost of fifty cents. Suppose this was not the case? Instead of IT, we would have ended up with Ballpoint Technology (BT), and have been faced with a very different corporate world.

THE CEO AND BT

Looking at today's corporate charts, we can see that effective management of BT is one of the most pressing problems a CEO has to face. The ballpoint technology department is generally centralized. Specialist professionals, or "scribes," have merged to maximize the efficiency of the use of the *Pen*. They have developed complex techniques for high-speed writing, ink conservation, fluid flow optimization, as well as interfacing to other systems of registration such as pencils. Requests for use of the scarce writing resource are prioritized against corporate goals, but there is still a two-year backlog of documents waiting to be enscribed. A CBO (Chief Ballpoint Officer) has recently been appointed to advise the CEO on an appropriate groupwide BT strategy.

One of the most effective ways for a CEO to change his own attitude toward computing is to *use* a computer. Many CEOs adopted this approach when the spreadsheet became available, and some found it genuinely useful. However, the problem with the spreadsheet, from a CEO's viewpoint, is that there are no interesting problems to solve. The recent availability of full-scale executive information systems that fit onto desktop or laptop PCs has changed the ground rules. It's a genuinely valuable exercise to scan the business trends and exceptional problems for your divisions, subsidiaries, and competitors; it sharpens up the whole apparatus of performance review and budget negotiation. Equally important, when you sit down to use such a tool, is that you realize that computers are simple and inexpensive, and you don't need to be intimidated by IT at all.

In implementing executive information systems for many CEOs, I've noticed that after a month or two of use, a CEO starts to form a robust and effective "top-down" view of the information that's coming up the pyramid. He develops rather strong opinions about whether anyone really needs to know about all those left-handed salespeople. He begins to see why the IT people want you to spend a substantial amount of money on real-time information flow at every management level, because that's a technically exciting progression from real-time information flow at the transaction processing level. In essence, you find yourself using your executive information system as a shortcut toward developing the same kind of personal rapport and gut feel for discussions about IT as you already possess for discussions about marketing, engineering, and everything else.

There is light at the end of the IT tunnel, and it doesn't have to be the light of an oncoming train. Your IT group contains many outstanding people who will make excellent businessmen. Your business subsidiaries contain many outstanding people who will thrive for a year or two in IT. There is no need for confrontation; this can be a win-win strategy. The stakes are enormous. Apart from saving a literal fortune on unnecessary IT developments, you will find that the redirection of IT effort toward real business goals will provide major bottom-line improvements.

The honeymoon with IT is over; let the real marriage begin. If nothing else, the enlightened partnership that will follow should save you from the kind of horror stories that emerge when computerization goes wrong, as it did for a well-known London department store that decided to mailshot its account customers. Unnoticed in the 100,000 letters was one delivered to:

Mr. H.R.H. Prince,
Charles Buckingham Palace,
The Mall, London, SW1
Dear Mr. Prince,
Have you ever considered the benefits of buying a new car? Just think what your neighbors in "The Mall" would say if they saw you driving into Charles Buckingham Palace in a brand new Ford Fiesta complete with motorized sunroof and matching alloy wheels?

Apparently, the neighbors' views were not recorded.

Robert Bittlestone is president and chief executive of Metapraxis Inc. During his nine-year career with the firm, he has been instrumental in launching both the London and New York offices, and aiding in the development of the award-winning chief executive information software system, RESOLVE.

Knowledge in a Box

Winston J. Wade
President
US West Information Technologies

*Expert systems and artificial intelligence are computer technologies
that attempt to imitate the reasoning process of human experts.
Applications of this "knowledge in a box" invariably have been
back-office operations. Now front-office uses, no longer technology in
search of a problem, are beginning to reach CEO desks.*

A critical rule in technology development is that market solutions inevitably drive technology, not vice versa. Technologies get adopted because they serve a business purpose, not because
they are technically possible. Perhaps the classic example of a technology in search of a market is the videophone, developed in 1968.
It was a technological triumph but did not succeed in the market.

Artificial intelligence (AI) will surely prove to be no exception to
this rule. But for the sake of illustration, consider the following
fanciful—and not market-based—vision of the future. The next time
you have to make a long-distance call to a large client, imagine
doing it this way.

Instead of picking up a phone, you simply touch your touch-
sensitive screen and speak a few simple commands. "Please
return Mr. Harima's call," you instruct the screen.

"It's 7:00 P.M. in Japan," a well-modulated voice reminds you.
Within seconds, an image of your client appears on the screen and
the meeting begins. With another touch of the screen, the conversation is automatically translated from Japanese to English and
from English to Japanese.

"I'm sorry to be calling you so late," you tell him. "I see from our quality report that our diagnostics have detected and repaired a few minor problems in your system. Is that why you called?"

"No, we haven't noticed any problems," Mr. Harima assures you. "I just wanted to add on an associate who would like to discuss your new product."

As the third party is added to the call, you use your touch screen to call up an expert sales adviser system that displays account information on the Japanese company and sales copy points for your new products in different quadrants of your screen, both invisible to the client. The system recommends a solution that can easily be integrated with their existing systems— then runs a short videotape of the product.

"We will discuss this with our engineers and get back to you," Mr. Harima says, ending the conversation with a bow. After you return the bow, the screen goes blank for a moment. Then it is filled with an image of your daily newsclip report, assembled automatically from a survey of 50 international newspapers. As you scan reports of significance to your company, the well-modulated voice reminds you, "I've scheduled Ms. Worthing for a 9:00 A.M. meeting. . . ."

A hypothetical office setting of tomorrow? Perhaps. A typical office? Perhaps. But as noted earlier, technology won't be the deciding factor. The market will determine whether or not today's fantasy becomes tomorrow's actuality. Some of the AI technology that would make this transpacific meeting possible is already out of the labs, helping businesses meet marketplace demand, manage global competitive challenges, and increase worker productivity.

But some of the technology in the scenario may never reach a broad market. An intelligent scheduler, complete with voice synthesis and recognition capabilities, might be useful, but with a seven-figure price tag, it's not likely to reach every manager's desk. And how many of us will ever read a customized newspaper with articles culled from thousands of publications on topics that we've preselected? A similar technology is available now; however, at least initially, the cost of subscribing to a service like this might be more than $50,000 a year. That hardly guarantees the kind of return on investment that stockholders would support.

For some, however, the scenario described will smack of deja vu, of the promises the AI industry made less than a decade ago. Many of those promises have yet to come true. After investors had poured millions into start-up companies, we watched the industry chug through fits and starts and very nearly fizzle. The futuristic claims of AI seemed overly ambitious at best, and completely unrealistic at worst. Of course, those in the fledgling AI industry saw things differently. A large initial investment was necessary in order to get the ideas out of the labs and into development, they said.

The truth is probably somewhere in the middle. The early disillusionment with AI certainly resulted from technology driving business solutions rather than vice versa. Too much effort was focused on basic research at the expense of marketable applications. When developers created expert systems applications, they focused on "proving" the technology rather than on developing effective business applications. On top of that, early systems were difficult to use, expensive, and nearly impossible to integrate into existing systems environments. No wonder the business world was disillusioned: AI was hardly the panacea we were led to believe it would be.

The industry had not yet matured, but we are learning from our naivete. Rather than letting the potential of the technology dazzle us, we must take a hard look at its impact on our business productivity. Can AI technology help us differentiate ourselves in the marketplace? Can it help us produce more work with the same resources? Can it help us provide better, faster service to our customers? Can it increase our profit potential? The answer to all of these questions is yes: AI remains one of the biggest and most promising technological research fields, and great progress will definitely be made over the next decade.

AI APPLIED

Although the commercialization of AI is relatively recent, the concept is not new. The field began more than 30 years ago when researchers studying intelligence saw analogies between computer problem solving and human problem solving. When computers were first introduced, they freed people from tedious day-to-day calculations. Now with AI, computers are beginning to handle day-to-day decision making. In fact, advances in one branch of AI, neural network technology, suggest that machines may not only have the capability to mimic human decision making, they may actually be able to learn and reason like humans.

There is a vast difference, however, between simply automating a task and endowing a machine with decision-making capabilities. Knowledge-based systems compute with knowledge, not just numbers; with rules of thumb, not repetitive instructions. The key is in symbolic logic—programs that use symbols that are much more flexible and powerful than numbers. Programmed with a set of rules and a knowledge base, the system can then make logical inferences as well as routine calculations.

As researchers have sought to apply AI technology to business problems, a variety of solutions, or branches of AI, have emerged. Those fields include robotics, computer vision, speech synthesis and recognition, natural language processing, neural networks, and expert and knowledge-based systems. Manufacturing industries are putting substantial emphasis on robotics and computer vision, two techniques for solving real-world problems with devices that interact with their environment in an intelligent way.

Other AI disciplines include speech and language. As the name implies, the goal of speech synthesis is getting machines to think and verbalize like humans. Speech, of course, can already be synthesized; now research is focusing on adding intelligence to that process so that systems can perform tasks such as conversion of electronic text to speech. Speech recognition encompasses two areas: recognition of all human speech and recognition of individual voice patterns. Like fingerprints, no two voice patterns are exactly alike, so the field has great potential for voice-based security. High-level work in natural language processing will help machines understand any language, despite syntactical and idiomatic hurdles.

Neural network research is the most exciting and futuristic field of AI, with tremendous promise for telecommunications and other industries. By mimicking brain functions and processing large amounts of information simultaneously, neural networks can actually learn as humans do. Our researchers are investigating the use of this technology for speech and speaker recognition research, and for data and image compression so we can send more information over less bandwidth.

To date, however, nearly all applications of AI are knowledge-based systems. These systems capture knowledge from a variety of areas, then use it to make humanlike decisions. Expert systems, a branch of knowledge-based systems, rely on the expertise of one or more human experts. Knowledge-based systems may use both human and nonhuman sources of information. These systems are increasing productivity, improving accuracy, and reducing costs by making knowledge and expertise accessible to others.

RESEARCH MEETS THE REAL WORLD

Development takes place through the interaction of corporate and academic research organizations, as well as intercompany research alliances, plus one other very important group: the clients who will actually use the systems. It would not be prudent for companies to wait until the scientists are through testing their proofs. Theoretical research is driven and directed by these needs. And operational issues—such as portability, maintenance, and integration with existing systems—are critical design elements, not mere afterthoughts.

Does this marriage of research and the real world contribute to a competitive business? Consider these success stories about several knowledge-based systems that have added measurable value to business.

Streamlined customer service

A large customer service system currently nearing deployment will dramatically streamline the ordering process for central office-based telephone services for businesses. This "translations" system promises to reduce what can be a two-week process to just minutes. It will eliminate an unwieldy paper chase, replacing dozens of pages of eye-straining forms that must be filled out by hand before switching equipment can be programmed.

Intelligent network diagnosis and maintenance

More than half of all knowledge-based systems currently in existence serve diagnostic functions or diagnostic decision support. Because it takes more time to find network failures than it does to fix them, machines can now do the finding and people can do the fixing. Such a system alerts maintenance workers to the source of network problems. These new knowledge-based systems enable machines to do the fixing as well. One system identifies, then resolves, line assignment problems. In addition to providing customers with better service, these systems also free up experts' time for more challenging problems.

Expert sales advice

Customer service representatives are using and praising the new AI system mentioned earlier that helps them pass along informed sales advice to residential customers. Using customer account information, demographic data, and equipment inventory from multiple databases, the system makes intelligent sales recommendations. If the representative's screen indicates the customer has a family with three teenagers, for example, the adviser would recommend a second "teen line." Soon, the system will be able to pull in data that will indicate if facilities are available to provide that extra line.

Strategic planning

Strategic planning is a complex maze, with a multitude of possible actions and reactions. A strategic planning system can simulate the effect of different actions on company planning by using "What if?" reasoning. If advertising is decreased by x dollars, what effect will it have on sales? What is the impact on quality if training dollars are increased? Corporate planning departments use this system to evaluate the ramifications of many actions they are considering.

The new systems will encourage a fundamental shift in the way we view knowledge. Knowledge is a corporate asset, and it should be managed as such. Like capital and financial assets, it must be preserved and leveraged to our advantage.

New technology will be designed to provide "industrial strength" knowledge representation capabilities that can be easily integrated within conventional systems. Key to the technology's success will be its compatibility with existing standards; researchers and developers will need to work cooperatively with industry standards organizations to ensure that this happens.

THE HUMAN IMPACT

The effectiveness of any computer system depends on the people who run it. Therefore, it is essential to consider the impact that these systems will have on people. As U.S. industry faces a declining pool of technical talent, it is also essential that we make the best use of our human resources. Knowledge-based systems will extend worker productivity and provide them with tools that do more with less. In many cases, the systems will free up some of our companies' brightest experts who have been chained to routine tasks. One network troubleshooting expert had been on call—and getting called—24 hours a day, seven days a week for six months. Since the installation of a knowledge-based help desk last year, she's been promoted to a new position, where she is making even more valuable contributions to her company.

We can't deny, however, that there will be resistance to systems that replace human beings. After all, that's been the case throughout the industrial age, and there's no reason the information age should be any different. We must encourage our people to accept change as a normal part of our business operations—and as an opportunity for developing new skills. Some readily accept new challenges; others need more encouragement.

SMART SYSTEMS, GOOD BUSINESS

When does an AI solution make sense for a business problem? How does a company get started with a new technology? The first consideration is not the potential for the technology, but the business need that it addresses. Be careful how you apply cost/benefit analyses. Many companies choose only to undertake high-cost, high payoff applications. That may be a mistake. As development tools have become more affordable, tighter, more focused projects can provide smaller but incremental long-term investments.

The role of these new systems is to democratize technology, translating its complexities into solutions that can solve real-world business problems. And despite our fascination with the marvels of technology, we should avoid pursuing technology for its own sake. Technology does not need to go looking for applications. Rather, business and market needs should seek out appropriate technology to achieve desired goals.

Winston J. Wade is president of US WEST Information Technologies. He is also president of US WEST Advanced Technologies, as well as a vice president of Englewood, Colorado-based US WEST, its $8.4 billion parent firm.

The Networked Corporation

Patrick J. McGovern
Chairman and Chief Executive
International Data Group

In a global economy, top-heavy corporations often tumble.
Maintaining a small company mentality (without thinking small)
gives employees the freedom—and the challenge—to grow.

W hen I am driving along Route 128 in Massachusetts or Route 101 in the Silicon Valley, I use an eyeball measurement to evaluate the companies that line those highways. The number of cars in the parking lot after 6 P.M. is inversely proportional to the size of the company. The smaller the company, the more cars and lights on in the building. In the large companies, the parking lot is a desert.

This phenomenon is one that reinforces a business lesson I learned right after graduating from MIT. I was associate editor of a computer magazine and my job was to travel around the United States and visit computer companies. I noticed immediately that the people I met at the smaller companies were more excited by their work, about product opportunities and contact with customers. The bigger the company, the less satisfied the people were. There was frustration with internal competition to get ahead, not to mention much less contact with the customer.

The conclusion is obvious: small is better. Without a doubt, a small organization creates a greater challenge to the individual to succeed. I learned in biophysics that the performance of an organism is directly related to the challenge to that organism.

Unfortunately, the success of small leads to problems. Companies get bigger; some are already large and cumbersome. But the very success that makes organizations burgeon with revenues and earnings can eventually result in stagnation and lost business opportunities. So the question is, how can you create a small company environment and still continue to grow and prosper?

The answer is the networked corporation and the facilitator is technology. Technology breaks down barriers that blocked the door to the next generation corporate environment. Networked computers, sophisticated but affordable communications capabilities, and strategic use of information systems suddenly create a myriad of possibilities; the possibility of small, for example.

When I started International Data Group (IDG) in 1964, the lessons I learned from my previous job weren't lost, but the technology simply didn't exist to allow the effective creation of a networked organization. Still, I knew this was a goal to pursue and time and again, I was proved right.

I am hardly surprised that the term "globalization" is suddenly on the lips of CEOs and business school professors. The concept of creating a truly global business organization was at the core of my vision for IDG. When we reached $1 million in sales, I started to view markets outside the United States as the future for the business. I even put International in our name.

Skeptics scoffed at the idea of a publishing company, of all things, being able to operate and flourish on a global basis. Even today, a leading economics columnist stated: "Newspapers will never become a truly global industry."

Perhaps so, as a total industry. But in my opinion, it seems as though companies like The New York Times or McGraw-Hill have simply overlooked this opportunity. No one, myself included, could ever have predicted the impact that technology would have on the advent of true globalization. Without that vision, publishers felt they had a unique product that couldn't be duplicated overseas and preferred licensing their products instead.

I saw it differently, even without a crystal ball on technology's role. We were filling a need in the United States: providing information about a burgeoning computer industry. Other countries would inevitably have those same needs. Readers everywhere want the same thing: to be more effective in business through the use of technology. Throughout the 1970s and 1980s I was on the road constantly, planting the seeds in Europe, South America, Australia, and the Far East.

My goal was to allow the local publishers, editors, and reporters to determine what their markets required. By the year 2000, I fully expect that up to 70 percent of our business will be generated outside the United States.

Headquarters identifies the mission—in our case, to be the world's leading supplier of information about the information technology industry. We create a set of common values, send the message, provide support, advice, and training . . . but success or failure is determined by the local business unit.

Today, we have 68 business units operating in 40 countries with 3,500 employees. We've grown at a 20 to 30 percent rate per year for 25 years. Headquarters staff is just 18 people and our costs are only 1.5 percent of revenue (as opposed to an average of 3 to 5 percent).

I'm convinced that our success is based on a decentralized approach to doing business, on our ability to stay "small." By so doing, we can evolve with the market and constantly identify new customer groups.

The most successful business units in the company validate my concept. Those with one goal, (i.e., one publication under its wing), perform the best. I've seen units over the years start two or three publications. The first publication does well but the new baby has trouble. It has either too much or not enough love. These struggling publications spring to life when set out on their own in separate business units.

The other side of the equation is that this concept lets me sleep peacefully knowing that our company does not depend on the success of any one business unit to survive. If China's recent crackdown had resulted in the closing of our Beijing operation (it didn't), IDG would go on.

AUTONOMOUS BUSINESS UNITS

I constantly fight the spread of hierarchy who extol the top-heavy approach. "Why don't you have central paper buying rather than each individual publication finding its own source?" the experts ask. "Such economies of scale would certainly produce an immediate increase in margin," they say. That may be true, but taking away operating freedom would cause key people to leave the company and in a few years, stagnation would set in. If you allow a small group of people to take an idea, nurture it, build it, and make it happen, the chances of success are enhanced beyond measure.

Ken Olsen saw this clearly at Digital Equipment Corp. in the early 1960s when he became frustrated with a suddenly stagnant young company. He found that when things went wrong, everyone turned to him to place the blame. In a stroke of business genius, he restructured the company. Each product group became an autonomous business unit responsible for the individual success or failure of that product. Each unit would compete for corporate resources but would share certain centralized functions such as manufacturing and sales.

Olsen's concept lit a fuse. Digital's sales and earnings took off and throughout the next two decades, this product line strategy propelled the company beyond the $5 billion barrier in revenues. Though he eventually reorganized again in the early 1980s, Olsen never gave up on the concept of individuals having great responsibility and driving their own businesses to success. Today, Digital is a $13 billion giant and is fighting IBM toe to toe.

It was no coincidence that as Digital grew, its internal network spread like a giant web around the organization. Top management understood intuitively that such a decentralized approach required a highly refined communications capability. Without information in this environment, one can easily get blindsided by a wave of change or innovation. Today, Digital has a vast international network that allows more than 70,000 of its employees to communicate instantly via computer-based systems.

Adopting a decentralized, networked approach is certainly a lot easier for smaller companies, but it is not an untenable concept for giants either. AT&T, for example, recently replaced five of its major business units with 19 business units in order to spread increased responsibility to lower levels of management. Robert Allen, AT&T chairman, simply got tired of the turf wars and endless committee-made decisions. He wants individuals to take responsibility and expects the move to make AT&T much more responsive and quicker to market. This is a reorganization worth keeping an eye on.

T.J. Rogers, head of the highly successful Cypress Semiconductor Corp., has also embraced the concept. Despite its success, Cypress is breaking itself into smaller, independent operations. According to *Electronic Engineering Times*, this marks the first time a healthy electronics company has undertaken such a move. Why do it?

"Cypress would be move vital as ten $100 million companies than as a single $1 billion company," Rogers stated.

My advice to Fortune 500 CEOs is: Don't be afraid to divide things up, throw out a challenge. Most people are only working at 15 percent of their capacity. If you give them a challenge, their skills and capabilities most definitely will flower. People will be happier and business performance will increase. Best of all, a lot of sour-faced middle managers will disappear.

I saw a clear example of this when I was establishing the first joint publishing venture with the Soviet Union. In Moscow, I met with a group of negotiators who ranged in age from their thirties to fifties. Gorbachev's mandate for change was exciting for those in their thirties. The older bureaucrats, on the other hand, feared the change. They had four-foot-high piles of requests on their desks and perceived perestroika as a threat to their careers. It was clear to me that the way to succeed in this venture was to align myself with the people in their thirties.

Of course, breaking down the barrier of overstuffed bureaucracy is no guarantee of success, nor is it the only necessary step to the networked organization. Technology has become the great enabler, the steam roller that is flattening organizations. Ironically, the path of computer technology mirrors the philosophy of the networked corporation.

Like massive, top-heavy bureaucracies, computing was dominated not long ago by huge, powerful mainframes, which controlled the flow of information out into the company. With the advent and proliferation of personal computers and networks, the individual is now empowered with technology at the desktop. More and more, the mainframe is becoming a data repository, no longer in control, but rather a source for information that is turned into knowledge by the end user.

Suddenly the mainframe and the personal computer are partners in the network rather than the master and the slave. Analogous to corporate headquarters, the mainframe can no longer dictate, it must allow other machines to have autonomy in the network.

The combination of networked technology with a small group of talented, motivated professionals is a powerful one. Our flagship publication, *Computerworld*, is a prime example. Long dominant in its market, *Computerworld* started spinning off other publications several years ago while seeking ways to increase market share. Headquarters lost sight of what had made *Computerworld* special. We missed some very important industry trends, had bloated unresponsive management, and most important, lost sight of our customer, the reader.

Inevitably, *Computerworld* suffered; readers began to desert, key staff people left as well, and morale was way down. In the past two years, *Computerworld* became its own business unit. Aggressive and talented management was put in place, virtually all the key players coming from within the company. New production technology and graphics equipment was brought in, allowing not only for a complete redesign, but for longer news deadlines, which allow readers to get the very latest information on their desks.

The mission was refocused, the product reevaluated and overhauled, and the tide turned dramatically. With a sleek new look and an ever vigilant ear to the reader, *Computerworld* not only dominates its market, but continues to be impressively profitable in a sluggish technology market.

As technology gets lower in cost, it has driven the realization of this organizational structure. We use electronic mail extensively throughout our company, which allows the immediate transmission of news and the sharing of resources around the globe. We've instituted our IDG News Service, which allows stories gathered by our more than 120 computer-related publications to be shared electronically around the world on a daily basis.

THE GLOBAL NETWORK

All our autonomous units can benefit from the global network; they share market knowledge accumulated by 25 years of publishing experience. Since no business unit has a corner on expertise, knowledge can be and is shared. A technique for improving circulation in Norway works just as well in the United States. The Australian PC publication can acquire essential marketing expertise from *Infoworld* or *PC World*. I wasn't prepared for this when I started out, but I found to my great delight that there is a tremendous amount of transferability of skills around the world.

Indeed, I remember when we set up our first international managers meeting in 1978. Everyone assumed it would be a nice social event but there'd be little exchange of useful information. When I traveled to each country in prior years, they emphasized how unique their market was. Of course, when I'd ask for their four-year plan, they'd set up easy goals so they'd look like heroes to headquarters. We constantly pushed for more aggressive goals.

I actually expected the individual country managers to be reluctant to share anything for that reason. But at the meeting, just the opposite occurred. The Germans stood up and bragged about how good they were and announced ambitious goals for themselves. Then the Americans, then the French, and so on. Soon, there was a lively exchange of ideas and information. I saw the benefit of using the forces of natural interpersonal rivalries to work for you. By instituting a worldwide employee stock ownership plan, we've generated even more desire for success. Now the Brazilians have all the more reason to help the French or the Japanese. They all own part of the business.

And this experience puts the networked organization into a different perspective. Technology is the vehicle, but it is the people who provide the fuel, who give shape and dimension and power to the concept. This seemingly obvious tenet is constantly getting lost in corporate hierarchies where CEOs are now asking why they are spending large percentages of budgets on technology and seeing little productivity increase.

Layering on technology offers no strategic advantage if the culture and environment aren't structured to allow individuals to flourish. We are not in business to acquire technology. We are in business to allow people to fulfill their potential, to give them something useful and exciting to do.

I agree with *Boston Globe* economist Robert J. Samuelson, who recently wrote: "Companies will increasingly flourish—or fail—on how well they become multicultural organizations. They will need

to create effective cooperation between people of different nationalities. The marketplace for ideas and technology is now worldwide. Companies are the means of transmission."

Patrick J. McGovern is founder, chairman, and chief executive of the Framingham,
Massachusetts-based International Data Group (IDG). IDG is a supplier of information
services on information technology. Its subsidiary, IDG Communications, is publisher of
more than 120 magazines and newspapers, including *Computerworld*, a business trade
publication printed in the United States.

5

INNOVATION AND PRODUCT DEVELOPMENT

The Endless Incubator

How can an old joint venture, with joint ventures of its own, stay young? Dow Corning does it by using what it knows about partnering to link up with its own industrial customers.

4,200 products later, Dow Corning is still on the cutting edge of materials technology. New applications are constantly being bred out of new materials because the company exists to transfer technology. The company's Silvue coating, an abrasive-resistant silicon film, glazes auto headlight covers, but it also protects the lenses in the sunglasses many people wear.

Formed in 1943 by Dow Chemical and Corning Glass Works, both of which are represented on the Dow Corning board, the firm also stays ahead by generating joint ventures of its own. Some of the many Silvue applications were developed by Anaheim, California-based SDC Coatings, a joint venture between Swedlow, Inc., and Dow Corning.

Dow Corning doesn't hesitate to go overseas for its partners. The company's Japan Group includes Dow Corning Toray Silicone, a joint venture involving silicon research and development. Dow Corning Europe, with headquarters in Brussels, has research and development centers in the United Kingdom, France, West Germany, and Belgium. Manufacturing operations are strung out across the continent because the company wants to be "globally aligned" to "focus on customer expectations."

It is clear that one meaning of the alignment concept is sharing technology and working closely with customers worldwide in the earliest stages of product development. President Lawrence A. Reed emphasizes that Dow Corning has changed from an insular but respected technology developer to a marketer that uses shared research to get in earlier on customer product development. "We're in the labs together," he proclaims. A University of Minnesota chemical engineering graduate, Larry Reed joined Dow Corning in 1964. At the end of 1984, he became the company's sixth president. Reed has raised sales revenues to over $1 billion. Appointed president in 1988, he's now setting these goals for the 1990s: (1) pushing new product sales to 25 percent of all sales by 1993, (2) raising overall sales to the $3 billion level, and (3) earning $300 million in profits "minimum."

This won't come cheap. Reed put $80 million more into capital expenditures in 1989—raising the total tab to $306 million. The key measure of innovative success, new product sales as a percentage of all sales, has been moving up from a low of 14.3 percent in 1984, when Reed was made president, to 19.8 percent in 1989. But that's still below the 21.2 percent achieved in 1979. The alignment strategy that has helped Dow Corning stay young and made it an endless incubator should meet the test. But getting there isn't easy, as Reed explains here.

> **People are treating joint ventures like they're a brand new thing. But yours is probably one of the oldest and started with two U.S. firms in 1943. Does it really make sense to continue as a single-industry joint venture for so long?**

We're not an industry. Organic silicon chemistry is a technology. We were set up commercially, in fact, by the same kind of industry groups that we now deal with. We're more like semiconductors, where the technology is also thought of as an industry.

> **Can you go wherever technology takes you—even if it leaves, temporarily, silicon-based chemistry?**

The answer is yes, our autonomy is certain if we in fact believe that through that technology we can somehow differentiate ourselves. We're a technology-based company that really deals with the needs of customers in all industries. Our plan is to absolutely ensure that we are at the places where technology is being invented and that we are working with the innovative companies of the world on new applications.

NEW MATERIALS BREED NEW PRODUCTS

What applications are on your mind currently?
There's a whole raft of them. In order to get differentiation in the next generation of products, whether it's automobiles or electronic equipment, choosing new materials is the first-level decision. It's those materials which will then allow for new features that can be utilized.

In ceramics we're talking about materials that will last much longer under heavy-wear conditions, that can operate at higher temperatures, that have more structural integrity. They're already being used on the hubs of a new generation of CDs.

In materials technology one of the things that is fascinating is that a compound, initially pointed at one kind of an application, can be used in something that appears to be extremely different. It may be surprising to some people that personal care is a high-tech industry. New shampoos use silicone technology today. Then there are the defoamers that go into everyday detergents—they're related to the pulp defoamers used in paper mills—but people don't think a detergent has anything to do with high technology.

> **Is there anything that's in the development stage where you have a new technology or process with a product transfer?**

We have a joint venture with Phillips Petrolium called AgriSense, which is experimenting with the controlled release of insect sex hormones as an attractant. This was spun out of developing technology in quite a different area. Our technology that's involved with hairstyle came out of original applications in automobile polishes and now has applications in clothing, too.

SPEEDING UP THE WORKPLACE

How does this breeding of new applications affect your own cycle time?
We have set for ourselves an internal objective to reduce our time to commercialize a product by 70 percent. That's what our objective is. But your question is broader because it impacts on how

we work with our customers. What we're really trying to do is assist our customers in shortening their own cycle times.

Historically, within our company and between companies, we've had a "hands-off," or keep-your-distance mentality: the research division did its thing, and then they passed it on to development, where something else got done. After going through manufacturing, somebody would decide they'd better talk to the customers and see if anybody wants what we've made. Usually, we would have to make some modifications and then repeat the process.

After struggling to shorten our own cycle time, we came up with a new idea: We decided to look ahead to where we think we ought to be five years or ten years from now. We set in motion, several years ago, a process that we have come to call our "renewal process." We have literally opened the books in all individual sectors to find ways that we can make step changes that are ultimately going to improve the way that we do business with our customers.

We set out to really define what happens all the way from the idea to when the product gets out the door. Instead of looking at this sequentially, as a process of independent steps, we have looked at this process as a continuum. And that continuum includes the customer.

Have you put the difference between what you were doing before you concentrated on how value is added and what you do now on paper?
The models that we originally had would encompass a whole wall. But we worked that down to two charts.

COMPETING BY COMMUNICATING

Has your new process brought you closer to your customers, or is it merely a matter of an executive proclaiming that his company is customer-driven?
We now conduct regular surveys of our customers. We did one three years ago, and parts of it weren't that pretty. They talked about problems in dealing with us, using the kind of words you don't like to see. We took them to heart. We were thought to be . . .

Arrogant?

Correct. Our customers respected our scientific capabilities, but were less than complimentary, in some cases, about how well we listened to them, and how well we really worked with them in solving problems as they perceived them.

How does this fit in with a networked approach to materials research? How does that work?

We've established a computer system that networks all of our people. All of our technology people are linked. As a new technology or a new application is being discovered, the information is made available for consideration for other kinds of customer needs. We have groups of people getting together at meetings around the world, sometimes three times a year, to talk about the advances in their respective fields and what the customer needs are.

Just how tightly do your customers let you embrace them?

What you have to do from both sides is develop a true partnership mentality. You have to have an extreme level of confidence in the other party, because both of you are giving away secrets. Historically, that was never done. In our case, it's secrets about our technology—and this very much requires CEO involvement. I really don't want to discuss specifics because in all of these cases where we have very close relationships with customers, we treat their information as proprietary.

Is there an example you can talk about?

It's fair to say that we're in the labs together with Procter & Gamble. We're sharing research information, we're sharing marketing information, and we're exchanging information on what the company is looking for in their end products that would differentiate them from the competition. We have seen this with Ford, another company that is changing rapidly. Now they're relying on the testing we're doing. They probably wouldn't have done that in the past.

The front-end of exchange of ideas with customers is critical today. We sit down with marketing people and technical people, and brainstorm jointly. We ask what the customer needs to solve problems, to achieve product differentiation, and if what's needed is worth it to both of us.

Today, we're working with Malco Products, a company that is very active in the pulp and paper industry. We're jointly working on new defoamer technology that will allow much higher efficiencies and require less energy. We started out with one product concept, one issue; but their people are very active in the oil service industry, and they now see other kinds of applications that will require some other materials, and in turn those new materials will help in solving other problems in the paper industry.

This gets into the issue of global competitiveness. If people take customer satisfaction seriously, by definition that's a step change requiring some substantial level of innovation. Our customers may see ways to extend the life of their products and give themselves a competitive advantage they need to compete with the Japanese.

A JAPANESE TARGET

Japan's Ministry of International Trade and Industry (MITI) has targeted high-performance materials as a growth technology of the 1990s. Can the United States meet this challenge?
The Japanese have targeted advanced materials as one of their areas for the 1990s. Typically they have evolved their technologies through what initially appeared to be relatively mundane consumer applications. For example, who would have thought of using a ceramic material in a tennis racket? In the United States our thinking would probably have been to put it into a new engine. In the process of developing the material and using new fabrication techniques, the Japanese gain experience. But in our case there's a significant difference. We are participating with leading-edge Japanese companies.

Are you getting as much transferred to you as is being transferred from here to Japan?
The exterior climate is now more conducive to working together. And we have been working very, very hard on this whole idea of interdependency and exchanging information, and, frankly, also

taking a much more aggressive role to ensure that technological information is being transferred in both directions.

ENVIRONMENT AND THE FUTURE

What is your greatest worry for the 1990s?
Regulation and the use of good science versus emotive reasoning in dealing with environmental problems is a major concern. Every responsible person who is involved in a major industrial company today recognizes that we must work toward an improved environment for our future. Nobody will deny that. The issue is how can we do it in the context of current scientific information. There's a scientific illiteracy that exists in the country today in the general populace, in our legislators, and in many well-intentioned people in other kinds of groups.

The concept of "chemical phobia" is far too widespread. If we have a problem, everybody wants to solve the problem, but let's do it in a way that makes some scientific sense. Too much "superfund" cleanup money is being spent on attorney fees. We're working very hard to try to think about where we might have some potential exposure, even for the wrong reasons. But we have very clearly made the decision that we will provide all of the information that we know how to provide, and in a timely way, to the general public.

Creating Innovative
Corporate Cultures

Roy Serpa
President and Chief Executive
Instamelt Systems

*Future productivity and profits depend on how well we foster
innovation and entrepreneurship in our corporate cultures.*

I n his book *Innovation & Entrepreneurship,* Peter Drucker warns
us that "today's businesses, especially the large ones, simply
will not survive in this period of rapid change and innovation,
unless they acquire entrepreneurial competence." Entrepreneurial
competence will evolve only if managers encourage innovation
within their corporate cultures.

The need for innovation has become more critical as the Western
economies face the loss of technological leadership, the elimination
of jobs, and the often painful processes of rationalizing and restructuring. Rationalizing involves the closing of noncompetitive or obsolete production facilities, whereas restructuring is the strengthening
of areas where there is the best opportunity to improve performance.

Rationalization and restructuring must be followed by a period
of renewal and revitalization if the Western economies are to avoid a
greater depression in the 1990s. The keys to renewal and revitalization are invention and innovation. Invention is the process of orig-
inating a concept or device, whereas innovation is the process of
introducing something new to meet an unidentified need. The best
source of innovation is the entrepreneur—someone who organizes,
operates, and assumes risk for new business ventures. Corporations

must change their cultures to create climate that will stimulate increased innovation and a more entrepreneurial management style.

SHAPING CORPORATE CULTURE

What is corporate culture and why is it important to managers? Anthropologist Clyde Kluckhohn defines culture as "the set of habitual and traditional ways of thinking, feeling, and reacting that are characteristic of the ways a particular society meets its problems at a particular point in time." Every developed society has a unique natural culture, industrial culture, and distinct corporate cultures. The industrial culture is influenced by the natural culture, the world economy, government and regulatory institutions, academia, and—in the United States—the free enterprise system. A favorable environment can encourage investment, invention, and innovation, whereas an unfavorable environment can discourage such activities and retard economic growth.

The industrial cultures in many Western countries have placed an inordinate emphasis upon short-term performance, yet innovation requires patience and long-term commitment. The financial community, labor, and management have often pursued short-term results at the expense of the long-term viability of industrial resources. If allowed to continue, this situation will pose a serious threat to the long-term economic health of our industries and our companies.

The industrial culture, specific industry, competition, technology, market, and especially the style of past and present management influence each corporate culture. Company values, recognition, rewards, and sanctions shape the beliefs and behavior of a culture. As management recruits, rewards, promotes, and discharges personnel, it sends signals that affect what people think and do. Quantity, quality, service, and value needs of customers shape the culture's combination of capabilities and limitations. The technology required to participate in the marketplace dictates the necessary skills and types of personnel that are part of a culture. All corporate cultures exist within an industrial culture and must conform to its rules of behavior in order to survive.

Each corporate culture is a product of unique values, beliefs, and rules of behavior. The rules or norms of behavior reflect the perceptions that individuals share of the prevalent values and beliefs of the company culture. Values are the core of organizational culture, influencing the beliefs and attitudes of individuals and groups. Beliefs are the mental convictions about values. They are largely shaped by the consistency or inconsistency between the value statements and actions of superiors within the organization. In the case of consistency, beliefs reinforce the norms of behavior that would be expected to evolve from the stated values. In the case of inconsistency, different beliefs—and therefore different norms—evolve according to the actions of superiors.

DEVELOPING AN ENTREPRENEURIAL MANAGEMENT STYLE

In the years ahead we must modify our management styles and become entrepreneurs as well as administrators. Our past aversion to risk-taking must be replaced by a greater willingness to invest in new products, new technologies, and new markets. We must focus more on the long-term and the innovative task as well as the operating task if our economy is to provide increased opportunities to a growing work force.

Performing innovative tasks requires understanding the value and benefits of technology. Corporate managers don't need to be technologists, but they must integrate technology into their approach to the marketplace so that the inventions of technologists can be commercialized. Our ability to combine innovation with invention will determine our success in achieving our economic potential.

How can you tell whether or not a corporate culture lacks an entrepreneurial management style? Obvious indications are a loss of market and technological position, the lack of new products, new technology, and new business positions, and languishing new product projects. Typical behavior in such a culture would include ignoring or discouraging new ideas, avoiding risk-taking, punishing failure and giving no special rewards for success, focusing exclusively on the present or immediate future performance of the company, and committing all resources to sustain existing products, processes, and markets.

FIGURE 5–1

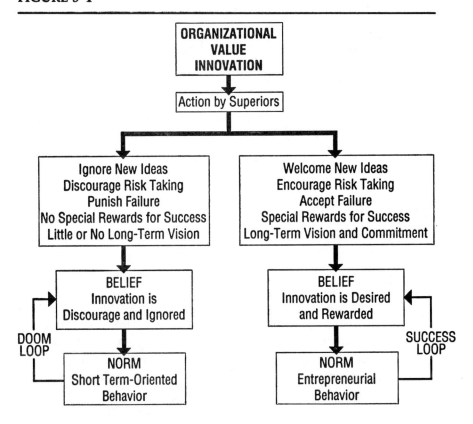

MAKING THE TRANSITION

The presence of such indications and behavior in a company does not necessarily mean that innovation is not a value of the culture. As Fritz Steele, author of *The Open Organization* and a noted authority on innovation states, "Sometimes, they [people] are just blind to the lack of congruence between their expressed values and their behavior." An isolated incident or series of incidents can cause discontinuity between the concept and the norms of behavior.

An example of discontinuity and continuity is illustrated in the diagram. Innovation is an expressed value of the corporate culture. The sequence on the left outlines the actions of superiors that are inconsistent with the value. The resulting belief fosters a short-term, maintenance management style. This creates a "doom loop" in which the stated value is not realized. In the sequence on the right, superiors' actions are consistent with the value, creating a "success loop" that fosters entrepreneurial behavior.

A "doom loop" can be broken and an innovative culture created when the senior executive becomes aware of the need for change. He or she must provide an example consistent with the value of innovation and must nurture the process of changing existing behavior. This commitment must be communicated to other top managers with the explicit direction that their participation will be required to create new norms of behavior. The first step is to ask managers to submit new ideas for products, processes, and markets on a regular basis in their monthly reports. They should also be prepared to discuss these new ideas at monthly management meetings. A part of each meeting's agenda should be devoted to ideas for improving the future performance of the corporation, and the senior executive should acknowledge all contributions with positive comments and with specific assignments for subsequent evaluation.

Next, the management team debates the evaluations, which must be accompanied by proposals for the commitment of resources. Those approved for action are implemented, and the manager who originally submitted the idea acts as executive sponsor. Each manager's performance should be judged both on his service as executive sponsor and on his short-term performance in the assignment. Special recognition, cash bonuses, and promotional rewards should be given to everyone involved as well as the executive sponsor. If the project is unsuccessful, other opportunities should be assigned without any punishment or loss of prestige.

As these new norms of behavior become evident to those in the corporation, their belief that only short-term performance is recognized will be gradually replaced by the belief that both short- and long-term performance will be rewarded. An innovative corporate culture will evolve as the success loop takes hold.

One company that has improved productivity and profits through innovation is Ameritech, one of the seven regional companies spun off from AT&T. Employees have submitted ideas that have reduced expenses, generated new revenue, and developed new lines of business resulting in $2 million of increased net income. A more dramatic example of innovation occurred at the SMH Group, makers of Omega, Longines, and Hamilton watches. In the 1970s, when the Swiss watch industry was on the verge of extinction, a team of engineers at SMH created an innovative design that reduced the number of parts in the average quartz watch from 90 to 51. The result was the Swatch watch, a consumer product phenomenally successful throughout the world.

WHAT CEOs CAN DO

What specific contributions can we make to create more innovative corporate cultures? First, we can try to better understand our own corporate culture. We can identify the true values, beliefs, and rules of behavior rather than the espoused nonoperational ones, then determine the gaps and act to close them. Special attention to fostering belief in innovation and entrepreneurial behavior can make them operational values. Secondly, we can encourage better management of our technical resources. We need to focus on technologies that fit our organizational capabilities and strategy, then facilitate their transfer to the marketplace. Thirdly, we can encourage teamwork within our function, across functions and divisions, and between related companies. Recognition and rewards should be given for team as well as individual performance. Most importantly, we must better understand our customers' existing and potential needs and be responsive to them.

The creation of innovative cultures in our large corporation demands priority attention if the Western economies are to reach their economic potential and create jobs for a growing labor force. Management, labor, and government must work together to strengthen our industrial cultures through the cooperative long-term commitments of resources and the willingness to make short-term sacrifices.

Roy Serpa is president and CEO of InstaMelt Systems, Inc., manufacturer of the Insta-Melt Rotary Extruder and affiliate of Midland, Texas-based oil and gas producers, Wagner & Brown. Involved in the plastics industry for more than 20 years, Serpa has worked extensively in developing new business ventures, technology transfer, and acquisitions.

Junk Your 'Linear' R&D!

Donald N. Frey
Professor, Industrial Engineering and Management Science
Northwestern University

To capture innovation from diverse sources, don't rely on traditional, centralized programs. The parallel paradigm speeds up market-driven ideas.

T he general perception in the United States is that we are in danger of being out-innovated by foreign competitors—particularly the Japanese—and that formal research and development may no longer be the key to leadership. Europe shares a similar perception about the United States and Japan. Despite a lack of formal research and development (R&D) programs, the Japanese have risen to become innovative, competitive economic powers. They dominate world markets by successfully commercializing some of our basic technology. This realization has led Europe and the United States to a renewed recognition of the importance of commercial innovation. Sources of innovation are diverse and do not necessarily include R&D laboratories. For example, studies have shown that customers of industrial concerns are an important source of innovation, and salespeople of these concerns play a key role as both communicators and originators of innovation. Getting innovative products to the marketplace today requires a new concept of R&D

The assumption that economic success stems from acquiring—unilaterally at the company level—enough proprietary research findings, is no longer generally true. There will continue to be rare exceptions, such as biotechnology and superconductive ceramics, based on new and revolutionary scientific findings. But they will soon mature into broadly available technologies. The spread throughout the world of science and technology, plus the sheer volume of new research, makes it almost impossible for any one firm to corner the market. "Airplane ticket" research is the new order of the day, and an attitude of "not invented here" is likely to prove fatal. Science and technology need to be considered a pool from which all companies can extract what they need for a particular innovation.

The growing universality of science and research makes innovation more frequently market-driven instead of technologically driven. External forces affecting industrial R&D include the restructuring or rationalization of American industry through takeovers (hostile or friendly) and other forms of recapitalization. Restructuring and rationalization tend to sharpen the focus of R&D on the short term, which translates into short-term product or process development and little long-term research. Managements concentrate too much on survival in the takeover world—frequently with excessive debt. They do not make long-term investments because they see the risks as excessive. In the short run, these rationalization forces are probably irresistible. In the long run, the restructuring fad will likely run its course. Meanwhile, however, less costly and more time-efficient methods for innovation, including innovation produced through R&D, are needed to help correct this short-term behavior.

In recent years reductions or decentralization of large industrial research labs to accomplish this goal have been well-publicized. Intermediate-sized firms, such as Borg-Warner and Cincinnati Milacron, are doing the same thing. In 1975 I dissolved the central research laboratories of Bell & Howell to decentralize R&D and thus innovation development. The result? A number of successful major innovations followed in the next 10 years, compared to none in the previous decade. The rationale of these actions is that central R&D is too far from the marketplace to avoid failures of new products ill-suited for that market, too removed from customer ideas or influence, and too slow to exploit new technologies—some of which may not even have been considered in an inward-directed R&D organization. While not all R&D laboratories are being totally decentralized, all are under various forms of pressure to change. Specifically, there are three emerging trends in industrial R&D: a stronger focus on short-term development, with less focus on long-term research; the creation of more innovation-oriented R&D in a different context; and a different mode of R&D operation, with more emphasis on speeding up market-driven innovation.

THE PARALLEL PARADIGM

While some centralized R&D organizations are being replaced by decentralized functions, most R&D organizations have also changed in functional content, becoming multifunctional, and in degree of permanence, more flexible. The term *multifunctional* rather than *multidisciplinary* is used because the latter has become identified with science rather than with parallel business functions used to develop the various elements of new products. The old "hand-off," or linear methodology, is too slow and fraught with downstream organizational barriers that contribute to failure. Simultaneous and parallel development involving engineering, manufacturing, and marketing is gaining sway. Given the market-driven character of most new innovation, marketing must play an integral role from the beginning, as must engineering and manufacturing, in order to achieve timely, competitive cost and quality.

Impermanence has become the new style in R&D. Ad hoc organizations or teams are being created for specific innovation. If successful, a team can be the core of a new business or product line. If unsuccessful, it is dissolved, with members sent to new ad hoc teams. The team can report to various authorities. If innovation is vital to the survival of the firm, the team often reports to an operating entity (if management can be trusted to innovate). Occasionally, it may temporarily report to a staff entity—if no existing operating business can handle the assignment, or if the innovation has no fit to existing operations.

What remains of an "old" R&D, whether centralized or decentralized, can be better used as a methodology for solving technical problems that arise in the operation of innovation teams. So a new R&D paradigm, which can be called "multi-input," "multifunctional development in parallel," or "parallel" for short, emerges.

In the process, management structure organization, reward systems, and methods for choosing innovation investments are in flux. A great deal of experimentation will occur as the new paradigm becomes more fully developed.

SERVICE-SECTOR CONSIDERATIONS

The emergence of the service sector as a dominant force in the U.S. economy has raised some additional and specific R&D issues. This sector has questionable productivity growth and little identifiable or formal R&D. A service-sector firm has two aspects with two different R&D needs: the service or professional function performed, such as healthcare, law, and banking, and support information systems. While R&D—to further the professional purposes of the firm—is being conducted extensively in such major sectors as healthcare and education (at both the federal and firm level), the comprehensive study of information technology and systems for the service industries is just now starting. Much of that research has not yet fully considered multirecording media, including paper and microfilm, in addition to electronics or multitransmission, whether through the post office, deliveries, or electronic means. As with R&D in the manufacturing sector, studies of successful information system innovations for service industries indicate that decentralization with multifunctional teams at the operating level, rather than at centralized MIS (with the possible exception of corporate standards setting), is vital for effective and timely execution.

INFORMATION SYSTEMS "R&D"

Information systems "R&D" is two-tiered, relying on customized software as well as commercial hardware and software. The growing and intense operational nature of economically successful information systems—which contrasts with the more traditionally centralized and isolated MIS systems—is resulting in the creation of ad hoc teams to develop new information systems. These teams are multidisciplinary and multifunctional because of the often

intense customer and people contact involved in service sector
information systems. But the service sector needs more than just
efficient information systems, it needs effective ones. This can be
achieved by designing a system to suit the specific strategy or
purposes of the firm—for example, to improve market share, customer satisfaction, responsiveness, or cash flow.

The R&D paradigm is shifting from the increasingly unsuccessful and unrealistic "linear" model to a "parallel" model incorporating ad hoc multifunctional teams. Regardless of whether these
teams are decentralized to operating units, they have a single
project orientation with multiple units. Any part of the more
traditional centralized R&D that remains can be used in two ways:
by ad hoc teams external to the laboratory to solve problems that
are uncovered in the team's innovation development, or to technically improve the innovation once it is an established product or
business in the marketplace.

Major issues in technology transfer—the interaction between
public R&D and private innovation—are now emerging. The private sector has a much bigger hand in development than research,
but research is increasingly done better in the broad-based science
and applied-science research institutions. These include private
and public research universities, government research laboratories, and profit and nonprofit private research laboratories. Government research laboratories present special problems in technology
transfer, but efforts are being made to correct these problems.

Science today is simply too broad, too international, and changing too fast for any one company to master it all. Increased private-
sector financial support to institutions can come directly through
grants and contracts, or, for tax-supported laboratories, indirectly
through tax dollars. How well each side understands the other's
needs will determine the degree of the financial support they receive. Greater understanding will also produce more realistic expectations of economic growth on the part of our political institutions.

Frey, dismayed with the barriers to commercialization of his own research, when research engineer at Ford and then former Professor of Engineering at the University of
Michigan, became a strong advocate of cross-educating students in engineering and
manufacturing. Formerly chief executive of Bell & Howell, he presently teaches at
Northwestern University.

Why CEOs Are Not Creative

Edward de Bono
Chairman
Edward de Bono Associates

Creative leadership has taken a back seat in the information age. CEOs may want to rethink the policy of not fixing it until it's broken.

H ere is the paradox. The excellent Patriot missile, which was so much in the news for its success in downing Scud missiles, was developed by Raytheon. At the same time, it was Raytheon that invented the microwave oven and did nothing about it; years later the Japanese made it a huge commercial success. This paradox exactly summarizes why 23 years' experience in the field of creative thinking has convinced me that American chief executives are not creative. The U.S. tradition is to regard creativity as peripheral and boxed into specified areas: technical R&D, software development, advertising, product packaging, and so on.

This attitude is neither unusual nor surprising. There is no U.S. business school that has a serious or satisfactory course on creativity. There are 10 sound reasons why creativity is not yet regarded as central to American business, or given an important enough priority.

1. The belief that more information will solve your problems. There was a time when information was indeed the limiting factor and more information made for better decisions. This is no longer

the case; ideas are the limiting factor today. Nor will analysis yield new ideas. The mind can only see what it is prepared to see (even scientists are only just beginning to realize this). We need to start ideas in our hands—with creativity.

2. There is an emphasis on problem solving even to the extent that all thinking is called "problem solving" in American psychological usage. People are taught problem solving and promoted on their problem-solving abilities, giving rise to what I call Catch 24: "To reach a senior position in an organization, you have to be without or have kept hidden exactly those talents you will need when you get there."

3. America was a pioneer society, and in any pioneer society action is always more important than thinking. As a result, U.S. executives are uncomfortable with concepts and want "hands-on" action. I have worked in 45 countries around the world, and I can say that U.S. executives are more uncomfortable with concepts then executives of most other countries. Yet today, technology is becoming a commodity, and future profitability is going to come from application of concepts.

4. U.S. executives rely a great deal on analysis and market research, in contrast to the Japanese who prefer to risk direct market tests (they try out 1,000 soft drinks a year). Negativity is far higher in the United States than in Japan because of traditional Western culture. This is being enhanced by an emphasis on teaching "critical thinking" in schools, when what should be taught is constructive and creative thinking.

5. The current fashion and emphasis is on "housekeeping," as in cost cutting, quality, people care, and so on. All these things are necessary for the competent running of an organization, but they are not sufficient. Water is necessary for soup, but soup is more than water. Quality is fine, but quality of what? Quality of what we have been doing and should now be changing? Even the word *management* means managing what *is* rather than creating what *can be*.

6. The false notion of competition as pushed by people like Michael Porter and the Harvard Business School. Competition is really only for survival and for keeping up. Competition is one of the things necessary to establish a baseline. For success we need to go beyond competition. The word *competition* means "seeking

with" or being content to run in the same race. We need to move on to the more advanced concept of sur/petition, which means "seeking above" and creating your own value monopoly.

7. The U.S. watch industry has been almost wiped out through a failure to realize that watches had become jewelry rather than just timepieces. What Swatch did for Switzerland could have been done by Timex if there had not been complacency about what was selling quite well. Complacency is the biggest enemy of creativity. To think you are doing well or are creative enough is eventually fatal.

8. The transistor was, of course, a U.S. invention, but major development and use took place in Japan. IBM was offered the xerography process but turned it down because of a failure to foresee the need for office copiers. The focus on "what is" makes chief executives blind to "what can be." Everyone knows of other corporations to which these things apply, but few CEOs have the vision to realize these things apply to their own corporations.

9. Short-term thinking encouraged by the need for quarterly stock analyst reports and judgment only on short-term results. This encourages manipulation (market and financial) rather than creativity.

10. U.S. business has always been opportunistic rather than opportunity developing. There is emphasis on "me-too," *Son of Lassie, Rocky V.* As Sam Goldwyn is reputed to have said: "What we need are some brand new cliches"—something new so long as it is the same as before and known to work.

A whole change in attitude toward creativity is required if U.S. business is going to reap the benefits from available capital, a large home market, personal effectiveness, and business competence. Success in the global market is going to need a baseline of competence on which to build the sur/petition that is going to be needed. That sur/petition is going to be fueled by concepts, and concepts need serious creativity.

Edward de Bono, a former Rhodes Scholar, is the chairman of Edward de Bono Associates, the author of 34 books that have been translated into 24 languages, and the founder of the International Creative Forum, which brings together worldwide corporations to analyze business creativity.

6

HUMAN RESOURCE DEVELOPMENT

Dial 911 for Teamwork

All the Baby Bells have had growing pains in adjusting to competition. When he became CEO, Bell Atlantic's Ray Smith realized his company had a wrong number in culturally adapting to its market.

T he cover of Bell Atlantic's 1990 Annual Report shows a blue chip that bears the words "The Bell Atlantic Way." Inside the report, in addition to the details and highlights of another good year (revenues $11.525 billion, up 7 percent; net income $1.312 billion, up 22 percent), there are also four pages devoted to an account of the psychological transformation of Bell Atlantic's employees into a "high-performance culture." They are now doing things "The Bell Atlantic Way," a mode of positive thinking symbolized by the blue chip.

Regardless of what cynical outsiders and competitors (and perhaps even a few untransformed insiders) may think of this, there's no question that Bell Atlantic performs like a blue chip company— last autumn, Barron's called it "the Cadillac of the industry." In 1990, in addition to a stock split, the brashest of the Baby Bells outperformed the composite results of the other six regionals, and its stock ended at an all-time high, up 380 percent from 1984.

Bell Atlantic is not alone in its prosperity; seven years after their creation, all of Ma Bell's offspring have become huge and highly profitable companies in their own rights. If all seven had been recombined with AT&T in 1989, their aggregate revenue would have exceeded General Motors' by over $2 billion, and their aggregate profit would have exceeded the automaker's by $6.7 billion.

Although they are regionally exclusive in their basic telephone businesses, the Baby Bells compete with one another abroad and even in the United States for serendipitous acquisitions and new lines of business. Cash-rich and growth-hungry, they are now seen as a threat by Ma Bell herself. In a letter to *The New York Times* this April, Randall L. Tobias, vice chairman of AT&T, warned that if the regionals were freed from the current antimanufacturing regulations and retained their monopolies, "AT&T and other U.S. companies would thus lose any business incentive to continue making heavy research and development commitments."

The aggressive Baby Bells want to be freed of almost all of the restrictions imposed by the federal legislation that created them. Those restrictions seem embodied in U.S. District Court Judge Harold H. Green, the nemesis of the ambitions of the regionals. Since 1986, Judge Green has held the line in preventing them from getting involved in manufacturing and information services—the two most desirable areas of enterprise. While the judge and Congress consider the issues, the Baby Bells themselves are hardly treading water. In addition to heavy investment in cellular (wireless) operations, cable TV (outside their regions), and business systems here in the United States, they are ranging the entire globe in search of opportunities.

As Ray Smith, Bell Atlantic's chairman and CEO, recently told the *Harvard Business Review,* "The old Bell System was like a great football team with the best athletes and the best equipment. Every Saturday morning, we'd run up and down the football field and win 100 to 0 because there was no one on the other side of scrimmage; we were a monopoly." Ray Smith was a star player on that team.

Born and raised in Pittsburgh, he joined the local Bell company in 1959, after getting a B.S. in industrial engineering at Carnegie Mellon. While he studied for further degrees in electrical engineering and business, he held posts in Bell of Pittsburgh's traffic, commercial, personnel, and operations departments. By 1976 he had become director of budget and planning at AT&T, and by 1983 was heading Bell of Pennsylvania and Diamond State Telephone. When those companies joined New Jersey Bell and Chesapeake and Potomac Telephone to become Bell Atlantic in 1984, Smith went with them. In 1989 he succeeded Thomas Bolger as the regional's CEO, and he added chairman of the board to his duties later that same year.

Under Bolger and Smith (who was CFO and then COO from 1985), the new corporation aggressively developed its lucrative region, installing fiber-optic cable (which carries signals 10,000 times faster than copper) and computer-operated switches to lower costs and increase product capacity. It also established itself in the fast-growing cellular market and moved into business systems, where it competes with AT&T, among others. Along the way it also created the world's largest independent computer service company, Bell Atlantic Systems Service (formerly Sorbus Inc.). The new regional's stockholders were happy investors.

Despite these accomplishments, Smith says he was disappointed with his colleagues' attitudes when he became CEO. As he told the *Harvard Review,* "In my first year as CEO, I was intensely frustrated because people didn't immediately understand my notions of empowerment, accountability, and teamwork. I finally learned to be less impatient."

The result of Smith's frustration and patience is "The Bell Atlantic Way." His work and pronouncements have resulted in reactions that range from *Fortune's* description of him as one of the "most visionary architects" of the communications megaindustry to another Philadelphia CEO's wry comment that he has "the biggest ego you'll ever meet."

IMPLEMENTING CULTURAL CHANGE

What is "The Bell Atlantic Way?" What actual change does it represent in the way the company works, in how it deals with itself, with its competitors, and with its customers?

I have to use the phrase "cultural change," although it's almost become a cliche. It was clear to us that the conventions we had for dealing with each other as businesses within a monopoly were totally inadequate. There was internal competition, trickiness, not team building but team competition. The structures, the language, the training, the promotion policies, the resource allocations—all of those things promoted internal battles.

What have you done about the situation?

We've created a new set of conventions, and we've trained 18,000 of our managers in them. We're now in the process of training

65,000 employees for three days, with substantial reinforcements after that. It's a huge, multimillion-hour training commitment to a new set of conventions of behavior.

Now you all carry a blue chip. What does it mean?
The chip just means first things first, meaning first your family and your own particular brand of spiritual and intellectual life and your health, then your company, and in your company your customers and then your employees. We call it "The Bell Atlantic Way," and that's a phrase that is used a million times a day in our company—people say, "That's not the Bell Atlantic Way."

BEFORE AND AFTER

What were you like before "The Bell Atlantic Way?"
Oh, I was a turkey manager. When I managed Pennsylvania, I saw the other companies as my competition. I truly believed that if I completed 100 percent of my objectives, I was fulfilling all of my objectives to the corporation. Now if everybody believes that, you'll have an organization that is destroyed before long, because sometimes in order to complete 100 percent of my objectives I have to sacrifice my teammates. If I had known then that my job was to see the whole company achieve 100 percent of its objectives, I would have behaved differently. I might have ended up with 91 or 92 percent and another manager would have been 98 percent and another 89 percent, but the whole thing would have been 100 percent. I didn't understand that I made one basic assumption, and it's the huge mistake that American business makes.

When did you reach your epiphany?
My lightning bolt came when I began to realize that for every profitable line that we had, every single product and every niche, we had competitors. That we moved slowly and were typical of large, bureaucratic organizations in that we thought improvement was incremental. We made incremental decisions, and as a result we missed out on achieving excellence. I presumed that I was going to get this job four or five years ago, so I began to think: How should we prepare this organization to be a team? Then I

remembered Rollie Massimino, who right around that time was the basketball coach for Villanova. He took a bunch of short kids and won the NCAA championship.

What's the Massimino method, and how does it apply to the business world?
He takes a bunch of scrappy high school kids, all total individuals, into the woods to camp for three weeks, and they come out speaking like team members. They understand accountability, they know that the only achievements are team achievements. You never hear Rollie's or any other successful coach's players complaining about each other. You wouldn't hear that. Now you've got a 19-year-old who just lost the NCAA championship talking on national TV. He's scored more points than anyone. It's easy for him to say, "Listen, I did my bit, but it's really marketing's fault." But he doesn't say that. He says, "They had a better team. They played very well. We did our best. We have a wonderful team. We worked very hard." He speaks like a team player, he thinks like a team player. Well, if Rollie Massimino and other great coaches can create team members who use creativity and have fierce individual accountability, why can't we? We've all got MBAs!

The Power of "Team"

Allan Cox
President
Allan Cox & Associates

Corporations that won't think team, won't make it.

T he chief financial officer and director of a large and respected corporation recently told me, "I haven't had a performance appraisal in over 20 years."

He went on to clarify that he had been evaluated on his numbers routinely, but as far as his actions and attitudes—his actual behavior on the job—were concerned, he had been left on his own.

I can already hear a few chuckles from some readers: "My God, if this guy's been moved through the chairs over a 20-year period, and reached the point where he's been made CFO and elected to the board, how much feedback does he need?"

This CFO and his fellow executives—including the CEO—are embarking upon a rigorous feedback discipline that measures their actions and attitudes on the job. This discipline is one facet of a corporatewide "re-birth." It's working: The numbers are up. The fact that top management is spending time and effort on developing themselves is sending the message throughout the company that what matters are actions and attitudes in support of carefully considered, clearly articulated values.

THINK "TEAM"

One of these key values is "team." The CFO doesn't know how to lead a team. He suspected this, but nobody ever told him—until his boss, peers, and subordinates gave him feedback through questionnaires and other evaluation instruments.

The rigors through which this giant corporation is willing to put itself is an indication we are in the midst of an organizational wave in worldwide business. Moreover, the "team" has become the organizational atom. Pure and simple, corporations that won't think "team" won't make it.

We have been beaten by the Japanese because they have made management-by-teamwork second nature. Yet team-building is rightfully viewed by many CEOs as ineffective, because it has often been applied as new patchwork to old clothing. True to the biblical parable, because it's not woven throughout the entire fabric of an organization, it tears loose and doesn't live up to expectations.

Team-building has been practiced in most cases as a special activity—and carried out by second- and third-level human resources professionals or consultants. These functionaries are brought in to "do" team-building as a freestanding project. When I suggested it to the management committee of one company, its members said, "We have more in mind than that, we did that three years ago. We're looking to do something else."

What these executives didn't understand is that team-building is unending. They saw it as an activity that is an end in and of itself, rather than a way of managing their entire business. But, by using the right kind of processes and guidelines, the development and implementation of their strategic plan could become a magnificent example of team management in action.

So as not to lose the power of "team," we should convert our language from team-building to team management to adjust our perspective, and then make two demands on team management. The first is that it does real work. The second is that it be corporatewide.

THE ORGANIZATIONAL WAVE

My book, *Inside Corporate America,* is a study of 13 major corporations from the three segments of business: consumer, service, and industrial. The book is based on a 400-item questionnaire completed by 1,086 managers in the 115 headquarters, subsidiaries, and divisions of these corporations. This group is comprised of 515 top and 571 middle-management executives.

One finding was disturbing. The respondents were asked to note the impact on their career success in their companies of "being a student of organizations." Two percent of top executives rated the impact as "very positive." Twenty-six percent rated it as "somewhat positive." The remainder spread their responses between "neutral," "somewhat negative," and "very negative." This is worthy of our attention.

The earliest emphasis in American business was on manufacturing and lasted for almost a century. Then the emphasis was on sales (for a shorter time); then marketing for yet a shorter time. Next came finance, which lasted about 15 years, ending around 1980.

Now we've entered a period that's global, not merely American, and one in which no solitary discipline or swing of the pendulum will serve us well. Some say, "we're going back to basics on manufacturing," and that's true. But sales and marketing also lay claim on our current rhetoric with the notion of "staying in touch with customers." And with the emphasis on shareholder value in running our businesses, finance is as important as ever.

We can call this period the organizational wave, and picture it as a subterranean volcano over which business and corporate life teeter. We can't see it, but we sway with its rumblings while signs of internal eruption are everywhere.

Some of these eruptions are structural. The merger, acquisition, and LBO phenomenon is a case in point. This is likely to increase; the stock market may become the greatest futures game of all, since any corporation in the world that draws attention to itself—for reasons good or bad—can have its assets valued and put in play overnight. CEOs must balance the long- and short-term skillfully and acknowledge that the measure of their worth is shareholder value over time.

Some of the eruptions are behavioral. Loyalty is gone; free-agency in professional sports is a good example of talent-for-hire. But it didn't start in sports, it started in business in the 1940s with the headhunter, and has extended to all organizational spheres, including university faculties and hospital staffs. Lifetime employment of the Japanese corporation is already eroding and likely to be increasingly influenced by our style. In this country, John Akers presides while IBM lays off employees. Nonetheless, the surveys of Daniel Yankelovich and others show that people from the top of the corporate hierarchy to the bottom still need and want to belong. They covet being productive and valued for their contributions. Authoritarianism no longer works. Participation is the rule.

We face countless variables, contradictions, and potential breakthroughs, while only a fourth of our top executives think being a student of organizational life is important. This is a crisis and not enough CEOs have grasped what Allen-Bradley president Tracy O'Rourke has: "The competitive environment, the technological environment, and the social issues inside a company are changing more rapidly than ever, and management is going to have to stay up with that rate of change. That's causing us all to have to really dedicate ourselves to a productive business life of renewing, reeducating, and constantly retraining ourselves. We've never had to do that before and it's going to be hard. You have to apply yourself and take time to do that. All of us convince ourselves that we don't have the time."

THE ORGANIZATIONAL ATOM

We must mobilize an all-out effort to teach our executives management-by-teamwork. The team is the organizational atom— the focus of power—and if the CEO is going to take the responsibility for sensitizing his organization to its own resourcefulness, then he must start there. What is called a team most often isn't. The "management team" of most companies is usually a case of mistaken identity. Meetings aren't "team" either, though a team can't exist without meetings. In its June 21, 1988 issue, *The Wall Street Journal* good-naturedly pointed out the banal quality of most meetings. The article, titled "A Survival Guide to the Office Meeting," stated that executives spend an average of 17 hours a week in meetings and another 6 in preparation for them.

Given the colossal waste of time and corporate resources, we would be smart to convert this waste to an investment in making meetings work. For example, the CEO of a well-known automotive manufacturer hosts a monthly dinner meeting of his direct reports. The meeting is meant to be informal, but he's made it clear he also expects it to be an occasion when issues and matters of concern to the business are brought up by attendees. These meetings have degenerated into small-talk socializing. The CEO complains that when he asks for substantive business issues to be raised, he's met with perfunctory comments, shallow questions, or just plain silence. Frustrated, he threatened the group at a recent meeting by saying that whoever didn't have something significant to offer at the meeting, wouldn't be invited back to the next one. He'd keep shrinking the group, he said, until he ended up with someone he could talk to.

HOW TO HARNESS "TEAM"

If we want to see and feel the power of "team" throughout our organizations, we're going to have to measure and reward team behavior. This is simple in concept but requires dedication from the CEO. The good news is that such an initiative is intensely gratifying and the best bet for increasing shareholder value over time.

Management-by-team is taking the design-oriented idea of quality in products and using it as a guiding light for ensuring the quality of our total management. Through a comprehensive, corporatewide design of team management—and its measurement—a company can build in total quality performance. Effective team management has to be designed to meet two demands: first, to do real work, and second, to be corporatewide. As Larry Perlman, president of Control Data, tells his people: "We are the competition." Gary Dillon, CEO of the highly successful $1 billion manufacturing business soon to be spun off by Household International, educates his people with a similar message: "We have found the edge and it is us."

As a CEO, you are best advised to undergo a team-effectiveness workshop. With the aid of a resource person skilled in team methods, you and your officers will be able to evaluate the merits of infusing team management throughout your company. With such a workshop behind you, you may well conclude you're a believer and have the determination to see this through. There are eight action steps you can take.

1. *Appoint a task force that will lay the groundwork for the team management system.* "Egad!" you protest. "Not another task force. That will consign the project to oblivion right from the start. Just like a blue ribbon panel in Washington."

My reply is that it will fail only if you let it. Since "team" is to do real work, think of the meaning of task force. It's a team with a real task. Complain all you like, but there's no other way. If you don't begin the effort with your own people (who know the organization best), then this already taxing challenge is doomed to fail for lack of the ideas you'll need. From where else, for example, could team management measurements come that satisfy most participants?

2. *Make the task force interdisciplinary and have it number between five and nine people.* "Team" is a small group in this range, and a team management system will set about improving the performance of groups of this size throughout your company. Pick the executive who reports to you who has the best interpersonal skills and put him or her in charge of the task force. Inspire them with your conviction. Make them accountable for conceiving a distinctive team management system. Then leave and let them get to work. But stay on the case.

3. *Draft (or revise) a corporate values statement that reflects the spiritual side of your organization.* (If these values emerge as contradictory to the mission of your strategic plan, you have even more work to do.) To do this, select a second interdisciplinary task force that you will head. Be sure that one member of the team management task force also sits on this one. Your corporate values statement might include an item that reads something like this: "The manager's first job is to nurture the competence and self-esteem of his or her subordinates."

4. *Develop and articulate behavior benchmarks that support team management.* It's one thing to have goals as an expression of your corporation's mission and strategy, but quite another to have "getting there" actions and attitudes that are specified and can be measured. Your company will want to develop its own benchmarks, but you probably can use some guidance on this as well as from a number of organizations such as the Center for Creative

Leadership in Greensboro, North Carolina, Development Dimensions in Pittsburgh, Forum Corporation in Boston, University Associates in San Diego, or our firm.

5. *Realize this is a large-scale indoctrination/teaching project, and your entire corporation is the classroom.* What is being taught are small-group leadership techniques. The message sent to each manager by his boss is: "You are a team member in this group, but on the next level down you are a team leader. What you are learning here you must teach and apply there."

6. *Keep the two demands of effective team management before you at all times.* First focus teaching techniques on real issues. Second, make team-management corporatewide.

7. *Reward your achievers.* The achiever's profile is comprised of commitment to team, risk, balance, and results. No values statement or team management exhortations will be subscribed to or implemented with any verve unless your people are measured against specific behavior benchmarks and rewarded both financially and emotionally for making them part of their job objectives and delivering results.

The required actions and attitudes in support of the achiever's profile need to be made a central feature of your incentive pay and performance appraisal procedures.

8. *Make sure your chief human resources officer is enthusiastic about what he's supposed to accomplish.* Lack of vitality in organizational thinking is underscored by the fact that many corporations have placed weak people in charge of human resources. Fortunately, this is changing. Your human resources officer, if not the key point-person in the administration of team effectiveness, will nonetheless be an essential player in its outcome.

When embarking upon the establishment of corporatewide team management, you're likely to have mixed emotions. Bound up with your anticipation of raising corporate performance a few notches, you may also encounter fears of misdirected effort, poor execution, and outright failure.

But the difference between winners and losers on the corporate playing field is the difference between managing through "team" versus doing it poorly or not at all. This demands perseverance, because while the initial stages of team management—well executed—yield immediate benefits, the real payoff is over a decade away. Remember the Chinese proverb: "A journey of a thousand miles begins with one step." Practice balancing the long- and short-term in the service of shareholder value, and you'll be a visionary who keeps his eye on today.

Allan Cox heads the Chicago-based consulting firm that bears his name. Founded in 1969, this firm specializes in top-management team effectiveness and mission development. Cox is author of six books, including the recently published, *Straight Talk for Monday Morning*. He serves as board chairman of The Center for Ethics and Corporate Policy in Chicago.

At the Heart of Leadership: Courage

Rodman L. Drake
Former Managing Director and Chief Executive
CRESAP

Cowardly lions who are still holding on in the 1980s will be running for cover in the 1990s.

C ourage is probably the oldest quality we associate with leadership. As children, we learn the stories of David facing Goliath, of Leonidas at Thermopylae, of Washington at Valley Forge, and we understand that leaders are undaunted by great odds. When we are older we learn of the kind of courage that puts community and principles above self-interest, as when John Adams defended the British soldiers who had committed the Boston Massacre. And we learn that leaders show perhaps their greatest courage—and sometimes greatest sacrifice—when coming to self-knowledge, as Lear did.

But strangely, we seldom talk about courage today. That neglect is to our detriment as chief executives and to the detriment of our companies. Specifically, we need courage to do what is probably the hardest thing any leader ever has to do: change ourselves and the parts of our organization closest to us. We need the courage to make changes right at the top—not just from the top. We need the courage to pick a successor who may go against organizational tradition, when tradition is merely another word for inertia. Finally, we need the courage to step aside for that successor.

Without the courage to do these three things, we cannot make our organizations more productive, more responsive, more flexible, and continuously adaptive to the global economy—the goals we all aspire to in this era of ceaseless change.

CHANGES AT THE TOP

We know that if our companies are to thrive in the radically changed environment of global competition, we must transform them. They need to become more productive, to stay close to the marketplace no matter where it is, to respond quickly to the changes in the marketplace (or rather, marketplaces), and to be flexible yet purposeful—not running off in all directions at once. In short, we all generally believe that the key to survival lies in redefining the company strategy for a new age in business and overseeing a change process that ensures that the strategy is implemented. And this is true. But when we set out to transform our companies, we too often take half-measures. In some areas we do well—for instance, we do a terrific job of transforming the shop floor. We make our manufacturing operations more productive through just-in-time inventories and quality circles, and more flexible by breaking down labor-management barriers and getting operations, research and development, and marketing in sync. We've been successful at instilling a new ethos of teamwork, in which the individual wins when the team wins and the team wins when the company wins.

In the past decade we've also gotten better at transforming staff functions and middle management (though we've not always been so effective at managing some of the human consequences of that transformation). Because of competitive pressures and advances in information technology, staff functions have become more streamlined and more focused on the concerns of the business. Staff managers have been able to turn more attention to supporting the work of making and marketing the company's products and services by leading, facilitating, or simply participating in work teams with peers in line positions.

For middle managers, organizations have become flatter, with many jobs eliminated. The survivors' jobs have been transformed from coordinating processes to producing products or services. And their ethos has shifted from bureaucrat to entrepreneur. They measure their success in real achievements—not in titles, office size, or place in the pecking order.

For the shop floor and middle management, then, we've done a good job of getting everybody's focus back where it belongs—on winning in the marketplace. We've been able to do that because we've managed to restructure the work to put the focus there.

In too many companies, though, we have not applied these imperatives to the part of the company where they can do the most good: the very top. The changes necessary to the survival of our companies stop at the threshold of the executive suite. The rest of the company may have become leaner, flatter, and more flexible, with managers focusing on product not perks, but the top still looks and acts like the traditional bureaucratic pyramid.

Restructuring a corporation is undeniably painful for CEOs. It's trying to see employees agonize with change and uncertainty, and, in some cases, loss of employment. But in the reflective moments after the announcement of a restructuring, most CEOs I've known and worked with lament that they haven't gone far enough. I'm often forced to agree. They've built up the courage to restructure, but they haven't had the courage to capitalize on the opportunity by making changes where they will have the greatest long-term impact on corporate performance: among the CEO's direct subordinates.

Consider Colby Chandler, the CEO of Kodak. He's embarking on Kodak's fourth restructuring in six years. Over the last several years his top management group has remained virtually unchanged. One has to wonder if Chandler has had any second thoughts about his management team in the face of the continued need to restructure Kodak.

Too often we see senior managers behaving in an all-too-human way, resisting change in themselves that they insist on in the rest of the organization. They want to preserve their spots at the top of "their" organizations—as though the company were a collection of fiefdoms. After a lifetime of learning how to work the hierarchical organization, they measure their success in terms of commanding a greater and greater share of the company's total resources, and in terms of the success or excellence achieved by their unit. They do not measure their success by their own ability to do whatever job needs to be done for the success of the company.

Some observers, including *Business Week*, believe this kind of ossification at the top was one of the reasons for United Technologies' floundering performance a few years ago. Then UT's new chairman, Robert Daniell, came in with the courage to make changes at the top—courage to redirect company resources into research and development, and courage to break down the lines between fiefdoms by bringing his senior managers together to share ideas and experiences in what he calls "The Saturday Morning Club." Unfortunately, Daniell's kind of reform-at-the-top initiative is all too rare, especially among incumbent CEOs.

This is not to say that senior managers are more venal or obstreperous than other members of the organization—only that they have learned to do well what the traditional organizational structure and incentive system has told them to do.

Nevertheless, this tip of the traditional pyramid becomes the rock against which even the most elegant transformation strategy may founder. To transform that tip, the CEO needs not only vision, but personal courage, and a lot of it. The experience of Roger Smith at GM is revealing. He took steps to breathe new life into the executive ranks when he brought in Ross Perot with EDS and Elmer Johnson, a Chicago lawyer, as part of a restructuring effort. Johnson, in fact, was a dark horse to succeed Smith. But those efforts at transformation did not succeed. Both Johnson and Perot are gone and Smith's tenure will end in August 1990. Smith is easily the most courageous GM chairman in modern times, but he apparently didn't go far enough to implement his convictions.

At this level, transformation means facing company employees and saying, "We've got to change." It may mean telling a colleague of 25 years that the division he's built cannot get the same share of the company's resources that it once did because our overall strategy requires that we change emphases in the business. It may mean saying to every member of the senior management group—including yourself—that the values and structure that have worked so well in the past will not work for us in the future. Now the question is, what do we do, not to the rest of the company, but to ourselves?

NONTRADITIONAL CANDIDATES
AS SUCCESSORS

One thing we may have to do is disappoint the ambitions of those executives closest to us. To transform our companies for the future, we may need the courage to pick a successor who goes against the grain of organizational tradition. The successor may have to come from an unorthodox place and have some unorthodox qualities, including a well-managed failure in his or her resume.

Traditionally, CEOs and their boards have looked for candidates from the generation of executives immediately below the chief executive—people who usually got where they are by being safely successful. These executives constitute the tip of the traditional pyramid. But just as they may—through no real fault of their own—pose the final obstacle to organizational transformation, this group may also be exactly the wrong place to look for the next generation of leadership.

At the very least, it is not automatically the best place to look. For companies undergoing radical strategic change—redefining what businesses they are in and how they will do business—the traditional pool of candidates for CEO usually consists of executives who have been successful at what the company used to do, not what it is doing now, and not what it is going to do.

The choice of Doug Yearley to be the new chief executive at Phelps Dodge reflects this type of thinking. Phelps Dodge, an old-line mining company, restructured and diversified into industrial products. When selecting the new CEO, the board opted for Yearley, the head of the industries product group.

For instance, a financial services company might have had a tradition of competitive excellence as a wire house. Its top people got to the top because they knew how to run that kind of business. But suppose the company now shifts strategies and expects to increasingly emphasize merchant banking and trading. Its new CEO had better be expert at running those kinds of businesses. But candidates of that sort may not be in the usual pool. Compounding the problem, those who are in the pool believe that they are entitled to the top jobs and that choosing a newcomer would deprive them of their legacy.

In this illustration, both logic and strategy say to look outside the usual pool for the next CEO: look beyond the organization, or look at a younger generation of executives in the organization who are leaders in the new direction of the business. But tradition, personal relationships, and simple anxiety about the unknown can weigh strongly against logic. Frequently, a traditional successor will even look good for several years, riding on the company's momentum. In many cases, however, the degree of change required will be far beyond the capabilities of the executive who grew up in a stabler environment. Such a choice only postpones the inevitable and creates pressure for more wrenching change at a later date. Again, what we need is courage to follow our best convictions about the future.

We need to see more leaders take the kind of bold step Reg Jones took at GE when he picked Jack Welch as his successor. There were several "safe" candidates whose progress up the corporate ladder fit the GE culture like a glove, but Jones sensed that the culture needed a shock and had the courage to act on his conviction.

It's not enough to go against the grain in defining the pool of candidates; CEOs and boards also need to reject tradition in defining the qualities they seek in those candidates. Typically, they have followed the principle that nothing succeeds like success. That seems a safe and prudent course. But I think it is the wrong one.

In picking successors, we need to look for candidates whose resumes include failures. But well-managed failures. By this I mean failures that came from breaking new ground and from which the executive and the organization learned something that made their next effort a success.

Ed Hoffman, who was selected to be the president of Household Finance Corporation (HFC) in 1987, is an ideal example. In 18 years at Citibank, the charismatic biophysicist experienced several failures, including one of the few instances in the bank's history when its foreign banking interests were nationalized. Ed was senior officer in Colombia when the government forced it to take a majority partner. He is also reported to be the key figure in convincing John Reed to write off Citibank's Latin America debt. Because of these managed failures, Ed was the ideal candidate to handle the massive, but successful, restructuring at HFC.

In the new competitive environment, everyone cannot win every time. We need leaders who are not wiped out by a setback, but who see it as valuable information that helps them adjust what they and their organization are doing.

Ken Susnjara of Thermwood Corporation is a good model for this kind of "fortunate fall." As *Industry Week* tells the story, in 1986, Thermwood was in trouble, so Susnjara stepped down from the corporate helm and became a salesperson for Thermwood products. From the sales experience Susnjara learned that what fascinated the people in research and development bore little or no relationship to what customers wanted. He also discovered that management decisions that look terrific in a boardroom can take on an entirely different cast when viewed through the eyes of a distributor-salesperson. When he returned as CEO in August 1985, Susnjara set about restructuring the company. He shut down the marketing and research and development facilities and established a three-division structure organized along product lines. He then cut executives' salaries by two-thirds to three-quarters and put the executives on productivity based compensation. As a result, Thermwood returned to profitability.

Susnjara wasn't unhinged by his company's setback, he learned from it. And he responded by changing himself, then his organization. That's the quality we need to look for in picking our successors.

STEPPING DOWN

The CEO's final act of courage is to step down when the time is right, and not outlast his or her own effectiveness. Each of us who leads an organization has our own signature way of looking at the world, at our company's place in it, at the way we think business ought to be done. When we are effective, our signature way of doing things matches the needs of the organization.

But in a continuously changing business environment, our way is unlikely to be the right way every time. And while we might all like to feel we are infinitely flexible, able to adapt to any situation, the truth is we are only relatively flexible. Each of us has a core way of acting and seeing that makes us who we are. The challenge, then, is to understand before anyone else when that core way of acting no longer best serves the interests of our organizations.

The late Bart Giamatti showed that kind of courage when he stepped down from the presidency of Yale at the age of 48, after spending eight years restoring fiscal stability and building the confidence of alumni. Bart was enormously popular with students and alumni, and admired by the faculty as a scholar and administrator. He could have stayed for many years. Bart once wrote about Matteo Boiardi, the 15th century Italian poet, that "Boiardi's deepest desire is to conserve something of purpose in a world of confusion." At Yale, Bart's great concern was to preserve the traditional values embodied in a great institution of learning. What is not well known is that in conserving these values, Bart was not able to attack a range of important problems at Yale. He was too much of an "insider"—with a web of relationships built during his tenure as a faculty member. Ultimately, he had the courage to recognize that he had accomplished much, but that the university needed a different set of skills. Baseball was fortunate to benefit from Bart's talents, and Yale moved on successfully to a new era of leadership.

On the other side of the coin, Harr Gray, Bob Daniell's predecessor at UTC, is an example of a leader who stayed too long. During his tenure of 14 years, he built UTC through a series of acquisitions from a $2 billion company into an $18 billion company. But Gray's success as a builder led him to pursue growth after several disastrous acquisitions and the loss of leadership in key business sectors. To top it off, he stayed beyond his normal retirement date under the guise that there was no qualified successor. If Gray had retired five years earlier, his record would have been exemplary.

Stepping down is hard. But it is not the hardest thing. Looking into ourselves and recognizing our own limitations is the hardest thing—especially when those limitations used to be the strengths we relied on, strengths that don't fit the world of our business any more. Many of us don't have the chance to stay too long, because the age at which we got the job is relatively close to retirement. But I believe most CEOs should not stay beyond 10 years, no matter how successful they've become. Even that span can be too long for some leaders, no matter how great.

This is different from the athlete's desire to go out a winner. It is the leader's desire to go out leaving the organization capable of winning. It is the most eloquent and courageous gesture a leader can make.

Rodman L. Drake is the retired CEO of New York-based Cresap, an international management consulting firm. He followed his own advice and stepped down in 1990 after a 10-year tenure. He is currently an independent investor and director of several corporations. Drake is a graduate of Yale and has an MBA from Harvard. He has written numerous articles on business management.

The Magic of Ownership

Jude T. Rich
Chairman
Sibson & Co.

If companies want executives to act as owners, they have to reward them as if they were owners.

S hareholders have grown accustomed to seeing some high-flown claims in proxy statements. Each year, companies implore them to believe statements on the order of: "If you approve our stock option, restricted stock, and performance share plans for executives, you will transform executives into owners! People will work harder and smarter! Performance will improve!"

While these long-term incentives can help attract and retain executives, such plans typically have little or no impact on actions and decisions, with the possible exception of a handful of senior managers. Our firm's surveys and interviews with hundreds of large-company executives show that most behave no differently because they participate in long-term incentive plans. These plans often do not work as advertised because they lack the "magic" of ownership.

REASONS FOR FAILURE

Why don't these incentive plans treat executives as owners? For starters, most of these plans call for little or no risk of capital. Even when stock is placed in executives' hands, executives usually sell the shares as soon as possible. Some companies have tried to overcome these problems by avoiding outright grants of stock or cash payouts based on easily attainable financial objectives. Instead, very large option grants are used, sometimes with restrictions on sale, after exercise. A few companies have even sold executives stock, or had executives purchase debentures that are convertible into common stock.

These approaches certainly help treat the top handful of executives more like owners, but what about executives, for example, in a $200 million division of a $5 billion company? Owning stock in a huge corporation won't make an executive behave like an owner of his small division. Given the current level of consolidation (nearly $900 billion in mergers and acquisitions in the past five years), long-term incentives in the future will have to be based, in whole or in part, on business unit performance in a majority of large U.S. companies. Better still, these incentives should simulate an equity ownership in the business unit whenever possible. In fact, a recent Sibson survey of 100 of the largest U.S. manufacturing and financial services companies shows that 18 percent now use long-term incentives based on business unit results. A similar survey five years ago showed only three companies with business unit plans.

Having a "piece of the action" stimulates the ownership and entrepreneurial spirits of executives, and can dramatically increase their commitment to business success. Anyone who doubts this claim should talk to a management team that has recently led an LBO of their company. Suddenly, the expensive corporate headquarters becomes disposable. Overhead melts away like ice. Marginal businesses and product lines disappear. Such is the magic of ownership, and the accompanying management risk.

SELECTING A LONG-TERM INCENTIVE DESIGN

Most executives would agree that tailoring incentives to business unit results makes sense. But many units are not standalone businesses. Frequently, businesses share resources, such as plants and sales forces. Also, transfer prices may be set by the parent corporation at levels that differ from the open market. So it follows that the degree to which incentives can be based on business unit versus corporate results depends on the level of interdependence and synergy among the businesses. Thus, the key factor in tailoring incentives to business unit results will be the corporation's fundamental strategic approach.

To classify a company's strategic approach, we can draw on Harvard's Michael Porter, who, in a 1987 *Harvard Business Review* article, identified four approaches:

Portfolio Management. Acquiring sound, attractive, undervalued companies. Retaining (or supplying) experienced managers and running the companies as autonomous units.

1. *Restructuring.* Acquiring underdeveloped, sick, threatened organizations (or industries on the threshold of significant change). Intervening actively, often selling off restricted units.

2. *Transferring Skills.* Developing or acquiring a position in new industries. Transferring proprietary expertise among units.

3. *Sharing Activities.* Achieving competitive advantage by sharing proprietary capabilities to lower cost/increase value differentiation.

"Portfolio management" is exemplified by ITT with its varied portfolio of hotels, insurance, automotive parts, and electronics. By contrast, PepsiCo transfers the company's considerable consumer products, distribution, franchise management, and other skills to a series of related consumer products businesses.

Companies like IBM and P&G share sales forces and manufacturing facilities among their businesses. Developing simulated ownership incentives in such interdependent businesses requires some difficult cost and asset allocations to establish the true value of each business. So companies that "share activities" are also likely to share a single long-term ownership plan. For example, when Sperry and Burroughs merged and integrated, a single plan consisting of a long-term cash incentive based on corporate performance, restricted stock, and options on Unisys stock was used.

The starting point for designing effective incentives is to decide whether to differentiate the unit's plan from that of the corporation, based primarily on the corporation's overall strategic approach. Then, the type of long-term incentive to accomplish the desired degree of differentiation can be selected, since these plans can be viewed along a continuum that ranges from highly differentiated plans to a single, common plan. We'll look at three companies that used this framework to design effective business unit incentives.

THREE CASE STUDIES

Health Care

A multibillion dollar health care company fits Porter's definition of a company that "shares activities." The company is functionally organized. Research, sales, and other resources are managed centrally. The CEO decided the company became so large that the stock option plan had little meaning to most of the top 100 executives.

To encourage a greater sense of ownership, he offered his team a large amount of debentures, convertible to common stock. Executives had to borrow to gain the right to convert to common stock in the future. If the company's stock did not appreciate, the executives were saddled with a crushing debt service without offsetting gains. On the other hand, rapid stock price growth would make them rich.

In this case, the interdependence of the various functions within this company prevented simulating business unit ownership. However, greater ownership was created using a corporate incentive plan.

Publishing

A major publishing company had attempted to launch a new magazine for some years without success. When a particularly innovative concept surfaced, the CEO established an autonomous legal entity completely separate from the other publishing properties.

To simulate ownership in the magazine venture, the key management and editorial staff were removed from the corporate stock option and restricted stock plans. Since these plans had provided regular gains for years, executives were put "at risk" in this speculative venture.

In place of the corporate plans, phantom stock was created in the new venture and shares were allocated to key players. The stock's initial value was set at the company's first-year cash investment to launch the business, plus any incremental cash contribution. In addition, the parent company's total cash investment was increased by the three-year Treasury bill rate each year. This "internal value" of the new venture was then subtracted from the "external market value" of the venture, which was set at 10 times annual cash flow, to determine the total gain in value. The 10 times multiple was based on analyses of sales of similar magazines over the past five years. The venture's executive team held 10 percent of the phantom stock, representing entitlement to 10 percent of the gain in the business's value.

If current projections are accurate, the executive team will increase the value of the business by $150 million within six years. The venture's top team will split $15 million of this gain. These executives will have earned this reward, given the effort and personal sacrifices they have made as "owners" of this venture.

Utility

A diversified utility had for some time owned two autonomous subsidiaries, one in real estate, the other in broadcasting. Clearly, this utility is acting as a "portfolio manager." Over the years, the performance of these subsidiaries was disappointing. Not surprisingly, all subsidiary executives were on corporate annual and long-term incentives. The president of the real estate business made a strong case that his industry typically shared a "piece of the action" with executives, rather than a more traditional utility incentive plan.

The company developed an annual incentive plan that paid out based on key strategic milestones for each of the two business units. In real estate, the annual incentive is based on such factors as zoning approvals and development progress.

SARs AS INCENTIVES

But the real key to success is a long-term incentive that simulates equity for the top executives. This plan uses stock appreciation rights (SARs) redeemable for actual subsidiary company shares.

These rights become exercisable over a four-year period, after which an executive can either allow the SARs to run (for up to six more years) or cash them in for real subsidiary shares. When an executive leaves the company or retires, he then has to sell his shares back to the parent company. The company reserves the right to buy back shares in four annual installments if an executive leaves before retirement. These installments provide a tax-deferral mechanism to the executive and avoid affecting the business unit's cash flow materially in any given year.

To illustrate how these SARs work, consider the president of the real estate subsidiary's plan. Assume the company's initial investment is $10 million. One million subsidiary shares are created. Thus, the price per share is $10. It is agreed that the president will have a 7 percent "ownership" opportunity, or 70,000 SARs with a strike price of $10 per share. At the time of the SAR grant, of course, there is no gain.

Next, the potential value of the real estate business over 5 and 10 years is projected. This enables the company to estimate the potential gain to executives for the 7 percent phantom ownership. The actual value of the real estate subsidiary will be determined by an independent appraisal every three years, or upon the resignation of the president.

This approach enables the executives to participate in the appreciation of the value of the business as though he were a partial owner. The participating executives are extremely enthusiastic about this plan, and the subsidiary's performance to date has outstripped original projections.

Although incentives usually cannot be counted on to motivate top executives to work harder, the executives in this business openly admit that they have worked both harder and smarter as a result of the incentive. Moreover, the company has been able to attract new executives with small portion of "ownership" and has lost none of its key players.

In sum, to influence the actions and decisions of business executives, long-term incentives should be differentiated from corporate plan based on the degree of business unit interdependence with other units. This interdependence depends on the corporation's fundamental strategy. Further, long-term incentives should simulate or create real equity of the corporation or business unit for the executives. In this age of increasing entrepreneurialism, ownership is magic.

However, compensation is only one of the many "levers" that management has to reinforce a corporate strategic approach and to motivate executives to carry out business unit strategies. Too often, senior managers believe that the solution to their problems is to design a new incentive plan. But incentives are often not the real problem. There are many elements organization effectiveness, including reporting structures, systems, management style, shared values, and how people are selected, developed, and coached.

Companies should consider all of these levers before tinkering with the compensation program. An integrated program of change using each of these levers, including compensation, has a significantly better chance of success than simply changing the pay plan.

Jude T. Rich is chairman of Sibson & Company, a management consulting firm. An authority on compensation for all levels of employees, he consults with many major U.S. companies on compensation, human resource management, and organizational issues. Previously, Rich was a partner at McKinsey & Company.

Managing the Skills Gap

Michel Besson
President and Chief Executive
CertainTeed

The work force crisis is as much about upgrading management style as it is about educational or training needs.

M ost U.S. companies today are basking in the work force benefits of the post-World War II baby boom. That may be one reason why so many employers find it hard to take the impending work force crisis seriously. Forty-five percent of the 4,000 who responded to a recent Hudson Institute/Towers Perrin survey said they were unconcerned about any mismatch between the skills of workers and the jobs they will be expected to perform. Obviously, the unconcerned have never talked with Elizabeth Brock, president of a small industrial pallet company in Dacula, Georgia. A critical skill in the manufacture of wooden pallets is measuring lumber. "In my office," she says, "I have a great big poster of an inch on a ruler. I show employees one inch; they don't know what I mean by a half-inch. So I teach them a half-inch, and then a quarter-inch. A sixteenth or a thirty-second of an inch is way beyond them. I'm at the point where I'm taking people I have to train in the basics." Nor have any unconcerned employers spoken with us at CertainTeed. We are a diversified building materials company that is going through some significant changes. And every last one of these changes—from statistical process control to computer-integrated manufacturing on the assembly line—is calling for rising levels of competence, and, just as important, a new managerial mind-set.

DEMOGRAPHIC DILEMMA

Workforce 2000: Work and Workers for the Twenty-First Century, a Hudson Institute report commissioned by the U.S. Department of Labor, analyzed economic and demographic trends for the coming decade. The study found that 80 percent of the new entrants into the labor market between now and the turn of the century will be women, minorities, and immigrants, many caught in the cycles of culture that mitigate against educational and occupational achievement. At the same time, the nature of the workplace itself is changing. According to *Workforce 2000,* more than half of all new jobs created between now and the year 2000 will require some education beyond high school, and nearly a third of those jobs will require a college degree. Workers will have to be able to follow instructions in manuals, understand and operate computers, communicate with charts and graphs, and work productively in teams. Workers will have to become true members of a work force shaped by new managerial incentives.

Every time work becomes more complicated, or more is expected of workers as participants in management, the trainability threshold rises. Yet today, in a time of rising thresholds, education levels among job seekers have hit a new low. The statistics are fast becoming well-known: One-fourth of all U.S. high school students fail to graduate, and only 7 percent of 17-year-old American students are able to perform jobs that require technical abilities. The U.S. Department of Labor is projecting work force growth of 21 million between 1986 and 2000, down 10 million from the previous 15 years. But it isn't just the numbers game that matters. Robotics, the redesign of work and the workplace, flexible working schedules, outsourcing, support for child and elder care, extension of the retirement age, and immigration—these factors in the right combination should make up for any shortfall in numbers. It's the shortfall in education and trainability that has a growing number of CEOs worried.

INVOLVEMENT WITH EDUCATION

As employers try to compensate for that shortage, in-house education becomes a hidden tax on U.S. industry. Bill Wiggenhorn, the director of Motorola's training program, estimates that it costs $200 to train a U.S. worker in statistical process control, a basic manufacturing technique. Teaching the same process to a Japanese worker, he says, costs 47 cents. The Japanese simply hand their employees a book. American workers must first learn to read and do basic math. IBM's education and training costs have reached $1.5 billion a year, or $5.5 million more than the entire annual operating budget of Harvard University. Employers nationwide already spend more on education and training ($210 billion) each year than the total annual bill ($189.1 billion) for all U.S. elementary and secondary education, public and private. But all evidence suggests, even at this early stage in the work force crisis, that remedial education costs are rising fast. A few years ago, when the dimensions of the crisis first became apparent, companies, CertainTeed among them, began "adopting" schools. Since then, in New York City alone, 60 public schools have been adopted. Nationwide, there are now roughly 140,000 such partnerships. While many have produced gratifying results, the concept may have raised too many false expectations on all sides. As educators and students have discovered, "adopting" can mean anything from donating antiquated equipment, to internships, to an all-expense-paid college education for any student who graduates with a satisfactory grade average. Moreover, there is little evidence that a successful partnership can promote the systemic change the current crisis requires.

THE WORKPLACE IS A CLASSROOM, TOO

There are at least as many ways to help schools as there are points of light in George Bush's universe. Some of the most promising, if controversial, were suggested on Labor Day last year by his Commission on Workforce Quality and Labor Market Efficiency. In its report, *Investing in People: Strategy to Address America's Workforce Crisis,* the Commission said business should help restructure public school curricula to emphasize personal competition less and teamwork more, develop problem-solving abilities, and combine academics with applied training. At CertainTeed, as management has worked to lower the levels of responsibility, we have become keenly aware of these needs. The more involved in management the employees become, the more critical are the skills of teamwork, problem solving, and application. I have always believed that a company's main concern should be the logical and constant growth of its business. By being profitable, a company can meet its obligations to employees and society. The job of business, then, is to train educated employees so that they have the necessary skills to perform effectively. But a company cannot train today's undereducated workers unless they are taught the basics. David Kearns, CEO of Xerox, has been making a strong case for business involvement in a political constituency for educational reform, to which state governors are the key. In the federal budget, education ranks as a minor item, averaging well under 10 percent. In state budgets, education is the largest expense, averaging some 40 percent. But simple-minded generosity is out. More businesses are starting to follow the advice of former Education Secretary William Bennett: "More generosity should come with strings attached." Business has a major role to play in strengthening educational quality and communicating cultural encouragement. But the workplace, not the schoolroom, is its best resource.

COMMUNICATION ON THE JOB

Let's look now at what business has been doing to empower the present work force. Is there an industry or firm of any size in the United States that has not by now heard of W. Edwards Deming or Joseph Juran, or brought in one of their disciples as a consultant? These people, heralds of a too-long-delayed revolution in management and corporate culture, are living reminders that Japan's managerial revolution was made in the United States. There is nothing "Japanese" about teamwork and continuous improvement; they are matters of organized common sense. If they worked marvels over there, they can work miracles here.

To bring about equal revolutionary change in U.S. industry, corporations must enhance communications so that they remove the logjam that prevents innovation, creativity, and quick decision making. When you enhance communications, people have a better sense of the direction and goals of the corporation and of their own contributions toward those goals. They understand what others are doing and how they can help. The building materials industry is a very tough, very competitive industry. If you're going to be a tough, aggressive company in the 1990s, you're going to have to give your people the tools they need to communicate. CertainTeed, for example, is in the midst of implementing a major philosophical change in the management of its information systems, moving toward a network of desktop PCs and minicomputers and away from dependency on a centralized mainframe system. These tools will enable us to support teamwork and make decisions faster at lower levels of management than ever before. We're moving in the direction of building a single mentality on continual quality improvement, respect for each other, and the recognition that the better trained our people are and the better the tools we put into their hands to make decisions, the faster the company will be able to move in bringing new, more innovative products to market. I still hear some American managers talking about the failure of U.S. schools and families to teach good work habits. American workers are "spoiled," I am told. "What we need are people who show up on time, stay on the job, keep records accurately, show initiative, stick with problems until they are solved, and tell the truth. And, by the way, whatever happened to company loyalty?"

Quality circles and similar programs have taught us that the peer pressure inherent in teamwork can do more to correct a perceived shortcoming in work habits than lecturing and discipline from above. We've also learned that improved communications between customers and industrial teams does more for quality and productivity than a desperate appeal to company loyalty. Critics, including the members of the Commission on Workforce Quality and Labor Market Efficiency, have complained that too much of the training effort has been devoted to middle and upper management, and not enough to supervisory, technical, clerical, and line employees. Such critics need to be reminded that every knowledgeable observer has placed the blame for U.S. industrial decline not on the American worker—but on the American manager. If that verdict is justified, and I believe to a large extent it is, then most of the training is going exactly where it will do the most good.

PUT THE MANAGER BEFORE THE HORSE

We know that to effect a cultural change we must rely on our middle managers most of all. For it is the middle-level managers who will give the workers the autonomy to become decision makers. Participatory management is far more subtle and difficult, but usually more rewarding and even pleasurable than simply telling others what to do. CertainTeed, for example, like its French parent, Saint-Gobain, consists of numerous highly autonomous business units. To form a mutually reinforcing bridge between the managers of these units we have created what we call Club Liaison. Modeled after an in-house club in France called "Hexagon" (a geometric symbol that closely resembles the outline of that country), Liaison is organized into six self-governing regional chapters of between 18 and 30 members each. The chapters meet twice a year in the spring and fall, usually at a different hotel, resort, or conference center. Meetings are scheduled typically over two days in the middle of the week. The members—plant managers, sales managers, credit managers, service center managers—come together in the afternoon of the first day for a reception followed by dinner. The after-dinner speaker is usually a corporate executive, often a group president. Corporate executives such as I may attend, but only by invitation, and an invitation is considered an honor.

Liaison, like any private club, exists primarily to encourage friendship between its members. Protocol is ignored. Each chapter decides on its own rules. The only given is an operational format that encourages a mutual exchange of ideas, experiences and information. This usually takes the form of a roundtable meeting on the morning of the second day, when the men and women of the chapter informally share experiences, discuss problems, and report on new accounts. The meetings often close with a visit to a customer—to a vinyl window fabricating facility, for example, or to a plant that builds modular homes, or to a CertainTeed manufacturing operation.

Club Liaison continues to demonstrate its value to the company with every chapter meeting. At last fall's gathering of the Midwest Chapter in Kansas City, the manager of our plastic pipe fittings plant happened to sit next to a new member, the vice president of manufacturing at the recently acquired Air Vent Corporation. The vice president began distributing his firm's product brochures, and the manager from the plastic fittings plant noticed illustrations of roof ventilator parts that appeared to be made of molded plastic. He asked who made them and learned that they were supplied to Air Vent by an outside firm in Michigan. CertainTeed's Kansas plant had machine time that the manager was anxious to fill; so he struck up a conversation and, after the meeting, took him to lunch. Today, the deal they made is saving Air Vent tens of thousands of dollars a year. It also increased machine utilization at the Kansas plant by more than 10 percent. This is only one small example of scores of new arrangements that, shaped by greater openness in the workplace, are boosting corporate earnings. Because it helps people talk to each other, Liaison is making a valuable contribution to managerial know-how and marketing efficiency throughout the corporation.

THE OPEN WORK PLACE

Training at CertainTeed is not limited to the higher echelons of corporate and field management, however. We recently launched the first module of a comprehensive long-term training program for all 400 of our front-line supervisors. Each will be involved in at least 10 two-week seminars over the next five years. Training in statistical process control has become a fact of life for CertainTeed's work force in many locations. We also have turned to Lehigh University to help bring our people up to speed in computer-integrated manufacturing (CIM). As one employee commented, the people at Lehigh "saved us many months of research. They were able to demonstrate what works and what doesn't." Currently, we are exploring with Lehigh's faculty and students a variety of new avenues through which to expand the relationship and expedite employee growth.

Such approaches can be surprisingly productive and profitable. But not by themselves. The options for work force empowerment are endless, but most require greater scheduling flexibility, worker participation, innovative compensation schemes, and similar options. Many of the latter have to do with the capacity of business to resolve conflicts between family needs and workplace requirements for stable attendance, punctuality, and concentration on the tasks at hand.

These human issues are important. Cultural adjustment is a necessity of globalization in the workplace. U.S. managers must continually ask, "What possible effects will this have on others, and how will they likely respond?" With this in mind, for managers, we offer a variety of special training programs conducted by a combination of in-house and outside experts. There are courses in negotiating skills, in finance for nonfinancial managers, and in goal setting.

Authoritarian regimes, whether in companies or in countries, can be very efficient. The American industrial dilemma lies in the choice between the deceptive calm of an authoritarian status quo and a commitment to struggle toward a distant, and by no means certain, redefinition of the workplace. In the 1990s we face the near certainty of a smaller, older, more heterogeneous work force. There is nothing we can do about that. But there is much we can do about employee competence, productivity, and cohesiveness. We are already making necessities of these virtues by using new technologies, participatory management, and international organization. Success will do more than merely close the gap between work force qualifications and job requirements. Success will transform the workplace, and lift U.S. industry to unprecedented heights of productivity.

Michel Besson is president and CEO of CertainTeed, a building materials producer, and wholly owned North American subsidiary of the French conglomerate Saint-Gobain.

Investing in People

David L. Crawford
Associate Professor
The Wharton School

On Labor Day, we honor the U.S. work force amid growing concern about its quality and its future. We can change that future, but we must act now.

O n Labor Day 1989, the Secretary of Labor's Commission on Workforce Quality and Labor Market Efficiency (Workforce Quality Commission) began its final report saying, "America's ability to shape the course of the twenty-first century will depend largely on the productivity of the American workforce. Competitive advantage has replaced military might as the principal source of global influence." Those sentences were written before the walls came tumbling down, but recent developments in Eastern Europe only reinforce the argument.

Our concern about work force quality is motivated in large part by our fear that our nation's standard of living is in jeopardy. Today we enjoy a standard of living that is very high relative to other nations, but without aggressive corrective steps, the traditional American dream of a more prosperous life for each successive generation may prove unachievable for large numbers of our children.

DEMOGRAPHIC AND ECONOMIC TRENDS

As we look to the future, we see demographic and economic trends that pose significant threats to our global influence and standard of living. Many of these trends were described in *Workforce 2000*.

The Aging Work Force

As the "baby boomers" age and the "baby busters" enter the labor force, the average age of the labor force will increase. There will be a growing need to retrain experienced workers in order to meet requirements for new skills because new workers will be in short supply. A few employers are already responding creatively to the aging work force. Days Inn, for example, has hired and trained retired persons to handle computerized reservations. Unfortunately, a new survey conducted by Towers Perrin and the Hudson Institute shows that most employers are doing little or nothing to respond to the aging work force.

The employed percentage of the total population will shrink soon after the turn of the century, when the baby boomers begin to retire. Since the employed must produce all the goods and services consumed by the population, the productivity of the future work force must increase to carry a heavier burden. If productivity does not increase quickly enough, the average standard of living will fall and intergenerational political debate will become much more heated than it is today.

The Feminization of the Work Force

More than 60 percent of the people entering the labor force between now and the year 2000 will be women. The continuing movement of large numbers of women into the work force will cause more stress for workers, both male and female, who have to cope with both family and job demands. To attract and retain the desired skills in tight labor markets, employers will feel pressure to provide "family friendly" work environments featuring schedule flexibility, dependent care programs, leave programs, and the like. Some employers, particularly some large employers, have already begun to introduce such innovations. IBM, for example, provides employees with schedule flexibility, dependent care referral services, and extended personal leaves. In addition, IBM conducts training programs that sensitize managers to problems that employees may encounter as they try to balance family and job demands. Unfortunately, as many have suspected and the Towers Perrin/Hudson survey confirms, many employers are doing little or nothing to help employees balance the demands of work and family.

The Growing Minority Role

Minority group members, particularly blacks and Hispanics, will be the other major source of future labor force growth in many parts of the country. It will be increasingly important to improve the labor market skills of minorities and to remove any remaining labor market discrimination. If we can accomplish the former, the latter is likely to be easier than ever before because of anticipated shortages of skilled workers. There will be a real opportunity to bring formerly disadvantaged populations into the economic mainstream, but only if we, as a nation, invest in their labor market skills.

Freer World Trade

There seems to be a general trend toward more open world markets. As U.S. firms face more and more foreign competition, the productivity of their workers will become more and more important. Adaptability of U.S. workers will also become more important when changes in world markets lead to rapid changes in the skill requirements of U.S. employers.

Technological Change

We expect that technological change will increase the skill requirements of many jobs. Already, some truck drivers are asked to operate handheld computers; some janitors are asked to operate complicated machinery and deal with fractions in measuring cleaning materials. The days when illiterates could easily have high-earning careers in manufacturing and other industries are gone forever.

In a valuable new book, *Leadership for Literacy*, Forrest Chisman reports the unfortunate fact that "at least 20 to 30 million adults do not have the basic skills required to function effectively in our society." Each year more such adults leave our high schools as both dropouts and graduates. Millions of adults are almost unemployable because they are unskilled and untrainable—untrainable because of illiteracy and innumeracy.

To make matters worse, many people believe that technological change is accelerating, so that the life cycles of products, technologies, and industries are becoming shorter. Shorter cycles will result in more rapid obsolescence of workers' skills, heightening our need for retraining systems. Illiterate workers may be able to do some of today's jobs, but they will be very difficult to retrain in the future.

The Skills Gap

The confluence of these trends is going to produce a "skills gap"—too few people who have the skills that employers want and too many people who do not. Some employers will not be able to hire the types of workers they need to compete in international markets. Employers will bid up the wage rates of the skilled workers they can find, thereby creating higher production costs and diminishing competitiveness. At the same time, many unskilled workers will be unable to attain the standard of living that they have come to expect.

The number of high-skilled, high-paying jobs will not grow as it would if skilled workers were plentiful. Some employers will be tempted to relocate production to foreign countries. Other employers will "downskill" jobs—that is, redesign production processes to accommodate low-skill workers. From a national perspective, these are not attractive solutions. Downskilling on a widespread basis would increase the number of low-wage jobs. The preferred solution is to increase the skills of U.S. workers so that good jobs can be created and filled.

WHAT WE CAN DO

The important question is, what should we do to close the skills gap? Many people have sought simple, quick, and preferably inexpensive fixes. Such "silver bullets" do not exist, and we must stop wasting time and energy looking for them.

The only promising approach is a national commitment to a broad spectrum of substantial and sustained investments in America's human resources. This commitment must be joined by every level of government and the private sector, but the leadership and a substantial portion of the new funding must come from the federal government. The bipartisan Workforce Quality Commission, appointed by former Labor Secretary Ann McLaughlin, called for such a commitment on Labor Day 1989 in its report, *Investing in People: A Strategy to Address America's Workforce Crisis*. A year later that call seems to have produced very little action.

This country has never had a coherent national program of human resource development; we must establish one now. Our program must address a wide range of problems, from the developmental needs of preschool children to the retraining needs of 55-year-old workers with obsolete skills. Following are some of the most important features of such a program.

Preparing Children for School

Most experts agree that the Head Start program is a cost-effective way to address the developmental needs of disadvantaged preschool children. At current funding levels, however, less than 40 percent of eligible four-year-old children and very few three-year-old children can enter the program. We should move immediately to include all eligible three- and four-year-old children and any five-year-old children who are not in kindergarten.

Incentives for Students

No amount of school reform is going to come to much unless students have incentives to put effort into their studies. New incentives would be created if employers began to use evidence of school achievement to evaluate young job applicants. If good students could count on getting good jobs, we would have more good students, but right now employers have difficulty identifying the good students. The Workforce Quality Commission proposed the development of understandable high school transcripts and voluntary achievement tests to document student achievements in a wide variety of academic and vocational areas. The

Worklink project organized by the American Business Conference, the National Alliance of Business, and the Educational Testing Service is already developing a computer system that could make school and test records available to employers. In an important new report, *America's Choice: High Skills or Low Wages!*, the Commission on the Skills of the American Workforce (Skills Commission) has proposed the use of a Certificate of Initial Mastery that would certify basic competencies to employers and others. The use of vocational education can be increased, since many students who do not succeed in traditional courses learn better in applied contexts. All of these promising ideas await government implementation and employer cooperation.

Just as the labor market could provide incentives for some students, the promise of postsecondary education or training, could be used to motivate others. If no student or parent thought of cost as a barrier to postsecondary education, academic interests and career aspirations would certainly be heightened. A few philanthropists have created such mind-sets for small groups of disadvantaged students and parents, but only a greatly expanded government program of grants and loans could make the mind-sets universal.

Adult Basic Education

No matter what is done to improve the schools, there will always be a need to provide basic education for adults. Some will need a "second chance" to escape illiteracy and innumeracy; others will need an opportunity to learn English as a second language.

This country is strongly committed to public education of children and teenagers, but adult basic education is supplied by an uncoordinated patchwork of ill-conceived and underfunded public programs, untrained volunteers, and corporate programs created out of desperation. Government should take responsibility to provide effective professional basic education to adults on demand.

Government Training Programs

The major government job training legislation in this country is the Job Training Partnership Act (JTPA). Current JTPA programs reach approximately 5 percent of the eligible population, and it is the wrong 5 percent. Less than two years ago I visited a JTPA program that was training people to use word processors. I was told that to enter the program, one had to be a high school graduate and type 40 words per minute. At that time (and still today), employers in most cities were eager to hire such people without benefit of prior training in word processing. This is an admittedly extreme example of what has come to be called the "creaming" problem of JTPA. We must refocus JTPA on the basic skill needs of the disadvantaged population and increase its funding level, which has fallen by over 25 percent in real terms since 1982.

Employer-Provided Training

While government should be responsible for basic education, employers should be the principal source of investment in job-specific skills. Some well-known companies are already making substantial investments in their employees' skills. More than half of BellSouth's employees participate in training programs in a typical year. Michel Besson described in these pages some of the management initiatives and innovative training programs of CertainTeed. These commendable efforts notwithstanding, the Towers Perrin/Hudson survey shows that many employers are choosing not to make such investments. The reasons for their choices are complicated and not always well understood, but we clearly need more employers to see their employees as opportunities for investment rather than as costs to be minimized. As the skills of trainable, experienced workers become obsolete, employers should see the trainability as a valuable asset that will be difficult to buy on the open market.

Public policy can help create an environment that encourages private investment in workers' skills. The Workforce Quality Commission proposed a special corporate income tax incentive to encourage employer-provided training. The Skills Commission proposed that the U.S. mandate employer expenditures for training as do most of our major international trading partners. One way or the other, we need to increase private investment in workers' skills.

BUDGETS AND OTHER REALITIES

In the year since the Workforce Quality Commission published its final report, I have given dozens of speeches on work force issues, and someone always asks about the "budget realities." We should, of course, be concerned about the federal budget deficit, but we must also be concerned about the national skills deficit.

Amid talk of $50 billion, $100 billion, and even $168.8 billion budget deficits, keep in mind that even an extra $5 billion per year divided among Head Start, student grants and loans, adult basic education, JTPA, training incentives, and related federal programs could produce dramatic improvements in the coming years. Yes, we must have more investment by states and the private sector, but the federal government must provide leadership and new funding. Unfortunately, I see no hope that the federal government will provide either effective leadership or significant new funding unless the business community demands them.

Budget realities are not the only realities. Just as you business leaders have mobilized forces for school reform, so too can you force politicians to recognize the reality expressed by the Workforce Quality Commission: "We must not accept a workforce that is undereducated, undertrained, and ill-equipped to compete in the twenty-first century." That is exactly what we are talking about if we do not get serious about investing in people.

David L. Crawford is associate professor of economics and management at the Wharton School. He is also president of Econsult, an economic consulting firm in Philadelphia and Washington, D.C., and former executive director of the Secretary of Labor's Commission on Workforce Quality and Labor Market Efficiency.

Whatever Happened to Corporate Loyalty?

Charles Jett
Partner
McFeely Wackerle Jett

The old loyalty is dead. While CEOs may be naive to think a new loyalty has replaced it, the text of the unspoken agreement between employer and employee has been amended.

'M aybe you cannot be loyal to—or expect loyalty from—anything that does not bleed when cut." This cynical response to our 1990 Survey on Corporate Loyalty is a stinging indictment of the prevailing attitude among managers toward corporate loyalty. No doubt loyalty has changed during the past decade. So much so that mere mention of loyalty now elicits a variety of wry grins and incredulous stares from those who have—in light of their own circumstances—redefined the term.

Unrelenting waves of corporate takeovers, mergers, LBOs, corporate downsizing, layoffs, and the like have eroded what we once knew as corporate loyalty. Some CEOs and the companies they lead have so underestimated the power of loyalty that their organizations' cultures are changing. And corporate leaders who believe their time can be better spent on questions of more tangible substance—production, marketing, or competition—may want to rethink and move the issue of employee loyalty to the very top of their to-do lists.

A finding from our nationwide survey helps define the issue: While nearly nine of every 10 executives say, "I am loyal to my company," nearly half also say, "I am always interested in other career opportunities." A contradiction? Perhaps. Or maybe it signals the emergence of a new loyalty. Regardless, it is certainly an issue that demands more attention from more CEOs. Why? Because respondents to our survey are not first-line supervisors or entry-level employees. They are more than 500 top executives at the nation's leading companies—a population thought impervious to flagging loyalty just a decade ago.

Some responses also indicate too much distance between CEOs' perceptions and reality. For example, CEOs believe more so than any other group of executives surveyed that their companies are loyal to employees. But CEOs are by no means naive. Only 1 in 20 says loyalty is on the rise, and more than 8 of every 10 say boards of directors and chief executives should be concerned with the issue of loyalty.

HOW IT GOT THIS WAY

Just when did we reach this point in our views on loyalty? The vast organizational changes of the 1980s forced tough business decisions and the elimination of thousands of jobs once thought secure. Fully one-third of middle management lost jobs during the decade due to the glut of takeovers and what seemed to be every company's determination to become "lean and mean."

Those who kept their jobs saw substantial change. The focus on cost-cutting to enhance short-term profitability led to severe cutbacks or outright elimination of management development programs. Career tracks became less certain, less clear. Strong signals were being sent each way—from company to manager and back again—that loyalty had gone the same route as the buggy whip.

Many of the actions taken by companies seemed sensible for the times. After all, the nation's business schools were unleashing hordes of ambitious and well-educated baby boomers into this environment. Through prudent use of emerging management information systems, managers could handle far more duties with smaller staffs than ever before. "Downsizing" became fashionable as well as profitable.

The message was clear: Individuals recognized the increased competitiveness of corporate management. Without exception,

TABLE 6–1
Measuring Loyalty Now

	Strongly Disagree	Disagree	Neither Agree Nor Disagree	Agree	Strongly Agree
In today's competitive business climate, companies are becoming less loyal to their employees.	2.2	17.6	7.8	53.3	19.1
Employees' loyalty toward their companies today is stronger than 10 years ago.	19.3	64.8	12.0	3.6	0.2
We work as a team.	2.0	9.5	18.5	56.2	13.7
Corporate loyalty is on the rise.	13.1	60.0	21.5	5.1	0.4

students and managers alike were increasingly aware of the de-emphasis on management development within many major corporations. Everyone seemed to be looking for a way to become a better career manager as competition grew for upper-level management jobs. These trends and other observations led our firm to survey executive and corporate loyalty. The results help quantify the seriousness of the issue, and pose some questions that all of us should ask of ourselves and our companies.

THE NEW LOYALTY

For example, our survey suggests that while one loyalty is dying, another is springing to life. In essence, the old loyalty is akin to an employee's near blind faith in an organization and its leaders, and the new loyalty represents the increased importance of self-interest.

The top executives we surveyed feel that new contracts of understanding are being formed between employer and employee. These contracts affect both business operations and careers—as was the case with the old loyalty—but the relationship appears now to have more strings attached.

Clearly, the old standard of working hard and applying yourself no longer holds. This unwritten contract has been undermined. People with 20 years and more of good service are laid off—often with no more compassion than that afforded a new hire who doesn't work out.

The new loyalty is a more specific contract. The employee still expects to be paid and to be given career advancement opportunities in return for providing services, and the company still expects performance and productivity in return for providing compensation and career opportunities. The difference from the past: A realization that nothing is forever. Companies and managers would like longer relationships, or so they say, but are willing to accept less.

THREE CASE STUDIES

What is this level of acceptability within your company, within yourself? The answers are important because they affect productivity and our competitiveness worldwide. Briefly, let's look at three examples of managing loyalty—one done right, one done wrong, and one that might yet be too close to call.

McKinsey & Company, a recognized management consulting firm, typically hires the best and brightest from the nation's top business schools. The firm is not shy about the performance expectations of its new people. Simply put, the policy is: "Up, or out."

McKinsey set a goal to hire exceptionally talented people. And if these people didn't become good consultants, the firm felt it was doing all parties equal harm by keeping them around.

On the surface, such a policy appears very threatening. In practice, however, it has developed an intensely loyal group of partners and managers and probably the most loyal alumni association of any business in the nation. It is interesting to note that most consultants who leave McKinsey do so voluntarily. Very few, in fact, are asked to find more suitable work.

The message: McKinsey was bold enough to make clear its expectations of performance. The firm put its cards on the table early on and established effective two-way communication on a routine and frequent basis. Departing McKinsey consultants benefited from their experiences, and they benefited further by leaving early enough in their careers to apply those job experiences elsewhere. Quite frankly, most simply find it difficult to be this honest with people.

Kodak is an example of a good company that sacrificed loyalty during the past decade. Many employees thought a life-time job at Kodak was as certain as death and taxes. However, on January 17, 1986, this myth exploded when 500 surprised, angry, and confused employees experienced the harsh reality of being fired. What about loyalty?

Some consider Kodak historically loyal to its employees—a long record of cradle-to-grave caring. The jobs were always secure. Unfortunately, this kind of contract of understanding isn't as strong as it appears. Wouldn't it have been more loyal for Kodak to inject reality into this contract by not perpetuating the myth of lifetime employment security? Isn't it more loyal to employees who will not be moving up the ladder to gracefully and compassionately terminate them early enough to pursue careers elsewhere?

There is nothing wrong with a great company like Kodak taking steps to meet international competition. But its immediate business needs and its traditional concern for employees didn't jibe. The company and its employees have learned a painful—yet productive—lesson about direct, upfront communication.

One of Tom Watson, Sr.'s, principles in building IBM was fostering respect for its people. For years, the company practiced a full-employment concept, holding onto its people in good times and bad to ensure a quality work force for the ultimate long-term benefit of the company.

Then in the mid-1980s, somewhat harder times came. John F. Akers, IBM's CEO, embarked on a massive retooling of the company's approach to business. Simultaneously, he tackled the redirection of IBM's talented work force.

The result: some 37,000 jobs eliminated since 1985, some 20,000 employees reassigned, retrained, and redeployed at high short-term costs, and three waves of early retirement programs prompting the departure of one-third of the company's senior executives. Costs were trimmed by more than $1 billion. Is this loyalty?

IBM made clear its intentions and did not fear bold moves to restructure the organization to meet competitive challenges. Even though IBM's people are perhaps more readily hired than the people laid off from most companies, the company was not loyal under its old standard. Yet, it appears the company is better positioned now for the 1990s. The culture has changed, and the new loyalty is more openly talked about and practiced. The jury is still out, but IBM just might be in better step with the times than ever before.

BUILDING CORPORATE LOYALTY

Returning to our survey, let's see what can be learned about today's executives' perceptions of loyalty. The typical respondent to our survey is a 49-year-old male from the Midwest who holds an advanced degree and serves as a chairman, chief executive, or chief operating officer. Others are vice presidents of various staff and operating functions. Most have worked for more than one company before assuming their current position.

These executives believe that company loyalty is positively affected when:

• Upper management provides an organizational structure and management style promoting teamwork and professionalism;

• Employers and employees behave more as associates or partners; and

• Employees see clear career advancement opportunities.

Most of the executives place a high value on loyalty and believe that:

• Employees learn loyalty lessons by example from managers;

• Productivity increases when managers demonstrate loyalty to employees;

• Career advancement within a company requires visible acts of loyalty; and

• Employee turnover drops when companies demonstrate loyalty.

These same executives also reveal that actions one might expect to affect loyalty in fact do not. For example, they say hiring from outside the company is not disloyal to company employees and increasing compensation is not an effective means of creating loyalty.

So what can be done to improve or turn around the decline of corporate loyalty in American business?

Most executives say loyalty should be a topic of discussion not only in every boardroom but at every level in every corporation.

The first step toward improving corporate loyalty is to make it a permissible issue for open discussion in your companies. Consider making loyalty to your employees part of your organizational mission.

CEOs should use some commonsense guidelines in nurturing a healthy corporate loyalty within their organizations. Seven principles are paramount: (1) Recognize that top management generally gets to where they are by being good career managers—by practicing loyalty to themselves. Nothing less should be expected of quality people who are climbing the same corporate ladder. (2) Establish an environment of "career partnership" between the company and its employees. Clearly articulate what kind of managers the company is trying to develop. Establish contracts of understanding between the company and its people. Insist on routine and frequent two-way dialogue between the company and its employees regarding the status of the contract.

It's also important (3) to periodically put the cards on the table regarding the status of the business and the kinds of people needed to support its growth and maintenance. (4) The firm must recognize that each individual including the company itself has the opportunity and the right to consider others to fulfill its needs. In essence, if either party fails to provide quality service to the other, then each should be expected to seek or provide that service elsewhere. Management must (5) be aggressive in moving people around in the organization, both to improve and expand their skills and provide variety in their jobs. If possible move them up; where appropriate move them laterally; where necessary move them out. Create (6) a little tension in the company that can be relieved only by quality performance and meeting expectations. Encourage company employees to set the same standards and create a level of tension for the company to perform for them.

Finally (7), beware of the political loyalists, who can be recognized by their tendencies to look good at the expense of others and their reluctance to give credit where it is due. A sure sign is their unwillingness to hire or promote high-potential people who they may find threatening. Political loyalists are easily spotted by subordinates, and are rotten apples capable of subverting even the most well-intended plans to improve the loyalty environment. Get rid of them.

Some clear truths exist today about how we run our companies. Perhaps our survey findings about corporate loyalty should not surprise us as much as our slowness in recognizing the changes and taking action on this issue. The need is imperative. After all, more than 80 percent of the CEOs in our survey say you can improve productivity by showing loyalty to employees.

Sure, it's a tough subject to get your arms around. But maybe for the first time we need to admit that loyalty has changed, problems do exist, and that as CEOs we're not as close to solving these problems as we should be. Today might be a good time to spark discussions and actions within your company. What you hear could change the way you do business.

Charles Jett is a partner in McFeely Wackerle Jett, a Chicago-based executive search firm.

Coping With Work-Force Inadequacy

Jude T. Rich
Chairman
Sibson & Co.

As declines in education make competent help harder than ever to find, companies are taking steps to make sure their supply of workers keeps up with demand.

As the "baby bust" generation comes of age in the next decade, U.S. companies face a critical shortage of employable workers. For one thing, the U.S. workforce aged 16 to 24 will remain constant in the next decade, but 12 percent more jobs will be created. Forecasters predict that immigrants and older workers reentering the workforce will help to close this gap, but these forecasts are fairly speculative. At the same time, over 25 percent of these new workers will be functionally illiterate and nearly that many will be innumerate—both results of the decline of this country's public education system.

American companies face billions of dollars of added cost to improve the supply of capable new workers. But the complete solution will also include efforts designed to reduce the demand for more people. By increasing the productivity of current employees, forward-looking companies plan to manage the demand side of this equation.

"Supply siders" are already spending more money in order to improve the supply of capable new workers. Some have taken a more aggressive recruiting approach and have increased entry-level pay. Others have sought out new employee sources, including the disabled, empty nesters, and retirees. Flexible work schedules and child and elder care benefits are being provided as inducements. Still other companies have addressed the failure of the education system by "adopting" local schools and helping to improve basic skill development. In fact, many companies now conduct extensive on-the-job remedial training in the three Rs.

The incremental cost of competing more aggressively for a limited supply of qualified workers and huge spending for re-education will have significant impact on a company's cost position relative to competitors. Hardest hit will be labor-intensive businesses, particularly financial and other service companies, where labor costs run as high as 40 to 70 percent of the total cost structure. U.S. firms that can avoid these cost increases—and still maintain or increase the quality of their products and services—will possess a major advantage.

Enter the "demand siders." To avoid significant cost increases and still cope with the inadequacy of the workforce, a few innovative companies are managing the demand side of the equation, as well as the supply side. These companies reason that they will be significantly better off if they can reduce the demand for new workers, rather than simply spend the money necessary to increase their supply.

To reduce the demand for new workers, these companies have taken three major initiatives. They have (1) pruned marginal businesses and products, particularly where future recruiting and training costs will reduce returns on investment; (2) reduced unnecessary work; and (3) increased overall productivity.

PRUNING MARGINAL BUSINESSES

A basic step is to take into account the rising costs of getting and training new employees when deciding whether or not to prune marginal businesses and products. In some companies, pruning can also free employees from poor-performing businesses and products for use in areas with higher expected margins and returns. The reason: current employees are typically far better qualified than new work-force entrants. As one company's chief executive said: "It's a lot cheaper to retrain a well-educated employee on how to operate a different machine or handle a different customer service need than teach a new worker how to read and write."

A number of studies have indicated that as much as 25 percent of all work done in America today could be eliminated. One of the most notable examples of rooting out and eliminating unnecessary tasks is General Electric's "Work Out" program. GE had already pruned its major businesses until each one was ranked number 1 or number 2 in its market. As a next step, GE eliminated work that no longer added value to the product or helped meet the customer's needs. While each GE business has approached the Work Out program somewhat differently, all make a relentless effort to reduce unnecessary work and include a slogan of "speed, simplicity, and self-confidence." Incentives are provided for productivity increases.

Ford Motor Company automated its parts warehouses to bring parts to warehouse workers rather than have workers walk around to find parts. Warehouses were reduced from 18 to 8, and 600 mostly entry-level jobs were eliminated.

Another way to eliminate unnecessary people is to avoid permanent staffing for peak needs in service-intensive businesses. BankAmerica pioneered the practice of increasing teller staffing only during particular hours or days. A number of companies use part-time employees or "floaters" who move from location to location, or function to function, to avoid overhiring to meet customers' needs during peak periods. Similarly, companies also encourage their field management to consider additional overtime, rather than hire new employees. While overtime rates are high, the total cost of recruiting, training, and paying both wages and benefits to new workers is often higher.

MOTIVATING IMPROVED PRODUCTIVITY

A 1984 study by Daniel Yankelovich showed that only one in four U.S. workers was working at his or her full potential, and recent studies suggest little improvement in the past seven years. Clearly, the demand for new employees can be dramatically reduced by better productivity. The Department of Labor estimates that a 1 percent increase in productivity eliminates the need for nearly 1.5 million workers.

One major incentive for employees to deliver this latent productivity is to give them greater figurative "ownership" of results. While U.S. industry has made major strides in worker involvement through quality circles and other means, too many decisions are still made from the top down. But new company cultures are developing in which managers coach, counsel, and coordinate, and give down-the-line employees the responsibility to solve problems and get results.

But incentives need to be tied to measurable results reasonably within control of employees to really motivate change. Nucor offers a prime example of effective incentive use among rank-and-file employees. Nucor divides employees into groups of 25 to 35 and gives them responsibility for tasks from start to finish. Incentives are based on measures the group can control, and can be equal in size to base salaries. The incentives are complemented with quality circles and other employee involvement programs. Nucor leads the steel industry in productivity and sports a 20 percent return on equity.

MAKING A COMMITMENT

Whatever steps are taken, companies need to balance reducing demand for employees with a commitment to providing high quality products and services. This, in part, means instilling a "nobler purpose" in the workplace. At McDonald's, for example, employees are trained to create an environment of "quality, service, cleanliness, and value"—an environment that acts as a surrogate to Mom's own kitchen. Johnson & Johnson's credo describes the company's first obligation as meeting the quality requirements of the doctors, hospitals, and families the company serves.

Employees are likely to be motivated more by a nobler purpose than simply making more money for shareholders or helping top executives earn larger bonuses. Of course, altruistic motivation must be balanced with personal financial incentives if nobler purposes are to work. But nobler purposes must be backed up by quality control or enhancement programs to offset the potential for reduced customer service or quality when work is being eliminated.

A major opportunity to compete effectively in the 1990s will be the ability to reduce demand for new employees while maintaining quality. Capitalizing on this opportunity will require rethinking why and how work is performed.

Jude Rich is chairman of Sibson & Co., a Princeton, New Jersey-based human resources consulting firm.

Teamwork Starts at the Top

Roy Serpa
President and Chief Executive
Instamelt Systems

The type of teamwork needed in the 1990s can be compared to a jazz band. Improvisation is not only accepted, but encouraged by the other members of the group. Nevertheless, each improvisation should support the group performance.

R ecently, the Management Center Europe, a Brussels-based management development organization, surveyed 350 senior executives and found that they believe the single most important leadership quality is the ability to build effective teams. Only 56 percent said that their superiors possessed this ability. Bill Mainguy, the managing director of the Management Center Europe, stressed the need to have senior executives surround themselves with good people and good teams. He went on to say that getting people to work together is essential to making things happen and avoiding the subversion of executive decisions.

Whether it is the institution of quality improvement programs, the transfer of new technology to the plant floor, or the implementation of a new marketing strategy, teamwork is a paramount factor for achieving success. Teamwork is needed because our industrial environment is complex and dynamic, and it requires contributions from many individuals with diverse skills of different professions in a variety of functional areas. Rapid, reliable exchanges of information must occur to ensure prompt, effective decisions and action. However, many of our corporate cultures continue to encourage individual performance and foster interpersonal competition. Individuals compete for recognition, salary increases, and promotions. As organizational cultures value individualism rather than teamwork, the belief is that individual performance is desired and that the rules of behavior foster primarily individual ambition and self-seeking.

According to Edward L. Hennessy, Jr., chairman and CEO of Allied Signal, "We must learn once again how to translate great ideas into high-quality products, fast and inexpensively. One way many American companies are facing up to the problem is by forming teams of marketing, manufacturing, and R&D people at the earliest stages of new product development. This collaboration enables them to get products off the drawing board, into production, and out to the marketplace much faster than traditional linear systems."

EXAMPLES OF TEAMWORK

Unfortunately, few examples of teamwork within organizations appear in the business press. We read about the General Electric plan in Shelby, North Carolina, that uses a team system to change product models a dozen times a day to produce lighting panel boards. Productivity at that facility increased by 250 percent compared with GE plants that produced the same products in 1985. While productivity skyrocketed, employee turnover fell from 15 percent in the first year of the new system's operation to 6 percent four years later. Another example of teamwork occurred during the mid-1980s at Cincinnati Milacron, where a multidisciplinary team of 10 men and 1 woman shortened the development time of a new injection-molding machine from two years to nine months.

At Ingersoll-Rand, James D. Stryker, the head of business development, guided a multidisciplinary, multifunctional team that reduced the development time on a new tool from three years to one. N.R. Kleinfield, writing in *The New York Times*, stated about Stryker: "He pondered the sorry development process, best seen as a succession of walls. Marketing would think up a product and throw it over the wall separating it from the engineering department. Engineering would work up a design and toss it over another wall to manufacturing, which would make the product and hurl it over a wall to sales. Those people would then try to sell it to customers who perhaps did not want it in the first place.

More recently, the General Motors Saturn plant has organized work teams that are responsible for productivity, quality, and costs. These teams develop and refine work methods, assign tasks, participate in equipment design, select tools, and pick their leaders and team members.

At a recent *Chief Executive* Roundtable, Charles E. Exley, Jr., chairman and CEO of NCR, expressed his belief that the giant strides made in information technology allow decision making to be made at lower levels in large organizations by well-informed team members.

The foregoing examples that have been discussed in the business press describe the teamwork that is possible within our large corporations. Rarely do we read of teamwork at the senior executive levels of these corporations. A notable exception took place at the Ford Motor Co., by the example set by Donald Peterson and Harold (Red) Poling (now former chairman and current chairman, respectively), who fostered teamwork by starting with Ford's senior executives. They were convinced that if the people at the top couldn't work together, it would be unrealistic to expect the people below them to be team performers. The significant advances achieved in quality improvement and increased competitiveness at Ford were no doubt influenced by "starting at the top."

TEAMWORK AT THE TOP

All too frequently in many corporations, the lack of teamwork is apparent at the executive level where the executive staff rarely operates as a team. Executives have risen to their positions by being individualistic, aggressive, and tough-minded managers. They have dealt effectively with powerful superiors and peers frequently on a one-on-one basis. In other cases their progress resulted from maintaining a low profile while avoiding risk, confrontation, and controversy. Rarely have these executives facilitated the performance of subordinates, peers, or superiors in a team situation. In the past, directing individual performance at the executive level was adequate for the economic environment. The management of differentiated activities by individuals and functions was more important than the integration of the activities of specialists and groups across functional lines.

In his book *The Fifth Discipline*, Peter M. Senge, director of the Systems Thinking and Organizational Learning Program at MIT's Sloan School of Management, refers to "the myth of the management team." He explains that "all too often, teams in business tend to spend their time fighting for turf, avoiding anything that will make them look bad personally, and pretending that everyone is behind the team's collective strategy—maintaining the appearance of a cohesive team."

During a two-year period I served on the executive staff of a major corporation. As the junior member reporting to the president, I had the opportunity to observe a group of executives representing three fully integrated divisions: finance, research, and human resources. This staff met monthly to review corporate performance and make strategic decisions. Each executive represented his division or function and pursued his individual agenda. Issues, problems, and decisions were approached from an individualistic perspective favoring those courses of action that strengthened personal status and well-being. The trust, openness, and mutual commitment to common objectives just didn't exist. There was an obvious competition for individual attention, reward, and resources. Common problems confronting the corporation were rarely approached cooperatively, but more often pursued parochially. The chief executive would leave strategy implementation that should be executed collectively in the staff's hands only to find later that either no action or unilateral action had been taken.

Another personal experience with the lack of teamwork at the executive level occurred when I served as the assistant to the senior executive who headed the division of a major multinational company. This executive's style was predominantly to conduct his relationships with his departmental executives on a one-on-one basis. Rarely were these subordinates encouraged to exchange views or discuss differences of opinion. At staff meetings, con-

FIGURE 6–1
Teamwork in Action

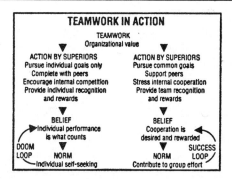

frontation was avoided, and a false sense of harmony was engendered. There was limited integration of effort between the staff as each pursued individual goals, strategies, and priorities. Confusion, ineffectiveness, and inefficiency reigned among the lower-level employees within each function as they struggled to perform their duties in those areas where interfunctional dependencies existed. The communication, coordination, and cooperation required for effectiveness and efficiency between functions were strained because of the example set by the executives.

The annual and five-year business plans were nothing more than financial forecasts pieced together with the independent thinking of each executive rather than an integrated strategy toward common objectives. The senior executive did not recognize the need for teamwork since he was not, by nature, a team player. He made no effort to build a team. During his 10-year tenure, competition continued to dominate the market for his major product line. He prepared no successor, and thus his replacement came from another division. Although he and his division survived, it is highly unlikely that this style of management will survive the 1990s.

Similar situations occur in many of our corporations because of the predominance of cultures that reward only individual effort—rather than teamwork—and the reluctance of executives to share power. Having observed this lack of teamwork on many occasions, I recall a statement made by Samuel Culbert and John McDonough in their book *The Invisible War.* "We observe selfish, divisive, and competitive values within the corporate organization; power plays, struggles, one-upmanship, game playing, empire building, fractionalized commitment, facade behavior, manipulations, lying, and theft." That statement may seem harsh, but interfunctional rivalries at the executive level discourage teamwork and encourage selfish, self-centered, individualistic behavior.

THE CHIEF EXECUTIVE'S CHALLENGE

The chief executive must instill trust among his senior executives since it is a prerequisite to teamwork. A recent survey of 400 managers conducted by Robert Kelley of Carnegie Mellon University found that one third of them distrust their direct bosses and 55 percent don't believe top management. The genuine team environment allows each individual to be candid and direct before decisions are made. An atmosphere of mutual trust permits the constructive exchange of views to take place without personal animosity. Each executive team member feels comfortable in contributing to the problem-solving and decision-making processes so that the final course of action will be one that all members of the team can implement with personal dedication.

Although many corporations claim that teamwork is an organizational value, the actions of superiors, especially at the executive level, are often not consistent with that value. These executives pursue individual goals, compete with each other openly, encourage destructive internal competition, and provide only individual recognition and rewards. The resultant belief within the organization is that individual performance is what counts. That belief encourages individual self-seeking rather than teamwork. A "doom loop" is formed wherein the behavior reinforces the belief.

In order to instill teamwork throughout our corporations, the example must come from the top—the chief executive and his/her staff. If subordinates at the mid-management level observe their superiors pursuing common goals, supporting each other's efforts, stressing internal cooperation, and providing team recognition and rewards, they will believe that cooperation is desired and rewarded. That belief will foster behavior that will contribute to group effort. The behavior will reinforce the belief and establish a "success loop." Robert Lefton, president of Psychological Associates, claims that less than 40 percent of the effort expended by corporate teams can accurately be described as "teamwork."

To establish teamwork as a value, the chief executive must ensure the following:

1. He must make it clear to his immediate subordinates that part of their performance evaluation will be based on their actions as executive team members.

2. He must encourage each executive to identify and discuss individual and organizational objectives with the entire executive staff.

3. He must encourage them to request support from each other and to act as resources to each other when appropriate.

4. He must establish specific objectives that require the participation of two or more staff members.

5. He must create task force assignments that are rotated to allow executives to team with as many peers as possible.

6. He must reconcile differences by candid, confrontational problem-solving sessions.

7. Most importantly, he must discourage individual self-seeking and pseudo teamwork.

As the executive staff functions more as a team, their example will create the belief within the organization that teamwork is valued. In time, the executive staff will realize the benefits in effectiveness and efficiency that will accrue to them individually as well as collectively. Before long they will become team builders within their organizations, and teamwork as a norm of behavior will evolve.

Roy Serpa is president and CEO of Instamelt Systems, a supplier of technology and equipment to the plastics industry. This is his third contribution to *Chief Executive*.

EXECUTIVE COMPENSATION, ACCOUNTABILITY, AND CONTROL

Pay Is the Message

David R. Meredith
Chairman and Chief Executive
Personnel Corporation of America

Money talks, and so does CEO pay. Taking a hard look at the way corporate leadership is rewarded, Chief Executive's *fifth annual survey of chief executive compensation concentrates on the messages sent by CEO pay packages. Those words tell plainly when a CEO's grasp exceeds his reach.*

T he popular press is at it again. Banner headlines denounce CEO pay packages, claiming that pay is too high—both relatively, in terms of company performance, and absolutely—meaning that it is up significantly from last year. There are even proposals from Senator Levin of Michigan and others to mobilize the government to stop perceived abuses in executive compensation.

We believe that consultants, the press—and even the government—should actively participate in the debate over CEO pay. Their role, however, should not be to offer knee-jerk criticisms of absolute pay levels, based on inaccurate numbers and a misguided view that a clear, bright line can be drawn to separate excessive and appropriate levels of compensation. Free markets—not regulated ones—do that best. The role of the critics ought to be to encourage open discussion of pay, and to show the investing public not just "how much" CEOs get paid, but also how that pay is delivered.

To argue that CEO pay is too high on an absolute basis is spurious. To illustrate what we mean, let's look at the pay package for Michael Eisner, chairman and CEO of Walt Disney Enterprises.

It's one of the most frequent examples cited by the popular press and erstwhile federal protectors of shareholder interests. We value his 1990 pay package at $71.9 million, second highest in our survey. Many have complained that it is absolutely too high, regardless of what he may have accomplished during his tenure. But just "who" is complaining? Do the critics include:

• The stockholders, whose shares have increased in value almost $7.2 billion above the industry norm?

• The employees, who work for a company that is growing and providing expanding opportunities for both employment and career advancement?

• The communities, whose economies are steadily bolstered by the revenues the company generates?

• The customers, who continue to flock in record numbers to Disney theme parks, Disney movies, and Disney stores? If the stakeholders are happy, where's the beef? Chrysler shareholders may have a beef. Between 1987 and the end of 1990, the value of their holdings (including dividends) dropped by $1.7 billion. We calculated Iacocca's pay in 1990 at a hefty $2.2 million—almost $1.1 million more than the competitive average. (See Table 7-4.)

HOW HIGH IS UP

Is pay unjustifiably up from 1990 while company performance is down? We all agree that 1990 was not a good year for the shareholder. We disagree with critics when it comes to the CEO. In fact, we find overall that CEO pay declined in 1990 from 1989 levels. This is illustrated in Table 7-1, which shows that from 1989 to 1990, pay has declined. It's down 11.9 percent, at the $1 billion sales level, and 17.9 percent, at the $8 billion sales level.

CEO pay fell in 1990 for two basic reasons. First, the operating performance of most companies declined from 1989 to 1990. Since a significant part of CEO pay consists of annual incentives based on operating performance, it is not surprising that total cash compensation for the CEO community, which had been growing at an 8 to 10 percent annual clip, increased by only 2.5 percent—less than half the rate of inflation. (Again, see Table 7-1 for an industry-by-industry breakdown of differences in cash levels from 1989 to 1990.)

TABLE 7-1
Comparison of Industry Total Cash and Total Pay Levels 1989–1990

Industry	(1) Percent Differential Total Cash 1990/1989	(2) $ Competitive Pay at Sales of $1M— 1990	(3) $ Competitive Pay at Sales of $1M— 1989	(4) Percent Differential 1990/ 1989	(5) $ Competitive Pay at Sales of $8M— 1990	(6) $ Competitive Pay at Sales of $8M— 1989	(7) Percent Differential 1990/ 1989
Aerospace	8.6	765,693	1,190,340	−35.7	1,270,268	1,269,753	0
Automotive	1.5	588,926	566,028	4.0	914,123	1,208,396	−24.4
Banking	−7.4	591,934	777,166	−23.8	906,952	1,698,435	−46.6
Chemicals	14.6	854,706	975,427	−12.4	1,480,351	2,320,900	−36.2
Computers & Technology	2.5	897,104	977,806	−8.3	1,188,971	1,956,423	−39.2
Electronics	2.2	699,169	877,110	−20.3	1,721,125	1,780,519	−3.3
Financial Services	−4.1	1,246,765	1,138,186	9.5	1,512,315	1,708,872	−11.5
Food & Beverage	3.0	815,775	893,191	−8.7	5,838,606	4,568,533	27.8
Industrial Equipment	7.5	810,125	879,171	−7.9	1,562,364	2,571,103	−39.2
Oil & Gas	17.3	560,132	627,944	−10.8	1,765,063	1,963,452	−10.1
Publishing & Broadcast	2.5	925,807	1,415,696	−34.6	8,595,941	4,153,218	107.0
Retailing	1.3	877,134	1,031,674	−15.0	1,416,816	1,991,852	−28.9
Transportation	1.3	528,937	566,296	−6.6	1,846,566	3,064,756	−39.7
Utilities	11.0	407,798	482,140	−15.4	800,411	901,310	−11.2
Median	2.5	NM	NM	−11.6	NM	NM	−17.9

More importantly, the stock performance of most companies was lower in the 1987 to 1990 period (this year's performance measurement period) than in the 1986 to 1989 period (last year's measurement period). And since a critical element of CEO pay involves long-term equity-based awards, which we value using the measurement period's growth rate, this part of CEO pay declined as well.

So what is wrong with this? Doesn't it support the view that "pay for performance" is becoming a reality? We don't think so. For while CEO pay did, in fact, decline in 1990, stockholder returns fell off the cliff. The median annualized return to shareholders was about 3 percent for the 1987 to 1990 measurement period, down 70 percent from the annualized 10 percent median return of the 1986 to 1989 period. This means that a typical CEO, who may have been accustomed to earning $1,000,000, saw his pay cut to $850,000 in 1990. On the other hand, an investor, accustomed to dividends and capital gains of $1,000,000 per year, had to settle for $300,000.

This gap suggests two facts of life regarding CEO pay. First, while most companies link the CEO's pay package with the interests of the shareholders, too many use pay packages that don't have enough leverage. By leverage, we mean how much the value of the package depends on changes in the price of the stock. Pay leverage includes not just upside potential but an equally powerful downside risk. Leverage can make CEO fortunes mirror those of the shareholders. (See Box 7-1 for a definition of leverage.)

Box 7-1

Methodology and Terms

CEO pay data for the most recent fiscal year were analyzed from annual reports and proxy statements for a sample of 221 companies that represent a cross-section of small, medium, and large companies, and low, medium, and high performers in 14 separate industries. In cases where the CEO changed in midyear, we chose the CEO who served the longest during the year.

(continued)

Box 7–1 (continued)

Company Performance is measured by summing the growth in stock price with all dividends for a four-year period, then calculating the compound growth rate that would yield this return based on an investment in the stock at the beginning of the period. (As a simplifying assumption, dividends are not "reinvested," except where significant payouts have resulted from capital restructuring.)

Competitive Pay is calculated through regression analysis ("lines of best fit"), comparing revenues with CEO pay for each company in an industry group.

Actual Pay is salary, annual bonus, and annualized present value of long-term incentives (as illustrated by the following valuation of stock options):

• Assumption: options exercised in five years.

• Exercise value established by projecting the option price for five years at the rate the stock price increased over the previous four years.

• Future gain (exercise value less option price) discounted by 8 percent to determine value.

Pay Factor is the percent difference between Actual and Competitive Pay.

Performance Factor is determined by subtracting the median Industry Performance from Company Performance.

Return Above/(Below) Industry is the difference between growing the market value of the company at the Company Performance rate versus the Industry Performance rate.

Pay Above/(Below) Competitive is the dollar difference between Actual and Competitive Pay.

Pay Premium (Penalty) per $100 in Performance is calculated by dividing Pay Above/(Below) Competitive by Return Above/(Below) Industry.

NM relates to companies in which pay and performance are not aligned. Linkage is absent.

Leverage Index is the percentage increase in the value of actual pay assuming a 15 percent annual stock price growth rate over the value of actual pay assuming a 0 percent annual stock price growth rate.

CEO Capitalization Index is a measure of ownership calculated in the same way as the Leverage Index, except that the numerator includes the appreciation in value of all the CEO's stockholdings (assuming 15 percent annual stock price growth) plus the value of total performance pay (at 15 percent growth).

TABLE 7–2
Leverage Indices

Index	1990	1989
(1) Above 0.75	91	73
(2) 0.26 to 0.75	48	65
(3) 0.00 to 0.25	82	83
(4) Total	221	221

Note: Leverage Index is a measure of the degree to which the value of the pay package is dependent on stock price appreciation.

Second, and even more troubling, the historical trend toward more highly leveraged pay packages seems to have stopped. In each year of our study, fewer CEOs had low-leverage pay packages than in the year before. In 1991, though, the drop was insignificant, from 83 low-leverage pay packages in 1989 to 82 in 1990. In other words, even though most companies are "getting it right," from a CEO compensation standpoint, too many others are adhering to pay philosophies that provide a very weak link between the CEO's interests and those of shareholders. As a result, they are discouraging prudent risk-taking by shifting pay increasingly toward the security of fixed compensation.

RISK IS DOWN

The net result is that some CEOs—with the tacit endorsement of their Boards and Compensation Committees—are surrendering the potential for wealth creation in order to minimize their downside financial risk. This is illustrated by the fact that the median pay premium (i.e., extra CEO pay for each $100 in above-market shareholder returns) fell from $.74 to $.48 while the median pay penalty (i.e., reduction in income for each $100 in below-market shareholder returns) increased only slightly from $.25 to $.29. We contrast these slender premiums and penalties to those in pay packages of CEOs who lead leveraged buy-outs and privately owned ventures. In LBOs, the pay premium is powerful—as much as $10.00 to $20.00 for each $100.00 in value created for the

TABLE 7-3
Companies Whose Pay Is Aligned with Performance

Industry	1990 (%)	1989 (%)	Differential (%)
Aerospace	80	73	7
Automotive	54	93	-39
Banking	69	88	-19
Chemicals	63	69	-6
Computers & Technology	87	63	24
Electronics	56	71	-15
Financial Services	50	57	-7
Food & Beverage	75	71	4
Industrial Equipment	58	92	-34
Oil & Gas	88	59	29
Publishing & Broadcasting	78	61	17
Retailing	63	69	-6
Transportation	67	87	-20
Utilities	56	63	-7
Overall	68	72	4

shareholders. The penalties for poor performance are equally dramatic and motivating—the potential loss of the CEO's investment and certainly the loss of his job.

Viewed in this light, the ire of the press pundits and other erstwhile protectors of the public interest ought not to be directed at the absolute level of CEO pay but at how pay is delivered. More specifically, and in the true spirit of Adam Smith and his successors, the fundamental question that ought to be raised today is: "Do the CEO and the stockholders share a common economic destiny—one where the CEO's rewards reflect those received by the company's investors?" Our research shows that the answer to this question is—sometimes yes, and sometimes no. When the answer is "yes," the CEO is in a position to motivate, inspire, and take appropriate risks—in effect, to truly lead his organization. When the answer is "no," the CEO has forfeited this powerful leadership tool and perhaps lost a golden opportunity to communicate and lead the organization to achieve its mission.

TABLE 7–4

Home Runs and Strikeouts

This chart depicts 10 extreme cases of disparity between the pay and performance factors found in this year's survey.

CEO	Company	Pay Factor (%)	Performance Factor (%)
High Pay/Low Performers			
Kirk Thompson	J. B. Hunt	43	(11.2)
Leslie Wexner	The Limited	42	(5.1)
J. D. Robinson III	American Express	62	(3.4)
Stanley Zax	Zenith National	51	(7.8)
Lewis B. Merrifield III	Pic 'N' Save	32	(28.3)
Low Pay/High Performers			
Carl Lindner	Chiquita Brands	−88	14.3
James Eiszner	CPC International	−48	5.7
John Lobbia	Detroit Edison	−37	14.1
John Schiff	Cincinnati Financial	−38	10.9
R. Zimmerman	Service Merchandise	−28	24.0

WHAT PAY SAYS

The CEO's pay package sends a critical message to the organization as well as the shareholders. If a large part of the package is tied to increases in shareholder value, the message is clear—the CEO is saying, "I believe in this company's future." If increases (and decreases) in shareholder returns fail to influence the pay package's value, the message is equally clear—and equally uninspiring to investors and employees. These messages provide powerful insights into the CEO's confidence in the future of the company, regardless of the company's historic performance:

• If linkage is high and company performance is high, the CEO's message is: "I can keep it going and continue the 'win-win' results we've achieved." This calls to mind Frank Shrontz at Boeing and Andrew Grove at Intel. Both clearly operate in fiercely competitive environments. They battle foreign competitors who receive substantial government subsidies. Both have declared through the medium of their compensation packages, "We're doing great, and we're going to keep it that way"—Shrontz through an award of 52,500 options and a leverage index of 1.36, and Grove through three years of awards totaling 290,000 options and a leverage index of 2.36. These leverage indices compare to industry medians of 0.78 in both cases.

• If linkage is high while performance is low, the CEO's message is: "I believe in the future, and I'm committed to making it happen." There are two conspicuous examples in the banking industry—Willard Butcher of Chase Manhattan and Walter Shipley at Chemical Bank (prior to executive realignment following the Chemical/Manufacturers Hanover merger). Both institutions have been experiencing serious performance problems (−14.2% for Chase, and −15.8% for Chemical), but through the medium of pay, the CEOs are making statements of enthusiasm about the future. Butcher's cash compensation was cut 26.9 percent in 1990, but he was awarded 45,000 options and 80,049 performance shares, which helped boost his leverage index to 0.72, compared to an industry median of 0.58. Shipley's cash was down 35.3 percent in 1990 while three-year awards of 142,000 options and 74,000 restricted share units led to a leverage index of 1.02. Both are clearly betting their opportunities of future wealth on their abilities to turn their banks around.

• When the linkage between the economic fortunes of the CEO and stockholders is low, the message is just as articulate to the investment community. More specifically: If linkage is low and performance is high, the CEO's implicit message, even if unintended, is: "The ride may be over—I am not sure I can keep this up." Emerson Electric has been a great performance story during Charles Knight's career as CEO (a four-year annualized return to shareholders of 10.8 percent versus an industry median of 2.5 percent), but his pay package encourages speculation that the great performance might not continue. His pay package—heavy on cash ($1.7 million in 1990) and performance shares (worth about $400,000 in underlying value in 1990) in comparison to options (65,000 over the years 1988 to 1990)—generates a skimpy leverage index of 0.21. In this case, the cash and underlying value portions are so high that they overwhelm the stock-based pay.

TABLE 7–5

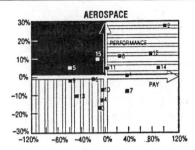

AEROSPACE

Company	CEO	Sales ($millions)	Company Performance (Ind. Perf. −4.0%)	Competitive Pay ($000)	Actual Pay ($000)
1. AAR	Ira A. Eichner	445	−4.0	629	935
2. Boeing	Frank Shrontz	27,595	20.8	1,717	3,455
3. GenCorp	A. William Reynolds	1,775	−23.6	880	839
4. General Dynamics	Stanley C. Pace	10,173	−18.9	1,347	1,316
5. Grumman	Renso L. Caporali	3,990	−0.9	1,072	475
6. Lockheed	Daniel M. Tellep	9,958	−5.5	1,340	1,082
7. M/A COM	Thomas A. Vanderslice	375	−15.0	603	883
8. Martin Marietta	Norman R. Augustine	6,126	6.0	1,190	1,519
9. McDonnell Douglas	John F. McDonnell	16,246	−8.8	1,509	578
10. Northrop	Kent Kresa	5,490	−13.3	1,159	1,138
11. Parker Hannifin	Paul G. Schloemer	2,453	1.4	953	984
12. Rockwell International	Donald R. Beall	12,379	7.8	1,413	2,387
13. Rohr	Robert H. Goldsmith	1,079	−13.3	780	369
14. TRW	Joseph T. Gorman	8,169	1.4	1,277	2,457
15. United Technologies	Robert F. Daniell	21,550	4.2	1,617	1,455

AUTOMOTIVE

Company	CEO	Sales ($millions)	Company Performance (Ind. Perf. −8.2%)	Competitive Pay ($000)	Actual Pay ($000)
1. Arvin Industries	James K. Baker	1,687	−8.2	647	585
2. Chrysler	Lee A. Iacocca	29,797	−8.9	1,103	2,189
3. Cummins Engine	Henry B. Schacht	3,462	−9.0	740	442
4. Dana	S. J. Morcott	5,225	0.8	798	739
5. Eagle-Picher Industries	Thomas E. Petry	699	−39.9	550	588
6. Echlin	Frederick J. Mancheski	1,601	−8.4	641	575
7. Federal-Mogul	Dennis J. Gormley	1,134	−4.0	601	679
8. Ford	Harold O. Poling	97,650	6.7	1,374	1,222
9. General Motors	Robert C. Stempel	123,276	8.3	1,435	1,159
10. Navistar	James C. Cotting	3,854	−17.0	755	475
11. Paccar	Charles M. Pigott	2,778	14.2	710	1,463
12. SPX	Dale A. Johnson	708	−7.5	551	624
13. Standard Products	James S. Reid, Jr.	652	−14.9	543	479

■ LOW PAY, HIGH PERFORMANCE   ▥ LOW PAY, LOW PERFORMANCE   ☰ HIGH PAY, HIGH PERFORMANCE   ☐ HIGH PAY, LOW PERFORMANCE

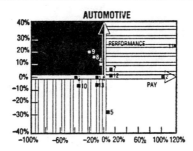

Pay Factor %	Performance Factor %	Return Above/ (Below) Industry ($000)	Pay Above/ (Below) Competitive ($000)	Pay Premium/ (Penalty) per $100 in Perf.	Leverage Index	Capital- ization Index
49	0.0	0	306	0.00	0.26	5.36
101	24.8	10,071,690	1,738	0.02	1.36	10.80
−5	−19.5	(529,182)	(41)	(0.01)	0.12	1.43
−2	−14.9	(1,187,085)	(31)	(0.00)	0.87	2.26
−56	3.1	91,828	(598)	NM	0.86	4.69
−19	−1.4	(159,404)	(258)	(0.16)	0.78	4.10
46	−11.0	(129,137)	280	NM	3.89	6.47
28	10.0	842,549	329	0.04	2.03	4.85
−62	−4.7	(431,719)	(932)	(0.22)	0.07	61.66
−2	−9.3	(520,639)	(21)	(0.00)	0.00	4.39
3	5.4	250,479	31	0.01	0.31	3.80
69	11.8	3,060,230	975	0.03	0.18	3.27
−53	−9.3	(144,936)	(411)	(0.28)	1.58	4.51
92	5.4	509,022	1,180	0.23	0.86	3.77
−10	8.2	1,928,548	(162)	NM	0.00	11.63

Pay Factor %	Performance Factor %	Return Above/ (Below) Industry ($000)	Pay Above/ (Below) Competitive ($000)	Pay Premium/ (Penalty) per $100 in Perf.	Leverage Index	Capital- ization Index
−10	0.0	0	(62)	NM	0.18	4.99
99	−0.6	(102,571)	1,086	NM	2.29	11.17
−40	−0.7	(16,571)	(298)	(1.80)	0.47	2.24
−7	9.1	482,618	(60)	NM	0.68	4.85
7	−31.6	(220,283)	38	NM	0.29	1.39
−10	−0.2	(4,781)	(66)	(1.38)	3.70	14.80
13	4.3	69,165	78	0.11	0.80	4.21
−11	15.0	8,361,397	(153)	NM	2.33	8.89
−19	16.5	13,600,153	(277)	NM	3.43	9.14
−37	−8.8	(227,847)	(279)	(0.12)	0.54	3.17
106	22.4	823,320	753	0.09	0.12	38.64
13	0.8	8,091	73	0.90	0.85	3.00
−12	−6.7	(59,754)	(63)	(0.11)	0.25	31.64

■ LOW PAY, HIGH PERFORMANCE   ▥ LOW PAY, LOW PERFORMANCE   ▤ HIGH PAY, HIGH PERFORMANCE   ▢ HIGH PAY, LOW PERFORMANCE

TABLE 7–6

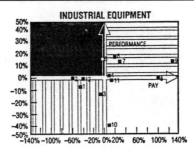

INDUSTRIAL EQUIPMENT

Company	CEO	Sales ($millions)	Company Performance (Ind. Perf. 5.7%)	Competitive Pay ($000)	Actual Pay ($000)
1. Briggs-Stratton	F. P. Stratton, Jr.	1,003	−1.9	811	435
2. Caterpillar	Donald V. Fites	11,436	6.0	1,749	682
3. Cincinnati Mlacrn.	Daniel J. Meyer	838	−8.6	766	675
4. Clark Equipment	Leo J. McKernan	1,445	7.1	910	991
5. Cooper Indstrs.	Robert Cizik	6,206	21.4	1,442	1,342
6. Deere	Hans W. Becherer	7,759	22.2	1,547	1,825
7. Dover Corp.	Gary L. Roubos	2,210	17.5	1,041	1,398
8. FMC	Robert H. Malott	3,722	5.5	1,227	2,503
9. Ingersoll-Rand	Theodore H. Black	3,738	17.0	1,229	2,803
10. Interlake	F. C. Langenberg	786	−34.6	751	799
11. Sundstrand	Harry C. Stonecipher	1,600	5.4	940	1,039
12. Timken	W. R. Timken, Jr.	1,701	2.9	958	590

OIL & GAS

Company	CEO	Sales ($millions)	Company Performance (Ind. Perf. 14.6%)	Competitive Pay ($000)	Actual Pay ($000)
1. Amerada Hess	Leon Hess	6,948	19.6	1,633	300
2. Amer. Petrofina	Ron W. Haddock	3,969	20.4	1,199	1,359
3. Ashland Oil	John R. Hall	8,552	2.7	1,831	1,721
4. ARCO	Ladwrick M. Cook	18,008	23.8	2,762	10,929
5. Cabot	Samuel W. Bodman	1,673	2.1	744	650
6. Chevron	Kenneth T. Derr	41,540	16.4	4,381	4,465
7. Diamond Shrck.	R. R. Hemminghaus	2,708	30.6	971	1,706
8. Exxon	Lawrence G. Rawl	105,519	14.6	7,330	6,415
9. Hamilton Oil	Frederic C. Hamilton	236	23.7	252	390
10. Mobil	Allen E. Murray	57,819	14.1	5,259	4,092
11. Murphy Oil	Jack W. McNutt	2,139	14.4	852	671
12. Pennzoil	James L. Pate	2,180	3.5	861	751
13. Phillips	C. J. Silas	13,603	25.7	2,366	4,296
14. Pittston	Paul W. Douglas	1,872	13.5	792	1,131
15. Quaker State	Jack W. Corn	874	−13.6	520	350
16. Sun	Robt. McClements, Jr.	11,812	3.9	2,189	972
17. Texaco	James W. Kinnear	40,899	18.0	4,344	6,391

■ LOW PAY, HIGH PERFORMANCE   ▥ LOW PAY, LOW PERFORMANCE   ☰ HIGH PAY, HIGH PERFORMANCE   ☐ HIGH PAY, LOW PERFORMANCE

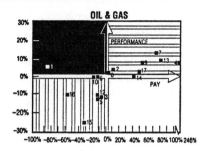

Pay Factor %	Performance Factor %	Return Above/ (Below) Industry ($000)	Pay Above/ (Below) Competitive ($000)	Pay Premium/ (Penalty) per $100 in Perf.	Leverage Index	Capital- ization Index
−46	−7.6	(165,091)	(376)	(0.23)	0.13	16.82
−61	0.3	49,483	(1,067)	NM	1.03	4.45
−12	−14.3	(266,702)	(91)	(0.03)	0.66	2.97
9	1.4	23,080	81	0.35	0.14	2.29
−7	15.7	1,934,899	(100)	NM	0.00	4.76
18	16.5	1,610,078	277	0.02	0.39	2.60
34	11.7	949,285	357	0.04	0.53	5.94
104	−0.3	(14,917)	1,276	NM	0.78	7.78
128	11.2	708,665	1,575	0.22	1.26	4.16
6	−40.4	(447,607)	48	NM	0.00	1.76
11	−0.4	(17,858)	100	NM	0.00	2.96
−38	−2.9	(78,058)	(368)	(0.47)	0.00	100.67

Pay Factor %	Performance Factor %	Return Above/ (Below) Industry ($000)	Pay Above/ (Below) Competitive ($000)	Pay Premium/ (Penalty) per $100 in Perf.	Leverage Index	Capital- ization Index
−82	5.0	622,996	(1,333)	NM	0.00	1,325.55
13	5.8	223,602	160	0.07	0.00	1.29
−6	−12.0	(1,040,902)	(111)	(0.01)	0.43	2.94
296	9.2	6,451,144	8,167	0.13	2.63	8.74
−13	−12.5	(518,943)	(94)	(0.02)	0.64	10.11
2	1.8	1,708,084	84	0.00	1.23	3.67
76	15.9	307,889	735	0.24	0.57	3.58
−12	0.0	0	(915)	0.00	4.12	7.94
55	9.0	225,105	138	0.06	0.00	98.84
−22	−0.6	(568,005)	(1,167)	(0.21)	0.72	6.12
−21	−0.2	(10,547)	(181)	(1.72)	0.25	4.29
−13	−11.2	(1,526,649)	(110)	(0.01)	0.95	3.44
82	11.1	2,144,147	1,930	0.09	0.91	6.91
43	−1.2	(31,073)	339	NM	0.50	4.85
−33	−28.2	(770,132)	(170)	(0.02)	0.30	1.69
−56	−10.8	(3,263,075)	(1,216)	(0.04)	0.72	7.40
47	3.4	1,883,626	2,047	0.11	1.93	4.81

■ LOW PAY, HIGH PERFORMANCE　▦ LOW PAY, LOW PERFORMANCE　▤ HIGH PAY, HIGH PERFORMANCE　□ HIGH PAY, LOW PERFORMANCE

TABLE 7-7

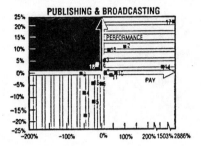

PUBLISHING & BROADCASTING

Company	CEO	Sales ($millions)	Company Performance (Ind. Perf. 3.2%)	Competitive Pay ($000)	Actual Pay ($000)
1. Affiliated Pubs.	William O. Taylor	536	−15.2	639	356
2. Capital Cities	Daniel B. Burke	5,386	14.5	2,303	4,715
3. CBS	Laurence A. Tisch	3,261	10.3	1,743	1,834
4. Commerce Clr. Hse.	Richard T. Merrill	716	−4.9	750	475
5. Dow Jones	Warren H. Phillips	1,720	−9.0	1,221	947
6. Dun & Bradstreet	Charles W. Moritz	4,818	−1.6	2,165	2,139
7. Gannett	John J. Curley	3,442	2.9	1,796	2,083
8. Jefferson-Pilot	W. Roger Soles	1,163	5.7	982	2,814
9. Knight-Ridder	James K. Batten	2,305	1.9	1,437	636
10. Lee Etprs.	Lloyd G. Schermer	274	3.5	440	714
11. McGraw-Hill	Joseph L. Dionne	1,939	2.5	1,305	1,719
12. Media Gen.	J. Stewart Bryan III	614	−1.1	689	659
13. Multimedia	Walter E. Bartlett	481	13.7	601	736
14. Time Warner	Steven J. Ross	11,517	6.4	3,513	56,324
15. Times Mirror	Robert F. Erburu	3,621	−0.9	1,847	1,265
16. Tribune Co.	Stanton R. Cook	2,353	7.8	1,454	1,201
17. Walt Disney	Michael D. Eisner	5,844	24.3	2,410	71,961
18. Washington Post	Katharine Graham	1,439	7.3	1,106	912

RETAILING

Company	CEO	Sales ($millions)	Company Performance (Ind. Perf. 9.2%)	Competitive Pay ($000)	Actual Pay ($000)
1. Dayton Hudson	Kenneth A. Macke	14,739	9.7	1,631	2,504
2. Edison Bros.	Andrew E. Newman	1,254	11.7	924	784
3. Family Dollar	Leon Levine	874	−6.3	850	500
4. Home Depot	Bernard Marcus	3,815	64.6	1,194	1,587
5. J. C. Penney	William R. Howell	17,410	9.9	1,695	1,513
6. K mart	Joseph E. Antonini	32,281	3.9	1,954	1,168
7. Longs Drug	R. M. Long	2,334	8.6	1,066	440
8. Mays	David C. Farrell	10,066	7.9	1,494	2,245
9. Pic 'N' Save	Lewis B. Merrifield III	475	−19.2	739	975
10. Sears	Edward A. Brennan	55,972	−4.3	2,219	979
11. Service Mdse.	R. Zimmerman	3,435	33.2	1,166	844
12. The Limited	Leslie H. Wexner	5,376	4.1	1,293	1,829
13. Toys 'R' Us	Charles Lazarus	5,510	15.2	1,300	5,415
14. U. S. Shoe	Bannus B. Hudson	2,719	−13.9	1,105	636
15. Wal-Mart	David D. Glass	32,602	27.4	1,959	2,166
16. Woolworth	Harold E. Sells	9,789	14.9	1,484	2,784

■ LOW PAY, HIGH PERFORMANCE   ▥ LOW PAY, LOW PERFORMANCE   ▤ HIGH PAY, HIGH PERFORMANCE   ☐ HIGH PAY, LOW PERFORMANCE

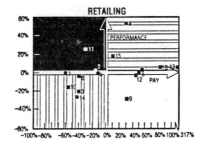

Pay Factor %	Performance Factor %	Return Above/ (Below) Industry ($000)	Pay Above/ (Below) Competitive ($000)	Pay Premium/ (Penalty) per $100 in Perf.	Leverage Index	Capital- ization Index
−44	−18.4	(757,387)	(282)	(0.04)	1.42	24.32
105	11.3	2,638,827	2,413	0.09	0.00	3.98
5	7.1	1,033,291	91	0.01	0.56	2.37
−37	−8.0	(343,646)	(276)	(0.08)	0.00	1.52
−22	−12.1	(1,719,035)	(274)	(0.02)	0.31	2.22
−1	−4.8	(1,748,803)	(26)	(0.00)	0.76	4.36
16	−0.3	(77,560)	287	NM	0.78	5.34
186	2.5	149,250	1,832	1.23	0.48	2.39
−56	−1.3	(143,027)	(801)	(0.56)	1.96	18.89
62	0.3	7,909	273	3.46	1.11	14.03
32	−0.7	(77,438)	414	NM	0.14	4.78
−4	−4.3	(101,588)	(30)	(0.03)	0.00	1.58
22	10.5	245,001	135	0.06	0.00	6.70
1503	3.2	607,234	52,811	8.70	56.95	72.00
−32	−4.1	(698,817)	(582)	(0.08)	0.00	34.34
−17	4.6	462,879	(252)	NM	0.25	16.61
2886	21.1	7,167,473	69,551	0.97	2.90	15.75
−18	4.1	377,827	(194)	NM	0.00	367.03

Pay Factor %	Performance Factor %	Return Above/ (Below) Industry ($000)	Pay Above/ (Below) Competitive ($000)	Pay Premium/ (Penalty) per $100 in Perf.	Leverage Index	Capital- ization Index
54	0.6	102,189	873	0.85	0.49	5.35
−15	2.6	47,555	(140)	NM	0.00	7.55
−41	−15.5	(308,308)	(350)	(0.11)	0.00	127.64
33	55.5	3,366,052	392	0.01	0.00	97.23
−11	0.7	176,832	(182)	NM	0.50	6.27
−40	−5.3	(1,487,928)	(786)	(0.05)	0.81	8.90
−59	−0.6	(18,283)	(626)	(3.42)	0.00	122.59
50	−1.3	(320,183)	751	NM	1.90	11.58
32	−28.3	(779,778)	236	NM	0.00	6.31
−56	−13.4	(8,406,573)	(1,240)	(0.01)	0.00	6.70
−28	24.0	452,597	(321)	NM	0.00	18.36
42	−5.1	(1,412,470)	537	NM	0.00	675.76
317	6.0	1,243,530	4,115	0.33	0.00	9.91
−42	−23.1	(804,072)	(468)	(0.06)	0.63	2.55
11	18.3	15,992,546	207	0.00	0.90	46.46
88	5.8	812,793	1,300	0.16	0.49	5.81

LOW PAY, HIGH PERFORMANCE LOW PAY, LOW PERFORMANCE HIGH PAY, HIGH PERFORMANCE HIGH PAY, LOW PERFORMANCE

TABLE 7–8

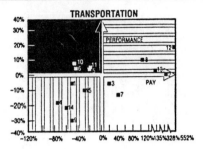

TRANSPORTATION

Company	CEO	Sales ($millions)	Company Performance (Ind. Perf. 3.0%)	Competitive Pay ($000)	Actual Pay ($000)
1. Alaska Air	Bruce R. Kennedy	1,047	−2.3	544	281
2. Alex. & Baldwin	R. J. Pfeiffer	674	3.0	417	1,787
3. AMR	Robert L. Crandall	11,720	−2.5	2,323	2,747
4. Cnsldtd. Frtwys.	Raymond F. O'Brien	4,209	−15.7	1,255	315
5. CSX	John W. Snow	8,205	6.1	1,875	1,485
6. Delta	Ronald W. Allen	8,582	6.0	1,926	1,215
7. J. B. Hunt	Kirk Thompson	580	−8.1	381	544
8. Norfolk Sthrn.	Arnold B. McKinnon	4,617	13.7	1,327	2,795
9. Pan Am	Thomas G. Plaskett	3,561	−28.3	1,135	538
10. Santa Fe Pac.	Robert D. Krebs	2,297	11.5	872	550
11. Southwest Air.	Herbert D. Kelleher	1,187	6.8	586	467
12. UAL	Stephen M. Wolf	11,037	20.7	2,241	14,609
13. Union Pacific	Drew Lewis	6,964	76.2	1,699	3,993
14. USAir Grp.	Edwin I. Colodny	6,559	−18.2	1,639	625
15. Yellow Freight	George E. Powell, III	2,302	−5.6	873	637

UTILITIES

Company	CEO	Sales ($millions)	Company Performance (Ind. Perf. 6.6%)	Competitive Pay ($000)	Actual Pay ($000)
1. Amer. Elec. Pwr.	W. S. White, Jr.	5,167	8.0	695	787
2. Arkla	Thomas F. McLarty III	2,436	6.4	544	526
3. Atlantic Energy	E. Douglas Huggard	717	4.8	366	388
4. Commonwealth Ed.	James J. O'Connor	5,262	8.4	699	607
5. Con Edison	Arthur Hauspurg	5,739	6.4	719	789
6. Detroit Edison	John E. Lobbia	3,307	20.7	601	381
7. Eastern. Utl.	Donald G. Pardus	452	−3.4	315	350
8. Kansas C P & L	A. Drue Jennings	761	12.5	373	364
9. L G & E Energy	Roger W. Hale	699	8.0	363	632
10. Midwest Res.	Mark W. Putney	894	5.0	393	367
11. Pacific G & E	Richard A. Clarke	9,470	6.8	845	1,111
12. Phil. Elec.	Joseph F. Paquette, Jr.	3,705	3.6	624	561
13. Public Service	E. James Ferland	4,800	6.5	678	607
14. Rochester G & E	Harry G. Saddock	831	3.6	384	250
15. Southern Co.	Edward L. Addison	7,975	9.5	800	954
16. Texas Utl.	J. S. Farrington	4,543	11.2	666	658

■ LOW PAY, HIGH PERFORMANCE   ▥ LOW PAY, LOW PERFORMANCE   ▤ HIGH PAY, HIGH PERFORMANCE   ☐ HIGH PAY, LOW PERFORMANCE

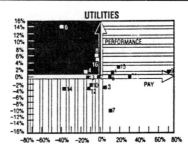

UTILITIES

Pay Factor %	Performance Factor %	Return Above/ (Below) Industry ($000)	Pay Above/ (Below) Competitive ($000)	Pay Premium/ (Penalty) per $100 in Perf.	Leverage Index	Capital- ization Index
−48	−5.3	(62,156)	(262)	(0.42)	1.71	4.88
328	0.0	0	1,370	0.00	1.18	5.52
18	−5.6	(721,695)	424	NM	0.00	3.02
−75	−18.7	(693,669)	(940)	(0.14)	0.00	4.20
−21	3.1	520,768	(390)	NM	1.97	5.82
−37	3.0	304,147	(712)	NM	3.08	8.96
43	−11.2	(251,314)	163	NM	1.47	4.50
111	10.7	2,753,542	1,469	0.05	0.50	3.44
−53	−31.3	(523,427)	(597)	(0.11)	0.29	3.80
−37	8.5	1,982,723	(322)	NM	2.10	4.90
−20	3.7	109,519	(120)	NM	0.00	21.64
552	17.7	1,860,207	12,368	0.66	3.02	7.65
135	3.2	967,485	2,295	0.24	0.79	4.28
−62	−21.3	(959,562)	(1,014)	(0.11)	0.00	5.18
−27	−8.6	(350,091)	(237)	(0.07)	0.23	55.74

Pay Factor %	Performance Factor %	Return Above/ (Below) Industry ($000)	Pay Above/ (Below) Competitive ($000)	Pay Premium/ (Penalty) per $100 in Perf.	Leverage Index	Capital- ization Index
13	1.4	364,364	92	0.03	0.00	1.81
−3	−0.3	(21,908)	(18)	(0.08)	0.00	5.58
6	−1.8	(63,742)	22	NM	0.04	1.91
−13	1.8	616,166	(92)	NM	0.00	1.53
10	−0.2	(49,543)	70	NM	0.00	1.20
−37	14.1	2,016,728	(220)	NM	0.00	1.41
11	−10.0	(217,509)	35	NM	0.00	1.38
−3	5.9	267,178	(10)	NM	0.00	1.40
74	1.4	52,286	269	0.51	0.12	1.12
−7	−1.7	(80,339)	(26)	(0.03)	0.00	1.60
31	0.1	60,322	266	0.44	0.27	1.96
−10	−3.0	(639,721)	(63)	(0.01)	4.20	5.37
−10	−0.1	(34,604)	71	(0.21)	0.16	1.68
−35	−3.0	(95,216)	(134)	(0.14)	0.00	1.21
19	2.8	1,092,837	154	0.01	0.64	2.60
−1	4.6	1,216,800	(8)	NM	0.00	1.50

■ LOW PAY, HIGH PERFORMANCE   ▥ LOW PAY, LOW PERFORMANCE   ▤ HIGH PAY, HIGH PERFORMANCE   ☐ HIGH PAY, LOW PERFORMANCE

TABLE 7–9

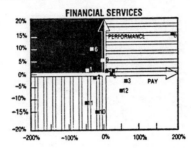

FINANCIAL SERVICES

Company	CEO	Sales ($millions)	Company Performance (Ind. Perf. –0.8%)	Competitive Pay ($000)	Actual Pay ($000)
1. A. G. Edwards	B. F. Edwards III	675	–0.5	1,202	634
2. Aetna	James T. Lynn	19,021	–3.0	1,639	1,067
3. American Express	J. D. Robinson III	24,332	–4.2	1,677	2,712
4. American General	Harold S. Hook	4,481	0.6	1,433	1,505
5. CIGNA	Wilson H. Taylor	18,164	–1.1	1,632	1,983
6. Cincinnati Fincl.	John J. Schiff	1,049	10.1	1,252	772
7. Dreyfus	Howard Stein	261	0.6	1,101	1,368
8. General Re	Ronald E. Ferguson	2,993	15.3	1,380	3,811
9. Liberty	Hayne Hipp	334	4.8	1,126	1,110
10. Paine Webber	Donald B. Marron	2,979	–15.8	1,380	1,122
11. Travelers	Edward H. Budd	11,313	–12.7	1,562	863
12. Zenith Natl.	Stanley R. Zax	468	–8.6	1,162	1,750

FOOD & BEVERAGE

Company	CEO	Sales ($millions)	Company Performance (Ind. Perf. 17.0%)	Competitive Pay ($000)	Actual Pay ($000)
1. Anheuser-Busch	August A. Busch III	10,744	15.2	7,718	1,796
2. Borden	R. J. Ventres	7,633	9.1	5,585	1,619
3. Brown-Forman	W. L. Lyons Brown, Jr.	1,017	17.3	829	1,096
4. Campbell Soup	David W. Johnson	6,206	21.4	4,591	12,058
5. Castle & Cooke	David H. Murdock	3,003	11.2	2,310	1,741
6. Chiquita Brands	Carl H. Lindner	4,273	31.3	3,225	400
7. Coca-Cola	Roberto C. Goizueta	10,236	27.0	7,373	31,070
8. CPC Intl.	James R. Eiszner	5,781	22.7	4,293	2,224
9. Flowers Inds.	Amos R. McMullian	835	–0.7	688	330
10. General Mills	H. B. Atwater, Jr.	6,448	25.3	4,761	7,508
11. Geo. A. Hormel	R. L. Knowlton	2,681	23.5	2,075	3,156
12. Gerber Prdts.	Alfred A. Piergalini	1,136	29.7	921	3,057
13. H. J. Heinz	Anthony J. F. O'Reilly	6,086	16.6	4,507	88,796
14. Hershey Foods	R. A. Zimmerman	2,716	13.2	2,100	1,420
15. Intl. Multifoods	Anthony Luiso	2,192	14.2	1,715	2,006
16. Kellogg's	W. E. LaMothe	5,181	12.3	3,870	2,126
17. Lance	J. W. Disher	446	4.8	380	235
18. McCormick	C. P. McCormick, Jr.	1,323	28.8	1,063	1,378
19. PepsiCo	D. Wayne Calloway	17,803	33.1	12,448	21,840
20. Quaker Oats	Wm. D. Smithburg	5,031	9.4	3,764	1,482
21. Ralston Purina	William P. Stiritz	7,101	11.3	5,216	4,742
22. Sara Lee	John H. Bryan, Jr.	11,606	19.3	8,303	5,425
23. Tyson Foods	Don Tyson	3,825	14.4	2,904	3,611
24. Wrigley	William Wrigley	1,111	25.1	901	1,409

■ LOW PAY, HIGH PERFORMANCE ▦ LOW PAY, LOW PERFORMANCE ≡ HIGH PAY, HIGH PERFORMANCE ▢ HIGH PAY, LOW PERFORMANCE

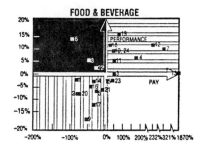

FOOD & BEVERAGE

Pay Factor %	Performance Factor %	Return Above/ (Below) Industry ($000)	Pay Above/ (Below) Competitive ($000)	Pay Premium/ (Penalty) per $100 in Perf.	Leverage Index	Capital- ization Index
−47	0.3	6,120	(568)	NM	0.06	11.61
−35	−2.2	(514,315)	(572)	(0.11)	2.50	6.09
62	−3.4	(1,473,744)	1,035	NM	1.16	7.22
5	1.3	234,274	72	0.03	0.79	8.32
22	−0.3	(48,574)	351	NM	0.00	1.74
−38	10.9	503,700	(480)	NM	0.39	56.76
24	1.4	63,807	267	0.42	1.33	18.32
176	16.1	4,214,954	2,430	0.06	1.42	3.68
−1	5.6	78,243	(16)	NM	0.66	44.88
−19	−15.0	(385,730)	(257)	(0.07)	1.03	8.63
−45	−11.9	(1,740,156)	(698)	(0.04)	0.80	4.19
51	−7.8	(134,145)	588	NM	0.00	10.48

Pay Factor %	Performance Factor %	Return Above/ (Below) Industry ($000)	Pay Above/ (Below) Competitive ($000)	Pay Premium/ (Penalty) per $100 in Perf.	Leverage Index	Capital- ization Index
−77	−1.8	(839,069)	(5,922)	(0.71)	0.04	20.81
−71	−7.9	(1,587,677)	(3,966)	(0.25)	0.00	7.49
32	0.3	25,326	268	1.06	0.17	245.90
163	4.4	1,104,717	7,467	0.68	1.05	2.90
−25	−5.7	(336,332)	(569)	(0.17)	0.49	212.66
−88	14.3	515,577	(2,825)	NM	0.00	2.65
321	10.0	9,984,033	23,697	0.24	0.97	55.86
−48	5.7	1,257,284	(2,069)	NM	0.86	1.86
−52	−17.7	(501,584)	(358)	(0.07)	0.14	8.70
58	8.3	2,140,876	2,748	0.13	2.40	15.69
52	6.5	299,289	1,081	0.36	0.53	5.80
232	12.7	767,298	2,136	0.28	0.66	2.55
1870	−0.3	(115,850)	84,289	NM	27.23	60.24
−32	−3.8	(508,740)	(680)	(0.13)	0.20	4.02
17	−2.8	(55,804)	291	NM	1.32	3.94
−45	−4.7	(1,789,598)	(1,745)	(0.10)	0.58	14.23
−38	−12.2	(422,822)	(145)	(0.03)	0.22	3.78
30	11.8	389,486	315	0.08	0.16	5.33
75	16.1	8,618,767	9,392	0.11	3.60	7.55
−61	−7.6	(1,388,343)	(2,282)	(0.16)	0.91	14.14
−9	−5.7	(1,651,656)	(474)	(0.03)	5.29	27.19
−35	2.3	571,187	(2,878)	NM	2.19	17.03
24	−2.5	(184,370)	707	NM	0.00	2.41
56	8.1	533,828	508	0.10	0.26	283.57

■ LOW PAY, HIGH PERFORMANCE   ▦ LOW PAY, LOW PERFORMANCE   ▤ HIGH PAY, HIGH PERFORMANCE   ☐ HIGH PAY, LOW PERFORMANCE

TABLE 7–10

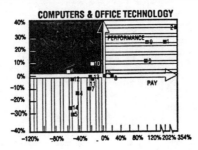

COMPUTERS & OFFICE TECHNOLOGY

Company	CEO	Sales ($millions)	Company Performance (Ind. Perf. −5.7%)	Competitive Pay ($000)	Actual Pay ($000)
1. Apple	John Sculley	5,558	21.6	1,132	3,416
2. AST Research	Safi U. Qureshey	534	30.4	824	3,785
3. Commodore	Irving Gould	887	7.3	883	1,750
4. Cray Research	John A. Rollwagen	804	−22.0	871	527
5. Data General	Ronald L. Skates	1,216	−37.6	921	464
6. Diebold	Robert W. Mahoney	476	−3.1	811	363
7. Digital Eqpt.	Kenneth H. Olsen	12,943	−14.9	1,269	982
8. Hewlett-Packard	John A. Young	13,233	−5.7	1,273	1,483
9. NCR	Charles E. Exley, Jr.	6,285	21.4	1,151	2,331
10. Pitney Bowes	George B. Harvey	3,196	4.5	1,050	852
11. Standard Reg.	John K. Darragh	716	−9.1	857	697
12. Tandem	James G. Treybig	1,866	−9.2	976	543
13. Tandy	John V. Roach	4,500	−7.3	1,100	874
14. Unisys	James A. Unruh	10,111	−31.5	1,227	596
15. Xerox	Paul Allaire	16,951	−5.7	1,316	1,358

ELECTRONICS

Company	CEO	Sales ($millions)	Company Performance (Ind. Perf. 2.5%)	Competitive Pay ($000)	Actual Pay ($000)
1. Ametek	Walter E. Blankley	661	−2.3	584	449
2. Analog Devices	Ray Stata	485	−19.3	511	505
3. EG&G	John M. Kucharski	2,474	4.4	1,035	553
4. Emerson Elec.	C. F. Knight	7,573	10.8	1,681	2,418
5. E-Systems	E. Gene Keiffer	1,810	5.2	904	981
6. General Signal	Edmund M. Carpenter	1,695	0.5	879	880
7. Harris	John T. Hartley	3,053	−5.8	1,134	1,501
8. Intel	Andrew S. Grove	3,921	28.8	1,264	5,944
9. Loral	Bernard L. Schwartz	1,274	−1.3	777	3,213
10. Molex	F. A. Krehbiel	594	5.8	558	408
11. Motorola	George M. C. Fisher	10,885	11.6	1,967	1,570
12. National Smcdtr.	Charles E. Sporck	1,675	−19.9	874	542
13. Raytheon	Thomas L. Phillips	9,268	4.1	1,834	1,369
14. Texas Instrmnts.	Jerry R. Junkins	6,567	0.9	1,580	599
15. Westinghouse	Paul E. Lego	12,915	4.1	2,118	2,281
16. Zenith	Jerry K. Pearlman	1,410	−25.8	811	450

■ LOW PAY, HIGH PERFORMANCE ▥ LOW PAY, LOW PERFORMANCE ▤ HIGH PAY, HIGH PERFORMANCE ☐ HIGH PAY, LOW PERFORMANCE

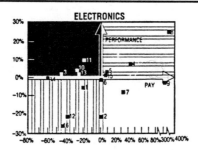

Pay Factor %	Performance Factor %	Return Above/ (Below) Industry ($000)	Pay Above/ (Below) Competitive ($000)	Pay Premium/ (Penalty) per $100 in Perf.	Leverage Index	Capital- ization Index
202	27.3	3,502,342	2,285	0.07	0.29	10.48
359	36.1	320,127	2,961	0.92	0.61	19.23
98	12.9	149,870	867	0.58	0.00	31.48
-40	-16.3	(996,412)	(344)	(0.03)	0.15	2.93
-50	-31.9	(531,264)	(457)	(0.09)	0.84	2.86
-55	2.6	55,048	(449)	NM	0.49	3.08
-23	-9.3	(3,496,041)	(287)	(0.01)	1.57	77.27
17	0.0	3,450	211	6.11	1.26	9.23
103	27.0	5,087,094	1,180	0.02	0.66	17.67
-19	10.2	1,135,870	(198)	NM	0.94	8.02
-19	-3.4	(57,055)	(161)	(0.28)	0.00	1.66
-44	-3.6	(182,322)	(433)	(0.24)	2.12	15.16
-21	-1.6	(196,822)	(226)	(0.11)	1.94	6.53
-51	-25.8	(2,295,175)	(631)	(0.03)	1.29	2.64
3	0.0	0	42	0.00	0.86	4.79

Pay Factor %	Performance Factor %	Return Above/ (Below) Industry ($000)	Pay Above/ (Below) Competitive ($000)	Pay Premium/ (Penalty) per $100 in Perf.	Leverage Index	Capital- ization Index
-23	-4.9	(112,074)	(136)	(0.12)	0.43	2.27
-1	-21.8	(483,953)	(6)	(0.00)	0.31	19.95
-47	1.9	70,311	(482)	NM	0.78	6.76
44	8.3	2,520,771	737	0.03	0.21	7.36
9	2.7	111,237	77	0.07	0.58	5.09
0	-2.1	(90,307)	1	NM	0.00	2.73
32	-8.3	(375,704)	367	NM	0.76	3.81
370	26.3	4,131,525	4,681	0.11	2.36	12.72
314	-3.8	(148,389)	2,436	NM	0.78	5.51
-27	3.3	139,474	(150)	NM	1.72	119.40
-20	9.0	2,037,737	(397)	NM	1.12	7.14
-38	-22.4	(755,497)	(332)	(0.04)	0.79	7.95
-25	1.6	325,996	(465)	NM	0.24	7.44
-62	-1.6	(209,021)	(981)	(0.47)	1.88	12.93
8	1.6	575,569	163	0.03	1.42	3.75
-45	-28.3	(449,559)	(361)	(0.08)	1.28	3.50

LOW PAY, HIGH PERFORMANCE   LOW PAY, LOW PERFORMANCE   HIGH PAY, HIGH PERFORMANCE   HIGH PAY, LOW PERFORMANCE

TABLE 7-11

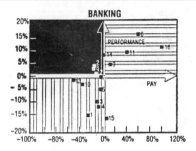

BANKING

Company	CEO	Sales ($millions)	Company Performance (Ind. Perf. −4.4%)	Competitive Pay ($000)	Actual Pay ($000)
1. Bank of Boston	Ira Stepanian	5,645	−20.6	844	650
2. Central Bancshares	Harry B. Brock, Jr.	513	−1.5	516	474
3. Chase Manhattan	Willard C. Butcher	13,709	−14.2	1,013	908
4. Chemical Banking	Walter V. Shipley	7,953	−15.8	906	836
5. Citicorp	J. S. Reed	38,333	−8.3	1,251	1,201
6. Comerica	Eugene A. Miller	1,324	12.4	627	1,014
7. First Chicago	Barry F. Sullivan	5,686	−5.0	846	808
8. First Tennessee	Ronald Terry	742	−2.2	557	493
9. First Virginia	Robert H. Zalokar	569	−0.9	527	604
10. Michigan National	Robert J. Mylod	1,237	−7.7	618	436
11. Old Kent Fin.	John C. Canepa	868	5.4	575	838
12. South Carolina Ntl.	James G. Lindley	697	−3.8	550	501
13. Union Bank	Taisuke Shimizu	1,516	−5.8	645	373
14. U. S. Trust	Marshall Schwarz	394	2.1	489	484
15. Valley National	Richard J. Lehmann	1,134	−21.3	607	625
16. Wells Fargo	Carl E. Reichardt	5,960	8.1	854	1,759

CHEMICALS

Company	CEO	Sales ($millions)	Company Performance (Ind. Perf. 9.4%)	Competitive Pay ($000)	Actual Pay ($000)
1. Amer. Cyanamid	George J. Sella, Jr.	4,570	10.2	1,277	1,795
2. Betz Labs	John F. McCaughan	597	22.1	746	1,140
3. Dexter Corp.	K. Grahame Walker	908	2.0	833	614
4. Dow Chemical	Frank P. Popoff	19,773	9.3	1,880	2,351
5. DuPont	Edgar S. Woolard, Jr.	39,709	10.8	2,260	2,188
6. Engelhard	Orin R. Smith	2,937	3.2	1,136	1,484
7. Ethyl Corp.	Floyd D. Gottwald, Jr.	2,514	9.5	1,090	959
8. Hercules	D. S. Hollingsworth	3,200	−4.6	1,162	761
9. Loctite	K. W. Butterworth	510	27.4	715	558
10. Lubrizol	L. E. Coleman	1,453	13.7	943	1,295
11. Monsanto	Richard J. Mahoney	8,995	9.3	1,527	1,408
12. Nalco Chem.	W. H. Clark	1,212	22.6	899	1,557
13. Olin Corp.	J. W. Johnstone, Jr.	2,592	2.4	1,099	874
14. Quantum Chem.	John Hoyt Stookey	2,618	13.0	1,102	771
15. Union Carbide	Robert D. Kennedy	7,621	−1.7	1,461	1,415
16. Witco	William Wishnick	1,631	−1.1	973	731

■ LOW PAY, HIGH PERFORMANCE   ▥ LOW PAY, LOW PERFORMANCE   ▤ HIGH PAY, HIGH PERFORMANCE   ☐ HIGH PAY, LOW PERFORMANC

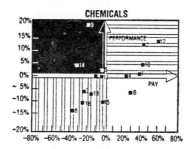

CHEMICALS

Pay Factor %	Performance Factor %	Return Above/ (Below) Industry ($000)	Pay Above/ (Below) Competitive ($000)	Pay Premium/ (Penalty) per $100 in Perf.	Leverage Index	Capital- ization Index
-23	-16.2	(779,316)	(194)	(0.02)	0.94	4.16
-8	2.9	41,291	(42)	NM	0.14	20.44
-10	-9.7	(975,825)	(105)	(0.01)	0.72	4.77
-8	-11.4	(895,266)	(70)	(0.01)	1.02	3.02
-4	-3.9	(1,038,906)	(50)	(0.00)	0.00	4.99
62	16.8	383,241	387	0.10	0.44	5.08
-4	-0.6	(34,514)	(37)	(0.11)	1.69	8.91
-11	2.3	39,134	(64)	NM	0.00	7.62
15	3.6	72,984	77	0.11	0.36	3.54
-30	-3.3	(54,590)	(183)	(0.33)	1.12	8.34
46	9.8	198,593	263	0.13	0.41	7.36
-9	0.6	9,896	(49)	NM	0.00	1.89
-42	-1.4	(29,453)	(272)	(0.92)	0.00	1.14
-1	6.5	80,469	(5)	NM	1.31	6.56
3	-16.8	(327,796)	17	NM	1.22	3.25
106	12.5	1,379,973	905	0.07	1.12	12.75

Pay Factor %	Performance Factor %	Return Above/ (Below) Industry ($000)	Pay Above/ (Below) Competitive ($000)	Pay Premium/ (Penalty) per $100 in Perf.	Leverage Index	Capital- ization Index
41	0.8	153,199	518	0.34	0.58	5.43
53	12.6	483,551	394	0.08	0.44	7.08
-26	-7.4	(192,939)	(219)	(0.11)	0.59	3.54
25	-0.1	(74,821)	471	NM	1.74	9.40
-3	1.4	1,427,519	(72)	NM	1.09	19.08
31	-6.2	(242,096)	348	NM	0.99	8.19
-12	0.1	10,262	(131)	NM	0.07	184.43
-34	-14.0	(1,510,122)	(401)	(0.03)	0.88	1.88
-22	18.0	514,906	(157)	NM	0.00	4.63
37	4.3	280,999	352	0.13	0.62	7.48
-8	-0.1	(24,460)	(119)	(0.49)	0.00	14.31
73	13.2	859,542	658	0.08	0.00	4.32
-20	-7.0	(282,960)	(225)	(0.08)	0.79	4.32
-30	3.6	230,835	(331)	NM	2.15	6.45
-3	-11.1	(1,579,190)	(46)	(0.00)	1.17	5.40
-25	-10.6	(411,200)	(242)	(0.06)	1.30	17.60

LOW PAY, HIGH PERFORMANCE LOW PAY, LOW PERFORMANCE HIGH PAY, HIGH PERFORMANCE HIGH PAY, LOW PERFORMANCE

Emerson's shareholders must hope that the fixed pay elements don't similarly overwhelm Knight's motivation to continue producing high stock returns.

• If linkage is low and performance is low, the CEO is sending a not-so-subtle message: "I am not putting my eggs in this basket —I'm running for cover." He may not intend to be saying this, but what else can one infer from the way John Reed of Citicorp was paid in 1989 and 1990? In 1990 his cash compensation was off only 19.1 percent, and his whole package was paid in cash (i.e., zero leverage). In 1989 it was all cash and restricted stock (a leverage index of 0.29). How should a shareholder interpret this signal?

So just what are forward-thinking companies doing when it comes to CEO pay packages that reinforce the drive for superior, shareholder-oriented performance? A lot, it turns out, with the specifics depending on each company's industry prognosis and competitive environment, its near- and long-term objectives, and the CEO's current ownership level. All these new programs have three key objectives in common. The first is to reduce fixed costs by minimizing salaries, cash bonuses, benefits, and perquisites. The second is to provide the CEO with the opportunity for major, lifestyle-changing wealth creation—an opportunity that pays off only if the shareholders win first. A newly hired CEO shouldn't have to wait and slowly build equity through annual stock option grants. In our opinion, a new CEO should be "jump started" through a mega-grant to get him thinking like an equity owner from day one. The third is to design CEO packages with an eye both to their motivational impact on the CEO and to the signals sent to the investment community. Of course, we are not in the business of providing investment advice, either to investors or to companies seeking to burnish their image. Instead, we believe companies should design pay packages that lead to higher performance through the alignment of the interests of the shareholders and the executive team. In a future issue we detail six different ways companies today are using compensation as a competitive weapon.

CEOs Can Resolve the Row Over CEO Pay

But do they want to? The issue, of course, is not absolute pay but setting pay in relation to performance and how to accomplish this beyond lip service. In the following at times heated exchange—few subjects draw blood quicker—among CEOs, CalPERS, directors, and compensation experts, most agree on the danger signals. How best to tie pay to shareholders' fortunes defies simple technique.

"The biggest barrier to teamwork is executive pay," said Douglas Reid, senior vice president, human resources, of Colgate-Palmolive, last spring at a Conference Board meeting. Reid said that employees accept the 90 percent differential in absolute pay, but it's the relative differences—when a top officer's pay increases when employees get no increase or, in fact, endure layoffs or termination—that cause them to seethe. He went on to say that Lee Iacocca during the 1980s had been a folk hero of his until last past year when Chrysler paid him $2.2 million as well as the repurchase of a second home that was noted in the proxy as an intercompany transfer. (Between 1987 and 1990 Chrysler shareholders saw the value of their holdings drop by $1.7 billion, a compound annualized 8.9 percent rate of decline.)

The popular business press and newspapers have already had a circus with Time Warner's Steven Ross. Although the $56 million he got—for a performance record below that of fellow publishing and broadcasting CEOs such as Tribune's Stanton Cook who got $1.4 million or Washington Post's Katherine Graham who took home $912,000—appears a bit absurd, his is not the most egregious case of imperial reach.

"If there's a rationale for all this other than greed I don't know what else could explain it," says Reid.

Most of *Chief Executive's* roundtable participants agree, but hasten to add that the extreme cases of avarice blind people to the reality that most CEOs' pay is aligned with performance (70 percent, according to PCA's Dave Meredith) in the sense that high performers get high pay and low performers get low pay relative to their industry. The typical chief of a billion-dollar firm gets $800,000, which ain't much compared to Mike Tyson's $30 million, or Madonna's $25 million (although it's better than General Norman Schwarzkopf's $103,000).

Described by some as an investor with an attitude, Dale M. Hanson, CEO of California Public Employees Retirement System, whose $65 billion portfolio is invested in some of the nation's biggest corporations, says he doesn't want to tell boards or CEOs how much to pay, but he sees plenty of danger signals that cause him to become more activist in holding management accountable. For example, CalPERS criticized ITT for paying its CEO Rand Araskog $30 million over a four-year period during which the company's stock fell 10 percent. It unsettled Sears Roebuck when it supported dissident shareholder Robert Monks's unsuccessful bid for a seat on Sears' board. It also unsettled Lockheed's Dan Tellop when it threw its support behind Harold Simmons' unsuccessful effort to gain control.

Not all of Hanson's activities are confrontational. He amicably persuaded GM's Bob Stempel to commit to maintaining a majority of outside directors on GM's board, even getting Stempel to have CalPERS lawyers help write the bylaws to make it possible. He also convinced companies such as Great Northern Nekoosa and USX to junk their poison pills in favor of so-called "chewable" pills that give management more time in the face of a takeover but that avoid share dilution.

Retired Citicorp CEO Walter Wriston, who holds directorships at GE, Chubb, Bechtel Investments, Sequoia Ventures, Pan Am, Tandem Computers, United Meridian, and ICOS Corp., blames the "ratcheting effect" of increasing pay levels on the misplaced notion by CEOs and directors of wanting to be in the first quartile. He disagrees with Stern Stewart's Joel Stern that CEO pay (as well as Wall Street's quarterly earnings pressure) forces leaders toward short-term thinking. "CEOs simply don't think the way most analysts think they do," he says.

Stern for his part argues that the quest for value is hopelessly confounded by obsolete financial management systems where the wrong goals and performance standards are measured. This results not only in many CEOs being overpaid, but a significant number being underpaid too. Willis Corroon's Dick Miller believes that, while not perfect, most CEOs are adequately compensated. However, he prefers to see the bulk of a CEO's personal net worth tied to the fortunes of his company. Universal Health's Alan Miller likes to see management own its own firm's stock and is uncomfortable when it doesn't. Views differ over how best to get stock into management hands. Stock options strike some as simply a giveaway where if the company does well, so does the boss, but if it doesn't, he doesn't lose anything either.

Nell Minow, who succeeded the aforementioned Robert Monks as president of Institutional Shareholder Services, believes that much of the problem with compensation arrangements arises out of the tenuous accountability between chiefs and the shareholders whose interests they are supposed to represent. There's a proven link between overpaid directors and overpaid CEOs, she argues. "I do not believe anyone who says that it makes no difference who hires and fires the compensation consultant or how many directors are independent." On this point CEOs and compensation experts disagree strongly. Roundtable participants suggest that directors too should be compensated in stock as much as possible to tie their fortunes to that of shareholders. Through greater monitoring of proxy resolutions, institutions will exert greater influence on management policies. Minow is developing a U.S. version of the U.K.'s ProNED, a clearinghouse/recruiting firm established by British institutional investors to generate independent director candidates for boards of public companies. A lively and at times sharp discussion hosted at New York's Mark Hotel about measuring performance at the top follows.

David Meredith (Personnel Corporation of America):
What makes compensation such an interesting phenomenon is the notion that compensation committees have really focused on the wrong question. They have focused on the question of how much do we pay, as well as what's a competitive rate to pay.

In my 25 years' experience, the first and oftentimes the last question that's asked by the compensation committee is what's the individual worth? What is the rate for the chief executive?

There's no question that there's a "ratcheting" activity. In our research we asked a sample of 225 CEOs where they wanted to position their company vis-a-vis competitive practices, and I think 93 or 94 percent of them said they wanted to be paying in the top half.

Walter Wriston (formerly of Citicorp):

That makes it hard.

Meredith:

Right, that makes it very hard. And when you actually asked them what they were paying, well, they were already paying in the top half.

But the focus historically is, how much should we pay? Nowhere near as much attention has been focused on the issue of what kind of chief executive behavior or what kind of action are we trying to reinforce with the pay system. In other words, how should we structure it?

That is the nexus of the issue, and one that has led us into a situation where we really aren't paying for performance. If you look through the research that we have done on it, you see that there is an increasing correlation, but not a very strong one, between the levels of pay and amount of pay that a chief executive gets and the kind of performance the company has turned in, performance measured against all industry or performance measured against the industry segments that they're in.

Joel M. Stern (Stern, Stewart & Company):

Have you refined your method of measurement of performance? Do you have a reasonably accurate measure?

Meredith:

We've taken a fairly simple notion, which is to say that we'll compare the performance in terms of total return to shareholders over the last four-year period and take it by industry. So if General Mills has outperformed Quaker, General Mills has outperformed Quaker from a shareholder perspective. That's the way I as an investor would look at it in terms of how I am doing. Are we doing better than those in the industry segment that we're investing in or are we not?

In looking at the historic approach that companies have taken to compensation, it was clearly an approach that provided a payoff to the chief executive for growing the business. The bigger the business, the bigger the competitive rate of pay for the position. That may or may not have been appropriate in the 1960s and 1970s, when they were trying to grow and make this a larger enterprise, but that was what was being rewarded. We've seen over the years, and it's a truism that has held in survey data forever, that for every doubling in size of the corporation, there's a 25 to 30 percent increase in competitive rates of pay for the chief executive. In other words, if you can get your corporation to be twice as big as what it is, you've got competitively about a 25 to 30 percent increase in pay. So the strongest indicator of pay has always been the size of the company. Performance is usually a secondary indicator.

Alan B. Miller (Universal Health Services):

But there's another factor in that it's more complicated to manage an operation that is growing or that is twice the size of another operation. The other thing is that if a company doesn't grow, regardless of the chief executive's pay, the people inside are not going to be very happy unless they have a place to grow. So the chief executive might be getting too much blame for trying to increase his salary by mindlessly blowing up the company to a tremendous size.

Meredith:

If size happens to be the right measure, so be it. But in our view, there are clearly other things like strategy development, product development, people development, facilities development, and the like that are all drivers of what is the value that will ultimately be created for the shareholder.

The disservice we have done from a compensation consultant's perspective is focusing on size as the beginning point. Every single presentation to a compensation committee that I've ever seen will start out with, "We looked at your industry segment and we did a regression analysis of sales versus CEO pay. Here is the 50th, here is the 75th percentile, and we'll go from there." The discussion virtually ends at that point instead of once you've figured ballpark, what do you want to do from a pay perspective? The real issue and the challenge of the late 1980s now into the 1990s is, how can we use pay to reinforce the kind of behavior that we want to encourage within the corporation?

Let's say that if the size of the company increases, we'll increase your base salary. If we increase your base salary, we'll increase your target bonus. Increase your target bonus, we'll increase the number of restricted shares you have. That's the ratchet. As opposed to saying let's put a number on the value of a chief executive performing at a given level and then start to focus on what the mix of the pay equation ought to be. I don't think the level makes a hell of a lot of difference. In fact, we know it doesn't. From an overall economics perspective, high-paid company CEOs don't perform any better than low-paid ones. So how should that pay be delivered? Let's say the CEO is getting 100 rubles. If you deliver 100 rubles in salary, the only incentive you have there is for the chief executive to keep his job. There is no up side for me, and there really is no down side risk other than losing my job.

Or you could transform it by putting a significant portion of the equation—some or all of your bonus, or trade in a portion of your salary—in the form of stock.

Stern:

When you talk about stock, are you talking about stock options or are you talking about restricted stock? Are they interchangeable to you?

Meredith:

No, not at all. Restricted stock grants underlying value. Stock options have value only if there is appreciation.

Stern:

Well, the studies that have been done on restricted shares indicate that when a company announces that it's paying its CEO restricted shares, then the stock price falls, and dramatically so. The reason for it is it seems to be an unambiguous signal that the prospects of the firm are not very great.

Meredith:

How about if it's done all in cash? If instead of granting compensation in part salary and part restricted stock, you grant it all in salary. That's an even more dismal signal. If you look at John Reed of Citicorp in 1990, it was all salary. He had had salary and options and so forth in the past. For 1990, the whole enchilada was in salary, as opposed to a Chemical or a Chase, where they had substantial grants of both stock options and restricted stock for their CEOs.

Wriston:

Except that John owns part of the company.

Meredith:

Yeah, not in his pay package, but he bought it on his own.

Wriston:

Which is another interesting factor that never gets in the equation.

Meredith:

Well, it should get in the equation. The ownership piece of it is a critically important one. It's how do I encourage more risk, more commitment. The LBOs and the venture capitalists dictate that you do that—put your money up or we don't want to invest. Public corporations tend not to do that.

OUT OF THE MONEY

Wriston:

How many companies have a premium option?

Meredith:

Very few.

Wriston:

I'd say they've got to be as rare as the dodo bird.

Stern:

The concept of having an out-of-the-money option should be very attractive to institutional investors because you're betting on the future. The trouble with stock options is it's a literal giveaway program. And it's diluted. If you have an out-of-the-money option program that somehow reflects on the cost of equity capital, then it's a nondilutive option, and it really does not hurt the shareholders to have those type of options either granted or purchased by the manager.

Meredith:

Hold on, there are other considerations here. The FASB regulations won't permit rising strike prices and treating the stock option as a capital transaction rather than as a compensation expense.

Stern:

That becomes a tax deductible item.

Meredith:

It's tax deductible under either circumstance. In fact, the one with the rising price option hits both the P&L and the balance sheet. With stock options, it's only a balance sheet transaction.

Stern:

As long as you're getting the tax saving, what difference does it make whether it's reducing earnings or if it's going directly as a charge to the capital account?

Meredith:

The difference that it makes is that the reported earnings are lower, and we know where reported earnings are lower you're going to drive some out of the market.

Dale M. Hanson (California Public Employees Retirement System):

I just don't agree with that. That almost fosters a short-term phenomenon. You can look at General Dynamics if you want to talk about incentive compensation where you basically watch the stock go down to the twos and erode by 50 percent, and now suddenly we put in this new, magic, 10-day formula and, lo and behold, now the stock is starting to come back up. But it's still not back to the level it was before, and now you have a CEO who's walked away with almost three times what his annual salary was. Are you telling me that that's sending the right signal? Particularly when people perceive institutions as living quarter to quarter? We are now embracing through CEO compensation something that is almost like day to day.

Meredith:

The issue is, what signal are you reading? Are you reading the signal that says I'm betting on the stock price coming back? Or do you want to leave a signal that says I don't care what the stock price is? I would think that as an institutional investor you would be concerned about what's going to happen to the stock price, and you'd want the CEO to be concerned about it as well.

Hanson:

I look at one thing, and that's total return. That's really the best key to the whole process. Everybody wants to beat the drum on international competition, but let's be honest. There's only one area right now where we stand out in international competition, and that's compensation. We're clearly the leaders in the world. [Laughter.]

CalPERS is an organization that is rightfully categorized as an activist. We're not embarrassed by that term; we're rather proud of our role in the issue of corporate governance and shareholder rights. We have a good track record.

There was a lot of media attention last year on our voting against the directors of ITT and Rand Araskog's salary. We put out a press release recently on a new agreement that we have reached with ITT, and because it was part of the kinder and gentler era and it was not confrontational, I have yet to see any national media pick the document up and run with the story. We have continued discussions with ITT, very positive discussions. Rand Araskog came to Sacramento and met with us. We talked about executive compensation. I give Rand Araskog a tremendous amount of credit for that. We've had several subsequent meetings in New York and have forged a new agreement as part of our 1992 discussions.

However, I do not think shareholders should be involved in setting CEO's salaries. That is clearly and rightfully the duty of the board. Hopefully, we can all agree that one of the critical functions of the board is to hire the CEO, to evaluate the management, and where appropriate, to hire management. The shareholders will increasingly be focusing on the board and asking if those directors are truly representing the shareholders. The board of directors is really the entity that we should be pouring our energies into.

The compensation committee should be hiring the compensation consultant, not management. It is surprising the number of directors that will come up to me and say I am absolutely upset with the fact that I am given this consultant and I had no say in his or her selection. Increasingly, there is going to have to be a separation of that process. In fact, more and more compensation consultants feel uncomfortable being hired by the CEO to work with the compensation committee. How can you truly be objective when your paycheck is coming from the individual for whom you're supposed to be studying the compensation package?

WHO'S PAYING WHOM?

Wriston:

Where do the paychecks come from if the comp committee hires him?

Hanson:

Well, they still come from the company, but I think the compensation committee should certainly be doing the interviewing and selection.

Wriston:

Then the paycheck doesn't matter?

Hanson:

Let's just start with the premise that most CEOs also happen to be chairmen of the board. Is it appropriate for the CEO who is the employee to be hiring the compensation consultant that is going to be providing input?

Wriston:

Well, let's just assume the comp committee hires him, okay, and the company pays the check. Does that make any difference to the consultant?

Nell Minow (International Shareholders Services):

Absolutely.

Wriston:

I don't think it makes the faintest difference.

Minow:

I think it makes all the difference in the world.

Wriston:

I don't buy that for a minute. Who pays the bill? The corporation pays the bill. And if I'm a consultant, I don't care who hired me. All I care is whether the check clears.

Minow:

Well, the check is not going to clear if the compensation committee fires you. As long as they've got the power to hire and fire . . .

Wriston:

It doesn't make any difference. Unless the people in the comp committee personally pay the thing, what difference does it make? You're a consultant, do you care who pays you?

Meredith:

It doesn't make a bit of difference to me.

Minow:

Do you care who hires you?

Meredith:

It doesn't make a bit of difference to me who does the hiring. What our role is, is to try and help management run the business better and to advise them on the design of pay systems and the reinforcement of the kind of performance you want. That is the best way to get it done.

I frankly have a Herculean problem thinking that a bunch of directors can tell the CEO how he best ought to manage the company. If you can, then you ought to be the CEO, not the director of the company. It's absolutely ludicrous.

Hanson:

Then why don't you do away with the board of directors?

Meredith:

To check and balance.

Minow:

Where's the check and where's the balance? You're describing a check without a balance.

Wriston:

The balance is that you have to pick a CEO.

THE VALUE OF COMMITTEES

Stern:

Boards of directors have very valuable committees who understand what their true assignments are. There is a finance committee, there is an audit committee, there's a compensation committee. Each of those committee chairmen understand that they have a supranormal responsibility and that the outside specialist is hired by the chairman of the compensation committee with uniform acceptance by the rest of the compensation committee. The judgments that are made by that person will carry weight with the board, and the CEO will agree to the results. We're not talking about things that are very extreme at the very top and the very bottom.

The differences here are more in substance than in form. As for the issues that you are raising, even though I sometimes flap my wings here and I get very excited, I hate to admit it, but I agree with about 75 percent of what you say. You're only 25 percent wrong.

Hanson:

That's a very small part of being wrong. Our feeling very definitely is the compensation committee should have a say on the hiring of a consultant. You are going to be seeing this coming in increased volume and frequency in the future, not simply from the CalPERS, but from a number of shareholders, and that is that they would like to see outside directors evaluate the CEO.

But again, the shareholders should not set the CEO salaries. The public sector model of the issue shows that it simply does not work. Dale Hanson is the CEO of a $65 billion pension system, and I am paid exactly the same salary whether I perform well or I perform poorly. I am paid exactly like another director of another state agency, like we've all been cut out of little cookie cutters.

But you know, we talk about committees sitting down and saying, "Gee, we ought to be at the top corridor, based on our peers." That same committee should be looking at it on a total return basis and say, "But my God, we're sitting 472nd out of the S&P 500 and what we ought to do is tank the CEO."

THE CEO AS SHAREHOLDER

J.P. Donlon (*Chief Executive*):

Dale, obviously, in the first go around, you didn't like what you saw at ITT. What is it that you do like to see?

Hanson:

CEO compensation should be highly correlated to what is happening to shareholder value. If there is not a correlation between executive compensation and creation of shareholder wealth, then I think we really do not have a suitable process.

I am troubled in the area of stock options only in the fact that in many cases, unless there is some form of an indexation on options, it's basically a free ride. If the person that has the stellar performance is going to be able to exercise that option, the person who's had sub-stellar performance will probably also be able to exercise it because the market is just rocking that company along.

Wriston:

What do you mean by indexation?

Hanson:

That you're looking at what the entire market is doing as far as moving up, and is this company just riding along the free ride, or is it that individual's performance that has brought the value of the stock up?

Robert G. Paul (Allen Group):

If the market goes down 1,000 points, 30 percent, then are you saying the option prices should be reduced by that?

Hanson:

The pricing of options gets into another issue: If you're constantly resetting that price, then what is the long-term incentive in that process? Gee, you couldn't make it there, so we're going to bring the hurdle bar down two feet and see if you can do it there!

Meredith:

But the reload options that you're talking about—in terms of taking the old options and granting new ones at a reloaded price—represent 3 or 4 percent of corporate practice today. That's not a common practice, and it's one that's looked on with great dismay in most corporate boardrooms I know about.

Stern:

If the managers took part of their bonuses each year and used that to buy stock options with a rising exercise price, but they did it every year, they would have something real to lose. That's number one.

The second thing is, I want to build in a rising exercise price on those options because shareholders are entitled to the first returns; only the excess returns for superior performance is what management should participate in.

Wriston:

Aren't management shareholders?

Minow:

If they are shareholders, then let them profit as shareholders. Only then should they get those returns.

Stern:

Come on, we're talking about two different types of people here! You're talking about the very senior management, and I'm talking about people who are two or three direct reports down who participate, too. It's something that appeals more broadly than just to the very senior management.

Of course, it has to be something that is not just a giveaway, but something that provides a real incentive for performance. If the person is going to be treated like a shareholder, then it goes up or down independent of that person's activities. That's not an example of pay for performance.

Wriston:

I just don't believe that short-term thinking is that widespread among senior management. You might have seen that once in one company.

Stern:

No, I haven't! I've worked for over 2,000 companies, and . . .

Wriston:

Really, 2,000 companies? Can't you keep a job?

Stern:

With respect, Mr. Wriston, it happens a lot. About 85 percent of total comp for people who are within three direct reports from the top takes the form of senior liability claims on the company. That's wages, retirement benefits, and medical benefits. If pay for performance is going to become an appropriate incentive structure, we have to change 85/15 to at least 50/50. I cannot get people to cut their salaries to get the 50/50. So what I'm willing to do is enlarge the potential bonus for earning superior returns, however measured. He [Meredith] has a technique, I have a technique, someone else has a technique. Whatever the technique is, we're going to give people a greater bonus for achieving it.

If the lion's share of the bonus is put into a bonus bank, and they only get one-third of it for the year and the other two-thirds is subject to negative charges if they underperform in future years, you can be darned sure people are going to have a longer term perspective and be interested in sustaining it. Every year a new bonus goes into the bonus bank. They buy more options with it, and so they're building up a very handsome return.

Arnold Pollard (*Chief Executive*):

Joel, aren't you kidding yourself in one of your fundamental premises? You're saying that employees should be forced, in effect, to take a significant percentage of their annual bonus—which might be set at a higher total return to accommodate your plan—and reinvest them in shares. Well, what's the difference between getting a nominal "bigger" dollar bonus, all of which you can't have and some of which must be reinvested in shares, versus getting paid a smaller bonus with options included in the first place?

Stern:

Gee, I thought you were much friendlier when your question began. I'm surprised nobody's nicer to me, given my lovely personality. But I'll try to answer your question anyway.

I have great fear that people might operate for the short run. Right now, people get bonuses based on current year performance, and they can take their check and walk. I want to make sure they really sustain a change in the value of the company.

The payoff for people with a rising exercise price such as we referred to earlier, if they do well, should be about $22 for every dollar they invest in those options. If they do well. But they have to stay 10 years to do it. They have to keep up the good performance for a long time.

Meredith:

But in the real world, they won't let you cut the 85 percent of the cost that's fixed on an arbitrary, sign-it-up basis.

Alan Miller:

It should be mandatory that you cut it to a 50 percent fixed cost. All it really means is you're increasing the total compensation equation because you can't get away with paying substandard salaries involuntarily.

Stern:

My plan is what I call a value-sharing plan. The only way that these people will earn higher compensation is if the incremental performance is quite substantial. The shareholders can't lose under a plan like this.

Paul:

If management is presented with that program, they will take voluntary pay cuts.

Meredith:

Voluntary, yes, mandatory, no.

Paul:

No, if you let it be known that this is the program they'll be in if they want to be an executive of the company, they're going to do it.

Stern:

People don't have to reduce their compensation for this thing that we're talking about to work. We're suggesting that we don't want to have to go into a company and say to people, we're going to have to change your culture and attitude about compensation. We're simply saying, listen, if you think the prospects here are excellent, we want you to participate in the value that's generated from those improved prospects. I see nothing wrong with that approach to the problem.

Alan Miller:

The nonrisk takers will leave. You will have less people to talk to.

Wriston:

The top executive should gamble a large percentage of the compensation. But put that down three or four levels with a person with a spouse and three kids, you get into real problems. The only way you do it is to pay more money. So what they do is they change the plan in the middle of the recession.

Richard Miller (Willis Corroon):

We did that back in the last recession for the top three levels of management. And it was a killer. It was the worst morale killer that I've ever seen.

Stern:

I'm on the board of a company that had that problem. We wrote a memorandum to our employees saying we have a problem now, and there are two choices to us: We can lay off a significant percentage of the salaried work force or we can take a pay freeze. We of the board would like to do a freeze instead of laying people off. And there was no problem.

Hanson:

Well, public employees face this about every two years and, obviously, particularly now in a recessionary period, it's common that the first thing you're going to look at is not freezing but cutting salaries. I arrived in California in 1987, and I'm on board for of all 30 days, and the human resources person came to me and said it's time for management bonuses. You have 33 managers and you have $5,000 lump sum to distribute.

I looked at him and said, "Surely you jest." He said, "I'm not kidding and don't call me Shirley." That is no way to have incentives. What do I say? "Oh, by the way, you are going to be paid 10 percent less than what you were paid the previous year. I have no merit I can give you. You can't even cash in your vacation because the state has a budget problem." I made a conscious decision to work in the public sector. But by the same token, I certainly would not subject corporate America to that mindset.

Meredith:

But that's what you're doing when you're hiring their consultant for them.

Hanson:

I totally disagree with you. Directors are there to represent the interests of shareholders. They are there to hire the CEO. They are there to evaluate the CEO. And how many directors evaluate CEOs today? Very few.

Meredith:

You're working from a bad data base.

Hanson:

Well, good, I would like to see your data base!

Richard Miller:

I've probably hired every consultant that our company has used since I became the chief executive officer some 23 years ago, and I've never had a complaint before from any of the committees because I felt that the consultants we were hiring were professionals. The board members felt the same way. If they weren't happy, they shouldn't have elected me chief executive. All consultants are professionals, and they're going to report in an independent manner regardless of who selected them.

Hanson:

We have now come full circle to the point where we're saying we all like the emperor's new clothes, and that's garbage. This would not be written up monthly in every major magazine in the country if there was not a problem. All of a sudden, I'm hearing no problem, it ain't broke, don't fix it. That's crap.

Minow:

I absolutely agree with Dale that shareholders should not set pay. And I also think that the compensation committee should be made up of independent outside directors. We looked at one company where the head of the compensation committee was the CEO's father!

It's important for shareholders to get involved in making sure that the directors are good, that they do a good job, that there are enough independent directors to provide some constructive feedback. It's no coincidence that overpaid directors have overpaid CEOs.

Wriston:

It's not that directors are stupid or don't work for the shareholders. Some of that is true, but most of it is smoke. The real problem directors face is liability in litigation. A year ago I told one of my boards that it was a seminal day in my life: My wife's lawsuits against her as a corporate director exceeded mine on that day and were up to $500 million. So when you talk about a director's compensation, there isn't anything you can pay him or her that will compensate for that liability. Unless you've been sued for $100 million, you don't know what the hell you're talking about.

Minow:

But do the lawsuits against you and your wife really deter you from accepting a directorship? When was the last time any director was personally liable?

Wriston:

Every day that you're alive.

Minow:

I don't believe that's true. Chancellor Allen of the Delaware Court, who presides over more of these cases than anyone else in the world, says that a director has a better chance of being hit by lightning than being found personally liable.

Wriston:

Yeah, well just try taking that chance to the bank. It's nice to say that as an observer, but it's another thing when the marshall walks in with a damned subpoena, believe me.

BUT SERIOUSLY . . .

Richard Miller:

There's a lot of greed out there, but in general, most boards have very hard-working directors. They take their jobs seriously. The committee chairmen take their jobs seriously. For the most part, they do damned good jobs.

I'm happy with the way things have been set. Of course, there are exceptions. In every field and in every part of business there are always going to be exceptions.

Donlon:

What do you think will most drive compensation considerations in the future?

Richard Miller:

I would like to see heavy stock options for CEOs. I am always disappointed when I pick up a proxy, and I see that the chairman who has been chairman for 5 or 10 years has 5,000 shares of stock, and he's been taking home $1.5 million a year. He's cashed in the options that he's gotten. That's the way they do things in Great Britain and in other parts of the world, and they have this partly because of the tax laws. But not in America. People should have a bulk of their personal net worth involved in the stock of the company that they lead. My personal net worth, the bulk of it, is in Willis Corroon shares, and it's been that way all my business career.

Stern:

My interest in the subject really came about by trying to understand the phenomena of the 1970s and 1980s—the unfriendly takeovers. I came to the conclusion that the underperformance of corporate America was more a function of this institutional government regulatory phenomenon that was institutionalized by the act in the 1930s. And that the incentives for improved performance that we're really getting to here really originated with the threat of an unfriendly takeover.

When that went bye-bye, a lot of people said well, I guess we don't have to worry. What's fascinating is that we're lucky the Dale Hansons of the world have come along and said you do have to worry. Because I really care about whether or not shareholder value maximization is an issue of importance to you—the CEO—or a member of the board of directors.

The reason why we should be concerned about how directors are paid and how the CEO is paid is because we should be interested in whether or not goals are set in terms of value maximization. Our interest is really not in how people get paid. It doesn't matter that Michael Eisner makes a lot of money as long as it's associated with outstanding performance. The real focus should be on whether or not people are being motivated to perform well, and then we can worry about how well they get paid. You can compare it to baseball players. Everybody's so concerned about whether those guys are getting overpaid. I liked Don Mattingly's comment when he was asked if he was worth $3 million a year. He said, "Well, the alternative is worse. If I don't get it, it goes to George [Steinbrenner, former general partner of the New York Yankees]." In other words, there is money available from all these TV revenues, and all they're doing is allocating funds.

Hanson:

We have a number of CEOs who deliver a tremendous amount of value to shareholders for what they're being compensated. Shareholders and directors and clearly the media will be focusing more and more on compensation—it is becoming, who will be the poster child of the year? At least over the near future, Steve Ross, you've got yourself locked up closely. You're not going to hear us complain about

Michael Eisner. Michael Eisner has delivered a tremendous amount of value to the shareholders. He has a compensation package that is at risk. If he does not hit certain targets, he's not going to be sitting with the godzillion dollars.

But there are others that have for a long time been poor performers who continued to have high levels of compensation, and at some point in time, the board is going to say, what are we paying this person for? Is this individual really and truly providing value to shareholders? Or is he or she basically only functioning for himself or herself? This is going to be an issue for the 1990s in corporate governance, and we would be foolish if we didn't think that. With the amount of attention the media gives to this, it has become a feeding frenzy.

Index